PERSPECTIVES ON SOCIAL PSYCHOLOGY

Edited by

Clyde Hendrick

University of Miami

LAWRENCE ERLBAUM ASSOCIATES, PUBLISHERS
1977   Hillsdale, New Jersey

DISTRIBUTED BY THE HALSTED PRESS DIVISION OF
JOHN WILEY & SONS
New York   Toronto   London   Sydney

Lawrence Erlbaum Associates, Inc., Publishers
62 Maria Drive
Hillsdale, New Jersey 07642

Distributed solely by Halsted Press Division
John Wiley & Sons, Inc., New York

Library of Congress Cataloging in Publication Data

Main entry under title:

Perspectives on social psychology.

Includes bibliographies and indexes.
1. Social psychology.   I. Hendrick, Clyde.
HM251.P426   301.1   77-22024
ISBN 0-470-99295-6

Printed in the United States of America

Contents

Preface

There are many approaches to — or perspectives on — social psychology. The purpose of this volume is to provide a relatively elementary overview of five of the more important perspectives. Chapter 1 reviews the nature of social psychology as an experimental science. Chapter 2 considers social psychology from the perspective of symbolic interaction, an approach traditionally more congenial to sociologists than to psychologists. Chapter 3 deals with social behavior from a developmental perspective. The developmental perspective has not been central in social psychological thinking since the 1930's; the work of Piaget, Kohlberg, and even Freud, however, has finally had the impact during the past decade, so that "social development" is currently emerging as a viable perspective. Chapter 4 conveys some of the excitement that the study of social behavior in other species can generate because of its relevance to human interaction. A few years ago, "animal social psychology" was an uninteresting byway. The growth of ethology as a discipline has transformed that byway into a major avenue, to the effect that any comprehensive social psychology must carefully consider the data and principles derived from ethological research. Finally, Chapter 5 presents a concise overview of the relevance and use of mathematical models in social psychology.

This book serves a need not presently met by any other volume. The first volume of the *Handbook of Social Psychology* presents the traditional theoretical approaches, such as S-R, field theory, role theory, etc. However, no volume previously published has attempted to treat social psychology from the point of view of the various general perspectives on the field. The current volume should therefore serve a very helpful integrative function.

The book should be of value to several audiences. In particular, it should be useful as a text for advanced undergraduate courses in social psychology, and in graduate seminars as well. We hope that the integration and syntheses of the various chapters might also offer something for the seasoned professional. The volume should be especially useful in classes where it is employed as the basic text and supplemented by selected reading of the primary source materials here cited.

I am grateful to the authors of the chapters for their dedication to scholarly excellence, and for getting the chapters done on schedule. I also wish to thank the staff of LEA for their efficiency and expertise which moved the book to publication almost painlessly. Sue Hendrick deserves special thanks for typing the drafts of Chapter 1, which at one time was almost twice as long as the final version. Finally, the excellent assistance of Cheryl Oros in compiling the index is much appreciated.

CLYDE HENDRICK

1
Social Psychology As An Experimental Science

Clyde Hendrick

University of Miami

INTRODUCTION

Social psychology is many things and has numerous facets. Today it is predominantly an experimental laboratory science. In fact, Klineberg (1965, p. 10) identified the experimental approach as the most direct trademark of the discipline. Social psychology is a relatively young discipline, having arrived at a mature status only since the Second World War. Murphy (1965) discussed three historical characteristics that led to the emergence of this new discipline. First, agreeing with Klineberg's emphasis, Murphy noted the forging of an experimental method that was potentially applicable to social behavior. Second, there was a turn toward a social direction in general experimental psychology. Finally, enough data and materials had to accumulate so that systematic texts could be written and courses offered.

During the 30 years since the Second World War, social psychology has become a burgeoning discipline. Sahakian (1974, p. 126) speaks of the discipline optimistically, stating "Today . . . social psychology stands in all of its majesty, with society depending on it for the investigation and solution of a number of its major problems." At present this optimistic assessment is not generally shared, and a period of reassessment which will be discussed in a later section in this chapter, has begun.

Experimental social psychology as a discipline may be characterized in several ways. It is, first of all, a scientific community of people (Crane, 1972) who tend to share a similar scientific language, a relatively common way of professional life, and a similar value orientation. The value orientation involves consensus on a variety of things; the most prestigious publication outlets; who does good or

1

bad research; the most desirable academic settings in which a social psychologist may lead a professional life; the important leaders or role models in the discipline; etc. The discipline may have a system of social stratification the same as any other science (Cole & Cole, 1973); indeed, social psychology may even contain a power structure of sorts (Strickland, 1976; Lubek, 1976), in which a relatively small minority of people control access to publication outlets, grant funds, and entry into the job market. The value orientation is initially transmitted in graduate training and is reinforced by face-to-face contacts at professional meetings, informal communication networks, and the gate-keeping function of publication outlets and hiring practices.

Experimental social psychology may also be characterized by its methodological orientation. The orientation relies heavily, almost predominantly, on the laboratory experiment for the conduct of inquiry. The high priority given the laboratory experiment is also part of the shared value consensus of members of the discipline. The lore of the laboratory experiment is massive, and this chapter will be concerned in a major way with the nature of experimentation in social psychology and the presuppositions underlying this approach.

Finally, experimental social psychology may be characterized as a substantive content discipline, a discipline that focuses on some areas of human life and ignores other areas. The focus on content proceeds in two ways. Some researchers focus on theory and its development. Currently, most such theories focus on specific topics (for example, attraction, attitude change, dissonance, etc.), although there is still some concern with general theoretical systems such as field theory, psychoanalytic theory, and S-R theory.

The second way in which content is dealt with is to focus on a phenomenon in question, to ascertain the various interrelated empirical variables that bear on the phenomenon in one way or another. This focus is on the variables relevant to the social phenomenon or process and is little concerned with theoretical development, although there may be nominal hypothesis testing to satisfy an earlier ethic that research should be conducted to affirm or deny a theory. With this focus on the collection of facts and empirical relations in a specific content area, the literature within that area tends to grow prodigiously, become encapsulated within itself, and effectively get cut off from other areas that would be closely related from the perspective of a general theory. For example, the research on interpersonal attraction proceeds in its own fashion independently of the research on attitude change. Even a simple theory of modest scope could view pro and con feelings toward people as one specific type of attitude formation and change, and thus the study of attraction would become a subunit of the general area of attitudes. Logical though such a grouping might be, the two topics remain separate as a perusal of introductory social texts will quickly testify.

This tendency for encapsulated content areas to develop in social psychology has led to discontent and a sense of fragmentation and probably has contributed to the sense of malaise or crisis currently existing in the discipline. The crisis in social psychology is given extended treatment in a later section.

In summary, experimental social psychology is best characterized in several ways. It is a network of social relationships among a dispersed group of academic scholars who share a common set of professional values and a communication network. Experimental social psychology, in contrast to many other social sciences, places high value on the manipulative laboratory experiment as the best path to the accumulation of social knowledge. Finally, there is considerable concern with miniature theories (for example, attraction, impression formation, etc.), but there is perhaps even stronger concern with the empirical study of the phenomena per se, with only secondary interest in the development of strong theories about the phenomena.

The Matter of Definitions

There are many definitions of social psychology. Most experimental social psychologists would agree with Allport (1968a) that the "focus of interest is upon the social nature of the individual person" (p. 3). Relative emphasis on the social system or the individual may vary, but most experimentalists perhaps tend to emphasize the individual. This emphasis is captured well by Allport's classic definition. "With few exceptions, social psychologists regard their discipline as *an attempt to understand and explain how the thought, feeling, and behavior of individuals are influenced by the actual, imagined, or implied presence of others" (p. 3).*

Moscovici (1972) defined three kinds of social psychology, but would agree that the type specified by Allport's definition is dominant. Moscovici called this approach *taxonomic,* with the aim of determining "the nature of the variables which might account for the behavior of an individual confronted with a stimulus" (p. 50). Social stimuli, according to this approach, are on a continuum with nonsocial stimuli, not essentially different in nature (see also Stotland, 1965). This study of effects on the individual necessarily concerns itself with reactions to an environment; hence, social psychology is susceptible to various kinds of behavioristic influence.

Moscovici also noted a *differential* social psychology, which is concerned with personality characteristics. The differential approach uses trait variation in attributes (for example, leadership, achievement motivation) as the mechanism for explaining social behavior. This approach is popular but it is not dominant. There is a suspicion of "merely correlational" research, in which variables are manipulated by "chronic" variation as opposed to the active "acute" manipulations of the laboratory experiment. Thus the differential approach does not have the prestige among social psychologists that the taxonomic approach has. There has been a tendency among some researchers during the last decade to combine the chronic and acute manipulations to form a subdiscipline of "experimental personality." Whether this approach will become a viable discipline in its own right remains to be seen.

A third approach to social psychology identified by Moscovici was called *systematic*. This approach tends to focus on the phenomenon of dependence and interdependence among individuals. Zajonc (1966) stressed this definition. The study of social relations or interaction among individuals was perhaps the original vision for an experimental social psychology. Certainly it seemed to be Lewin's general approach to the study of group processes. However, the study of interaction in all of its complexity proved too difficult for the laboratory experiment. The conception of independent-dependent variable is not well suited for capturing the interlocking dynamics of ongoing interaction. Consequently group processes qua group were not studied very much. The systematic approach to the study of groups was transformed into the taxonomic approach, so that the study of conformity, communication, etc. was essentially translated into the effects of other individuals (for example, social pressure) on one individual's response (for example, a measure of conformity).

The taxonomic approach reflected in Allport's definition is without doubt the dominant approach to social psychology today. It is well suited to an S-R, independent-dependent variable, unilinear causal view of social behavior. As developed in later sections, this approach reflects a philosophy that underlies most of experimental social psychology. Only recently have attacks (e.g., McGuire, 1973) been leveled seriously at this predominant view.

It will be useful to examine briefly the two major metaconcerns of experimental social psychology — the nature of theory, and the experimental approach.

Theory in Social Psychology

General theoretical orientations have had considerable impact on social psychology. They are still drawn upon for general ideas and moral support, but no one thinks seriously any longer of "testing" or "confirming" these general theories. The first volume of the most recent edition of *The Handbook of Social Psychology* (Lindzey & Aronson, 1968) is devoted to such systematic positions. There are discussions of stimulus-response, Freudian, cognitive, field, and role theories in social psychology. Perhaps the best statement is that these theories are not really theories in any specific sense, but rather approaches or guiding orientations that provide a language for the conduct of research, and, to a limited extent, may suggest the direction for research.

The trend during the last two decades has definitely been toward smaller theories that deal with limited topics, what Robert Merton (1957) called theories of the middle range. There are a great many such theories. Undoubtedly, Festinger's (1957) *dissonance* theory has been the most popular and productive of research.

In some respects this trend toward miniature theories is surprising. No doubt the general orientations were seen to be inept, but no one attempted to replace them by better general theories. Rather the trend was toward selected topic theories. This trend is surprising in the sense that it violates the urge toward general explanatory paradigms. Lewin's call for theories of unrestricted universality was very clear. Also, some of the theories of the natural sciences were considered as suitable models to follow in this regard.

Moscovici (1972) presented an interesting analysis of this issue which is worthy of note. Moscovici felt that the decline in theory is due to (or at least correlated with) the growing empiricism in social psychology. There are three aspects of this empirical trend.

1. Social psychologists are in general antispeculative in outlook. In the same sense that experimental psychology eschewed philosophy earlier, social psychology today eschews anything tainted with metaphysics and beyond the realm of empirical proof.

2. Theories are variously regarded. One approach is to view theories as conventions (free and somewhat arbitrary creations) that are fruitful as long as they generate research. In this way, theory is a language and a tool that is subordinated to the empirical method. Theories viewed in this way are not "grand thought devices," but simply disposable tools. If they do not work they can be discarded. The need for a convenient tool would lead to neater, more precisely stated theories that are more productive in empirical research. Increased emphasis on precision would usually lead to more circumscribed content domains. To the extent that this argument has merit, one would expect that the use of mathematical models in social psychology will increase greatly in the future, an approach that Harris (1976a) has vigorously advocated.

3. The growing emphasis on experimentation and away from the observational approach of the field is also conducive in a different way to the miniaturization of theory. To be most efficient the laboratory experiment requires a very narrow theory for test. In fact, it requires a specific hypothesis, ideally cast in an if-then implicational form. The purpose of experimentation is in this way subtly transformed from testing general theories to testing a specific hypothesis, which does not necessarily have a broader epistemological context than the bare statement of the hypothesis itself.

In this role social psychologists often devote enormous energy to testing hypotheses. Because hypotheses are often personal creations, there may be considerable emotional investment in them. Researchers set out to "confirm" their hypotheses, and they can draw considerable support from the philosophy of science for the "logic of confirmation." In this way, experiments often seem to serve the function of justification of the hypothesis rather than the discovery of new knowledge. McGuire (1973) presented an incisive discussion of the demonstrational nature of many hypothesis testing experiments. Social psychologists do not tend to follow Popper's (1968) conception of falsifiability of a theory in which one's pet hypothesis must survive the "destruction test" of an experiment.

In general then, theory construction and testing in the broad sense has been subordinated to the logic of confirmation of hypothesis testing in a narrow specific sense. Moscovici suggests what he conceives to be a more fruitful conception of theory formation as a dialectic competition between theory and experiment. "Experiment and theory do not stand in a transparent relation to one another; it is the role of the theory to make experimentation unnecessary, and the role of experimentation to render the theory impossible" (p. 46). This position seems to advocate an adversary relation between theory and experimentation, instead of the usual conception of a complementary relation. There may be considerable merit in this conception, and it would be of interest to see the conception developed more fully.

There are several consequences of the decline in theoretical emphasis. One consequence is that social psychologists are sometimes accused of belaboring the obvious, of testing commonsense aphorisms. Another consequence is that the death rate of new knowledge is almost as rapid as its birth rate. Several commentators have complained about the lack of cumulativeness in research data. A third consequence of the change to miniature theories is the relative isolation of different research areas, which results in a sense of fragmentation, as was noted above.

The trend toward specific, small-scale theories seems undeniable. On a positive note, such theories are often testable in a way that was not possible with the more general formulations. Over a number of specific experiments it is often possible to obtain a sense of confirmation or disconfirmation for the theory. Precision of statement is necessary for the testing process. Undoubtedly, if anyone were smart enough to create a theory of social behavior both very general and very precise, it would be done. Until the Einstein of social psychology emerges, however, we must make do with the miniature theories.

The Experimental Approach

Social psychologists have always been concerned with method and have used (and still do) a wide variety of them. One volume of *The Handbook of Social Psychology* is devoted exclusively to methods. However, it is clear that the laboratory experiment (and secondarily the field experiment) is considered the most useful methodology. In fact the ordering of topics in the methods volume of the *Handbook* gives a reasonable assessment of the prestige rank ordering of the various methods. The initial, excellent chapter by Aronson and Carlsmith (1968) is concerned with experimentation. The remaining chapters, in order, are concerned with data analysis, attitude measurement, simulation, observational methods, sociometric techniques, interviewing, content analysis, cross-cultural research, and the significance of animal studies.

The experiment, as it has developed in social psychology, is rather narrowly conceived. The experiment is viewed as the active manipulation of one or more sets of environmental events that are conventionally thought of as independent variables. Some aspect of the subjects' overt or verbal behavior is measured and considered as the dependent variable. The data are usually analyzed by parametric statistics, most often analysis of variance. The emphasis is on causal relations viewed as the orderly connection between independent and dependent variables, as in Aronson and Carlsmith. The active, acute manipulation of independent variables is considered desirable to ascertain more precisely the nature of causal relations.

This view of experimentation seems to be the dominant one. This type of experiment has been called the *nomological* experiment by Lachenmeyer (1970), who notes a problem in identifying this one type as the only legitimate form of experiment. He feels that this emphasis slights the observation-inductive end of the theory construction process in favor of the deductive-verification end. There are many other types of experiments, such as measurement refinement and methodological studies, pilot studies, pure fact-finding studies, experiments to discover the existence of an object or process, and perhaps even crucial experiments on occasion (Lachenmeyer, 1970). Descriptive studies of the kinds of social behaviors that exist and the range of variation in such behaviors seem not to be very popular with social psychologists.

Since the emphasis of the present chapter is on social psychology as an experimental science, most attention will be devoted to research that used laboratory experiments. It will not be the purpose to discuss the vast number of specific procedures and techniques used in the conduct of social experiments. Adequate summaries of these procedures already exist (e.g., Aronson & Carlsmith, 1968; Hendrick & Jones, 1972). Considerable attention will be devoted to the issues and problems of laboratory research and to the set of assumptions on which this research is based.

In summary, experimental social psychology emerges as a discipline that is strongly attracted to the manipulative laboratory approach. The orientation tends toward hypothesis-testing within the context of small minitheories. The content domains are diverse, and the discipline in fact consists of many separate empirical areas, with few conceptual links between areas.

Several topics will be considered in the remainder of the chapter. The next section will present a brief history of experimental social psychology. Following that presentation, an attempt is made to examine in some detail the philosophic presuppositions which undergird the discipline. Another section directly confronts some of the recent issues that have collectively been referred to as the crisis in social psychology. A brief concluding section provides a prognosis for the future of experimental social psychology.

HISTORY OF EXPERIMENTAL SOCIAL PSYCHOLOGY

A definitive history of social psychology has not been written. Most social psychologists are ahistorical in their interests. Consequently, passing acquaintance with Allport's (1968a) chapter in *The Handbook of Social Psychology* is usually the modal amount of exposure that most social psychologists have to the history of their discipline. Even Allport's scholarly work was mostly concerned with the "ancient" tradition and devoted a scant six pages to "The Beginnings of Objective Method." Recently, the sanctity of Allport's history has been challenged by Samelson (1974), who argued that Allport's rendition of Comte is in actuality an origin myth that rationalizes the present purposes and goals of social psychology.

The unexpectedness of this criticism of Allport's version of the history of social psychology serves as a reminder of how little historical scholarship on social psychology actually exists. Perhaps the lack of interest in historical issues is in the process of change. An interest group has formed that publishes a mimeographed bulletin, the *Newsletter of the History of Social Psychology Group*, edited by Lorenz J. Finison.

Baumgardner (1976) advocated a critical history of social psychology as a means of understanding the crisis in the discipline (see page 49 for an extended treatment of the crisis). Much of the history of science has a presentist bias and is written in a fashion to justify present outlooks, methods, theories, etc. Further, until recently, histories of science tended to focus on the internal development of a field, that is, the evolution of the theories and scientific content internal to the field. According to Baumgardner, a critical history would include consideration of the internal development of a field within the social contexts, with all of their extrascientific factors, in which the field develops.

Baumgardner (1976) presented an interesting example of such an extrascientific influence in the history of social psychology. During the second decade of this century, William McDougall's instinct theory was very influential in the development of social psychology and won the approval of no less a thinker than John Dewey. During the 1920s, instinct theory fell into disfavor (Dewey also turned against it). The history books usually attribute the shift to the behaviorist revolution, initiated by John Watson, and the circularity of the instinct concept. However, Baumgardner showed that the shift to an equally extreme environmental-functional emphasis was not based on hard empirical data. Rather, the shift was due in an important way to political/social attitudes. McDougall's psychology was meant to be applicable to real world problems. Once the full social implications of instinct theory became clear, the incongruency of those implications with the social amelioration values of McDougall's supporters led them to abandon instinct theory very quickly.

There are undoubtedly many more important examples of how the social context helped shape the directions in which social psychology developed. The development of a critical history of social psychology would be an important contribution for the assessment of the current status of the discipline, and would hopefully provide a rational directive for its future development.

A recent text by Sahakian (1974) comes closest to a systematic conventional history of social psychology. The major sections detail the rise of social psychology from antiquity to 1908, the initial modern era from 1908 to 1930, the formative years of the thirties, and the modern contributions including those from psychoanalysis, Lewinian field theory, cognitive consistency, and learning traditions. The book is a scholarly contribution and merits reading.

Beyond Allport's chapter and the Sahakian volume, there are several other interesting general contributions. A volume edited by Klineberg and Christie (1965) commemorating the opening of a department of social psychology at Columbia University is of interest, particularly the chapter by Gardner Murphy, "The Future of Social Psychology in Historical Perspective." A short article by Gordon Allport (1968b) in Lundstedt reviewed "Six Decades of Social Psychology." Allport's benediction was, on balance, positive: "All in all, my own outlook is optimistic. I think that social psychology may yet become the central science for the understanding and amelioration of mankind. But the way is long and difficult and our wisdom is thin" (p. 18). However, he noted that we ignore our own history and that journal-article citation only uses references from the very recent past, a tendency detrimental to the broad wisdom we need.

An autobiography by M. Brewster Smith (1972b) is valuable for providing a personal flavor and one perspective on social psychology from the period since the Second World War. Smith stated that he never did an experiment except as a student. While, as he admitted, he is unusual in this respect, it is refreshing to discover that it is still possible to become a member of the establishment (and even President of the American Psychological Association) without it being necessary to manipulate an independent variable.

Other sources bearing on the recent history of the discipline include Steiner's (1974) article on groups, Smith's (1972a) question "Is Experimental Social Psychology Advancing," McGuire's (1973) yin-yang analysis of progress in social psychology, and Katz's (1967) parting editorial. Finally, an article by Stotland (1965) is useful in creating a perspective on the discipline.

The following sections will focus on the history of social psychology as an experimental, primarily laboratory, science. The initial section discusses the origins of experimental social psychology in the study of what is now called social facilitation. The second section looks briefly at the contents of the classic texts of the thirties. The third section considers the impact of Kurt Lewin. The full flowering to maturity is discussed in the fourth section, and the last section notes some very recent trends. It should be emphasized that the following account is necessarily selective; a full account would require an extensive volume.

The Origins in Social Facilitation

It is generally agreed that Triplett (1897) performed the first experimental investigation in social psychology (see Zajonc, 1966). The general context of Triplett's work was the question, "What change in an individual's normal solitary performance occurs when other people are present?" (Allport, 1968a, p. 64) Indeed, Allport noted that this first experimental problem was the *only* social problem studied in the laboratory for three decades. As is often common for research today, Triplett's research started with an observation from everyday life. He noted that a bicycle racer's top speed was greater when the racer was paced. Triplett designed a laboratory task in which children wound fishing reels, alternately alone and in pairs, and measured winding time under both conditions. Performance was generally superior in the pair condition, presumably due to its competitive nature.

Allport noted that this early work failed to distinguish between intentional competition and the energizing effect due to the simple presence of another person. It remained for F. H. Allport (1924) to draw the distinction between competition and simple social facilitation and to point out the difference between face-to-face interacting groups and coacting groups.

A massive amount of research was conducted in this general tradition. The research tradition was differentiated into "audience effects" and "coaction effects" (Zajonc, 1965). Much of the research found that coacting groups were superior in performance to solitary workers and the presence of an audience enhanced performance. But some studies showed a reverse effect (see Zajonc, 1966, for details of these studies). This research tradition was exhaustively summarized by Dashiell (1935) in Murchison's *Handbook of Social Psychology*. The inconsistencies in the data continued, and by 1950 this research tradition had fallen upon hard times, although scattered studies continued.

It remained for Zajonc (1965, 1966) to provide an elegant resolution to the inconsistencies and infuse the research tradition with new life. The solution was simple. Zajonc proposed that coaction as well as audience presence enhances performance of well-learned responses and impairs learning of new responses. This hypothesis accounted for most of the discrepant data. Further, Zajonc generated new data, both with animals (even the lowly cockroach) and humans. In so doing, Zajonc restimulated interest in this classic area of research, resulting in at least one book (Simmel, Hoppe, & Milton, 1968) and numerous journal articles during the last decade.

Two aspects of Zajonc's conceptual contribution should be noted.

1. Ideas are important. An area of research that accumulates inconsistencies becomes sterile and tends to become inward oriented toward technicalities of experimentation. Past a certain point of complexity and inconsistency, researchers leave the field for greener pastures. The research tradition simply dies. There are

undoubtedly many empirical areas of research in psychology which have met this fate.

I recall clearly some years ago working with a student on audiogenic seizures in mice. The student reported that there was no literature beyond a given date. Not believing him, I checked for myself, and it was true. The relevant reviews indicated that the field had become horribly complicated and unaesthetic. A confounding factor may have been the introduction of a new technique, electro-convulsive shock, which led to alternative research interests. However, it seemed clear that unexplained inconsistencies in the literature was the primary factor leading to almost complete abandonment of the study of audiogenic seizures.

It is interesting to speculate that without Zajonc's creative conceptualization, social facilitation would by now be a relic of dead research. At the very least, Zajonc gave the area a new impetus. This instance seems to be a classic example of the stimulating power of hypotheses to generate research that matters, is lively, and can generate wide interest.

2. General hypotheses tend toward cross-species validity. Zajonc's work well illustrated one tradition of experimental social psychology, that the laws describing human behavior should be consistent with the laws describing the behavior of other species. Hypotheses are stated generally and, in the hands of a skilled researcher, may be shown to hold true for "white rats, cockroaches, and elephants, as well as men" (Hendrick & Jones, 1972, p. 92). This conception is perhaps no longer held by the majority of experimental social psychologists, but Zajonc's work illustrates that for some areas of behavior, such universality is a reasonable aspiration.

As the first area of experimental research in social psychology, social facilitation posed a conceptual dilemma about the nature of the discipline that has not yet been resolved satisfactorily. At a general level, social facilitation is concerned with the behavior of an individual within a group context. The dilemma is whether the conceptual focus of the field should be developed at the level of the individual or at the level of the group (for an interesting discussion of the issue in context of the relation between environmental and social psychology, see Altman, 1976). Floyd Allport (1924) made an influential choice in favor of the individual. Allport's emphasis on the individual gained support from a growing interest during this period in the concept of attitude, a conception primarily intraindividual rather than intragroup in emphasis. The result was that, by 1930, the individual was well entrenched as the anchor point of analysis, yielding the classic definition by Gordon Allport cited in the introduction to this chapter.

The emphasis on the individual has not been uniformly consistent, however, and, in fact, there has been a shifting back and forth of the focus from the individual to the group. From the time of Lewin in the late 1930s through the 1950s, there was a redirection to a concern with group processes (Steiner,

1974) with a corresponding flight of researchers away from attitudes (McGuire, 1969a). During the 1960s, interest somewhat shifted from the group back to the individual once again. Theories of cognitive consistency and attribution processes were developed in abundance, and hundreds of research studies were conducted in pursuit of intrapsychic inconsistency reduction and attributional processes.

Based on the previous historical cycles, Steiner (1974) predicted that the age of the group will arrive again in the late 1970s. Current loss of interest in many of the consistency theories suggests a reasonable basis for Steiner's prediction.

The recurrent dialectical emphasis on either the individual or the group is perhaps the central quandry of social psychology. The discipline has never been able to decide, in a conclusive way, its basic unit of analysis. The hoary issue of the individual in the social context, and the relation between the two, concerns all of the social sciences. However, most disciplines seem to have opted more clearly than experimental social psychology for either the social context or the individual human for their central conceptual focus. However, the failure of social psychology to make a definitive choice is not necessarily bad and may become a catalyst in the evolution of a more exciting science over the long term; but this undoubtedly will be at a cost of some turbulence and sense of anomie for practioners of the discipline.

Experimental Social Psychology in the 1930s

Allport (1968a) noted that empiricism and positivism did not have much impact on social psychology until the 1920s. Beyond the work on social facilitation, experimentation really had very little impact until the 1930s. There was a wealth of research with related methodologies such as field studies (for example, Newcomb's Bennington study, reported in 1943), anthropological data, and attitude measurement (see Sahakian, 1974, p. 125, for details).

It seems relatively clear that Sherif's (1935; 1936) work on social norms was the first extensive use of modern experimental methodology in a systematic program of social research. This work combined a broad knowledge of anthropology and sociology with questions of individual processes in a small group context, under relatively rigorous laboratory conditions. Sahakian (1974) noted that Sherif's research directed social psychology somewhat away from the behavioristic orientation acquired from Floyd Allport and toward consideration of group processes. More generally, Sahakian credited Gardner Murphy and the "Columbia Contingent" with orienting social psychology toward an enduring experimental ethic. He stated that "experimental social psychology as a movement or lasting force is attributable to Gardner Murphy's creative and guiding efforts" (p. 137).

In view of Sahakian's assessment, it is perhaps useful to review briefly the three major texts published during this period, the 1935 handbook edited by

Murchison and the two editions of *Experimental Social Psychology* by Murphy (Murphy & Murphy, 1931; Murphy, Murphy, & Newcomb, 1937).

A Handbook of Social Psychology

Reading the Murchison volume is a sobering experience. Both in content and method, social psychology is today an almost entirely different discipline. If a field can change that much in 40 years, one trembles at anticipating the shape of the discipline 40 years hence and at the implications for the lasting value of current work.

The Murchison volume clearly reflects the impact of evolutionary theory. Only with this conception in mind, do chapter headings such as "Population Behavior of Bacteria" and "Social Origins and Processes among Plants" in a book on social psychology make any sense at all today. Consistent with the evolutionary trend, there was a strong emphasis on animal behavior, with discussions of insect societies, bird societies, and mammalian herds.

Sahakian stated that, with the exception of Allport's classic chapter on attitudes, the Murphy and Murphy chapter on the influence of social situations on children, and Yerkes's chapter on the social behavior of nonhuman primates, the Murchison volume failed to make a lasting contribution. One might add Dashiell's chapter on social facilitation to those exceptions, in view of Zajonc's (1965) rehabilitation of this research tradition. However, these exceptions are only 4 of 23 chapters, and the book basically reflects another era – and essentially another discipline.

Experimental Social Psychology

The first edition of this text in 1931 actually contained very little experimentation in the modern sense. There was a heavy developmental emphasis in the first two major sections of the book. The third section contained chapters on "The Individual in the Group Situation" and "The Cooperating Group," which reviewed the social facilitation and related literature. The chapter on attitudes was concerned almost entirely with descriptive and measurement research.

The 1937 revision retained the broad developmental emphasis, but there was by now some truly modern research to review, such as Sherif's (1936) book. The authors mentioned Piaget, Lewin, and Sherif as newcomers who were making solid contributions to the field. There was an interesting ambivalence toward experimentation and some second thoughts about the directions in which it might be heading. Recognizing at the same time the impact of the first edition, the authors stated:

> Despite the vigorous protests in Chapter I of our first edition against regarding experimental social psychology as the only social psychology, the publication of our book was unfortunately assumed to be further evidence that the experimental method must always come first and that all problems must fall willy-nilly into a form recognizable by the laboratory worker (p. 13).

At another point, in commenting on Sherif's work, the authors noted: "Experiment in these cases is the crowning touch, the technical perfection of the analysis. It must be emphasized, however, that the experimental method in all these cases *comes late*. It comes after the problem has been defined and its salient characteristics so well formulated that we know what can be controlled and measured" (p. 14).

This early foreboding was reflected by Murphy in retrospect in the Klineberg and Christie (1965) volume. Murphy noted:

> It may be that by using all the supposed basic principles of a scientific psychology, and even those of a scientific physics, we have to some degree biased their [the students'] vision of what a social psychology might become. I am not guiltless in this matter myself, because 30 years ago, in the hope of gaining respect for social psychology, I certainly overplayed many rather small and unimportant experiments, and certainly underplayed a number of large empirical movements which were not founded upon experimentation (p. 30).

To the extent that Sahakian (1974) was correct in attributing to Murphy credit for making experimental social psychology a "movement or lasting force," there is a grim irony involved. The seeds of both the current productivity and the severe problems of the discipline were apparently sown in part by Murphy's early approach. He was clearly cognizant of the potential problems inherent in a one-sided experimental approach, but was unable to check the forces he helped unleash. As Armistead (1974) noted, the plea of Murphy, Murphy, and Newcomb that social psychology concern itself with the life history of the person socially defined went unheeded, and "psychological social psychology has moved away from any such developmental approach, abandoning it to 'child' and 'developmental' psychology" (p. 14).

In summary, it seems clear that experimental social psychology as it is viewed today had its origins in the 1930s. Scholars such as Murphy and Sherif were seminal in orienting the discipline to its current direction. Their view was broader than today's view; their secondary emphasis on experimentation had by mid-century become the overwhelming primary emphasis. However, the narrative as to how this trend occurred cannot be complete until another individual is considered, one who far surpassed Murphy in his influence on the discipline — Kurt Lewin.

Kurt Lewin (1890-1947)

In reviewing Lewin's various books and volumes of papers, one cannot fail to be impressed with his dazzling creativity and wide variety of interests. His influence permeates the field, so much so that many of his ideas have become common property and no longer necessarily receive explicit citation.

This estimation is easily documented. Tolman compared Lewin to Freud (Sahakian, 1974, p. 313). More recently, in reviewing the series (*Advances in Experimental Social Psychology* edited by Berkowitz, Smith (1972a) noted:

> More than any other single figure, Kurt Lewin stands at the source of the experimental social psychology displayed in these volumes. The intellectual father of many of the senior leaders of the discipline, he stands as grandfather to a substantial number of the authors. For Lewin, basic and applied research, laboratory and field research, were complementary, not opposed. I hope that as systematic empirical social psychology emerges from its present "crisis," it may regain something of the Lewinian synthesis. (p. 95).

A useful intellectual biography of Lewin's life has been written by Marrow (1969). Lewin's academic career began at the University of Berlin, where he attracted many able students who produced numerous excellent experimental studies considerably before the 1930s. Such terms as "Zeigarnik effect" and "level of aspiration" have become part of the psychological language as a result of this early research.

An outstanding sourcebook on the early work of Lewin and his students in Germany has been compiled by DeRivera (1976) and includes extensive commentary. The volume contains translations of five doctoral dissertations on the following subjects: resumption of interrupted activities (Rickers-Oviankina). mental satiation (Karsten). relapses in relearning (Schwarz); dynamics of anger (Dembo); and success and failure (Hoppe). These early experiments formed the initial basis of the empirical-conceptual system that became known as field theory. The reports are rich in observational detail, and their leisurely pace provides an interesting contrast with the compactly written papers appearing in modern social psychology journals.

Lewin migrated to the United States in 1932, and, after three years at Stanford and Cornell, spent a decade at Iowa (Boring, 1950). In 1945 he founded the Research Center for Group Dynamics, which moved permanently to the University of Michigan after his death in 1947. One of the more impressive features of Lewin's life was his ability to attract large numbers of able students, both in Germany and in the United States. These personal qualities may have contributed almost as much to his lasting fame as his many fertile theories and experiments. Boring (1950) noted: "We shall not understand Lewin's place in American psychology in 1933-1947 except in relation to the enthusiasm which his generous, friendly, insistent zealotry created. Whether Tolman is right in comparing him with Freud history will decide. Those who were closest to him felt very sure of his genius" (p. 724).

Lewin's contributions to social psychology have many facets. He emphasized the importance of the development of psychological laws and systematic theory; the aphorism "there is nothing so practical as a good theory" was coined by Lewin. He stressed the necessity of experimentation: "As far as methodology is concerned, one has to emphasize that laws can be established in psychology only by an experimental procedure" (Lewin, 1937, p. 204). Lewin's conceptions of experimentation were intermixed with his philosophy of science, which also has had a substantial impact on social psychology. Some attention will be given to this impact in the next section. Finally, Lewin became quite involved in the solution of social problems after he migrated to the United States. He was one of the founding members of the Society for the Psychological Study of Social Issues.

Lewin's theoretical system was sometimes called topological psychology, but more commonly field theory. The approach combined elements of field notions from physics and Gestalt psychology and topology concepts from mathematics. The system was not so much a formalization as an approach or a language that could hopefully provide an appropriate set of concepts for the construction of psychological theory. At a general level, DeRivera (1976) describes field theory as:

> ... an attempt to describe the essential here-and-now situation (field) in which a person participates. It assumes that if one fully understood a person's "situation" (in the broadest meaning of this term), one would fully understand his behavior. Hence, the goal of field theory is to be able to describe fields with systematic concepts in such a precise way that a given person's behavior follows logically from the relationship between the person and the dynamics and structure of his concrete situation (p. 3).

The many specific concepts of Lewin's theoretical approach may be found in systematic texts on personality, motivation, and social psychology. Perhaps the specifics of the theory per se no longer stimulate new conceptions or experiments (DeRivera, 1976, p. 27), but the theory has had a powerful indirect influence in social psychology. Almost any topic heading in a social psychology text owes a partial ancestral debt to Lewin's conceptions; indeed, some of the headings probably would not exist were it not for Lewin's work.

In some respects social psychology's debt to Lewin may be more methodological than substantive. His ability to create relatively precise experimental analogues for social processes — phenomena such as leadership, social climates, group dynamics, social change, etc. — made possible a veritable explosion of experiments on social processes that had previously been intractable to experimental control.

Nevertheless, it is doubtful that either Lewin's ability at theorizing or his skill in designing innovative experiments would, considered separately, have assured his status in psychology. His genius lay in linking creative experimentation with construction and testing of theoretical hypotheses in a continuous back-and-forth dialogue. The gap between an abstract theory and the minutiae of an experiment is very large, and Lewin's field conceptions were very abstract while his empirical investigations were patiently detailed. The importance of the ability to bridge the conceptual and empirical realms is captured beautifully in the following quotation from DeRivera:

> The central core of Lewin's method is the tension between the abstract conceptualization of essential underlying processes and the concrete facts of the individual case. The conceptualization strives for breadth and elegant simplicity, the theorist attempting to relate his concepts to each other with mathematical precision. But at the same time, the raw facts of each existent individual case demand accountability for every detail of their case.
>
> It is important to realize that these are not, cannot be, separate endeavors. They cannot be, for they are simply the two poles of one dynamic whole. The facts have no meaning without the conceptualization, the theory has no substance without the facts. The tension of this dialectic must be embodied in the investigator (p. 15).

In addition to embodying the dialectic of abstract theory and experimentation, Lewin also kept in mind applications to real world situations and attempted to develop his conceptualizations in such a way as to maximize applicability to the real world. For example, in commenting on the famous studies of leadership styles and group atmosphere (Lewin, Lippitt, & White, 1939), Cartwright and Zander (1968) noted that Lewin was attempting several things. First, he was interested in leadership because of its practical implications for education, social work, administration, and political affairs. However, the leadership studies were not attempting to simulate groups in real life. Rather,

> . . . he stated the problem in a most abstract way as one of learning about the underlying dynamics of group life. He believed that it was possible to construct a coherent body of empirical knowledge about the nature of group life that would be meaningful when specified for any particular kind of group. Thus, he envisioned a general theory of groups that could be brought to bear on such apparently diverse matters as family life, work groups, classrooms, committees, military units, and the community (p. 19).

It is doubtful that the vast output of group dynamics research in the 1940s and 1950s would have occurred without this integral link of theorizing and hypothesis testing with experimentation and concern for social application.

A balanced evaluation of Lewin's place in social psychology leads inevitably to the conclusion that his formative influence was dominant, far surpassing that of most other contributors combined. In many ways, Lewin's influence in large measure determined what the very nature of the discipline would become in the two decades following the Second World War.

Experimental Social Psychology: 1945-1965

By midcentury, experimental social psychology was a burgeoning discipline. Lewin's influence gave strong impetus to the study of group processes during the 1940s and 1950s. At the same time, under the influence of Hovland at Yale, the study of attitude-change processes proceeded with vigor. During this period, the laboratory experiment was perfected as a powerful tool for the analysis of social phenomena. Complex factorial designs with sophisticated manipulation of variables and measurement of effects became common. Deception experiments became more and more frequent, eventually leading to a negative reaction (e. g., Kelman, 1968). During this period, the number of social psychologists increased greatly and their productivity kept apace so that, by the early 1960s, it was impossible for one person to keep abreast of the massively growing literature. Several excellent modern texts were produced during the latter part of this period (see Smith, 1966, for an excellent review of these texts), and this trend accelerated so that by 1975 there were perhaps 30 current introductory texts. Several excellent substantive summaries of research and theorizing during this period are given in the Koch series (e. g., Asch, 1959; Lambert, 1963; Sherif, 1963).

Two developments during this period deserve emphasis: the focus on method and the development of middle range theories. The concern with method was perhaps the predominant trend. "During the forties and fifties, a revolution in methods placed emphasis on an inward-turning laboratory method, where the investigator cut the problem down to manageable size and emphasized 'internal validity' rather than 'external validity' in his work" (Lambert & Weisbrod, 1971, p. 2). Katz (1967, p. 341) spoke of the impressive advance in methodology both in new techniques and research standards. Allport (1968b) made the same point, but with considerable reservation:

> The fifth decade brought also a frenzy of methodological sophistication. Factor analysis, mathematical models, computers, minute empiricism, multivariate analysis of variance, and elaborate mendacious experimentation began to flourish. Our addiction to the pompous and erroneous term 'methodology' betrays our preoccupation. We inflate our methods into 'methodologies' because we are so conscious of them and so childishly proud (p. 15).

This concern culminated in an entire volume devoted to methods in the most recent edition of *The Handbook of Social Psychology* (Lindzey & Aronson, 1968). In particular, the chapter by Aronson and Carlsmith indicates the high degree of sophistication that the laboratory experiment had achieved. A more elementary presentation is given by Hendrick and Jones (1972).

The second major development of the period was the trend away from general theories and toward middle range theories. This trend was noted by Moscovici (1972) and by Katz (1972), who also pointed out that experimentation has usually been in the service of testing single concept theories. The theory of the single concept did indeed become popular; theories of dissonance, balance, attitude change, and attribution predominated. No longer were general schemes such as Lewin's field theory seriously entertained. This trend to single concept theories led to numerous diverse and specialized literatures, often with little interconnection between them.

Substantively, the bulk of the research during this period was nominally concerned with either group processes or attitude change. The serious study of attitude change was primarily a post-World War II pnenomenon. Earlier work was largely descriptive. Murphy, Murphy, and Newcomb (1937) devoted one section to the experimental modification of attitude, but most of the studies reported were concerned with attitude change as a function of schooling and the effects of emotional versus rational political pamphlets. Prestige of the communicator also made a tentative, though crude appearance during that period. Finally, several studies sought a correlation between information held and attitude, a question that eventually emerged as the issue of the relation between learning and persuasion. At the same time, theorizing on attitude became "top-heavy with conceptual elaboration, including contentious questions of definition, analyses into components, and distinctions between attitudes and related constructs" (McGuire, 1969a, p. 137). McGuire also spoke of the flight of young talent from the study of attitudes in the 1940s (presumably to groups), a trend which was not reversed until sometime into the early 1950s.

One work of note is a careful history of the attitude concept by Fleming (1967) who traced the concept back to its earliest origins. Fleming described attitude as a semitechnical word which has also triumphally invaded ordinary speech. His thesis was that " . . . from modest beginnings, 'attitude' had come by the middle of the twentieth century to embody a new conception of man, a redefinition of the distinctively human to encompass the impact of the last hundred years upon men's view of themselves" (p. 291). Gordon Allport (1968b, pp. 12-13) would probably have agreed with this assessment. After noting that the average life of popular concepts is perhaps two decades, he viewed attitude as an exception, calling it the "truly indestructible core concept in our science."

The turn away from descriptive attitude studies toward the manipulation of attitude change seems to have been due in large part to the pressures of World War II. The armed forces were greatly interested in problems of troop morale and propaganda. This interest led naturally to a focus on change. A number of psychologists and sociologists were involved in this program; the most important for present purposes was Carl Hovland. Originally trained in a behavioristic tradition, Hovland collaborated on a number of attitude studies while in the army. One program concerned the effect of films on troop morale. This work lent itself readily to the manipulation of independent variables.

Hovland continued this research after the war, attracting many students. McGuire (1969a, p. 138) stated that Hovland's ability to make attitude research exciting to young scholars was analogous to Lewin's gift for attracting students to group dynamics. This research continued at Yale, resulting in several volumes and many articles (the classic is Hovland, Janis & Kelley, 1953). The thrust of the work was loosely within a learning tradition, but was largely empirically oriented. This research is well summarized in several sources (e. g., Kiesler, Collins, & Miller, 1969).

By the early 1950s, the experimental study of attitudes was in full swing. The study of group processes also continued to boom. However, during the decade, interest in groups diminished somewhat. The gestalt emphasis of the Lewinian field somehow became totally encapsulated within the single head, resulting in a plethora of consistency theories, most notably Heider's (1958) balance theory and Festinger's (1957) dissonance theory. McGuire discussed (1969a) how this inward-turning emphasis led to an interest in attitude-change processes. By the mid-1960s, the consistency approach to attitude change had somewhat eclipsed the Yale learning approach. Toward the end of the period, the Lewinian inspired gestalt-balance approach had shifted in a slightly different direction, toward atttibution processes. The basis for this shift already existed in Heider's (1958) classic treatment of phenomenal causality, the roots of which partly lay in Lewin's field approach. Interest in dissonance and related areas of research remained very high during the early 1970s, but by 1975 the number of consistency articles dropped off somewhat, and attribution articles showed an enormous increase. Theoretically, then, the present era may be characterized as the age of attribution. This characterization represents only a slim central tendency of course, since there has been an exploding diversity of research in many areas. However, the assessment of the *major* interest as in attribution is probably a fair one.

The Recent Past

By 1965, the experimental approach was the queen of methods. In fact, in some quarters it was vaguely disrespectful to even consider using any other method. Experimental social psychology was at the height of its glory at this date. The field was growing rapidly, and there was much confidence in the future of the discipline. At about this time, the Society of Experimental Social Psychology was founded to provide an intimate forum for experimentalists. (See Hollander, 1968, for a brief history.) Shortly thereafter, a strong negative reaction occurred, which has since come to be called the crisis in social psychology. The roots of this reaction are complex and will be dealt with more fully in another section. It is sufficient to state here that one result of the crisis has been a broadening of the scope of respectable methods and the active pursuit of applied concerns. Lambert and Weisbrod (1971) dared to speak of a revolution in *comparative* social psychology, which remained underground for many years but which has now emerged as respectable company. The *Journal of Applied Social Psychology* was launched in 1971, an undertaking probably not possible a decade earlier. In part due to the influence of McGuire (e. g., 1967), research in natural settings (e. g., Willems & Raush, 1969) and field settings (e. g., Bickman & Henchy,1972; Sandowsky, 1972) has become more common. The seminal work by Webb, Campbell, Schwartz, and Sechrest (1966) also contributed to this movement. Sales' (1973) use of archival data to study the relation between threat and authoritarianism was also an interesting innovation in method. At the same time that new methods were being tried, social psychologists turned in a massive way to the study of the experiment in its own right. A whole literature on the social psychology of the psychological experiment has emerged (e. g., Rosenthal & Rosnow, 1969).

It is too early to tell whether the shift to other methods will persist, or whether it is just a passing fad. Fried, Gumpper, and Allen (1973) found only a slight increase in field studies reported in the *Journal of Personality and Social Psychology* for the period 1961-1970. Higbee and Wells (1972) studied the 1969 volumes of the same journal and found that nine out of ten articles involved experimental manipulation, the majority of which used college students as subjects, and four out of five experiments used an analysis of variance design. Higbee and Wells saw very little push toward field research.

Higbee and Wells's analysis may not well reflect present trends, since journal articles are based on studies conceived several years previously. It seems probable that the incipient diversification in methods will continue and even accelerate. The lack of guiding theories for creative hypothesis testing, the disenchantment with the experiment in other areas of psychology (Deese, 1969), the conception of new orientations toward research such as the adversary model (Levine, 1974), and the growing concern with the ethics of social experiments (e. g., Resnick & Schwartz, 1973) all conspire to ensure methodological diversity. At the moment, the future of social psychology would seem to be very open.

PHILOSOPHIC FOUNDATIONS OF EXPERIMENTAL SOCIAL PSYCHOLOGY

Overview

There seem to be at least two basically contrastive views of humanity within the social sciences. William James referred to these views as the tough-minded and tender-minded conceptions of people. In the recent past, these two viewpoints have confronted each other in the guise of phenomenology versus behaviorism (Wann, 1964). The arguments are summarized succinctly by Hitt (1969). A variety of issues are involved, including behavior versus consciousness, predictability of human behavior, objectivity versus subjectivity of human life, similarity versus uniqueness, humans as passive receivers of stimulation versus humans as active generators of stimulation, and so on. Most generally the dichotomies may be treated as the hard (or naturalistic) versus the soft (or humanistic) approaches to social knowledge.

There is little doubt that experimental social psychology is within the central tradition of natural science. Harré and Secord (1972, p. 5) identify three basic assumptions of this approach as it applies to the behavioral sciences.

1. A mechanist model of humans is the only one that will satisfy the requirements for making a science.

2. The principle of causation must be assumed in the minimal Humean sense — precluding metaphysical consideration of the mode of connection between cause and effect.

3. A methodology based on logical positivism provides the best approach to behavioral science.

Harré and Secord's list of assumptions is a fair assessment of the underlying presuppositions of the natural science approach to behavior. These assumptions lead to an emphasis on situationism (Bowers, 1973) and a search for environmental determinants of behavior. The situationist approach coalesces into a metaphysical view, in which stimulus-response connections are equated with causation (Rychlak, 1968), allowing behaviorism to serve as a guiding philosophy (Skinner, 1974). Further, stimulus-response (hence causation) is mapped onto the notion of relations between independent and dependent variables, in this way allowing experimental results to stand for causal relations (Hendrick & Jones, 1972).

The story is not really that simple. Actually, the philosophic traditions most directly affecting experimental social psychology are torturous in their complexity. The purpose of this section is to review some of those historical strands in the philosophy of science that are most relevant to social psychology. It will be useful to begin with a contrasting view of another approach for comparative purposes. For that purpose, the essentials of Verstehen sociology will be presented briefly. Following that, a major subsection will be concerned with the philosophy of natural science, particularly with the nature of causation and theoretical explanation. Another subsection will detail the specific influences of the philosophy of natural science on social psychology. Considerable attention will be given to the influence of Kurt Lewin. This material will culminate in an epistemological model, which is offered as the basic paradigm that social psychologists implicitly follow in the conduct of their scientific activities.

The Soft Approach: Verstehen Sociology

Psychology does not hold exclusive ownership of social psychology; sociologists own a share as well. In fact, about one-third of the social psychology courses taught in the United States are offered in sociology departments. There are of course many distinguished proponents of the natural science approach within sociology. However, I would urge that the modal approach of sociological social psychologists follows a different philosophy of science — that of Verstehen sociology.

Wilson (1970) identified two radically different approaches to sociology. The normative approach follows the natural science tradition with its emphasis on deductive theory and hypothesis-confirmation research. In contrast, the interpretative (Verstehen) approach assumes that adequate social explanation must deal with the interpretative meanings of an actor from his/her own standpoint. This approach denies that an understanding of meaningful subjectivity is possible from the external viewpoint of deductive science.

The origins of the interpretative approach are diverse. Wilhelm Dilthey was instrumental in forging it (see Truzzi, 1974, for a discussion), but, among sociologists, the work of Max Weber is cited most often (see Levison, 1974, for a concise discussion). Weber felt that causal explanation was ultimately necessary but that, for the social sciences, it could only be achieved through interpretative understanding of social action (Chua, 1974). By "action," Weber meant all human behavior to which an acting individual attached a subjective meaning. Weber used the term "understanding" to refer to the kind of knowledge that people have of their own experience, such as intentions, thoughts, emotions, etc. When this kind of understanding is generalized to other persons, it becomes interpretative understanding.

Weber distinguished two kinds of interpretative understanding (Levison, 1974, p. 60). The first was a direct observational understanding, as in the immediate grasping of the meaning of "two plus two." Another example is the observation of a person chopping wood. The very meaning of the act is given in the observation; we are not conscious of an inference process. The gestalt person-chopping-wood is immediately given in perception as a meaningful act.

A second kind of interpretative understanding Weber called explanatory understanding. This kind satisfies the "why" question by placing the act in a more inclusive context of meaning. For example, the question "Why is the person chopping wood?" may be answered by knowledge of the person's motives or intentions. For example, he/she may be chopping wood because that is his/her job; he/she is being paid to do so. Or he/she may be chopping for exercise or for needed firewood, etc. The point is that knowledge of the broader context gives immediate meaning as to why the person is engaging in a particular act.

Weber's discussion of two kinds of Verstehen implies a dimension requiring different degrees of inference. At one extreme the meaning is given directly by perceiving the act (for example, woodcutting). Socialization in a given group ensures the apperception of such meaning, and, indeed, social life would be impossible without such an immediate apperception of meaning. Requiring slightly more inference is the imputation of intent. With an overt act like chopping the assumption that the person is intending to chop wood requires very little inferential energy. Other more passive activities, (for example, staring out a window) may require considerably more inference to ferret out the intention. Finally, inferring the reasons or motives for the act may require the highest degree of inference. Weber's point was that even in motivational inference, a great many social situations are "standard" in the sense that the motive is "given" and "understood" by all actors observing the situation.

Thus, according to Weber, explaining another's behavior requires interpretative understanding based on the analogy of self-understanding of one's own subjective processes. Weber provided the basis for an interpretative sociology, but it required further tools for full development. One of the most important developments was the concept of *role-taking,* originated by Mead (1934), and elaborated by symbolic interactionists such as Blumer (1969). Role-taking means imaginatively projecting oneself into the place of the other, viewing the world from the other's point of view. Reciprocal role-taking allows the exchange or sharing of meaning and provides the foundation for interaction. Overt interaction may be viewed in this fashion as a meshing or "playing out" of reciprocal roles. (See Kelley, Osborne, & Hendrick, 1974, for an extended discussion of the distinction between role-taking and role-playing.)

In this view, social behavior rests on the exchange of shared meanings within the context of interaction. But meanings are not just exchanged in rote fashion. Rather, meaning is itself defined, revised, or changed during interaction. In this sense, roles are not so much played out as constructed in process by devising performances consistent with each actor's interpretative meaning of the situation.

The methodological implications of the interpretative approach require that interaction be studied from the point of view of the actor. Only by role-taking the actor's position, can his/her world be understood and explained. Since subjective understanding is required, literal description of behavior from an external point of view will fail to capture the true meaning of the behavior. Thus, the deductive-experimental approach to social explanation is inadequate. One must have a methodology that allows for the study of behavior from the subjective point of view of the actor. Many different techniques are used by adherents of the interpretative approach, but, as a general approach, *participant observation* seems to be the favorite method. At its best, this approach reflects the social process of living within society, a necessary condition for understanding society from the subjective view of its individual members. An excellent volume detailing this methodology has been prepared by Bruyn (1966).

Verstehen sociology provides an interesting contrast against which to view developments in the natural science tradition. Quite clearly, experimental social psychologists do not subscribe to the interpretative approach, either as a general philosophy of science or in terms of methodology. It may well be that social psychologists use this approach considerably within the *context of discovery,* but it is eschewed within the *context of justification* (see Levison, 1974). For example, in reading Aronson and Carlsmith's (1968) chapter on experimentation it is clear that a great deal of role-taking and subjective understanding occurs in devising experimental manipulations and in constructing the pseudoenvironments of deception experiments. However, this interpretative understanding is always implicit, part of the common-sense lore of experimentation. The explicit concerns are with the logic of confirmation in the justification of testing hypotheses.

Philosophy of the Natural Sciences

This material can best be developed by a partial historical approach. The first subsection examines briefly the ancient origins. The second subsection discusses the rise of empiricism in science. The third subsection discusses some of the more salient developments in this century. The discussion of the first subsection is heavily indebted to Losee (1972).

The Ancient Origins

Many of the major issues in the philosophy of science derive from Aristotle's philosophy. Aristotle's general conception of science was cyclical, progressing from observations to general principles (induction), and back again to new observations (deduction). The scientist should induce explanatory principles from observed phenomena, and then deduce statements about the phenomena from premises that include these principles. Induction was conceived in terms of simple enumeration, roughly analogous to the modern principle of mathematical induction. Deduction was conceived in terms of stylized argument using a few basic sentence forms (all S are P; no S are P; some S are P; some S are not P) that were essentially statements of class inclusion or exclusion. The argument followed a few set forms (for example, the syllogism), and validity of the argument was based only on the proper relation between premises and conclusion. Since validity followed from logical form, Aristotle imposed several extralogical conditions on scientific deduction: (a) a premise should be empirically true; (b) a premise should be indemonstrable to avoid an infinite regress of statements; (c) a premise should be more familiar or better known than the conclusion; and (d) a premise should in some sense *cause* the result shown in the conclusion. In this sense Aristotle viewed scientific laws as *necessary* truths.

The Aristotelian conception of causality is well known. Aristotle felt that an adequate scientific explanation must specify all four aspects of causation: the efficient, material, formal, and final modes. At a later period, due to Galileo's influence, only efficient and material causation were considered as true causes. In fact, considering the formal and final modes as causes seems quite peculiar today. In a fascinating history of the metaphor of growth and development, Nisbet (1969) showed how ancient Greek thinking was permeated with the notion of change based on the analogy of growth of living things. Aristotle's emphasis on all four causes makes good sense when the growth metaphor is accepted as the metaphysical basis for the operation of the natural world.

The Pythagoreans introduced another element into scientific explanation, the use of mathematics. They believed that what was real was the mathematical harmony present in nature. Mathematical relations that fit phenomena are the explanation of the phenomena. An alternative view was that mathematical hypotheses must be distinguished from substantive theories about the structure of the world. In this way, there arose the issue of "saving the appearances" by mathematical relations. The nature of mathematics was very unclear; for example, Ptolemy was uncertain whether his mathematical models were only computational devices or whether they mapped reality. The issue has evolved historically as the role of models vis-à-vis theory. Controversy still abounds. One rigorous discussion is provided by Braithwaite (1953).

Another trend in mathematization was the tendency toward the axiomatic approach, as in Euclid's geometry. This approach was generally consistent with Aristotles's development of deductive logic. Three ideals of the axiomatic approach as applied to science were: (a) axioms and theorems should be deductively related; (b) the axioms should be self-evident truths; and (c) theorems should agree with observation. Not everyone agreed with the requiredness of these three ideals. Some people argued that (c) was sufficient; as long as theorems agreed with observation, science could progress, and the truth or falsity of the axioms did not matter. In this way the question of the truth-value of theory came about. Arguing that only (c) is required is to adopt a conventional approach to theory, perhaps best represented in modern times by Poincaré. Viewing a theory as a convention emphasizes its pragmatic value or tool function, as opposed to the view of theory as expressing necessary truth.

At the same time that the mathematico-deductive approach was originating, the ancient atomists were busy forging a philosophy of nature. In contrast to the Platonic view, which mapped appearance onto reality in the sense of an imperfect copy mapped onto the original, the atomists argued for a radically different mapping. Underlying reality was different in kind from the world of appearance. The idea was introduced that observed changes can be explained by appeal to processes occurring at a more elementary level. Hence, the issue of reduction was born early, and it stubbornly persists. A second related point was that qualitative changes could be reduced to quantitative changes at the atomic level. The atomists paved the way for the quantitative view of nature as it exists in modern science.

During the Middle Ages, the notion of experimentation made a tentative appearance. The principle of Ockham's razor was enunciated, which in effect said that we should not ponder whether "nature chooses the shortest path," rather we should *talk* about nature in the simplest possible way. Thus, simplicity became an attribute of concept formation, rather than an attribute of nature per se. During this period, scholars also became more skeptical of the possibility of necessary truth. Nicolaus of Autrecourt reduced the concept of necessary truth to the minimal logical principle of noncontradiction. Nicholaus recognized that necessary knowledge of causal relations could not be obtained from deductive argument, because statements about causes do not imply statements about effects in the same sense that a premise entails a conclusion.

At the beginning of the modern period, Galileo constructed a new philosophy of science by excluding teleological explanation; by downgrading the importance of Aristotle's logic of classes; by upgrading mathematical models, particularly the notion of a functional relation; by restricting the concern of physics to the atomists' primary quantitative properties; and by affirming the Archimedean use of idealized constructs. Abstraction was valued, and the ideal of universal physical laws was esteemed. In the wake of Galileo's modern conception of science, Francis Bacon emphasized induction in science, and Newton perfected the axiomatic method, setting a standard for mathematical deduction that has persisted in the natural sciences.

The ancient origins of the philosophy of natural science were quite diverse. Some of the most important issues were: (a) the problem of induction; (b) the nature of deductive theory in explanation; (c) the status of causality; and (d) the relation between mathematics and substantive physical knowledge.

The Rise of Empiricism

Gross (1974) identified Hobbes as among the first philosophers to argue for the application of experimental and mathematical methods of the natural sciences to the study of human behavior. Hobbes developed a rather sophisticated mechanistic theory of learning in the atomistic-associationist tradition. However, his interests were quite diverse, and he attempted to apply his ideas to social, political, and legal behavior, as well as individual behavior. Somewhat later, John Locke extended Hobbes atomistic thinking to social behavior much more explicitly. Locke argued that the cause of things must be sought in their atomic motions, and in contrast to Descartes, who stopped at the "mind," Locke attempted to apply the "laws of motion" to mental as well as physical phenomena. In this way, mind was viewed as a natural substance, not different in kind from other physical properties of the world. This conception, perhaps more than any other, allowed the full flowering of an empirical social science. As an atomist, Locke was also a reductionist. Applied to social phenomena, his approach assumed that social or group behavior could be deduced from psychological postulates. This position is currently called *methodological individualism.* Most experimental social psychologists probably accept this methodological postulate, at least implicitly, but it is hotly debated in sociology, as might be expected. George Homans is one of the more distinguished proponents of this principle in sociology. (See Ryan, 1973, for an interesting collection of papers on this topic.)

This general empiricist approach was defined more sharply by David Hume, who held that all knowledge of matters of fact arises from sense experience. Consistent with this approach, he granted considerable importance to the "moral" sciences, because all science rests on the power of human cognizance. Further, the experimental method of reasoning could be applied to moral subjects in the same way as to the natural sciences.

The growth in skepticism during the Middle Ages about the possibility of necessary knowledge was elaborated in detail by Hume, resulting in his well-known analysis of causation. In brief, Hume viewed causation as a relation and not a sensible quality of objects. Causation was viewed as a complex idea of relation constructed from the simple ideas of: (a) perceived contiguity; (b) succession in time; and (c) a constant conjunction of two events over a series of instances. Thus causation was viewed as a law that applies to classes of events rather than individual events. Hume denied any intrinsic or necessary connection between cause and effect, except in the psychological sense of our belief in the appearance of a necessary connection. Most commentators agree that Hume's view of causation is most similar to the modern notion of correlation. By stripping the concept of cause of any metaphysical notion of necessary connection, Hume set the stage for the concept of a functional relation between behaviors, thereby greatly promoting empirical social science. Interesting brief discussions of Hume may be found in Eacker (1972), Lana (1969), Levison (1974), and Losee (1972).

Around the time of Hume, empiricism was advanced in another way by Berkeley, who criticized Newton for failing to distinguish mathematical theory from hypotheses regarding the true nature of events. Berkeley viewed forces in mechanics as constructions, useful in calculation, but having no bearing on real existence in the world. For example, equally plausible alternative theories may be proposed to account for the same phenomenon. In this way, Berkeley took a purely instrumentalist position on the status of physical laws; they were computational devices, nothing more. The reduction in status of theoretical entities by Berkeley was consistent with Locke's and Hume's emphasis on sense experience as the source of all knowledge. The approach indirectly placed value on empirical research, and the tradition grew in strength over the next century, reaching an apex in Mill's inductivism.

Kant attempted a synthesis of the divergent schools of empirical and rational thought. He agreed with Hume that empirical experience arises from sense impressions, but disagreed that such knowledge is purely given in the impressions. He proposed a theory of cognition, which distinguished between the content and form of experience. Sense impressions provided the raw material for knowledge, but the knowing person provided the principles for structuring and relating this raw material. Raw sensations of phenomena were ordered by forms of sensibility, the most basic being the forms of space and time. The resulting perceptions were related by the twelve categories of understanding (for example, unity, substantiality, causality, etc.) to provide specific judgments of experience. Finally, the judgments of experience were organized into a system of knowledge by the regulative principles of reason (Losee, 1972).

One of the most basic regulative principles was the notion of the purposiveness in nature. It was a neat solution for the question of necessity. Kant recognized that necessity in nature can never be proved in an absolute sense, but he urged that we adopt the principle as a working rule of procedure.

Kant was skeptical about the possibility of complete causal knowledge for still another reason. He noted that causal laws can establish only that particular states of a physical object or living organism follow from other previous states. But living organisms have a different status. Living organisms are self-organizing wholes, systems which consist of a series of part-whole relations. The organization of a system is a matter of reciprocal part-whole definition. The unilinear conception of causality as a flow of events is not well suited to capture the organizational properties of living beings.

This theme is reflected in modern times by the attempt of Gestalt psychology to create a conception of causality as a total explanatory field, rather than a unilinear flow of events. Some of this concern was also evident in the philosophic concerns of Kurt Lewin. Currently, Piaget's philosophy and psychology are heavily indebted to the Kantian synthesis, and in general Kant seems to have contributed greatly to the development of the modern systems approach.

It is clear that the origins of the philosophy of science do not present a unified front. Someone has called science a vast series of specific projects. Philosophizing about science seems to have followed a similar course. Nevertheless, it seems reasonable to point out one very general consideration that has been a point of contention over the centuries. That issue is the relative valuing of experience (or sense experience) as opposed to reason. The valuing of reason leads to a pleasure in speculation, to the construction of theory and the intellectual pleasure of deduction, and to the use of abstractions such as mathematics. The valuing of sense experience leads to concern with the empirical world, with manipulating or experimenting with it, and perhaps to a vague distrust of unchecked reason.

The tendency toward one or the other of these two extremes may well be a basic psychological disposition. In what was called an empirical approach to the philosophy of science, Mitroff (1974) studied the theoretical preferences of 42 eminent physical scientists concerned with the *Apollo* program. The point of interest was the type of theories these scientists preferred. Mitroff found very clear differences. At one extreme were the creative speculators, scientists enamored with esoteric theories and willing to defend them. At the other extreme were the pure data gatherers. The latter scientists believed in sticking to the facts and making only the most narrow extrapolation beyond them. Also, they tended to distrust the speculators.

This theory-preference-data-preference dichotomy may be seen even within a given philosophic or theoretical area. As one example, the preference for a systematized, deductive theory by Clark Hull is well known. Equally well known is B. F. Skinner's preference for data and his disdain for theoretical construction.

Yet both men were behavioristic in their approach to psychology. It may be that such general psychological preferences shape in part one's preferred philosophy of science. If true, one would perhaps expect cyclical changes of preference within a discipline over a period of time. For example, if founding members of a discipline were mainly empiricist in outlook, they would tend to attract first- and second-generation novices with a similar outlook. Over a few generations, a firm empiricist outlook would be established. When this approach began to produce few returns, a crisis in the Kuhnian sense would emerge, and "radicals" from the polar extreme, or rationalist tradition, would be attracted. In this way, the composition of the discipline in terms of philosophic preference would gradually swing toward the rationalistic, speculation-preferring end of the continuum. This analysis is similar to McGuire's (1973) analysis of the reasons for shifting preferences in methods, but it is conceived at the more general level of changes in metaphysical beliefs of members of a discipline. The analysis shifts Kuhn's (1970) focus slightly away from the importance of internal crisis as the instrument of change, and it views the result of internal crisis as causing a selective factor in group recruitment to emerge and eventually resulting in a new paradigm for the science because of the changed intellectual style of the group.

The Twentieth Century

Two developments in the nineteenth century require mention at this point because of their importance for twentieth century development. One development was John Herschel's distinction in 1830 between the context of discovery and the context of justification (Losee, 1972). Herschel emphasized the context of justification. Many procedures could lead to discovery, and a wild guess was just as good as a careful induction, if it led to scientific laws which could be confirmed. By stressing justification, Herschel initiated the study of science as an "idealized" set of activities, leading to the concerns of the twentieth century with questions of logic, deducibility, language, and syntactical constructions. The focus on justification to a considerable degree allowed the philosophy of natural science to become a normative discipline.

In contrast to Herschel's approach, a contemporary of his, William Whewell, argued for a philosophy of science based on the actual study of the history of science. He felt that there was only a relative distinction between fact and theory, a point more recently emphasized by Gergen (1976). His studies led to a cumulative view of science as a continuing progression that, on analogy, evolves over time from many small tributaries to one mighty river of knowledge. This view was consistent with the notion of progress, and the view prevailed as part of "common sense" until challenged by Kuhn's (1970) thesis of paradigm shifts.

Despite his common sense appeal and vast work in the history of science, Whewell's approach to the philosophy of science was overshadowed by Herschel's normative approach. During the past few years, the historical approach has received new vigor from some philosophers (e. g., Harré, 1970), as well as from students of the sociology of science.

The developments during the twentieth century were many and multifaceted. It will be convenient to organize the discussion around two topic areas: conceptions of causality and conceptions of theoretical explanation.

Conceptions of causality.   The history of conceptions of causality has been summarized in two outstanding volumes by Wallace (1972; 1974). The high tide of causal determinism was probably Laplace's famous statement at the end of the eighteenth century that, if an all encompassing mind could know the respective positions of all particles in the universe, that mind could perfectly predict past and future alike. This statement represented mechanism in its purest form. However, the skeptical trend introduced by Hume gradually gained favor. Also, developments in quantum physics led to Heisenberg's uncertainty principle in 1927, which showed the impossibility of precise prediction of events at the atomic level. This notion led to strong interest in statistical laws and probability explanation, and the notion of cause was gradually replaced by the concept of function. In 1958, Waismann declared "the decline and fall of causality" (Wallace, 1974, p. 163). In many quarters, it became not quite respectable to use the word "cause."

The tide has changed during the last 15 years, however. Nagel (1961) provided a reasoned argument for the use of causal laws in science. He listed four conditions that a law must satisfy to be called causal: (a) an invariable and uniform relation between cause and effect events; (b) spatial contiguity of the relevant events; (c) temporal contiguity with cause preceding effect; and (d) an asymmetrical relation, so that, if A causes B, B can not cause A. In general, however, Nagel was still within the broad Humean tradition of empiricism.

Wallace (1974, pp. 217-237) discussed an anti-Humean trend in current conceptions of causality. One important figure in this new trend was Curt Ducasse (e. g., 1969), "His main thesis was that causality and the causal relationship are directly perceptible in experience, and can only be explained, contrary to Hume, by positing some type of nonlogical or physical necessity as actually existent in nature" (Wallace, 1974, p. 226). Ducasse urged that, in a strict experiment, the relating of changes in one variable to changes in a second variable are directly observable; therefore, causal connections are directly observable. Wallace (1974) concluded that the net effect of Ducasse's work was to foster a withdrawal from empiricism and a return to realism.

Three other modern philosophers have stimulated a partial return to a realistic philosophy of causation: David Bohm (e. g., 1957), Mario Bunge (e. g., 1959), and Rom Harré (e. g., 1970). Bohm noted that the assumptions of mechanism were philosophical in character and, in the same sense, that Heisenberg's indeterminancy principle was a philosophical assumption. He argued that both causal laws and statistical laws have a place in science as alternate views of natural processes. Bunge (1959) rejected Hume's constant-conjunction formula. He felt that common sense as well as scientific practice treats causation as more than a relation. Causation is treated as a category of genetic connection between events that is a way of producing new things from old things. Bunge's formulation was that, if C (cause) happens, then and only then E (effect) is always produced by it. Thus Bunge's version of realism viewed necessary connection as an important attribute of causality and tended to localize the causal principle in nature, as opposed to localization in explanatory linguistic systems about nature.

Harré (1970) strongly attacked what he called the "event ontology" and the "logico-mathematical ideal of deductive explanation." His view was that the aim of science is to find the structures, states and inner constitutions of the phenomena of nature. The following quotation aptly summarizes his view of causation.

> The universe as we know it is *characterized* by the striking phenomenon of causation. It is not the case that an event of any logically possible kind follows one of a given kind. Provided we ensure, or are satisfied of the stability of the conditions in which the events occur, just one kind of event follows one of a certain kind, in most situations. This is so striking as to lead one to the idea that events are generative, that one happening generates another, and also that things have quite determinate and characteristic powers to produce definite kinds of events (p. 6).

The focus on characteristic powers of things is important. Harré stated that the discrimination and identification of things in terms of their powers rather than their qualities provides the basis for a metaphysics that is, in fact, closer to actual scientific practice than the ontology of events.

Harré's philosophy is important to social psychologists, and his work merits careful reading. For one thing, his philosophy seems congruent with the growing literature on causal attribution. There is the distinct possibility that this literature can provide a careful psychological basis for the philosophical metaphysic developed by Harré. Second, the work of Piaget (1974) on the development of causal conceptions in children promises to be productive for research on causal attribution, as well as providing a rationale for the realistic philosophy that conceives powers, capacities, etc. as inherent characteristics of objects.

Thus the thinking on causality in the natural sciences has swung full circle, from Aristotle's early view of necessity to the Humean approach of correlation, and back again to the notion of necessary connection in nature. Actually, these sophisticated changes have been partially lost on social psychologists, who tend to justify experimentation in terms of causal language. For example, "The major value of experiments is that they are better able to test hypotheses about causal relationships than non-experimental studies" (Mills, 1969, p. 412); and "In sum, the major advantage of the laboratory experiment is its ability to provide us with unambiguous evidence about causation" (Aronson & Carlsmith, 1968, p. 10). One should be warned, however, that Harré's realistic philosophy does not in his opinion justify experimentation as it is practiced in social psychology (e. g., Harré & Secord, 1972).

As the principle of causation came more into question at the beginning of this century, philosophers gradually detached the idea of explanation from the idea of cause. Most philosophic attention has been devoted to the general problem of scientific explanation.

Conceptions of scientific explanation.   Most of the controversy has revolved around the nature and importance of theory in scientific explanation. One approach that began with Berkeley has viewed theories as conventions, essentially downgrading their importance in scientific explanation. This view has continued in the present century. For example, Mach viewed theories as implicit summaries of facts, serving the function of economy in thinking. Duhem argued that theories do bind together sets of empirical laws, in a sense serving a representative function, but he denied that they serve any truly explanatory function.

Thus, the view of theories as conventions has numerous modern advocates, but this view has not been dominant. The major emphasis has been on theory as a deductive explanatory system. There have been numerous controversies on this issue, many of which still are not resolved. The more modern approach views a theory as beginning with a series of statements tied together by logical rules. At the beginning the statements constitute a formal calculus; they are devoid of empirical meaning. Only when some of the formal symbols are defined in terms of empirical phenomena does the calculus take on empirical meaning,, that is, become a theory. Certain of the statements are considered as "primitives" or assumptions of the theory. The formal structure of the calculus allows derivation of other statements, which may serve as "theorems," and which, because of the initial empirical definitions given to basic terms, may be subjected to empirical confirmation or disconfirmation (Braithwaite, 1953).

This approach culminated in the "covering law model" (e.g., Hempel, 1966). Following this approach, there are several requirements for an adequate deductive theory. First, the theory must contain some number of universal laws, L_1, $L_2, \ldots L_k$, and statements of antecedent conditions, $C_1, C_2, \ldots C_k$. From the conjunction of universal laws and antecedent conditions, a specific consequence, E, is deduced that can be subjected to empirical test. The covering law model is intended as a model for both explanation and prediction. The deduction of an empirical consequence that is confirmed is the explanation of that consequence. By the same token, the derivation of the consequence may, prior to its testing, be considered as a prediction of the specific events entailed by the consequence statement.

The covering law model has been widely popular. Its use has been advocated in many scientific disciplines, and it has even been urged on historians, but there have been criticisms as well. For example, if deduced consequence E turns out to be false empirically, all one can know empirically is that the total conjunction of all the premises is false. One does not know which one (or several) universal laws might be at fault, or whether the statements of antecedent conditions were incorrect. The net result is that it is impossible to perform a *crucial experiment* to test the theory. For an interesting account of other logical puzzles encountered in the deductive approach, see Salmon (1973). In general, however, the covering law approach probably still best represents the ideal of a normative philosophy of science in terms of a formal, deductive approach to theory construction and testing.

This section would not be complete without mention of the philosophy of logical positivism, which developed during the 1920s. The positivists had a narrow conception of philosophy, restricting its function to the clarification of assertions and questions. They sought a criterion of empirical meaningfulness. One such criterion was that only verifiable statements were to be considered as empirically significant statements. Thus was born the doctrine of verifiability. The basic approach was to construct an empiricist language and require that empirically significant statements be translatable into that language. At an early point, this was the approach of Rudolf Carnap (see Gardner, 1966, for a readable introduction to Carnap). However, the verifiability criterion proved impossible for the simple reason that it could not account for universal statements, a mainstay of nomothetic science. As a less stringent requirement, Ayer (1952) proposed confirmability as a criterion rather than verifiability. This attempt was later revised, in part because it was unclear. For example, a given statement may be considered an empirical generalization in one context and a definition in another context.

Popper (1968) shifted the emphasis to a search for a criterion of empirical method, rather than a criterion for meaningful statements. His approach is called the method of falsifiability, and he argued that proper empirical method requires' exposing a theory to the possibility of being falsified. Science was viewed as a series of conjectures, refutations, and new conjectures. The logic of confirmation is improper in the sense that statements cannot ultimately be proven true in any final sense. They can only fail to be falsified.

Logical positivism had enormous influence on the behavioral sciences, even though it did not survive as a viable movement. In general, the analytic work of positivism contributed to the growth of formal deductive models as the ideal in science.

Finally, Bridgman's (1927; 1936; 1959) operational criterion should be mentioned as an important development in the 20th century. This position is well known. The early view was that the meaning of a concept is nothing more than the operations performed to assign values to it. Bridgman later softened this position, noting that it is not possible to specify all conditions present when an operation is performed. Finally, unanalyzed operations and mental operations were allowed. Thus, what started as a very hard empiricist approach eventually became a relatively soft cognitive approach.

As noted previously, the philosophy of natural science is not unified in its approach. There are many controversies and changes in dominant viewpoints. The most salient tendency of the 20th century seems to have been the increased emphasis on explanation by scientific theories. The ideal for a theory is a formal logical system from which consequences can be deduced and subjected to empirical test.

Impact of Philosophy of Science on Social Psychology

The effects of the philosophy of the natural sciences are quite diverse, although some salient trends are evident. It is convenient to analyze these influences under four categories: philosophy of theory construction, generally; the influence of Lewin's philosophy of science; philosophy of experimentation; and philosophy of the subject.

Philosophy of Theory Construction

Two general themes relevant to social psychology may be noted. One theme emphasizes deductive theory construction. The second theme emphasized a dynamical approach to psychological explanation, due in part to the strong influence of Kurt Lewin, which will be discussed in the next subsection.

The roots of deductivism are relatively clear. They flow from learning theory and, in particular, the hypothetico-deductive approach of Clark Hull. This approach favored the elaboration of theoretical superstructure and used mediating hypothetical constructs and explicit theorem deduction from the postulates of the theory. Construction of such general theories of learning was quite popular during the 1940s, and, for a time, it appeared that the deductive approach to explanation might encompass psychology generally. It is difficult to envision now the great esteem in which this approach was held (e. g., Marx, 1963). It influenced many areas of psychology. McGuire (1965) spoke fondly of this general approach.

The demise of the grand deductive system began sometime in the 1950s. Koch's (1954) critique of Hull's system was highly influential. The rise of Skinnerean empiricism was another factor. The development of mathematical models by scholars such as Estes was still another important trend. The ease with which mathematical models could be invented and discarded tended to shift emphasis once again to the concept of theory as a convention.

Mathematical theories of learning also tended to deal with more restrictive domains than the general Hullian theory. In other areas as well, the trend toward limited domain and single concept theories became evident. This trend was equally true in social psychology, as noted in a previous section. In the recent past, the trend has moved toward testing single hypotheses of the if-then variety, whose formal relation to general theory is usually unclear. The current emphasis in social psychology on testing conditional propositions thus seems to be the final residue of the general deductivist approach to theory construction. The if-then form of statements is retained, but the rigorous deductive approach is not evident.

Lewin's Philosophy of Science

Perhaps the most important point for understanding Lewin's philosophy of science and its impact on social psychology was his conviction that psychology should be an autonomous science, self-contained, with its own system of concepts. This view stems from Lewin's more general notion "that a fundamental incommensurability separates sciences from each other; each science is a closed unit of systematically connected concepts" (Heider, 1959, p. 4). A scientific discipline constitutes a conceptual world, and, although connecting bridges between disciplines are desirable, each discipline is responsible for constructing it own conceptual world and associated methods, thereby gradually diverging from other disciplines. "These ideas form the background of [Lewin's] conviction that psychology should strive to build up a more or less autonomous realm of concepts which form a closely knit system, and that as it develops it should become more aware of its own proper nature, that it should segregate itself away from other sciences, for instance, physiology, and that it should in this way, purify itself" (Heider, 1959, p. 4).

Within this general perspective, Lewin believed that there was a right way and a wrong way to construct a science. His views are stated most systematically in a classic article published in 1931 (reprinted in Lewin, 1935) that contrasted the Aristotelian and Galileian modes of thought in physics. According to Marrow (1969), this paper was highly influential in psychology generally, as well as social psychology.

Lewin was convinced that psychology should develop a "dynamical", that is, Galileian approach to explanation. To develop this conception, he provided a contrast with the older Aristotelian approach to physics relative to the newer Galileian approach, and then applied this contrasting distinction to psychology. According to Lewin, Aristotelian physics depended upon valuational concepts, abstract classification, and the concept of lawfulness as frequency. Concepts were valuational in that they tended toward some perfect state, for example, perfect motion. Concept formation used the principle of class inclusion-exclusion, and the essential nature of a thing was determined by specifying its class membership. Classes tended to be viewed as paired opposites without the notion of continuous gradations so important to the concept of a variable. Finally, in Aristotelian physics, lawfulness was specified in terms of what occurred without exception, or at least most frequently. Thus lawfulness had a quasi-statistical character, and regularity was understood in historical — more precisely historico-geographic — terms. This approach leads to empiricism in the sense of fact gathering for purposes of classification.

Galileian physics depended upon: (a) the principle of homogenization; (b) use of genetic concepts; and (c) the notion of concreteness. Homogeneity meant a view of the world as a comprehensive, all-embracing unity. This approach deprived classification into abstract categories of its efficacy and, in so doing, helped change the class concept from the notion of a polar pair to the notion of an ordered series. The primitive principle of homogeneity also assured the possibility of commensurability of one concept with another concept, ultimately allowing the construction of a system of related concepts. Also, since the class concept gave way to the notion of an ordered series, quantitative relations among sets of ordered series became possible, yielding quantification of the dynamical relationship between concepts, or conceptual variables.

Lewin's notion of genetic concepts led him to distinguish between phenotypes and genotypes or, more generally, between descriptive and conditional-genetic concepts. The world is in a continuous phenomenal flux (phenotypes); however, there are underlying regularities or identities (genotypes), which generate the descriptive diversity of the phenomenal world. It was the task of Galileian physics to construct a basic set of related concepts that best maps the underlying genotypes of physical nature. In this way, the science of physics may be constructed as an elegant system of interrelated conceptual variables.

Finally, Lewin's specification of the principle of concreteness indicated that physical objects possess properties in definite degree or intensity. This basic conception grants the possibility of measurement of object attributes, something not really possible in Aristotelian classification systems. Assigning measurement properties to objects provides the basic foundation for coordinating the empirical physical world to the abstract set of concepts that constitute physical theory.

Lewin felt that psychology was struggling to become Galileian in approach. The concern with frequency, class representativeness, averages (statistics, generally), and historic or developmental explanation he believed to be a residue of the Aristotelian approach. Lewin argued that psychological laws must have unconditional general validity in the same sense as Galileo's laws of free-falling bodies. The quest for general validity emphasized ideal cases or constructs. This approach is very much within the Archimedian advocacy of the use of idealized constructs, although apparently Lewin viewed such constructs as mapping reality in the sense of a realistic philosophy, rather than in the sense of thought conventions as propounded by Poincaré. Since ideal cases rarely occur in nature, they must be constructed for careful study. This view leads directly to a preference for the experiment as the best tool for constructing situations.

There are several implications of Lewin's philosophy for social psychology.

1. Questions of frequency of occurrence are not very important. If a lawful relation between two variables is established, the relation is unconditionally valid. Apparent exceptions to the relation should be viewed in terms of what would today be called other interacting variables, rather than in terms of a statistical notion of frequency. The focus on the generality of variable relationships is ahistorical or, rather, moves beyond the question of historical regularity. "Historical rarity is no disproof, historical regularity is no proof of lawfulness" (Lewin, 1935, p. 26). Although Lewin had no objection to averages, medians, and the like as summary devices, he would object to significant differences established

by inferential statistics as an indicant of the underlying dynamical relation between psychological variables. Averaging cases may obscure or mix several different types of psychological relationships that are quite different from the psychological law the investigator thought was being established.

2. The quest for general laws led to an emphasis on the dynamics of events in concrete situations. For example, in the old physics, the direction of a physical vector was determined in advance by the nature of the moving object. In modern physics, the existence of a physical vector depended upon the relation of the object to its environment (Galileo's experiments on inclined planes presupposed such a relation). The whole situation in which the event occurs contributes to the event, hence is part of its dynamic. Conceptually, variations of the critical features of the situation are required, and these variations are related to the essential feature of the event in question (for example, the velocity of an object). In psychology, Lewin insisted that experimental analysis should be undertaken only within the context of an analysis of the situation as a whole (Lewin, 1951). This emphasis is well illustrated in Lewin's early work. In addition to conventional experimental manipulations, a great mass of descriptive material was obtained from subjects to ascertain the meaning of the situation from the subjects' point of view. In fact, the emphasis on the meaning of the total situation to the subject was so strong that it led DeRivera (1976) to characterize Lewin's research as experimental phenomenology. The general emphasis on observing subject behavior as a function of varying experimental arrangements was common to both Lewin's approach and that of today's experimental social psychologists. Today, however, full descriptive accounts of situations are seldom attempted; the emphasis is almost solely on the effects of the variable manipulation as measured by some objective means. The phenomenal meaning of the manipulation from the subject's point of view is seldom attempted.

3. The emphasis on an analysis of the total situation was congruent with Lewin's insistence on a psychological as opposed to a physicalistic approach to the development of psychological theory. Lewin felt that extreme emphasis on physical operational definitions led to a superficial concern with the physical world at the expense of the psychological world of the individual. Real psychological explanation resided within the life space of the individual, and it was within the individual's inner psychological world that meaningful explanatory constructs would be found. There is a basic incommensurability between physical operations and the psychological operations of the life space. Instead of purely physical operational definitions, Lewin advocated "coordinating definitions," which allowed a commensurate translation between theoretical psychological concepts and those aspects of behavior and experience that were actually measured.

Lewin's approach led to a clash with psychologists in the behavioristic tradition who strongly advocated physical operational definitions. In social psychology, the issue has evolved to the question of stimulus control versus psychological control in the manipulation of independent variables (Kiesler, Collins, & Miller, 1969). Advocates of stimulus control believe in precise standardization of the physical operations for all subjects in a given experimental condition. Advocates of psychological control argue that the variable should be changed for different subjects to bring all subjects to the same psychological state. The ambivalence created by the clash of Lewinian and behavioristic conceptions of operationism continues, although the behavioristic solution of stimulus control is most popular presently. (See Hendrick and Jones, 1972, pages 84 to 85, for further discussion of this issue.)

4. Lewin's conception of the dynamic relation of one variable to another suggested directly that psychological theory could be mathematically represented. Lewin tried various devices, for example, adapting topology to achieve such a representation. This emphasis was quite congruent with the general trend in psychology toward the use of mathematical models. However, the trend toward mathematization in social psychology has been sporadic, although there are strong advocates (e. g., Harris, 1976a).

5. The emphasis on an analysis of the total situation led Lewin to the basic assumption that *behavior is a function of the field at the time the behavior occurs.* This assumption led Lewin to distinguish sharply between systematic and historical causal explanations (for example, see Lewin's 1937 critique of psychoanalytic theory). Proper psychological explanation must be guided by a principle of causal *contemporaneity.* The past is gone, the future is not yet, and their effects can only be indirect by virtue of the individual's current memory of the past or anticipation of the future. The structure of the entire psychological field at the present moment is the causal locus that will explain behavior.

The principle of contemporaneity is both subtle and profound. It is also very difficult to apply effectively to the study of social behavior. Nevertheless, Lewin's conception may have had indirect effects on the direction and current practice of social psychology. The principle of contemporaneity is not intrinsically conducive to asking research questions about human development. As noted previously, a developmental emphasis dominated social psychology (for example, Murphy's writings) during the 1940s, but the discipline became largely ahistorical in interest during the 1950s. This shift may have been an unintended result of acceptance of the principle of contemporaneous causation with its emphasis on the here and now.

The emphasis on contemporaneity may have also contributed to the steady growth of cross-sectional, one-shot social psychology experiments. The increase in such research seems to have been correlated with the decline in interest in developmental issues. If all important causal variables are operative at the given moment, short duration experiments would seem to be a logical methodological consequence, especially since the general philosophy focussed on systematic rather than historical theorizing.

This evolution, to the extent attributable to Lewin's influence, is in many respects a perversion of his actual intent. The full descriptive analysis of the empirical situation was an important tenet of Lewin's methodological philosophy and his actual empirical practice. The stripping away of the rich descriptive analysis in modern social psychology experiments would be most unsatisfactory to Lewin, and it is doubtful whether he would consider many current experiments as making a meaningful contribution to knowledge.

Somewhat ironically, Lewin was quite interested in questions of psychological and social development. He would be unhappy that his philosophy of science might inadvertently have contributed to a demise of interest in developmental issues. Lewin's actual position bears a striking similarity to some of the research within the Skinnerean tradition.

> ... the modern experimental procedure is likely to become more and more "historical." This means (1) it will take into account the historical situation of the person as a whole; (2) it will often have to create experimentally a special history by letting the subject go through a series of situations in order to build up the situation one wants to study (Lewin, 1937, p. 203).

In summary, Lewin's philosophy of science embraced what Harré (1970) called an event ontology. Lewin's focus on idealized variables and dynamic relations seemed almost to require the laboratory experiment. His notion of systematic lawful relations between conceptual variables may have had the effect of minimizing the need for what is today called external validity, in the sense of demonstrating the relation across different populations of persons. The emphasis on contemporaneous causation may have inadvertently lent credence to the one-shot, cross-sectional laboratory experiment, even though Lewin's own beliefs tended more toward a time-series study within a given situation. Lewin's focus on conditional-genetic propositions was congruent with the trends in deductive philosophy and thus contributed to the current emphasis on testing specific implicational hypotheses. Finally, Lewin's emphasis on systematic, that is dynamic, theory and his devaluing of historical explanation may have contributed to the demise for several years of the study of social developmental trends. In conclusion, Lewin's philosophy of science, despite its breadth, led directly to a focus on and preoccupation with the laboratory experiment.

Philosophy of Experimentation

Several trends should be noted. The major event was undoubtedly the introduction of Bridgman's operationism via Stevens's (1939) classic article. As noted above, Lewin opposed a narrow operationism because he felt it deflected emphasis to physical rather than psychological variables. However, the principle of operationism (of various varieties) became a standard methodological principle in all areas of psychology.

The emphasis on hypothesis testing was noted previously. The stress on the logic of confirmation from the logical positivists was retained. Lewin's influence led to an emphasis on the search for functional relations, and, as noted previously, social psychologists tend to view such functional relations as exemplifying causal relations. The stress on functional relations is really just an analogy to the approach of physics, primarily because of the ordinal nature of the data of social psychology. At the extreme, the difference on a dependent variable due to simple presence-absence of the independent variable is often considered as evidence of a functional relation. Generally, inference statistics are used as evidence for such a relation, again in opposition to Lewin's general position.

In experimental research, great skill has been developed in manipulations of the independent variable (e. g., Aronson & Carlsmith, 1968). This skill is an outgrowth of Lewin's emphasis on construction of idealized cases and situations. McGuire (1969a) presented an interesting contrast between the Lewinian approach (the Festingerians), with its orientation toward the independent variable, and the learning approach (the Hovlanders), which emphasizes measurement of the dependent variable. There seems to be an element of truth to this contrast.

Lewin perhaps never clearly saw some of the problems of the laboratory experiment, especially the host of problems that revolve around the role of subject in a specific situation. His vision was on general laws, and he seemed somewhat unaware of the relativity of knowledge gained from the experiment. More important than Lewin's own views of the experiment were the effects of his views on later generations of social psychologists. Social psychology at present is still selectively and almost exclusively preoccupied with the laboratory experiment. It is a reasonable conjecture that this selectivity, with many of its attendant problems, is due in large measure to Lewin's influence.

An example may be offered to document this thesis. In an important paper, "Causal Interconnections in Psychology," Lewin (1936) specified a principle of concreteness. Essentially, he meant that only what is concrete can have effects. Lewin felt that this truism was often ignored by those who attempted to explain events by principles of development, adaptation, abstract drives, or in treating abstract principles as if they were concrete causes. Further, effects can only be produced by concrete individual facts that exist at a given moment (the contemporaneity principle). A related idea was that causal facts have a relational character. Events do not derive from the nature of a single object, but rather events result from an interaction of several facts, forming a relationship. A third relevant idea, as noted previously, was the "unconditional general validity of psychological laws" (Lewin, 1935, p. 23).

These three conceptual elements — concreteness of effects, relational character of psychological facts, and the general nature of laws — are undoubtedly susceptible to various interpretations. One line of implication was as follows. Festinger (1959) expressed the opinion that careful population sampling is not important in hypothesis testing experiments. The real point of the experiment is to show a relationship, because (following Lewin), if a relationship is found, a law relating concrete facts has been discovered. As a law, it must have generality. Hendrick and Jones (1972) took the next logical step by arguing that any population differences that would result in a different relationship from the one obtained in the laboratory from a sample of a specified population can be reconceptualized in terms of another conceptual variable interacting in some way with the first independent variable. In this way, population questions do not enter into the development of an abstract conceptual theory. Population differences can always be explained by discovering new conceptual variables.

This type of thinking has had strong consequences in the conduct of social research. For one thing, it has legitimized the massive reliance on sophomores as subjects, because population generality is intrinsically recast as a question of variable generality. The fact of such reliance on sophomores has led to severe questions of the external as well as the internal validity of psychological experiments (Campbell & Stanley, 1963). Beyond that, basic questions of triviality and the very meaning of social experiments have been asked recently.

This example was presented to show the subtle ways in which one of Lewin's ideas may have influenced the practice of experimental social psychology. Undoubtedly there are numerous other possible examples as well.

Philosophy of the Subject

According to Schultz (1969), the subject was originally conceived in psychology in the role of observer, sometimes as a reagent, in introspective studies. The role was honored because he/she was both observer and observed. With the rise of behaviorism, the role of observer was downgraded to that of lowly subject (sociology has always accorded more status via the term "actor"). The downgrading of the role of subject was concurrent with the growing conception of manipulation and control of variables in the laboratory. The subject's role gradually became one in which his/her behavior was defined, controlled, manipulated, evaluated, and reported by the scientist to a high degree of precision (Argyris, 1968). In general, the subject's role came to be viewed as a passive one with something of a blank-slate quality. More recently, there have been some attempts at rehumanization of the subject; the preferred term may come to be "human participants" (American Psychological Association, 1973).

The growth of single concept theories also contributed to the dehumanization of the subject role. The focus on a single attribute allows an experimenter to ignore the full individuality of the subject, much as the surgeon's focus on the appendix allows him to ignore the patient's body as an integrated whole.

This selective emphasis has led to some very peculiar practices, especially deception experiments. On one hand, social psychologists plan their experiments as if the single independent-dependent variable relation were all that existed in the situation. On the other hand, it is implicitly understood that the subject is really a self-activating whole, an actor in the sociological sense. Therefore strategies are required to get the subject to focus only on the narrow experimental plan the psychologist has in mind. This often requires deception, and the scenario is carried out as if only the narrow variable relation existed. However, the very existence of deception experiments presupposes the conception of the subject as a self-cognizing actor. This type of incongruity has been treated in an interesting fashion by Argyris (1975) in his distinction between theories in use and theories of action.

It seems clear that the current role of subject follows the notions of mechanism. The deductive approach to theory and the ideal of manipulation of variables require a relatively pliable conception of the subject so as to maintain simplicity of scientific approach. Currently, behavioral science cannot deal with people in the role of self-determining systems. This mechanical view of the subject's role has led to grave concerns over the ethics of human experimentation. Kelman (1968) is one of the more eloquent spokesmen on this issue. It may be that basic revision of the conception of the subject is in the offing because of the increasing pressure of ethical concerns.

Thus, the residual effects of the philosophy of natural science on experimental social psychology are: (a) retention of vestiges of the deductive approach as seen in numerous hypothesis testing experiments; (b) emphasis on functional relations between variables, providing eminence to the laboratory experiment; and (c) a mechanical, passive view of the human when he/she is in the laboratory in the role of subject. It will be useful to summarize these considerations in terms of a simple epistemic model, which guides much of the theorizing and experimentation in social psychology.

Social Psychology's Epistemic Model

In view of the previous discussions, the following model is proposed as that which experimental social psychology seems to follow. A representation of the model is shown in Figure 1.1.

The model is quite general and is applicable to some psychological specialties other than social psychology. It will also be familiar in one form or another to most readers. The model is deeply entrenched, serving multiple purposes as the model for theory testing, the model for the experiment, and the model for the subject. The model is based on the individual, but the word "group" could be substituted with no basic changes required. The model will be described briefly, and then its many functions will be detailed.

Classes of manipulable physical operations constitute the input side. These various activities are not random, but are viewed as manipulating a conceptual independent variable, which is ordinarily considered as both a theoretic entity and a substantive entity located within the individual. Activation of the independent variable, in the Humean view, results in or produces, in the necessary production view, effects. The nature of the theoretical linking relation is specified, preferably as a quantitative functional relation. The effects are on a conceptual dependent variable, which is manifest in various operationalized output

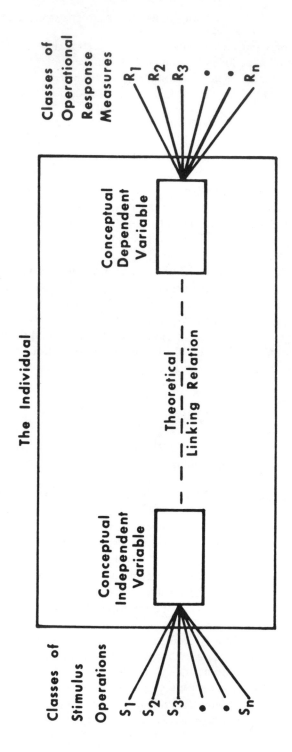

FIGURE 1.1   Social Psychology's Epistemic Model

44

measures of response. The model is unidirectional or, more generally, unicausal (McGuire, 1973).

The model may of course be easily expanded. More than one conceptual independent variable may be envisioned, and these variables may interact or operate independently. The logic remains the same whether one or many independent variables are used. Causal direction remains one way, but with several variables the flow is multicausal rather than unicausal. One approach that is excluded is the positivistic (McGuire, 1969a, p. 145), in the Skinnerean sense of omitting conceptual variables and linking input and output operations directly.

This general paradigm resolves many needs. It models the subject as an input-output creature, essentially passive in the unidirectional flow. Conceptual entities may be multiplied indefinitely within the model without imposing a self-determining view on the subject. Any possible feedback loops are reconceptualized, not as within the individual, but as environmental effects of the response that change the environment, leading to a different input situation, which again flows in sequence through the individual. Thus, feedback effects are viewed as a series of "snapshot" changes over time, coming from outside the individual, but not part of his/her basic structure.

The model also serves the needs of the manipulative laboratory experiment. It is the basic but very general S-O-R paradigm. Stimulus events are equated with independent variables that can be manipulated. Response events are conceived as dependent variables that can be measured. The basic requirement of relating independent and dependent variables is met in this way.

Finally, the model serves as the paradigm for hypothesis testing and confirmation. The conceptual variables within the organism are viewed in the theoretic sense as if-then conditional implications. Their relation is specified and thus serves as a psychological hypothesis. If the conceptual variable is manipulated and related (as predicted) in an orderly way to the dependent variable, the hypothesis is said to be confirmed. Confirmation of hypotheses in this way is viewed as supporting whatever theory may be at issue.

Thus the scope of the model is encompassing, satisfying a confluence of needs regarding theory construction and the conduct of experiments. It will be useful to point out several other specific features of the model as well.

1. The model works best for theories of the middle range, or what is called specific concept theories. Whenever two concepts are specified in a relation, the full mechanism of the model is potentially operative. The model is essentially a hypothesis-testing paradigm, and, even if a higher order theory is involved, the hypothesis is essentially "detached" from it for purposes of testing.

2. The distinction between operations and conceptual variables satisfies two requirements. First, it satisfies the requirements of operationism and its "hard-nosed" insistence on definitions of concepts by specifiable procedures. Second, it satisfies Lewin's counter-insistence on psychological concepts, particularly

idealized constructs. Thus, social psychologists have attempted to combine both positivism and the rationalism of idealized constructs.

3. The notion of a theoretical relation between two conceptual variables satisfies Lewin's dictum for systematic causality in the sense of lawful relations. The notion of the linking relation is viewed ideally as a functional relation, preferably in quantitative terms. In this way, at least, a residue of Lewin's emphasis on dynamic explanations is retained.

4. The ultimate metaphysical question of causality is left open. The theoretical linking relation may be viewed in the weak Humean sense of constant conjunction or in the stronger sense of necessary production.

Comparison of the Model with Lewin's Conceptions

It is of interest to compare the current epistemic model with Lewin's conceptions of theory and experimentation. The current model is essentially an evolutionary offshoot of the Lewinian model, but the two differ in some important ways.

In a loose sense the inner contents of the schematized individual shown in Figure 1.1 may be equated with the Lewinian life space. The life space consisted of all the relational concepts (genotypes) that, as an interconnected system, provided a valid psychological explanation of the individual's behavior. The external phenomena of stimuli and overt responses were less important (they were phenotypes). This focus on the central features of the life space to the relative neglect of input and output led Brunswik to characterize Lewin's system as postperceptual but prebehavioral, a characterization with which Heider (1959, p. 4 agreed but did not denigrate.

Lewin's focus on the conceptual structure of the life space led to a subtle difference in his conception of experimentation as compared to the current conception portrayed in Figure 1.1. The difference is made clear by Heider's interesting discussion of the observer-object partition. The scientific observer has a choice in the object selected for observation. The primary choice may be to focus on the direct stimulus and response observables (input and output), and the scientist's energies will be directed largely to relations between inputs and outputs. Or the observer can make the observer-object partition differently, namely, between the directly observable features of the world and the conceptual structure within the life space. In the latter case, input-output data are of secondary importance; they are mediational tools to give information about the genotypic constructs.

Current social psychology emphasizes the partition between the observer and the directly observable input-output relations. (This partition would rather naturally lead to the emphasis on stimulus control instead of psychological control, as was noted earlier). In contrast, " . . . for Lewin the partition between observer and object is at the life space; his primary concern is with what goes on in this life space; that is, where he expects to find the relevant variables, the nodal points which he expects to follow exact laws without exceptions" (Heider, 1959, p. 5).

The difference in observer-object partitions leads to different evaluations of the efficacy of experimental procedures. From today's vantage point, Lewin's approach was casual (even sloppy). Having subjects participate in many different experimental manipulations (with no worries about counterbalancing or the like), with detailed interviews about the subject's experiences between manipulations, seems hopeless for production of valid, precise data. From Lewin's point of view, however, the experimental manipulations were mere secondary phenomena whose job was to create a specified conceptual state within the subject. Tapping the subject's phenomenology in the interview situation while the experiment was in progress served the purpose of ascertaining whether the specified conceptual state indeed occurred and, if so, its relation to some other conceptual state of interest.

Lewin would be equally chagrined at the current emphasis on precision of relating observable inputs to observable outputs with so little attention to the conceptual intervening variables. He would argue that a given stimulus operation may create very different psychological states in different subjects and that a given response may have different meanings. When different cases are combined and compared by inferential statistics, valid knowledge about the conceptual variables is likely to be obscured, and the resulting clean input-output results are relatively meaningless because they are based on shifting and superficial phenomena (phenotypes), rather than accurately indexing the underlying genotypes.

Each point of view of experimentation has difficulties associated with it. Lewin's approach is not cognizant of the serious problems of demand characteristics, evaluation apprehension, carryover effects, and other assorted bias problems with which current researchers are intimately familiar. On the other hand, the objective focus on stimulus and response variables that exists today makes the individual something of a black box that requires endless speculation. It is an anomaly that research on intrapsychic phenomena (for example, dissonance, reactance, attribution processes, etc.), even when the manipulations are clean and the results clear, requires so much speculation as to what probably occurred inside the subject, given that the hypothesized input-output relations in fact occurred. It is a sobering experience to thumb through a current issue of *Journal of Personality and Social Psychology* and read only the discussion sections. Very often, there is extended discussion of what might have occurred inside the subject's head. One is left with the feeling that not much was learned after all about what the subjects were really thinking, believing, attributing, etc. One is also left with a vague puzzlement as to why and how the research enterprise happens to be so constructed that direct answers about intrapsychic processes seem virtually impossible to obtain. Obviously, some happy compromise between Lewin's approach and the current approach to experimentation is needed. Unfortunately, what that compromise might be is not at all clear.

Evaluation of the Epistemic Model

The current model has been in service for many years and has stimulated enormous numbers of social psychology experiments. In that pragmatic sense, it has been very useful. It may in fact be the model that most faithfully represents what humans most often are like in their daily lives. Argyris (1975) would associate the model under discussion with his Model 1 of human behavior. According to Argyris, humans (when following Model 1) are programmed to achieve their defined purpose, win and not lose, suppress negative feelings, and emphasize rationality. Humans have learned behavioral strategies to achieve these four values, the most important of which is control over other people. Argyris demonstrated how a number of important works in social psychology follow this model rather closely. He concluded that the basic structure of the social psychology experiment, especially the feature of control, is analogous to the structure of Model 1.

The primary question is whether the epistemic model of Figure 1.1(or Argyris' Model 1) is the only viable model on which to base a science of human social behavior. The answer would seem to be no; there are other alternatives, and, with increasing urgency, other alternatives are recommended.

The model has been criticized on various grounds. It has been argued that it is too simplistic, does not capture the true complexity of behavior, and ignores common-sense knowledge that humans are self-activating causal systems. McGuire (1973), after much labor, pinpointed the source of the crisis on the linear causal model which is depicted in Figure 1.1. Harré and Secord (1972) reached a similar conclusion. Presumably the solution would be to allow bidirectional causal relations among numerous conceptual entities within the model, in this way, creating a complex, self-regulative system that more closely approximates the complexities of actual human beings.

One may reasonably doubt whether the change from a passive S-R conception of the individual to a complex system conception will fully satisfy the concerns that have been expressed. Regardless of the multiplication of complexity within the conceptual system, the paradigm is still essentially external to the observing psychologist. The person as we know him/her in everyday life remains opaque, eluding the explanatory net.

In a penetrating discussion of Lewin's system, DeRivera (1976) concluded that Lewin failed to extricate the subject from an essentially passive stance. The system fails to capture the person as an actor from his/her own subjective point of view, who in that capacity is not only acted upon, but who is " . . . responsible for the very organization that then determines the forces upon him" (p. 30).

More generally, the epistemic model of Figure 1.1 and its many variants represent the external, objective approach to the study of social life. By its nature, the model cannot deal with or explain behavior from the subjective point of view of the actor. In contrast, the whole point of Verstehen sociology discussed at the beginning of this section is to explain social behavior from the point of view of the actor. The success of Verstehen sociology seems as debatable as the success of the epistemic model currently under consideration. DeRivera (1976) called for an integration of the objective and subjective perspectives in what he called the *human-science approach*. Such an integration would, of course, be highly desirable. Whether it can be achieved or not is quite another matter.

Social psychology has pursued its epistemic model with vigor for several years. At this point in time, a backlash has occurred, and there are serious questions about the nature and future direction of experimental social psychology. Many people speak of a crisis in the discipline. In order to examine the possibilities more carefully, it will be useful to devote some attention to this so-called crisis in experimental social psychology. This problem is considered in the next section.

CRISIS IN EXPERIMENTAL SOCIAL PSYCHOLOGY

To speak of a crisis in an abstract collective like social psychology is to engage in metaphor. The existence of a crisis is a matter of social definition. It exists because people say that it exists. The basic issue is to determine why they are saying it. This section will explore the issue and attempt an assessment. The crisis has now passed through a certain historical period. For our purposes, Ring's (1967) striking statement will be considered as the official declaration that a crisis existed. After considering Ring's views, a representative sample of other opinions will be noted, hopefully allowing for some clarity in defining the nature of the crisis. Another section will explore the crisis in the context of cultural-value changes within the discipline of social psychology. Some of the recommended directions for the discipline will then be noted. Finally, an assessment of the scope and implications of the crisis will be provided.

Statement of the Crisis

Kenneth Ring (1967) viewed experimental social psychology as "in a state of profound intellectual disarray" (p. 119). He contrasted the Lewinian vision of the close-knit interplay of theory, research, and social action with the current themes of social psychology. One theme is a humanistic, action-oriented orientation, a legacy of Lewin, which is represented by The Society for the Psychological Study of Social Issues. This orientation continues to receive lip service, but according to Ring, it is not dominant and has little effect on the practice of the discipline.

The scientific orientation was mentioned by Ring as a second value trend, and William McGuire was named as a distinguished representative. Presumably this "hard nosed" approach derives from the behavioristic tradition, which views science as a serious, no-nonsense business, soberly advancing the frontiers of knowledge by hypothesis-testing laboratory experiments. Ring believed that this orientation is also not a dominant one in social psychology.

The dominant orientation is a "fun-and-games" approach with an emphasis on "exotic topics with a zany manipulation" (p. 117). The focus is on the laboratory experiment, and the rules of procedure are:

1. Experiments should be as flashy and flamboyant as possible.
2. An effective, *amusing* manipulation is better than a merely effective manipulation.
3. Prosaic topics for study should be avoided.
4. One should never make an obvious prediction.

Ring traced the potential impact of the fun-and-games approach on undergraduate teaching, graduate training, and the development of the field. None of the implications is promising.

In concluding his indictment, Ring voiced the opinion that Lewin's conception of social psychology had not merely been compromised, but debased. Ring urged the reassessment of values by asking social psychologists to consider three questions before engaging in research.

1. Does the research deal with a problem of some broad human significance?
2. Is the research a part of a program of systematic inquiry or only a one-shot affair?
3. Does the research seem to entail the deception-experiment paradigm as a matter of course?

Ring's indictment is certainly a strong one. His analysis appeals to the notion of an abstract value system inherent in the discipline; researchers may follow the value system without consciously aspiring to do so. In contrast, Rowan (1974) presented an equally strong indictment but localized the source of malaise within the pragmatic concerns of the working day — with the need to get the research done and published. Rowan presented his own list of questions that, he believed, guide researchers in the conduct of their work.

1. Is it cheap? Can I do it with no materials other than duplicated score sheets — there is always plenty of paper about — and with existing apparatus?
2. Is it handy? Can I do it with the people I have on hand? Can I do it without moving too far from my office? Can I use my computer?
3. Is it convenient? Can I fit it into the life of my students without disrupting their habits in any way?
4. Is it brief? Can I get it over in twenty minutes — or an hour, if I can run several people at a time?
5. Is it publishable? Will it add to my book of records, whether it reveals anything worth knowing or not? Memo: interesting statistics can help; poor sampling will not be penalized (pp. 87-88).

These views state something of the current sense of crisis. The focus is on underlying values with the result that problems permeate nearly all aspects of professional life. To the extent that Ring's analysis holds true, the crisis cannot be ameliorated by merely excising a bad technique or tinkering with subject populations or manipulations.

Other Representative Views of the Crisis

Ring's official indictment is of course just one view. Such opinions might be expressed for any number of "sour-grapes" reasons. Since, as noted above, a crisis of this nature exists only in the sense of people saying that it exists, it is desirable to consider other viewpoints as well. A sample of relevant quotations is presented in Table 1.1 chronologically by author's name.

The earliest date of one of these criticisms, by Scriven, is 1964, but he might be discounted as an outsider — a philosopher, and besides his statement is sheer unsupported opinion. Another early harbinger, Smith, might also be discounted since, by his own admission (1972b), he is mostly an "armchair" psychologist. However, more recently, the indictments become more frequent, and when researchers such as Berkowitz, Secord, Katz, Riecken, and Steiner express a sense of crisis, an attack on the credibility of the witness seems less workable.

What is the gist of what these people are saying? Numerous things, some even contradictory, such as Moscovici's view that social psychologists lack a unity of interests and shared perspectives compared with Richards's view that social psychology is a self-contained, inward-looking discipline. One major theme is the problem with the product of research. Allport speaks of the narrowness of experimental research, which produces "elegantly polished triviality." Katz (1972) complains that experiments seldom provide new information because they are lacking in ideas. Riecken also bemoans the narrowness of research pieces that "seem to begin nowhere and to go not very far." Smith (1966) refers to the clogged journals and narrow empiricism.

This theme reflects the explosive increase in the literature, which tends toward brief reports. A sense of fragmentation and noncumulativeness may be inevitable, particularly if at an early point in one's career, the writer felt that he/she had something of the "big picture" of the discipline. The unified image cannot be retained when the literature grows as rapidly as it has in social psychology.

One tentative supposition is that the natural growth of a literature will lead to a sense of fragmentation. Harré and Secord favor the interpretation that the discipline continues to rely on a positivist methodology, which can no longer be justified, in a sense declaring that we subscribe to the wrong philosophy. Congruent with this emphasis, Armistead argues that social psychology ignores the context of social behavior. The lack of compelling theory is also noted by

TABLE 1.1

Quotations on the "Crisis" in Social Psychology

... many contemporary studies seem to shed light on nothing more than a narrow phenomenon studied under specific conditions. Even if the experiment is successfully repeated there is no proof that the discovery has wider validity. It is for this reason that some current investigations seem to end up in elegantly polished triviality – snippets of empiricism, but nothing more. Here surely lies the current challenge to social psychology (Allport, 1968a, p. 68).

When you combine the striving for general laws with a conception of the 'social' in terms of interaction between organisms and with the experimental, laboratory method, you end up with a social psychology that systematically ignores, both in its conceptualizations and in its predominant method, the social context in which social behavior occurs. This is the main reason why psychological social psychology is up a blind alley (Armistead, 1974, p. 15).

At any rate, it seems to me ... that social psychology is now in a 'crisis state,' in the sense that Kuhn used this term in his book, *The Structure of Scientific Revolutions*. We seem to be somewhat at a loss for important problems to investigate and models to employ in our research and theory (Berkowitz, cited in Smith, 1972a, p. 86).

The need for a comprehensive theoretical treatment of social psychology and for a reformed methodology we feel to be pressing, and to be evident from the increasing dissatisfaction with the state of social psychology, even within the citadels of the profession. The underlying reason for this state we believe to be a continued adherence to a positivist methodology, long after the theoretical justification for it, in naive behaviourism, has been repudiated (Harré & Secord, 1972, p. 1).

The concern with technology and the marginal interest in theory are related to what seems to me the most critical problem we face today in social psychology – the continuing and growing fragmentation of the discipline (Katz, 1967, p. 341).

Of the thousands of experimental studies published in social psychology in the past 20 years, the number that supplies new information to a cumulative body of knowledge is surprisingly small. A great deal of the experimental effort has been without impact not because of poor method, but because of the lack of ideas behind the work. The development of experimental social psychology has been costly if the energy input is compared to the significant output (Katz, 1972, p. 557).

It must be admitted that social psychology is not truly a science. We wish to give it an appearance of science by using mathematical reasoning and the refinements of experimental method; but the fact is that social psychology cannot be described as a discipline with a unitary field of interest, a systematic framework of criteria and requirements, a coherent body of knowledge, or even a set of common perspectives shared by those who practice it ... a solid foundation for the future has not been laid (Moscovici, 1972, p. 32).

TABLE 1.1 *(continued)*

TABLE 1.1 *(continued)*

Social psychology, as an academic and research activity, has developed as a self-contained and inward-looking discipline which has not only become separated from the phenomena it sets out to analyze but is also sterile as a source of human understanding (Richards, 1974, p. 233).

There is still, unfortunately, less cumulativeness than one might like to see. Individual research pieces often seem to begin nowhere and to go not very far. One sometimes gets the same impression from the journal literature in social psychology that one gets from listening to a conversation among golfers: everyone is talking, but only about his own game. With notable exceptions, there is a dearth of replications (Riecken, 1965, p. 15).

Pure research in social psychology is among the most unproductive fields of human endeavor today, ranking only with mathematical economics as being a kind of exciting game for people that like exciting games in this particular field, i. e., nobody except those who do it (comment by M. Scriven, In Wann, 1964, p.190).

... I am not too happy about the clogged state of our journals, filled with the products of project-supported busyness, in which fad and fashion, methodological fetishism, and what I remember Gordon Allport to have called "itsy-bitsy empiricism" make it easy to lose direction and significance (Smith, 1966, p. 117).

Near the end of the '60's, doubt and self-criticism became increasingly evident among American social psychologists — about the lack of cumulative gains commensurate with effort expended and of consensual paradigms to define the growing edge of scientific advance, about the artificiality and human irrelevance of some of the problems that had been pursued with great sophistication, about the instability of laboratory findings insofar as they often turned out to depend upon unexamined interpretations of the experimental situation by the human subjects, and about the questionable ethics involved in the deceptive manipulations that were typically required to attain some control over these interpretations. The field is still in crisis, with no predominant new directions clearly apparent, though there is greater emphasis on observation and experiment in real-life settings and on applied concerns (Smith, 1973, p. 611).

Starting three or four years ago, meetings of social psychologists became gloomy affairs. Self reproach became endemic as we struggled to justify our existence in a world beset by problems for which our discipline had provided very few solutions. Despair sometimes led to wholesale denunciations of laboratory research, to damning criticisms of the ethical and methodological qualities of our investigative strategies, and even to suggestions that we forsake our scientific tradition in favor of participation in social movements (Steiner, 1974, p. 106).

Berkowitz and by Katz (1967), but this theme is not as strong as the theme of narrowness of research. The lack of relevance for solving social problems is noted by Steiner and by Smith (1973). More specific issues, such as problems of replicability and the ethics of deception are noted only by Smith (1973).

The critics thus stress a variety of problems. The major theme seems to be the narrowness of research reports and fragmentation of the literature. This theme also undoubtedly receives some emphasis because of the lack of convincing general theoretical paradigms. More specific technical problems such as issues in subject deception also contribute, but they seem not be be the dominant concern. One is left with a general sense of malaise, that all is not well, but the statement of what is wrong is not very precise or specific. Indeed, when one examines the substantive literature, the sense of crisis is hardly apparent at all. "The origins of the crisis – indeed, even the existence of a crisis – do not readily appear in a survey of the research literature itself. The literature continues to grow at a fast rate; new theories are proposed, new research areas are investigated" (Elms, 1975, p. 968).

Very recently, some systematic attempts have been made to pinpoint the source of the sense of crisis. Elms (1975) discussed three types of problems; in general, the problems have more to do with psychologists and their working environment than with the inner content of social psychology as a discipline. The first problem is the difficulty in conducting precise scientific research; a difficulty more severe than in other disciplines, at least in the estimation of social psychologists. Quite recently, there has been an increased awareness that social behavior is even more complex than previously imagined, along with sensitivity to laboratory artifacts, and especially those deriving from experimenter-subject role interactions.

Somewhat incongrous with the first problem is that of " . . . many researchers' apparent expectation that research should be relatively easy to conduct, should readily produce clear-cut and statistically significant results, and should lead directly to the development of theories that are both sweeping and elegant" (Elms, 1975, p. 969). The statement of the existence of such a normative expectancy resonates quite well with the cynicism of Rowan (1974) noted previously in his list of the *real* working day concerns of social psychologists. Presumably this expectancy is developed during graduate and undergraduate socialization into the discipline. Students tend to be exposed primarily to the relatively simple designs of classic experiments; the increasing complexity of more recent research is either avoided or not emphasized. Once researchers discover just how difficult good research really is to conduct, they become discouraged and either abandon research or shift from one area to another as the complexity of a well-worked area increases beyond the tolerance point.

Finally, Elms (1975) noted several sources of outside pressures that have discouraged social psychologists. These include the demand for relevance, demands for the study of women and minorities – leading to a general reevaluation of the generality of much previous social research, and the end of easy grant money.

Deutsch (1976) provided an analysis of the crisis that is somewhat more general than Elms' analysis. Instead of locating the crisis in factors external to the discipline, Deutsch viewed the crisis as stemming from the dialectical interplay of certain properties inherent in the discipline. Further, "the crisis in social psychology is not new; we are in a perpetual crisis" (Deutsch, 1976, p. 134). One source of the crisis originates with the discipline's "unique focus upon the interplay between psychological and social processes. This focus puts social psychology in the constant position of imbalance in which it teeters from an overemphasis on the psychological to an overemphasis on the social" (pp. 134-135). Another source of crisis is that "social psychology also teeters between the abstract and the concrete, between saying something in general and saying something in particular" (p. 135). Deutsch felt that in recent years we have focussed so much on the abstractions of hypothesis testing in general that we know very little about the particularity of social behavior. This complaint is reminiscent of Lewin's advocacy of a full description of the concrete situation, coupled with a recognition that social psychology has largely ignored this stricture.

Finally, according to Deutsch, social psychology is under constant pressure to solve social problems, but unfortunately, the discipline can not by itself and should not aspire to solve any of the major social problems or our times. We must recognize the inherent limits of our discipline. This last point is related to Thorngate's (1976a) interesting thesis that the proper task of social psychology might not be so much to reduce ignorance as to reduce arrogance. There are limits to what people can know and do in the way of social change. One valuable function of social psychology would be to tutor society on the nature of those limits.

One feature common to the analyses of both Elms and Deutsch is the emphasis on the high expectations social psychologists tend to hold for their discipline — and the impossibility of fully realizing those expectancies. The recent realization that the great expectations can not be fulfilled may be in part a consequence of a unique feature of the discipline; its relative youth and the fact that most senior experimental social psychologists of the modern era have had careers that spanned the last few decades of massive growth and change. This correlation of the personal career-life cycle with maturation of the discipline suggests that the current sense of crisis may be construed as a cultural change among practitioners of the discipline which is due to the massive informational, conceptual, and social changes they have witnessed during their careers.

The Crisis as Culture Change

As noted previously, the enormous growth of a literature over a couple of decades will result in the appearance of great change. It is also true that the modern origins of the discipline some 20 years ago coincided with the beginnings of the careers of most of today's distinguished social psychologists. Over the years there was, so to speak, a natural correlation between personal development and growth of the discipline. From that perceptual vantage point, what started as a small tidy forest becomes an exploding jungle of unconnected thickets. For the new generation, however, which never knew the small tidy forest, a selected thicket patch becomes their forest, providing a sense of unity and directing research work. No doubt as the new generation ages and its thicket patch becomes innumerable small briar patches as specialization proceeds relentlessly, we will no doubt hear a new chorus of despair over the increasing fragmentation.

This analysis thus views the crisis as in part induced by the cultural change in the discipline as one ages. There may be a related factor at work. It may be that *young* men and women are best suited for the arduous toil and narrow focus of experimentation. As one ages, his/her perspective may broaden, and former wide horizons seem quite restrictive, leading one to explore new areas of knowledge and new ways of doing things.[1] Such a tendency would lead to the advocacy of change.

This analysis is of course quite speculative. I offer below two examples that illustrate the thesis of expanding horizons as cultural change. The examples were chosen because they are relatively clear and may serve as archetypes, in that sense they are intended to be somewhat independent of the intellectual endeavors of the individuals involved. The examples selected are the changing methodological views of William J. McGuire, and the recent, radical "social psychology as history" thesis of Kenneth Gergen.

Growth in Methodological Perspective: William J. McGuire

In a remarkable series of four articles McGuire (1965; 1967; 1969b; 1973) dealt with the problems of social psychology and offered solutions. His views have been influential (for example, the volume by Bickman and Henchy, 1972). In the process, his own views and proposed solutions have been modified considerably.

The first statement of a viewpoint was contained in a discussion of a paper in the volume edited by Klineberg and Christie (1965). This point of view is well illustrated by the following quote.

> Approaching research from the perspective of application rather than theory, I regard as inelegant and inefficient as trying to push a piece of cooked spaghetti across the table from the back end. To these gentlemen who have suggested this applied approach, I would say quite emphatically: "We are not here to turn out consumer goods." What do I see us turning out? Let me explain with an authentic parable (adapted from Stephen Spender). I always ask an undergraduate inquirer why he feels his vocation lies in social psychology. Sometimes the student replies "I think maybe modern psychology has something to offer (or at least could be made to offer something) on the problem of international tensions, on how to reduce them before we all blow ourselves up, and I'd like to work on it." To such I say gently, "My boy, you have a good heart. I admire you. But unfortunately I myself have little to offer you.

---

[1] This analysis implies that innovative ideas in social psychology may most likely come from people of seasoned maturity; more strictly technical innovations of method may come from the novice.

Perhaps you should speak to one of my colleagues here. Or have you thought of the law or the ministry?" But sometimes I get that other kind of student who replies: "I'm interested because I've got a hunch that a person might do some neat things in social psychology by using a little matrix algebra and difference equations." To this one I say, "My boy . . . welcome home." But lest I seem to be insisting that we work only from highly mathematical theories, let me make clear that I feel our social-psychological research should concentrate on hypotheses derived from any kind of basic theory. My objection is only to the selection of hypotheses for their relevancy to social action at the cost of theory relevance (McGuire, 1965, p. 139).

As noted previously, Ring (1967) identified this view as representative of the value structure of social psychology as basic science.

The second statement (McGuire, 1967) was a response to Ring's (1967) critique. McGuire now conceptualized the relation between basic and applied research as one of dynamic equilibrium. The current crisis was due to a perturbation too far in one direction, that of basic research. He predicted a "remelding of basic and applied research with increasing attention to the latter." The mechanism for the remelding was envisioned as theory-oriented research in natural settings. McGuire saw several attractions in testing hypotheses in natural environments, including: advances in mathematical modeling and computer simulation, greater availability of nationwide samples for survey research, improvements in content analysis, increasing availability of data archives, growth of interest among intellectuals in social affairs, pressures from granting agencies, and the frustration of scientists trying to prosper in the overcrowded world of laboratory research.

Negative reasons for the predicted move to natural settings concerned the growing problems with laboratory research. The problem of artifacts with attendant difficulties in generalization and theoretical interpretation were noted. Also, ethical issues of laboratory (and field) research were discussed.

All in all, McGuire's articles provide a reasonable cafeteria of proposed solutions for the crisis recognized by Ring. It is of interest to note the increased breadth of conceptual concern in McGuire's (1967) article relative to his 1965 statement. It is partly a matter of expressed attitude as well as substance. One gets the impression from the 1965 article (actually presented in 1961; see McGuire, 1967, p. 125) that nonmanipulative research in natural settings would be not quite respectable. In contrast, the 1967 paper positively embraces such research. And with that embrace, McGuire made such research legitimate — once again — to a considerable number of social psychologists.

One may critically ponder McGuire's proposed solution of course (as he did himself at a later date). Phillips (1973, pp. 5-16) presented a sobering picture of the reliability and validity of sociological data. Even the most basic data, such as interviews, questionnaires, and census data contain gross error, according to Phillips. If true, one wonders whether the relentless pursuit of research with the massive new data archives that McGuire recommended might not be something of a Pandora's Box, more inefficient in the amount of truth gained than the laboratory experiment with all of its cumbersome problems.

Tajfel (1972) offered a conceptual criticism and alternative to McGuire's summation of the problem as a tension between basic and applied research.

> I believe, however, that the first of Ring's problems, the conflict between pure and applied research, is also in the nature of a symptom. McGuire's solution, an increasing stress on sophisticated quantitative techniques applied to large populations or to great quantities of data from natural settings, is like burying the patient before he is quite dead in the hope that his descendants will present less of a problem. Experimental social psychology as we know it today is "irrelevant" only to the extent that it is a social science practised in a social vacuum and not because it is not applied. This vacuum is not due to the fact that we are attempting to do fundamental research; it is due to the social psychologists having often taken the wrong decision as to what kind of *homo* their discipline is concerned with: "biological," "psychological" or "sociopsychological" (p. 71).

Regardless of the pros and cons of the basic-applied dichotomy, the important point is the shift, a large one in my opinion, from a stern, hard-nosed approach to an ethos that welcomed both the laboratory and the natural setting.

McGuire's third statement is contained in a volume edited by Sherif in 1969 on interdisciplinary relations in the social sciences. In this article the theme of theory-oriented research in natural settings was explored more extensively. In fairness to McGuire, he did maintain that the manipulational laboratory experiment would continue to be the most efficient tool for the development of basic theory. However, the basic thrust of the article was toward the natural setting.

The conceptual emphasis was shifted somewhat and broadened. McGuire (1969b) regarded the crucial distinction as that between *creative* and *critical* phases of scientific research. The creative phase is the generation of hypotheses, and the critical phase is the testing of them. The previous distinction between basic and applied research was equated with the distinction between theory-oriented and action-oriented research, respectively. The basic-applied issue (or theory-action distinction) was viewed as pertaining to the creative, hypothesis-generating phase of research.

> One is engaged in basic research to the extent that in his creative, hypothesis-generating phase he derives his predictions from some theoretical conceptualizations with the aim of clarifying, testing, and developing the theory. One is involved in applied research to the extent that he derives his predictions during this creative, hypothesis-generating phase from the practical need for making an informed decision in a natural setting requiring action (p. 24).

In contrast, the distinction between *laboratory* and *field* research was viewed as pertaining to the critical, hypothesis-testing phase of research. "One is engaged in field research to the extent that he tests his hypothesis in natural settings, in the world he never made. One is engaged in laboratory research to the extent that he tests his hypothesis in artificial situations that he has contrived" (p. 24). Another distinction relevant to the critical phase is that between *correlation* and *manipulational* research. "By correlational research I refer to any hypothesis testing in which we do not ourselves manipulate the independent variable, but allow nature to do so. By manipulational research, I refer to the hypothesis-testing tactic of ourselves inducing the different levels of the independent variable . . ." (p. 24). The correlation-manipulation distinction is considered orthogonal to the laboratory-field distinction. Finally, the meaning of "experimental" is shifted from its habitual association with the laboratory to the more general meaning "to test."

In these various distinctions McGuire has performed a coup that serves an ideological function. Because if one accepts these distinctions, he can say that he is "engaged in experimentation so long as he is testing his hypotheses, whether in the laboratory or in the field, and whether by manipulation or correlational variation of his independent variable (p. 25). The possibilities are even more drastic since, if one were engaged in some practical, real-world problem that generated a hypothesis and tested in turn in the natural setting by correlational methods, he would be entitled to call his research an experiment.

McGuire's distinctions serve an ideological function because they legitimize and place on an even par settings and research practices that formerly served as poor cousins to the exalted laboratory experiment. In comparing McGuire's present approach with his 1965 position, it is evident that a considerable liberalization of what counts as good science has occurred. McGuire does retain his conviction that "basic research will prove of more practical usefulness than the same amount of effort put into applied research" (p.26), but he notes that history may prove him wrong.

In his more recent (1973) paper, McGuire made an even more radical departure. He now viewed the switch from theory relevance to social relevance for the creative, hypothesis-generating phase of research as "only a superficial cosmetic change that masks rather than corrects the basic problem" (p. 448). The newly emerging paradigm was now viewed as a minor variant of the traditional laboratory paradigm.

The basic problem, as McGuire saw it, lay in the continued acceptance and use of the epistemological model presented in the previous section.

> Socially relevant hypotheses, no less than theoretically relevant hypotheses, tend to be based on a simple linear process model, a sequential chain of cause and effect which is inadequate to simulate the true complexities of the individual's cognitive system or of the social system which we are typically trying to describe . . . the basic shortcoming of the theory-relevant and the socially relevant hypotheses alike is that they fail to come to grips with the complexities with which the variables are organized in the individual and social systems" (p. 448).

Further, hypothesis testing experiments are now viewed as more like demonstrations of knowledge already known, rather than real tests. The flight to the field is viewed as "a tactical evasion which fails to meet the basic problem" (p. 449).

McGuire's prescriptions (the seven koan) are complex and difficult to summarize briefly. He stresses the importance of hypothesis formation by a variety of methods. He urges more complex causal models with sufficient feedback loops to account for the real complexity of the world. He asks for more observation of people as opposed to data. Diverse social data on a variety of indicators are needed, taking into account both past and future as well as present perspectives of a population. More conventionally, he suggests upgrading and diversification of our analytic and statistical tools. The sixth koan might be summarized by the statement that perhaps it would be good for senior investigators to get back to the research themselves, rather than serving as chief administrator and financial officer of a grant-inspired social empire. For the meaning of the seventh koan, the reader is advised to check for himself (McGuire, 1973, pp. 455-456).

This odyssey into McGuire's intellectual development is offered as an example of the questions that haunt the discipline. Although McGuire is perhaps a few years ahead of most of us in this regard, I believe his intellectual struggles do serve as representative of the intellectual struggles of many social psychologists. We begin to see not just the social form of people declaring a crisis, but the underlying substance — the reasons and shifting values concerning methods and the nature of knowledge itself — that have led to this sense of crisis. The crisis may be in part "cultural," in the sense of intellectual change and maturity in individuals, but it is also epistemological as well. We turn now to one other, quite radical statement of the current crisis, the "social psychology as history" thesis of Kenneth Gergen.

Social Psychology as History: Kenneth Gergen

It was noted in a previous section that social psychologists tend to be ahistorical in interests, both in regards to the history of their own discipline and in the explanation of ongoing behavior. It was not always so.

> But though the concept of culture cannot be said to have solved any of our psychological problems, it has awakened us to an immensely important fact regarding the limits of what we are pleased to call social psychology. It must be recognized that nearly all the experimental work in social psychology ... has value and is definitely meaningful only in relation to the particular culture in which the investigation was carried on (Murphy & Murphy, 1931, p. 8).

Somewhere along the way experimental social psychologists forgot this limitation, due in part no doubt to Lewin's call for psychological laws of universal validity.

In an important paper Gergen (1973) rather rudely reminded us once again of our dependence on historical contingency. It was Gergen's thesis that:

> Social psychology is primarily an historical inquiry. Unlike the natural sciences, it deals with facts that are largely nonrepeatable and which fluctuate markedly over time. Principles of human interaction cannot readily be developed over time because the facts on which they are based do not generally remain stable. Knowledge cannot accumulate in the usual scientific sense because such knowledge does not generally transcend its historical boundaries (p. 310).

Several substantiating arguments were given. Gergen viewed science and society as a feedback loop in which members of the society may learn a behavioral principle and then use it in ways that will subsequently invalidate the principle. Such invalidation is especially likely because social psychological theory contains prescriptive biases (for example, it is bad to be a conformer), and people desire to avoid control over their behavior — even by psychological "laws." Thus, general knowledge of social scientific laws will result in enlightenment effects that will likely invalidate those laws. Thus, social psychology is firmly "wedded to historical circumstances" — the basic content and theory will necessarily change as historical circumstances change.

In some respects, Gergen's position is more radical than McGuire's position. McGuire called for a new, more complex model of causality. Gergen tended toward the view that causal models, however complex, will not solve the problems of social psychological knowledge.

A strong rebuttal to Gergen's position was soon forthcoming from Schlenker (1974), who argued in favor of traditional scientific-experimental practices. Schlenker's rebuttal contained five major points.

1. Theories must be phrased in abstract form so as to possess proper generality. Deductions are made by insertion of specific cases or instances into the general terms of a theory. If a theory incorporated specifics directly, it would not be sufficiently general to properly explain the wide diversity of existing phenomena.

2. The search for orderliness and regularity is a characteristic of natural sciences; the search for abstract underlying regularities is also a proper goal for the social sciences.

3. Inability to predict social events with precision does not imply that such prediction is impossible in principle. Instead, Schlenker followed the deterministic position that poor prediction is a matter of lack of knowledge of relevant intrusive variables. If such variables can be discovered and brought under control, predictability will emerge.

4. Schlenker emphasized the conditional nature of scientific hypotheses (if A, then B). To demonstrate scientific validity of an implicational statement, it is necessary that A be true as specified. Gergen's enlightenment effects may be considered as just another species of contaminating artifact that prevents A from holding true as specified. Such feedback effects (for example, subject awareness) do not pose any intrinsic threat to the establishment of hypotheses.

5. Gergen had argued that social psychology deals with facts that are largely nonrepeatable. Schlenker replied that all events are unique in both the physical and social world; thus uniqueness is per se no barrier to the development of a social science.

Schlenker's (1974) paper was a reasoned response within the neopositivistic philosophy of science, to which a substantial number of social psychologists subscribe. The issue was joined, and a vigorous controversy ensued. Manis (1975) essentially supported Schlenker's position, particularly on the issue of the search for regularity. He felt that " . . . the *processes* underlying social behavior are probably relatively stable, although they operate on an endless variety of social *contents* as we vary the time and place of our investigations" (p. 454). The emphasis on underlying processes seems to be within the Lewinian tradition that the search should be for the underlying genotype; the "endless variety of social contents" seems equivalent to the Lewinian notion of phenotype. In sharp contrast, Thorngate (1975) argued that there are about as many underlying regularities as there are theorists, and that "the most valid conceptions of social behavior are those which characterize it as having local organization and general disorganization" (p. 487).

A whole series of divergent viewpoints were expressed in a symposium of papers edited by Manis (1976a, 1976b). These papers included Gergen's (1976) response to Schlenker's (1974) initial critique; another paper by Schlenker (1976); as well as papers by Hendrick (1976), Greenwald (1976), Thorngate (1976b), Harris (1976b), Secord (1976), Godow (1976), and a summary-conclusions paper by Brewster Smith (1976).

One important theme discussed in several of the papers concerned the issue of underlying regularities, or "stable processes" in Manis's 1975 terms. Gergen (1976) argued that posited underlying regularities are hypothetical constructions, human inventions rather than substantial aspects of nature, in the same sense that a tree or a rock is a real aspect of nature. In a neat twist of the argument Gergen argued that because of the wide diversity of particulars in behavior, it is possible to find positive instances to support almost any hypothesized process or underlying regularity. The implication is that almost any social theory that might be proposed will be valid in some degree. Manis (1976a), instead of feeling discouraged with the hypothetical status of processes, noted that some of science's proudest moments involve construction of unseen processes or mechanisms that create order and coherence among an otherwise chaotic set of particulars. Thorngate (1976b) noted that Schlenker's argument implies that processes govern behavior, while Gergen's position implies an interaction between process and behaviors (that is, mutual determination). Finally, Hendrick (1976) pointed out that there may be a general value that what is unseen is considered more explanatory than what is directly observed. This value of the hidden mechanism is one of several general thought themes or themata in science identified by Holton (1975).

The critical issue involved in these discussions is the reality status, ontological status, of underlying processes. In Lewin's terms, what is the nature of the reality of the genotype? This question does not yield an easy answer, either in the physical sciences or the social sciences. Further, the reality status of a concept may change over time. For example, the concept of a gene was originally that of an unseen hypothetical construct. However, as research techniques improved, the gene gradually achieved the status (at least partially) of an existent entity with a definite physical structure.

In general, it seems likely that the reality status of a concept will ultimately depend on whether a viable physical structure can be imagined, sought and discovered. Ultimately all process concepts must be viewed as structure concepts, if the concepts are to be treated as more substantial than mere thought devices.

There are two divergent values on this issue. Some (e. g., Manis, 1976a) happily embrace the process concept as a pure thought device, if it serves a useful summary function in the integration of experience. Others seem to need an actual concrete embodiment of the concept, to be able to hold it in their hands so to speak. Most psychological concepts, at the level of psychological language, rather clearly do not have a direct physical substrate. The felt need for such a physical substrate no doubt accounts for the persistent tendency in psychology toward physiological reductionism.

It seems clear that in most cases it is not possible to either prove or disprove a reality status for posited underlying processes (Godow, 1976) in social psychology. The debate on this particular issue between Gergen and Schlenker would appear to be a draw. The next important issue, making the minimal assumption that processes are no more than thought conventions, is whether they indeed can serve as terms for general theories that make sense of and organize the diverse phenotypes of the phenomenal world. Schlenker argues that process concepts can serve such a function; Gergen argues that they have not done so yet in social psychology; Godow concludes that neither position allows a conclusion as to what might or might not happen in the future.

The issue finally seems to boil down to the mental set or attitude of each scholar on the issue. In part, the issue is one of expectation of what the discipline can accomplish and perceived discrepancy of results from that expectation. Some feel quite comfortable with lower expectations and feel that even if social psychology is mostly historical in nature, it still has much to contribute to current social life (e. g., Smith, 1976; Cronbach, 1975).

At the moment it appears that the advocacy of lowered expectations must also be applied to the analysis of the issue of "social psychology as history" itself. Careful study of all the relevant papers does not provide a clear basis for decision pro or con on the issue. To lower expectation even further, there is no evidence in these papers that the issue is even decidable in principle. The result is that no direct guide to action is provided. One indirect result may be that airing the issue will tend to further legitimize attempts at new methodologies and new approaches to concept formation. If such indirect results occur, the "history" episode may end, after all, on an optimistic note.

Conclusions

This section began with the speculation that the present sense of crisis in social psychology is due to: (a) the sense of fragmentation due to the explosive growth of social psychology literature; and (b) the correlation of the development of personal careers of today's distinguished leaders with the massive change in the discipline. The sense of perpetual change may lead to feelings of anomie with respect to present anchors and future directions of the discipline. This "culture change" hypothesis is congruent with Elms' (1975) contention that the crisis is a crisis of *confidence* rather than a paradigm crisis in the true sense.

Developmental changes in the methodological thinking of William J. McGuire and the issue of social psychology as history were explored for possible insights into the nature and causes of the crisis. There is some evidence for the cognitive (that is, expectational or cultural) interpretation of the crisis. No doubt there is also a genuine epistemological basis for the malaise; however, careful study of the various statements on the crisis do not indicate any definitive answers. The conclusion would therefore seem to be that we must not expect an aesthetic or logical answer, but must instead rely on the pragmatism of the various courses of action recommended as solutions to the crisis.

Recommended Courses of Action for the Crisis

Recommendations are diverse and do not fall into any strong consensual patterns. McGuire has offered the most specific suggestions; his views were presented previously and need not be repeated here. Gergen (1973) argued for several approaches: toward an integration of pure and applied research; a shift in emphasis from prediction to sensitization; development of indicators of psychological-social dispositions over time; research on behavioral stability in the historical sense; and the development of an integrated social history. Sensitization in place of prediction may seem like a regression from good science to many people. But as Smith (1976) noted, sensitization is "not to be sneezed at." If we ask what we do well as social psychologists, it turns out that good research seems " . . . typically to have the character of *demonstrations* identifying, legitimizing, and publicizing a new way of looking at some aspect of social phenomena" (Smith, 1976, p. 438). These activities in and of themselves may often have considerable social value in sensitizing people to look at their behavior in a new way (Thorngate, 1976a).

Both McGuire and Gergen urged an expanded breadth of vision for experimental social psychology, in methods as well as substantively. Allport (1968b) voiced a similar note. "Although social psychology has its own body of history, theory, problems, and methods, it is not a self-sufficient science. It thrives best when cross-cultivated in a rich and diversified intellectual garden" (p. 19). Such interdisciplinary breadth has long been advocated by Sherif, as illustrated by a recent volume (Sherif & Sherif, 1969). Lambert and Weisbrod (1971) foresaw a truly comparative social psychology, which uses a variety of methods for cross-cultural theory building and hypothesis testing.

Somewhat in contrast to McGuire, M. Brewster Smith (1972a) believed that advances will come most rapidly if social psychologists deal more directly with the basic human problems of everyday social life. He stated that "advances in basic theory may be as likely to emerge serendipitously in the pursuit of these problems as in frontal assault upon theory as such" (p. 95). Others mention broad alternatives. For example, Armistead (1974) offered a "reconstructed" social psychology consisting of a mixture of humanistic psychology, phenomenology, and Marxism. The continued growth of Verstehen sociology (e. g., Truzzi, 1974) may yet have a significant impact on experimental social psychology.

Harré and Secord (1972) presented an alternative model of humans as rule-following agents within the context of a realistic philosophy. Methodologically, this approach leads to an analysis of "episodes" and somewhat away from formal laboratory experiments. Harré and Secord's volume is important and deserves careful reading by social psychologists.

More recently, Secord (1977) specified four criteria for the solution of the crisis.

1. Person parameters must be included in our theoretical systems. Individual differences may often interact with treatment or dependent variables. If so, random assignment averages out person parameters, and resulting generalizations that apply to people in general are either trivial or banal. Lewin would be pleased with this recommendation, since the full specification of the person was one important aspect of the full specification of the field, which was required for adequate explanation.

2. Our theories "must include the conception that people are at times active agents who play some part in directing their own behaviors." Secord recognized that our current theories do not account for the subjective perspective or point of view of the person and are therefore lacking in an important respect. The problems of integrating both objective and subjective explanatory concepts were addressed in the previous section. It is a terribly difficult problem.

3. Secord called for a taxonomy of situations, or essentially, a theory of how behavior varies across situations. Until we have such a taxonomy, we will not be able to "characterize adequately those situations which are the focus of our laboratory or field investigations," and we will not be able to speak meaningfully about generality of results obtained in the laboratory. Whether such a taxonomy can be developed or not is an open question. It may well be that human behavior contains so much particularity that no meaningful taxonomy may ever be extracted (e. g., see Smith, 1976, pp. 339-340).

4. The last criterion is that we should also allow for behaviors that are not self-directed or even comprehended by the behaving person, an apparent concession to the Freudian notion of unconscious determinants of behavior.

On first appearance, Secord's prescriptions are quite reasonable, although there is a question of scale and what can be accomplished. In fact, in proposing how to find out if a phenomenon is governed by historical dependencies, Thorngate (1976b) gave about the same answer: "Gather data over persons, behaviors and time and observe what changes (relations, processes, etc.) and what doesn't. In practice, the task is fiendishly difficult and, I dare say, frightfully boring" (p. 404). It may be that development of a viable social science (or even to decide on the possibility of one) will simply require a willingness to drudge and grub — perhaps over several generations.

In summary, no unified direction to the solution of the crisis is in the offing, and diversity is the main characteristic of the proposed solutions. Increasing breadth of contact with other disciplines seems to be one theme, but the call for a radical reconceptualization of our bases of knowledge seems to be equally frequent. Clearly, a coping response is evident, an undoubtedly healthy trend. The present situation was perhaps best stated by Kuhn (1970), in his general discussion of scientific revolutions.

> Confronted with anomaly or with crisis, scientists take a different attitude toward existing paradigms, and the nature of their research changes accordingly. The proliferation of competing articulations, the willingness to try anything, the expression of explicit discontent, the recourse to philosophy and to debate over fundamentals, all these are symptoms of a transition from normal to extraordinary research (pp. 90-91).

One difficulty for social psychology is that it is not entirely clear what the old paradigm was. McGuire (1973) presented one analysis. Undoubtedly we have been operating under some version of Lewin's philosophy of science, uneasily grafted onto some version of the behavioristic philosophy. The knowledge model of the previous section was offered as the most likely candidate for the philosophy of science by which social psychologists have in the past conducted their research. This is the unidirectional causal model discussed by McGuire and against which he rebelled. With these difficulties in clearly articulating the old paradigm, however, it is doubly difficult to see the shape of any collective new paradigm. Indeed, it is not even clear that the paradigm approach has a compelling validity for social psychology as a conceptual tool (e.g., Elms, 1975). Perhaps the best summary statement is that we are somewhere in the coping process; it is somewhat unclear where we have been and most unclear where we are going.

PROSPECTS FOR THE FUTURE OF EXPERIMENTAL
SOCIAL PSYCHOLOGY

The major salients of the history and philosophic foundations of experimental social psychology have been discussed in this chapter. We have seen how the early optimism of the discipline gave way to pessimism and a sense of crisis. It seems reasonable at this point to pose the question of what the future holds for the discipline.

The continued existence of social psychology seems assured. The real issue is whether the modifier "experimental" will continue to be attached to denote a substantial part of the discipline. The experimental approach to psychology in general has been under assault recently (e. g., Gadlin & Ingle, 1975; but see Kruglanski, 1976 for a spirited rebuttal). There seems to be a general feeling that the experimental method has been overemphasized and that it misses too much of what is really important in human life.

Congruent with the unhappiness with the experiment have been the persistent calls for innovations in new methods. Some of this emphasis was noted in the previous section. There is increasing pressure for social psychologists to get involved in applied activities. An interesting analysis by Helmreich (1975) argued that the applied-theoretical distinction is pernicious to progress, and that the real effort should be devoted to the acquisition and application of sophistication "necessary to understand a complex, multivariate reality" (p. 558). An interesting series of responses to Helmreich's paper has been edited by Gross (1976). It seems highly likely that the growing interest in applications of social psychology will lead to new theories (perhaps even new approaches to theory), which in turn will feed back to create new and diverse methodologies.

In addition to attention to new methods and approaches to social psychology, there needs to be considerable attention devoted to the nature of the discipline, its practice, and presuppositions. Social psychology needs to be studied in detail as a discipline from a sociological perspective (e. g., Buss, 1975). Basic prescientific value commitments that affect scientific choices of social psychologists also need to be assessed. Such an assessment of psychology in general has been discussed by Coan (1973), who calls for the development of a "psychology of psychological knowledge." Finally, social psychologists could profit from detailed study of the philosophy of science. Most social psychologists seem antispeculative in outlook and tend to avoid philosophic issues. Ignorance in such matters does not lead to bliss. "The failure to recognize the relevant epistemological issues involved suggests that some of our difficulties may arise from the philosophical naivete of the average psychologist, rather than from any special characteristic of the field itself" (Forsyth, 1976, p. 457). Even our most basic notions may need to be reconsidered. For example, the primitive notion of a *variable* (Blumer, 1969) might well be reassessed for its applicability to social knowledge. Such reassessment is equivalent to a philosophical analysis, a conclusion stated by Winch's (1958) analysis of the social sciences. Such a detailed and systematic series of conceptual studies of the foundations of social psychology seems well past due.

Predicting the future of a complex social enterprise is always a risky business. One prediction is that the sense of crisis will soon subside, in the sense that people will gradually quit talking about it. It is conjectured, however, that the consequences of the crisis will not subside. The diverse new activities the crisis helped spawn will continue to grow and develop, and the world of social psychology will become ever more complex. The future status of the laboratory experiment is in some doubt. The experiment will persist, but whether it will remain the "queen of methods" is doubtful. Most likely the laboratory experiment will be demoted in rank to the status of coequal with a variety of other methods. By 1985, it may well be that social psychologists will look back on today's laboratory experiment with puzzlement as to how the experiment ever achieved the position of such exclusive eminence. Let us hope that such puzzlement will also be associated with a more productive and optimistic social psychology than exists today.

REFERENCES

Allport, F. H. *Social psychology*. Boston: Houghton Mifflin, 1924.

Allport, G. W. The historical background of modern social psychology. In G. Lindzey & E. Aronson (Eds.), *The handbook of social psychology* (2nd ed., Vol. 1). Reading, Mass.: Addison-Wesley, 1968. (a)

Allport, G. W. Six decades of social psychology. In S. Lundstedt (Ed.), *Higher education in social psychology*. Cleveland: Case Western Reserve Press, 1968. (b)

Altman, I. Environmental psychology and social psychology. *Personality and Social Psychology Bulletin*, 1976, *2*, 96-113.

American Psychological Association, Inc. *Ethical principles in the conduct of research with human participants*. Washington, D.C.: Author, 1973.

Argyris, C. Some unintended consequences of rigorous research. *Psychological Bulletin*, 1968, *70*, 185-197.

Argyris, C. Dangers in applying results from experimental social psychology. *American Psychologist*, 1975, *30*, 469-485.

Armistead, N. Introduction. In N. Armistead (Ed.), *Reconstructing social psychology*. Baltimore, Md.: Penguin Books, 1974.

Aronson, E., & Carlsmith, J. M. Experimentation in social psychology. In G. Lindzey & E. Aronson (Eds.), *The handbook of social psychology* (2nd ed., Vol. 2). Reading, Mass.: Addison-Wesley, 1968.

Asch, S. E. A perspective on social psychology. In S. Koch (Ed.), *Psychology: A study of a science* (Vol. 1). New York: McGraw-Hill, 1959.

Ayer, A. J. *Language, truth and logic* (2nd ed.). New York: Dover, 1952. (2nd ed. originally published, 1946).

Baumgardner, S. R. Critical history and social psychology's "crisis." *Personality and Social Psychology Bulletin*, 1976, *2*, 459-464.

Berkowitz, L. (Ed.). *Advances in experimental social psychology* (9 vols.). New York: Academic Press, 1964-1976.

Bickman, L., & Henchy, T. (Eds.). *Beyond the laboratory: Field research in social psychology*. New York: McGraw-Hill, 1972.

Blumer, H. *Symbolic interactionism: Perspective and method*. Englewood Cliffs, N.J.: Prentice-Hall, 1969.

Bohm, D. *Causality and chance in modern physics*. New York: Van Nostrand, 1957.

Boring, E. G. *A history of experimental social psychology* (2nd ed.). New York: Appleton-Century-Crofts, 1950.

Bowers, K. S. Situationism in psychology: An analysis and a critique. *Psychological Review*, 1973, *80*, 307-336.

Braithwaite, R. B. *Scientific explanation*. New York: Harper & Brothers, 1953.

Bridgman, P. W. *The logic of modern physics*. New York: MacMillan, 1927.

Bridgman, P. W. *The nature of physical theory*. Princeton, N.J.: Princeton University Press, 1936.

Bridgman, P. W. *The way things are.* Cambridge, Mass.: Harvard University Press, 1959.

Bruyn, S. T. *The human perspective in sociology.* Englewood Cliffs, N.J.: Prentice Hall, 1966.

Bunge, M. *Causality: The place of the causal principle in modern science.* Cambridge, Mass.: Harvard University Press, 1959.

Buss, A. R. The emerging field of the sociology of psychological knowledge. *American Psychologist,* 1975, *30,* 988-1002.

Campbell, D. T., & Stanley, J. C. Experimental and quasi-experimental designs for research on teaching. In N. L. Gage (Ed.), *Handbook of research on teaching.* Chicago, Ill.: Rand-McNally, 1963.

Cartwright, D., & Zander, A. (Eds.). *Group dynamics* (3rd ed.). New York: Harper & Row, 1968.

Chua, B. H. On roles, rules and interpretative understanding. *Journal for the Theory of Social Behavior,* 1974, *4,* 71-87.

Coan, R. W. Toward a psychological interpretation of psychology. *Journal of the History of the Behavioral Sciences,* 1973, *9,* 313-327.

Cole, J. R., & Cole, S. *Social stratification in science.* Chicago: University of Chicago Press, 1973.

Crane, D. *Invisible colleges: Diffusion of knowledge in scientific communities.* Chicago: University of Chicago Press, 1972.

Cronbach, L. J. Beyond the two disciplines of scientific psychology. *American Psychologist,* 1975, *30,* 116-127.

Dashiell, J. F. Experimental studies on the influence of social situations on the behavior of individual human adults. In C. Murchison (Ed.), *A handbook of social psychology.* Worcester, Mass.: Clark University Press, 1935.

DeRivera, J. (Ed.). *Field theory as human-science: Contributions of Lewin's Berlin group.* New York: Gardner Press, 1976.

Deutsch, M. Theorizing in social psychology. *Personality and Social Psychology Bulletin,* 1976, *2,* 134-141.

Ducasse, C. J. *Causation and the types of necessity.* New York: Dover, 1969. (Originally published, 1924).

Deese, J. Behavior and fact. *American Psychologist,* 1969, *24,* 515-522.

Eacker, J. N. On some elementary philosophical problems of psychology. *American Psychologist,* 1972, *27,* 553-565.

Elms, A. C. The crisis of confidence in social psychology. *American Psychologist,* 1975, *30,* 967-976.

Festinger, L. *A theory of cognitive dissonance.* Stanford, Calif.: Stanford University Press, 1957.

Festinger, L. Sampling and related problems in research methodology. *American Journal of Mental Deficiency,* 1959, *64,* 358-366.

Finison, L. J. (Ed.). *Newsletter of the History of Social Psychology Group.* Dept. of Psychology, Wellesley College, Wellesley, Ma. 02181.

Fleming, D. Attitude: The history of a concept. *Perspectives in American History,* 1967, *1,* 287-365.

Forsyth, D. R. Crucial experiments and social psychological inquiry. *Personality and Social Psychology Bulletin,* 1976, *2,* 453-458.

Fried, S. B., Gumpper, D. C., & Allen, J. C. Ten years of social psychology: Is there a growing commitment to field research? *American Psychologist,* 1973, *28,* 155-156.

Gadlin, H., & Ingle, G. Through the one-way mirror: The limits of experimental self-reflection. *American Psychologist,* 1975, *30,* 1003-1009.

Gardner, M. (Ed.). *Rudolf Carnap: An introduction to the philosophy of science.* New York: Basic Books, 1966.

Gergen, K. J. Social psychology as history. *Journal of Personality and Social Psychology,* 1973, *26,* 309-320.

Gergen, K. J. Social psychology, science and history. *Personality and Social Psychology Bulletin,* 1976, *2,* 373-383.

Godow, R. A., Jr. Social psychology as both science and history. *Personality and Social Psychology Bulletin,* 1976, *2,* 420-426.

Greenwald, A. G. Transhistorical lawfulness of behavior: A comment on two papers. *Personality and Social Psychology Bulletin,* 1976, *2,* 391.

Gross, A. E. Applied social psychology – problems and prospects: Some responses to Helmreich. *Personality and Social Psychology Bulletin,* 1976, *2,* 114-115.

Gross, G. Unnatural selection. In N. Armistead (Ed.), *Reconstructing social psychology.* Baltimore, Md.: Penguin Books, 1974.

Harré, R. *The principles of scientific thinking.* Chicago: University of Chicago Press, 1970.

Harré, R., & Secord, P. F. *The explanation of social behavior.* Totowa, N.J.: Rowman & Littlefield, 1972.

Harris, R. J. The uncertain connection between verbal theories and research hypotheses in social psychology. *Journal of Experimental Social Psychology,* 1976, *12,* 210-219. (a)

Harris, R. J. Two factors contributing to the perception of the theoretical intractability of social psychology. *Personality and Social Psychology Bulletin,* 1976, *2,* 410-416. (b)

Heider, F. *The psychology of interpersonal relations.* New York: Wiley, 1958.

Heider, F. On Lewin's method and theory. *Journal of Social Issues, Supplement Series 13,* 1959, 3-13.

Helmreich, R. Applied social psychology: The unfulfilled promise. *Personality and Social Psychology Bulletin,* 1975, *1,* 548-560.

Hempel, C. G. *Philosophy of natural science.* Englewood Cliffs, N.J.: Prentice-Hall, 1966.

Hendrick, C. Social psychology as history and as traditional science: An appraisal. *Personality and Social Psychology Bulletin,* 1976, *2,* 392-402.

Hendrick, C., & Jones, R. A. *The nature of theory and research in social psychology.* New York: Academic Press, 1972.

Higbee, K. L., & Wells, M. G. Some research trends in social psychology during the 1960s. *American Psychologist,* 1972, *27,* 963-966.

Hitt, W. D. Two models of man. *American Psychologist,* 1969, *24,* 651-658.

Hollander, E. P. The Society of Experimental Social Psychology: An historical note. *Journal of Personality and Social Psychology,* 1968, *9,* 280-282.

Holton, G. On the role of themata in scientific thought. *Science,* 1975, *188,* 328-334.

Hovland, C. I., Janis, I. L., & Kelley, H. H. *Communication and persuasion.* New Haven, Conn.: Yale University Press, 1953.

Katz, D. Editorial. *Journal of Personality and Social Psychology,* 1967, *7,* 341-344.

Katz, D. Some final considerations about experimentation in social psychology. In C. G. McClintock (Ed.), *Experimental social psychology.* New York: Holt, Rinehart, & Winston, 1972.

Kelley, R. L., Osborne, W. J., & Hendrick, C. Role-taking and role-playing in human communication. *Human Communication Research,* 1974, *1,* 62-74.

Kelman, H. C. *A time to speak: On human values and social research.* San Francisco: Jossey-Bass, 1968.

Kiesler, C. A., Collins, B. E., & Miller, N. *Attitude change.* New York: Wiley, 1969.

Klineberg, O. The place of social psychology in a university. In O. Klineberg & R. Christie (Eds.), *Perspectives in social psychology.* New York: Holt, Rinehart, & Winston, 1965.

Klineberg, O., & Christie, R. (Eds.). *Perspectives in social psychology.* New York: Holt, Rinehart, & Winston, 1965.

Koch, S. Clark L. Hull. In W. K. Estes, S. Koch, K. MacCorquodale, P. E. Meehl, C. G. Mueller, Jr., W. N. Schoenfeld, & W. S. Verplanck (Eds.), *Modern learning theory.* New York: Appleton-Century-Crofts, 1954.

Kruglanski, A. W. On the paradigmatic objections to experimental psychology: A reply to Gadlin and Ingle. *American Psychologist,* 1976, *31,* 655-663.

Kuhn, T. S. *The structure of scientific revolutions* (2nd ed.). Chicago: University of Chicago Press, 1970.

Lachenmeyer, C. W. Experimentation – A misunderstood methodology in psychological and social-psychological research. *American Psychologist,* 1970, *25,* 617-624.

Lambert, W. W. Social psychology in relation to general psychology and other behavioral sciences. In S. Koch (Ed.), *Psychology: A study of a science* (Vol. 6). New York; McGraw-Hill, 1963.

Lambert, W. W., & Weisbrod, R. (Eds.). *Comparative perspectives on social psychology.* Boston: Little, Brown, 1971.

Lana, R. E. *Assumptions of social psychology.* New York: Appleton-Century-Crofts, 1969.

Levine, M. Scientific method and the adversary model: Some preliminary thoughts. *American Psychologist,* 1974, *29,* 661-677.

Levison, A. B. *Knowledge and society.* New York: Bobbs-Merrill, 1974.

Lewin, K. *A dynamic theory of personality.* New York: McGraw-Hill, 1935.

Lewin, K. *Principles of topological psychology.* New York: McGraw-Hill, 1936.

Lewin, K. Psychoanalysis and topological psychology. *Bulletin of the Menninger Clinic,* 1937, *1,* 202-211.

Lewin, K. *Field theory in social science.* New York: Harper & Brothers, 1951.

Lewin, K., Lippitt, R., & White, R. K. Patterns of aggressive behavior in experimentally created "social climates." *Journal of Social Psychology,* 1939, *10,* 271-299.

Lindzey, G., & Aronson, E. (Eds.). *The handbook of social psychology* (2nd ed., 5 vols.). Reading, Mass.: Addison-Wesley, 1968.

Losee, J. *A historical introduction to the philosophy of science.* New York: Oxford University Press, 1972.

Lubek, I. A note on the power structure in social psychology. *Representative Research in Social Psychology,* 1976, *7,* 87-88.

Lundstedt, S. (Ed.). *Higher education in social psychology.* Cleveland: Case Western Reserve Press, 1968.

Manis, M. Comment on Gergen's "Social psychology as history." *Personality and Social Psychology Bulletin,* 1975, *1,* 450-455.

Manis, M. Is social psychology really different? *Personality and Social Psychology Bulletin,* 1976, *2,* 427-436.   (a)

Manis, M. Social psychology and history: A symposium. *Personality and Social Psychology Bulletin,* 1976, *2,* 371-372.   (b)

Marrow, A. J. *The practical theorist: The life and work of Kurt Lewin.* New York: Basic Books, 1969.

Marx, M. H. (Ed.). *Theories in contemporary psychology.* New York: Macmillan, 1963.

McGuire, W. J. Discussion of William N. Schoenfeld's paper. In O. Klineberg & R. Christie (Eds.), *Perspectives in social psychology.* New York: Holt, Rinehart & Winston, 1965.

McGuire, W. J. Some impending reorientations in social psychology: Some thoughts provoked by Kenneth Ring. *Journal of Experimental Social Psychology,* 1967, *3,* 124-139.

McGuire, W. J. The nature of attitudes and attitude change. In G. Lindzey & E. Aronson (Eds.), *The handbook of social psychology* (2nd ed., Vol 3). Reading, Mass.: Addison-Wesley, 1969. (a)

McGuire, W. J. Theory-oriented research in natural settings; The best of both worlds for social psychology. In M. Sherif & C. W. Sherif (Eds.), *Interdisciplinary relationships in the social sciences.* Chicago: Aldine, 1969. (b)

McGuire, W. J. The yin and yang of progress in social psychology: Seven koan. *Journal of Personality and Social Psychology,* 1973, *26,* 446-456.

Mead, G. H. *Mind, self, and society.* Chicago: University of Chicago Press, 1934.

Merton, R. K. *Social theory and social structure.* New York: Free Press, 1957.

Mills, J. (Ed.). *Experimental social psychology.* London: Macmillan, 1969.

Mitroff, I. I. On doing empirical philosophy of science: A case study in the social psychology of research. *Philosophy of the Social Sciences, 1974, 4,* 183-196.

Moscovici, S. Society and theory in social psychology. In J. Israel & H. Tajfel (Eds.), *The context of social psychology: A critical assessment.* New York: Academic Press, 1972.

Murchison, C. A. (Ed.). *A handbook of social psychology.* Worcester, Mass.: Clark University Press, 1935.

Murphy, G. The future of social psychology in historical perspective. In O. Klinberg & R. Christie (Eds.), *Perspectives in social psychology.* New York: Holt, Rinehart, & Winston, 1965.

Murphy, G., & Murphy, L. B. *Experimental social psychology.* New York: Harper, 1931.

Murphy, G., Murphy, L. B., & Newcomb, T. M. *Experimental social psychology* (Rev. ed.). New York: Harper, 1937.

Nagel, E. *The structure of science.* New York: Harcourt, Brace, & World, 1961.

Nisbet, R. A. *Social change and history.* New York: Oxford University Press, 1969.

Phillips, D. L. *Abandoning method.* San Francisco: Jossey-Bass, 1973.

Piaget, J. *Understanding Causality.* New York: Norton, 1974.

Popper, K. *The logic of scientific discovery* (K. Popper, Trans.). New York: Harper & Row, 1968. (Originally published, 1934.)

Resnick, J. H., & Schwartz, T. Ethical standards as an independent variable in psychological research. *American Psychologist, 1973, 28,* 134-139.

Richards, M. The biological and the social. In N. Armistead (Ed.), *Reconstructing social psychology.* Baltimore, Md.: Penguin Books, 1974.

Riecken, H. W. Research developments in the social sciences. In O. Klineberg & R. Christie (Eds.), *Perspectives in social psychology.* New York: Holt, Rinehart, & Winston, 1965.

Ring, K. Experimental social psychology: Some sober questions about some frivolous values. *Journal of Experimental Social Psychology, 1967, 3,* 113-123.

Rosenthal, R., & Rosnow, R. L. *Artifact in behavioral research.* New York: Academic Press, 1969.

Rowan, J. Research as intervention. In N. Armistead (Ed.), *Reconstructing social psychology.* Baltimore, Md.: Penguin Books, 1974.

Ryan, A. (Ed.). *The philosophy of social explanation.* New York: Oxford University Press, 1973.

Rychlak, J. F. *A philosophy of science for personality theory.* New York: Houghton Mifflin, 1968.

Sahakian, W. W. *Systematic social psychology.* New York: Chandler, 1974.

Sales, S. M. Threat as a factor in authoritarianism: An analysis of archival data. *Journal of Personality and Social Psychology, 1973, 28,* 44-57.

Salmon, W. C. Confirmation. *Scientific American, 1973, 228*(5), 75-83.

Samelson, F. History, origin myth and ideology: "Discovery" of social psychology. *Journal for the Theory of Social Behavior, 1974, 4,* 217-231.

Sandowsky, A. M. (Ed.). *Social psychology research: Laboratory-field relationships.* New York: Free Press, 1972.

Schlenker, B. R. Social psychology and science. *Journal of Personality and Social Psychology, 1974, 29,* 1-15.

Schlenker, B. R. Social psychology and science: Another look. *Personality and Social Psychology Bulletin, 1976, 2,* 384-390.

Schultz, D. The human subject in psychological research. *Psychological Bulletin*, 1969, *72*, 214-228.

Scriven, M. Comments of Professor Scriven. In T. W. Wann (Ed.)., *Behaviorism and phenomenology*. Chicago: University of Chicago Press, 1964.

Secord, P. F. Transhistorical and transcultural theory. *Personality and Social Psychology Bulletin*, 1976, *2*, 417-419.

Secord, P. F. Social psychology in search of a paradigm. *Personality and Social Psychology Bulletin*, 1977, *3*, 41-50.

Sherif, M. A study of social factors in perception. *Archives of Psychology*, 1935, *27*, No. 187, 1-60.

Sherif, M. *The psychology of social norms*. New York: Harper & Row, 1936.

Sherif, M. Social psychology: Problems and trends in interdisciplinary relationships. In S. Koch (Ed.), *Psychology: A study of a science* (Vol. 6). New York: McGraw-Hill, 1963.

Sherif, M., & Sherif, C. W. (Eds.). *Interdisciplinary relationship in the social sciences* Chicago: Aldine, 1969.

Simmel, E. C., Hoppe, R. A., & Milton, C. A. (Eds.). *Social facilitation and imitative behavior*. Boston: Allyn & Bacon, 1968.

Skinner, B. F. *About behaviorism*. New York: Knopf, 1974.

Smith, M. B. Three textbooks: A special review. *Journal of Experimental Social Psychology*, 1966, *2*, 109-118.

Smith, M. B. Is experimental social psychology advancing? *Journal of Experimental Social Psychology*, 1972, *8*, 86-96. (a)

Smith, M. B. Toward humanizing social psychology. In T. S. Krawiec (Ed.), *The psychologists* (Vol. 1). New York: Oxford University Press, 1972. (b)

Smith, M. B. Criticism of a social science. *Science*, 1973, *180*, 610-612.

Smith, M. B. Social psychology, science, and history: So *what? Personality and Social Psychology Bulletin*, 1976, *2*, 437-443.

Steiner, I. D. Whatever happened to the group in social psychology? *Journal of Experimental Social Psychology*, 1974, *10*, 94-108.

Stevens, S. S. Psychology and the science of science. *Psychological Bulletin*, 1939, *36*, 221-263.

Stotland, E. Experimental social psychology and its neighbors. *Journal of Social Psychology*, 1965, *67*, 315-323.

Strickland, L. H. (Ed.). The "power structure" in social psychology. *Representative Research in Social Psychology*, 1976, *7*, 79-86.

Tajfel, H. Experiments in a vacuum. In J. Israel & H. Tajfel (Eds.), *The context of social psychology: A critical assessment*. New York: Academic Press, 1972.

Thorngate, W. Process invariance: Another red herring. *Personality and Social Psychology Bulletin*, 1975, *1*, 485-488.

Thorngate, W. Ignorance, arrogance, and social psychology: A response to Helmreich. *Personality and Social Psychology Bulletin*, 1976, *2*, 122-126. (a)

Thorngate, W. "In general" vs. "it depends": Some comments on the Gergen-Schlenker debate. *Personality and Social Psychology Bulletin*, 1976, *2*, 403-409. (b)

Triplett, N. The dynamogenic factors in pacemaking and competition. *American Journal of Psychology*, 1897, *9*, 507-533.

Truzzi, M. (Ed.). *Verstehen: Subjective understanding in the social sciences*. Reading, Mass.: Addison-Wesley, 1974.

Wallace, W. A. *Causality and scientific explanation* (2 vols.). Ann Arbor, Mich.: University of Michigan Press, 1972, 1974.

Wann, T. W. (Ed.). *Behaviorism and phenomenology.* Chicago: University of Chicago Press, 1964.

Webb, E. J., Campbell, D. T., Schwartz, R. D., & Sechrest, L. *Unobtrusive measures: Nonreactive research in the social sciences.* Chicago: Rand McNally, 1966.

Willems, E. P., & Raush, H. L. (Eds.). *Naturalistic viewpoints in psychological research.* New York: Holt, Rinehart, & Winston, 1969.

Wilson, T. P. Conceptions of interaction and forms of sociological explanation. *American Sociological Review,* 1970, *35,* 697-710.

Winch, P. *The idea of a social science.* New York: Humanities Press, 1958.

Zajonc, R. B. Social facilitation. *Science,* 1965, *149,* 269-274.

Zajonc, R. B. *Social psychology: An experimental approach.* Belmont, Calif.: Wadsworth, 1966.

2

Social Psychology As
Symbolic Interaction

Russell A. Jones
Robert A. Day

University of Kentucky Medical Center

> *... nature is not so much her own ever-sweet interpreter, as the mere supplier of*
> *that cunning alphabet, whereby selecting and combining as he pleases, each man*
> *reads his own peculiar lesson according to his own peculiar mind and mood.*
>
> Herman Melville
> Pierre: or The Ambiguities

SYMBOLIC INTERACTION

The subject we shall discuss in this chapter is one that has appeared, and continues to appear, under many different guises and in many different disciplines. The guise under which our subject is known within sociology is "symbolic interaction," but, as we shall see, the issues and problems confronted by this perspective know no disciplinary boundaries.

Definition

The defining problem of our subject is the social construction of meaning, the imposition of some sort of order and coherence on what William James once referred to as the "booming, buzzing confusion" that constitutes the world of the newly born. The necessity of interpreting and understanding our surroundings is not, of course, confined to infancy, but continues and grows progressively more difficult and complex as we mature and our horizons broaden and our knowledge increases. In the attempt to make sense of the myriad stimuli that impinge upon us from both without and within: we place constructions on reality;

we turn to others to validate our perceptions; and we become very selective in what we perceive. In this chapter, we will look at some of the implications of such a view.

"Symbolic interaction" is not a theory. Rather it is a perspective, a viewpoint, a way of looking at certain types of social and psychological phenomena. Stone and Farberman (1970) note that the symbolic interactional perspective is defined by a concern for the generation, persistence, and transformation of meaning in our perceptions of reality. Further, meaning for the individual can only be established through communication with others. The particular others with whom one communicates, of course, are a major determinant — if not *the* major determinant — of how one will perceive and define objective reality. As Berger and Luckmann (1966) put it:

> Every individual is born into an objective social structure within which he encounters the significant others who are in charge of his socialization. These significant others are imposed upon him. Their definitions of his situation are posited for him as objective reality. He is thus born into not only an objective social structure but also an objective social world. The significant others who mediate this world to him modify it in the course of mediating it. They select aspects of it in accordance with their own location in the social structure, and also by virtue of their individual, biographically rooted idiosyncrasies. The social world is "filtered" to the individual through this double selectivity (p. 131).

Although there is a somewhat greater element of choice as to which social structure or at what point in a given structure adults find themselves, the essential features of the process of perceiving reality are the same for adults as those mentioned by Berger and Luckman. The definitions that significant others hold of reality are posited as being that reality. Differences in definitions are negotiable and, as Saul Alinsky frequently pointed out, the key to negotiation is power — in some form or other. The view we will be discussing in this chapter, then, is one that looks at the self as both an active and reactive information-processing agent engaged in an attempt to order the universe and make sense of it by a process of communication with others. As will become apparent, many of the ideas that we will be discussing are not new. To say that the ideas are not new may itself imply that they have to do with historically universal social phenomena of the utmost importance. We, of course, believe they do.

The Importance of Communication

The sine qua non of symbolic interactionism is communication. Communication, in any of its many forms, provides the process by which individuals can share their experience and perceptions with each other. Without communication, neither individual thought nor human society as we know it would be possible. Most human communication, of course, takes place via an exchange of symbols, hence, the phrase "symbolic interactionism."

In recent years, the analysis of verbal communication has become quite sophisticated. For example, suppose that a speaker wishes to convey a particular idea or refer to a particular topic. Often the speaker will hesitate and try to find just the right word to convey a particular notion; several words apparently come to mind and are rejected because they do not capture quite the right nuance. Rosenberg and Cohen (1966) have developed a model of speaker and listener processes that is predicated on the idea that what the speaker is really doing during such hesitations is attempting to take the role of the listener and evaluate the various response alternatives, that is, would a given response mean to the listener what the speaker intends it to mean? This notion of "taking the role of the other" is, as we shall see, an important one in the symbolic interaction approach.

Not all communication involves language, however, even among humans. In recent years, there has been an exploding interest in nonverbal communication. Many people appear to be rediscovering the importance of all the little signs and gestures that Freud (1938) described in *The Psychopathology of Everyday Life*. Freud believed that most, if not all, actions performed by a person were of communicative significance. Body position, errors, slips of the tongue, manner of dress: everything was assumed to convey something. In recent years, there has been a growing experimental literature that demonstrates that many of these "meaningless" behaviors are indeed taken to mean something, whether or not they are so intended. Jones and Cooper (1971), for example, have shown that the number of times an experimenter glances at a subject during an experimental session significantly affects the subject's mood, which in turn influences the subject's performance on a projective test. Somewhat paradoxically, it is almost impossible for two people not to communicate when they are in each other's presence. Trying not to communicate when in the presence of another is like trying to make your mind a complete blank — it simply cannot be done.

Given, then, the pervasiveness of communication in our day-to-day life and the statement that communication is central to the perspective we will be discussing in this chapter, the question which forces itself upon us is *why?* Why is communication so important? Surely humans could exist without communication. That is precisely what they would do without communication, exist. It is the ability to communicate that separates man from the lower animals. It is the ability to communicate, to exchange symbols, to symbolically "point" to things not physically present that allows the transmission and inheritance of culture and raises man above his biological imperatives. The ability to communicate, in short, makes man human. There is a point here which is easy to miss. Without the ability to communicate, man would have nothing to communicate. That is, it is only through a process of communication with others that we learn to label reality, both external and internal. This, of course, is a part of the basic question of social psychology: what is the relationship between the individual and society? The symbolic interaction perspective provides a way of looking at how the individual both shapes and is shaped by society.

Overview of the Chapter

It would be impossible to cover all of the material pertinent to symbolic interaction in a single chapter. Language development and usage, interpersonal exchange, reference groups, role theory, self-concepts, person perception, value
systems, deviance: the list of topics is very long indeed. Further, in order to be
complete, we would have to systematically explore the interrelationships among
these various topics. Are there, for example, identifiable stages in the development of self-concepts that correspond to certain aspects of language development?

Given the impracticability of such an encyclopedic approach, it seemed better
to select a few topics and cover them in sufficient depth to give the flavor of the
symbolic interaction approach. The topics that we have selected are rather closely identified with particular research methods. Hence we have also devoted some
time and space to an exposition of the methodologies themselves. As we mentioned above, many of the ideas that we will be discussing are not new. Thus, we
begin by taking a look at some of the philosophical ruminations from which
symbolic interactionism emerged.

HISTORICAL AND PHILOSOPHICAL ORIGINS

Most historical accounts of the rise and subsequent development of symbolic
interactionism as a viable theoretical perspective in sociology and social psychology have had the tendency of focusing almost exclusively upon American
social thought. Even more specifically, most of the attention has been directed
primarily to the departments of psychology, philosophy, and sociology at the
University of Chicago and/or the collaborative efforts of such key individuals as
William James, John Dewey, W. I. Thomas, Charles H. Cooley, George Herbert
Mead, Ellsworth Faris, and Herbert Blumer. This is hardly surprising for a theoretical perspective whose name was only first coined in a chapter written by
Blumer in 1937 (Blumer, 1937, p. 153). The broader influence of the European
training that many of these key individuals received and the relationships between symbolic interactionism and various diverse strands of European thought,
however, have often been overlooked or largely neglected. For this very reason,
we would like to briefly sketch out some of the more important historical continuities and similarities between the two.

The Scottish Moral Philosophers

The first discernible articulations of what was later to become known as symbolic interactionism can perhaps be found in the works of the Scottish Moral

Philosophers.[1] Give or take a few years, this group pretty well spanned the eighteenth century. The most notable members were Adam Smith, David Hume, and Adam Ferguson, But Thomas Reid, Francis Hutcheson, Dugald Stewart, Lord Kames, and Lord Monboddo were all members of the inner circle and made some rather significant contributions of their own. While they worked in a number of different areas (economics, history, philosophy, anthropology, and sociology), the Scottish Moral Philosophers were important to the present topic in at least three different, but related ways.

First, this was the first group to expose the futility of arguments based on the "true" nature of man. Here they were responding to the Social Contract theorists such as Hobbes, Locke, and Rousseau. They attacked the contract theorists because they believed that this kind of reasoning had done little more than lead social thinkers down a blind alley, in which the basic underlying philosophical assumptions resulted in deductive, circular reasoning. Hence, the postulates or assumptions (for example, Hobbes portrayed man as being "mean, solitary, brutish, nasty, and insatiable") could be either supported or refuted, but not really improved and further developed. This was simply because the nature of the real problem, according to the contract theorists, derived from the internal or instinctual nature of the individual. Thus, most of the contract theorists devoted their intellectual energies advancing explanations and descriptions of the state of the presocial individual. If this basic presocial human nature could be determined, they argued, then it might also be possible to reorganize society and its institutions in a new and hopefully better way. In attacking this line of reasoning[2], the Scots countered with a common sense approach which was grounded in moral philosophy, history, and ethnography.

Second, the Scottish Moral Philosphers, responding perhaps to the extreme idealists, felt that the existence of society was indubitable, that this fact must be accepted, and that the best place to begin was in studying its actual organization. Why should the social theorist try to create an imaginary, free-floating man in a vacuum? Accordingly, they argued that the focus should instead be upon real

---

[1]There are at least two fine overviews of these men and their works. They are Gladys Bryson, *Man and Society: The Scottish Inquiry of the Eighteenth Century,* (Princeton, New Jersey: Princton University Press, 1945) and Louis Schneider (Ed.), *The Scottish Moralists: On Human Nature and Society* (Chicago: The University of Chicago Press, 1967). The best sources, however, are the group's original writings.

[2]Here it should be noted that Smith's theoretical work itself has some internal inconsistencies. In *The Wealth of Nations* (1776), rather than relying completely on a distinctly "social" explanation to analyze the numerous and profound changes taking place in Europe, Smith at times fell back upon the argument of man's "inherent" tendency to "truck, barter, and trade" to enhance his position. This lapse into the kind of Social Contract reasoning he earlier had attacked, however, represents only a very small part of his overall theoretical argument.

groups of individuals and their moral sentiments (sympathy, "fellow-feelings," etc.). Underlying this facet of their reasoning, of course, was their belief in the possibility of ultimately discovering the causes of human behavior and their acceptance of Hume's empiricism as a method of proof. Thus, they stressed the systematic and empirical study of social organization, social interaction, and their underlying features.

Third, and most directly related to the matter at hand, this group frequently engaged in wide ranging psychological and social psychological treatises. These ranged from Hume's rather casual reflections, regarding the perceptions of the old by the young and vice versa and the particular manner in which local people responded to and parried with strangers and foreigners to create a sense of order, to Adam Smith's more systematic efforts in developing a viable social psychology. Several aspects of this work stand out. One of the most striking features consisted of their keen awareness of the limitations of pure human reason in interpreting and understanding the world. Even Hume, whose famous analysis of causation is still important reading today, was very skeptical of the ideas of cause and effect. What all of them were concerned with, to be certain, were the numerous intrinsic and extrinsic factors that filter out and shape both our social actions and what we consider to be truth or knowledge. The question that plagued them and the social psychologists of today as well was whether or not any such thing as universal human nature existed.

In *The Theory of Moral Sentiments* (1752), much of Adam Smith's analysis of the individual's attitude toward the self and the subsequent evaluation of the self sounds strikingly similar to the later writings of both Cooley and Mead. Here Smith suggested that the individual was provided with a "mirror" by society, which aided in looking at one's own character, sentiments, and physical and mental capabilities. This "mirror" consisted of both the perceptions of the individual held by various peers and the behavior exhibited to the individual by them. Thus, if we would think of ourselves as being spectators of our own actions, Smith felt we could be afforded "a looking-glass by which we can, in some measure, with the eyes of other people, scrutinize the propriety of our own conduct" (quoted in Schneider, 1967, p. xxvi). Here Smith also refers to the "impartial spectator." In Schneider's words, this term referred to "that man within the breast who may be said broadly to be the representative within ourselves of *others* in the society about us — of others who make our judgments of our own conduct and sentiments less partial or self-interested than they would be if we had not effected precisely that internalization whereby the others come to be represented with us" (p. xxvi). In short, Smith was saying that we judge ourselves and our own acts in much the same way we feel others judge us. The process of communication thus brings about understanding and sympathy through what amounts to playing the role of others. Furthermore, in Smith's viewpoint there were no "individuals" per se, but only organized relationships.

Others in the group — Ferguson and Stewart, for example — suggested that Smith should have used a more familiar term, such as "conscience," instead of "the man within the breast." Nonetheless, this section of his work clearly seems to be less concerned with the area of ethics than with social psychological problems, many of which were linked directly to some of the central concerns of symbolic interactionism. In other ways, some of his ideas seem to anticipate certain aspects of Freud's conceptions of the ego and superego.

The French Philosophers of the Enlightenment and the Romantic-Conservative Response

The French Philosophers of the Enlightenment (approximately 1725-1800) were also very important figures in the development of modern sociology and, as a result, they have had at least an indirect influence on symbolic interactionists. In a number of ways, they were tied directly in their thinking to the Social Contract theorists, the Scottish Moral Philosophers, and to the writings of Jefferson and Franklin in the United States. The philosophers who comprised this group — men like Montesquieu, Voltaire, Diderot, and Rousseau — were caught up in a climate of opinion that greatly emphasized the possibility of freedom, individuality, spontaneity, and individual perfectability. Consequently, a deep passion to set things right comes across strongly in their writings. Politically speaking, they were opposed to both the premises upon which power and authority had come to rest in the hands of the aristocracy and to the nature of existing social institutions in France.

The Enlightenment philosophers therefore aspired to create a new world based on reason and truth. Truth, however, came to be defined quite differently than it had been in the past, in that it no longer relied upon authority, tradition, dogma, and revelation as its basis. Instead, an attempt was made to bring together and synthesize two distinct philosophical approaches that had managed to remain separate and apart throughout the seventeenth century: rationalism and empiricism. Enormously inspired by the scientific achievements of the preceding centuries, as illustrated in the works of da Vinci, Galileo, and Newton, to mention only a select few, reason and observation thus became the underlying basis or model to be used in the pursuit of truth. Probably the strongest influences on the Enlightenment philosophers were the writings of John Locke and the work of Sir Isaac Newton. Locke's "possibilism," combined with Newton's methodology and the numerous accomplishments that followed in the wake of his work were extremely influential for the emerging positivism of the time. Taking these developments as their cue, many social thinkers thus began to argue that if science could reveal the workings of basic natural laws, then surely it was only a matter of time before similar laws could be discovered in the cultural and social realms as well.

The intention of this group, moreover, was that this new positive approach to truth or knowledge would help to change not only the way people reasoned about things, but also the very nature of the existent social order itself. The Enlightenment philosophers therefore represented not only the tendency toward positivism, which was soon realized, but also a tendency toward dialectical or critical thought as well. In the words of Zeitlin (1968), "The existing factual order was studied scientifically by these men in order to learn how to transcend it" (p. 9). In stressing the need for restructuring French society, this group of thinkers also provided implicit and explicit support for the political activists more directly involved in the revolutionary overthrow of the French aristocracy in 1789. Thus, the Enlightenment philosophers advocated an important and positive role for revolution in the reengineering of French society from top to bottom. After the irrational old order was torn down, they felt a new and hopefully better society could be constructed upon rationally based principles.

The Romantic-Conservative reaction in France, England, and Germany was a direct response to both the intellectual products of the French philosophers of the Enlightenment and the overt political events stemming from the French Revolution of 1789 and its aftermath. The Romantic and Conservative thinkers of the early nineteenth century abhorred the chaotic and disorganizing consequences for Europe of the French Revolution and generally attributed these consequences to those revolutionaries who had unwittingly and uncritically embraced the principles of the Enlightenment. According to the Romantic-Conservatives, the biggest mistake of all centered around the attempt to reorganize society solely upon rational principles.

Responding then to the exaltation of reason and empiricism, which had arisen in the eighteenth century, such diverse figures as Louis de Bonald and Joseph de Maistre in France, Friedrich Hegel in Germany, and Edmund Burke in England countered by extolling the virtues of emotion and imagination. The Romantic-Conservative reaction thus lead to a great revival of interest in the areas of art, poetry, and religion. In Zeitlin's (1968) words:

> In general, the Enlightenment conception of a rational mechanistic universe was now rejected. In every field – literature, art, music, philosophy, and religion – an effort was made to free the emotions and the imagination from the austere rules and conventions imposed during the eighteenth century. In religion, the importance of inner experience was restored; and in philosophy, the individual mind was assigned a creative role in shaping the world (p. 36).

In addition, the concepts of the group, the community, and the nation-state took on increasingly important roles in social theory. Historical traditions, culture, and personal loyalties were now seen as binding the individual to the group, community, and the nation-state. And, perhaps most important of all, the societal perspective once again regained an equal footing with that of the individual or perhaps even exceeded it. Certain developments in philosophy occurred, however, that were most pertinent to the future development of social theory in general and, more specifically, to symbolic interaction theory. Since most of these developments can be found in German thought, we will turn now to a very brief overview of them.

The German Influence

There are so many diverse ideas and influential thinkers of German origin in the disciplines of philosophy, psychology, history, and cultural studies, generally., that are pertinent to the development of symbolic interactionism that we can barely scratch the surface of these works here. Nevertheless, we will make a brief attempt, since the German influence is a vital and important part of the early intellectual development of this perspective. We would contend that, before one can fully understand the general world view and underlying philosophical assumptions of symbolic interactionism, it is necessary to historically examine some of these fundamental aspects of German thought. In many ways, the overall historical period in which these developments occurred and even the tone and substance of many of the arguments are congruent with parts of the writings of the Romantic-Conservatives in France and England. But the German Idealists addressed most of these issues much more directly, systematically, and analytically than the French and English writers had yet done. Finally, it should also be added that we feel an understanding of the history of ideas can help to enrich our ability to assess both the current state of social psychological theory and its possible future directions. In the case of symbolic interactionism, some of the most exciting contemporary work in the field centers around a number of different efforts to redirect, reexamine, synthesize, and better ground our research in such diverse German schools of thought as Marxism, dialectical historicism, the sociology of knowledge, phenomenology, Gestalt psychology and ethnomethodology (Denzin, 1969; Lichtman, 1970; Petras and Meltzer, 1973; Reynolds and Reynolds, 1973; and Zeitlin, 1973).

At the most fundamental and basic level, the Germans gave considerable thought to the question of how we actually go about obtaining our "knowledge" of the social world. Immanuel Kant (1724-1804), labeled by many as the last true epistemologist, was the most important and well-known of the early German philosophers who dealt with this issue. During his lifetime the two schools that the Enlightenment helped to bring together, rationalism and empiricism, periodically embraced one another, but they still remained separated in terms of their overall strategies for knowing the world. The rationalists (Descartes, Spinoza, Leibnitz) sought this unity by way of logical principles. The empiricists (Locke, Hume, and Berkeley) proposed to start with empirical facts to unify thought. And, although both groups believed that these two forms of knowledge would ultimately be synthesized, this had not yet been accomplished.

This was due to the fact that both schools believed that knowledge could be divided into primary and secondary qualities. Descartes, representing the rationalists, felt that empirical or sensory knowledge was notoriously variable. But he also felt that some forms of empirical kmowledge contained very real information about reality. Thus, he divided the sensory qualities into a secondary category, which depended upon the mind itself for their character. Obviously, the mind represented the primary category of knowledge for Descartes and the rationalists. For the empiricists, the situation was reversed. Sensory experience of the world was primary, and the role of the individual mind was given a secondary priority. When these distinctions between primary and secondary qualities were extended to their limits, rational and empirical knowledge ended up in apparently irreconcilable spheres. Knowledge applied to reality had no certainty for the rationalists and, conversely, the certain knowledge of the rationalists had no application to reality for the empiricists.

Building on the ideas of Hume, Locke, and Leibnitz, as well as many others, Kant attempted to solve this schism between the two schools. In effect, he attempted to overcome the bifurcation of nature itself. For Kant, the splitting up of nature into mind by the rationalists and the physical world by the empiricists was unsatisfactory and unrealistic. The result was that nature and reality itself were divested of all independence and process by the rationalists, while the mind in turn was effectively discarded by the empiricists, who reduced it to material particles. Kant's major accomplishment was the bringing together of this subject-object dichotomy into a more wide-ranging and complete conceptualization of the knowledge process. His major assertion was that you cannot have an object (fact or experience) without a subject (mind). Going further, Kant made a distinction between synthetic and analytic statements.

> A synthetic statement is any statement which adds some new item to the stock of knowledge about the world. It is a statement about the world, a statement of fact. Generally, there is only one way to arrive at a bit of factual knowledge; that is, to obtain it from experience. Synthetic knowledge is empirical knowledge. Analytic statements, on the other hand, do not require factual investigation. They are not statements arrived at in this manner. They are deduced from other statements already made. The conclusion of an Aristotelian syllogism is analytic. Such knowledge is not known after the fact (*a posteriori*) but before, or without appeal to facts (*a priori*) (Martindale, 1960, p. 217).

Kant went on to illustrate how it would be possible to arrive at *a priori* synthetic knowledge and thus felt he had helped to save science and also broaden the realm of what is considered to be knowledge.

In summary, Kant believed it was necessary to fuse both phases of the subject-object experience. Self-experience, that knowledge of one's place and time in the world, had to be combined with the object experience of empiricism before a more complete understanding of the world could be developed. Thus, the relationship between the knowing self and the world of objects became a crucial part of the thought of the German Idealists. In contrast to the Empiricists, the Kantian conception of knowledge assigned a creative and dynamic function to the mind: it actively shaped, organized, and processed the data of the senses into a particular conception of the phenomenon in question. In this fashion, he tried to free the mind from its dependence on solely external sources for knowledge. Similarly, he gave a renewed validity to truth derived from the intuitive and spiritual realms. If such concepts as causality and necessity were viewed as products of the creative mind, then why should scientific knowledge have greater validity than nonscientific knowledge? According to Kant, knowledge was present only when the experiential world was congruent with the categories of the mind. Kant's theory of knowledge, however, permitted the concerned intellectual to say virtually nothing about such things as justice, beauty, good, and evil, and, pushed further, the state of human affairs generally.

Georg Wilhelm Friedrich Hegel (1770-1831) attempted to synthesize the German Romantic-Idealist tradition and, in addition, added a definite historical dimension to it. He also confronted those issues Kant had ignored, justice, beauty, good, and evil; but this particular dimension is the most problematic aspect of his work. For present purposes, we will accentuate only his synthesis of the German Romantic-Idealist tradition and its historical and dialectical dimensions.

Accepting most of Kant's argument, Hegel, went even further in his philosophical synthesis. He felt reason was not only a faculty existing in the individual's mind, but that it reflected the process of historical development as well. Unlike those Enlightenment thinkers who viewed reason as a mere abstraction, Hegel saw it as an imminent force that would determine the structure and development of the world and its thought. In different places in his writings, Hegel referred to this transformed body of reason as though it were some worldly cosmic force, calling it by such terms as the Idea, the Spirit, or the Absolute. As such, he saw it as an impersonal, logical, and cosmic process that would eventually unite both the social and natural realms into one dynamic and organic whole.

For Hegel the process of history therefore represented the progressive unraveling of reason in the world. The overriding, ultimate cosmic reason of things and events became apparent only as the internal contradictions of society, its institutions, and their knowledge of the universe worked themselves out historically. Hegel referred to this as the dialectical process. By this he meant that any idea or thought system (thesis) necessarily calls out its opposite (antithesis). The function of reason is to reconcile this conflict (synthesis). Every state of reality thus passes into its own negation or antithesis. The negation brings a new synthesis into being, the same process occurs again, and the negation itself is even negated. In this ongoing process, thought is constantly being brought to a higher unity. Hence, the dialectical process represents both the self-development of existence and our knowledge of it. Every phenomenon directs us beyond it to the greater whole. Thus, it is possible to have not only knowledge of the here and now, but knowledge of the unknown and the future too.

Coming from the basic ideas of Kant and Hegel, a number of other intellectual developments burgeoned in Germany. We will only mention them briefly in passing here. Karl Marx, Wilhelm Dilthey, Max Weber, Max Scheler, Ernst Grunwald, and Karl Mannheim all helped to develop, among other things, the area known as the sociology of knowledge. In this perspective, the major concern is with the relationship between knowledge and other existential factors in a society or culture. In its broadest sense, it deals with the history of ideas (with emphasis on their structural sources or points of origin); the constraining and facilitating roles that social structure and culture play on the production of ideas; and the political, ideological, and philosophical assumptions underlying thought systems. The notion of Verstehen sociology also developed among these thinkers, most notably in the works of Dilthey and Weber. It called for going beyond the positivistic, empirical knowledge of the social world by penetrating into the subjective meanings that actors attach to their own behavior and to the behavior of others. The task of the social sciences, according to the Verstehen position, was to achieve an interpretative understanding of social behavior that explained its causes, its development, and its ultimate effects. It is interesting to note that Wilhelm Wundt, a German whom Boring claims was the "first" psychologist, argues that ". . . psychology is not the science of 'inner experience' because the distinction between inner and outer experience is not valid" (Boring, 1950, p. 332). Finally, in Germany the whole phenomenological approach began in the works of Edmund Husserl (1859-1938).

Overall, the German influence was important to the development of the symbolic interaction perspective in a number of ways. First, the interrelatedness of the subject and object worlds was stressed. Second, the social world and our knowledge of it was viewed as a process that was always undergoing conflict, change, and redevelopment. Third, our knowledge and interpretation of both the social and physical realms was found to be influenced and biased by a variety of divergent sources. Fourth, the importance of interpretation and meaning, as well as all of its contextual variations, was defined as the very essence of the social sciences.

The American Context and the Formation
of the University of Chicago

As mentioned earlier, most historical accounts of the rise and subsequent development of symbolic interactionism have tended to stress the importance of American social thought and, in particular, the activities of those pivotal individuals who were brought together at the University of Chicago. Since there are already a number of historical, theoretical, and philosophical treatises on this topic (Coser, 1971; Faris, 1967; Kuhn, 1964; Manis and Meltzer, 1967; Martindale, 1960; Mead, 1934; Mullins, 1973; Reynolds and Meltzer, 1973; Strauss, 1964; Turner, 1974; and Vaughan and Reynolds, 1968), we will only sketch out the major points here. The interested reader can refer to the more detailed and wide-ranging accounts, which are readily accessible.

In addition to the European influences presented above, American social thought incorporated other theories, ideologies, and philosophies into its way of looking at the world. Those that have not yet been mentioned and seem to us to be important include the following: (a) protestantism; (b) Darwin's theory of biological evolutionism; (c) the philosophy of pragmatism; and (d) behaviorism. We will only say a few words about each of them here.

Although it is difficult to know the extent of its impact on the later adherents of the perspective, Coser (1971, p. 348) has suggested that Mead and most of the early American sociologists were influenced by the strict puritanical atmosphere in which they were raised. Many of the liberal arts colleges were (and still are) run by different Protestant sects and, consequently, it is quite likely that the Protestant ethic, which was so much a part of American culture found its way either directly or indirectly into the curriculum. This ethic eventually moved many thinkers from the realm of the sacred to the secular world by emphasizing human perfectability. It also stressed ethics and searched for a new humanitarian basis for universal understanding and cooperation among individuals. In other ways, it merged successfully with the spirit of the frontier by emphasizing human mastery and control over the environment.

Closely parelleling many of the ideas of Hegel and other German philosophers was the interpretation of Charles Darwin's biological evolutionism rendered by certain American intellectuals. Both Mead and Cooley, for example, felt that Darwin's *The Origin of the Species* (1859) provided the empirical support for the revolutionary but factually inadequate writings of the German Romantics and Idealists. Darwin's careful and systematic analysis of the evolutionary development of different species of plants and animals enabled the social scientist to challenge mechanical conceptions of human action and to restate the issues of freedom, autonomy, and innovation in empirical, evolutionary and social terms (Strauss, 1964, p. xviii). Thus, Darwin's work on evolution became an important rationale for moving away from the mechanistic and individualistic conceptions that dominated much of the social sciences during this time. It is possible that Mead also derived the concept of the gesture from Darwin's *The Expression of Emotion in Man and Animals*. However, Mead, in particular, recast many of Darwin's ideas. Following Kant again, the mind was portrayed as being engaged in the instrumental process of insuring the organism's survival. As such, it was engaged in a continuous struggle for control over the environment. Thinking was viewed as an activity that both grasped and shaped the world so that it would be more favorable to human conduct. Furthermore, the most appropriate test of intelligence, according to this perspective, was its ability to solve everyday problems. This, of course, has direct ties with the philosophy of pragmatism.

There are many extremely complicated lines of mutual influence among Mead, William James, James Mark Baldwin, Josiah Royce, Charles Peirce, C. H. Cooley, W. I. Thomas, and John Dewey that simply cannot be traced in any detail here. Only a very detailed and specialized inquiry into the history of ideas could trace these lines precisely. Many of these individuals, however, were influenced by the philosophy of pragmatism, which was evolving during their lifetime, and some comments on this perspective seem in order.

In America, the chief spokesmen for pragmatism were William James (1842-1910) and John Dewey (1859-1952). Not surprisingly, Mead studied as a graduate student with James at Harvard from 1887 to 1888 and got to know him quite well by tutoring his children. Then, having returned from advanced studies in philosophy in Germany with Wilhelm Wundt and G. Stanley Hall, Mead accepted a job as instructor in the Department of Philosophy and Psychology at the University of Michigan in 1891. There he encountered both Charles H. Cooley and John Dewey, and all of them became well-acquainted with each others' ideas and work. In 1894, Mead joined Dewey at the University of Chicago in the Department of Philosophy. He remained there until his death in 1931.

Many writers have suggested that the philosophy of pragmatism was a distinct and uniquely American intellectual product. Ruggiero, for example, has stated that "pragmatism was born in America, the country of 'business,' and is, par excellence, the philosophy of the business man" (quoted in Martindale, 1960, p. 297). While it is true that pragmatism achieved much of its popularity during the era of the robber barons and the rise of monopoly capitalism in the United States, this seems to be an unfair and historically naive assessment of pragmatism. For pragmatism didn't really represent a single unified body of philosophical ideas; instead, it borrowed from any number of diverse sources, most of which were European in origin.

The work of James, Dewey, and Mead represents a continuation of Kant's efforts to bridge the gap between rationalism and empiricism or, as they were later called, idealism and scientism. All were engaged in efforts to resolve the issue of the subject (knower)-object (known) dichotomy. James became interested in pragmatism by way of his negative reaction toward the implications of mechanistic thought in science. Dewey, on the other hand, became interested in it by converting neo-Hegelianism into a more practical program.

James denied that the subject-object relationship was fundamental to our understanding of the world, by arguing that there was no such entity as consciousness. Moreover, sounding very much like today's existentialists and phenomenologists, he felt there was no original mind that preceded and could be differentiated from the objective, material world. This, however, did not mean that the mind did not perform a definite function. It did. Its function, which was originally spelled out in the *Principles of Psychology* (1890), became a part of what James later called the pure experience. The pure experience was simply the merging of this subject-object relationship into the immediate flux of life. Thus, subject and object were mere differentiations that could change places with one another if given different circumstances. Taken to its logical conclusion, James' pragmatism allowed him to view as truth anything that gave him pleasure.

Dewey's starting point was found in Hegel's philosophy, but much like Marx, he wanted to apply it to real material conditions. Over and over again, he emphasized the central value of intelligence and the concept of mental activity as a social process. But in contrast to James, the test of whether something was true or not had to take into consideration the more general material and shared world of others as well. Thus, Dewey stressed the importance of science, logic, adaptation, and a certain amount of instrumentalism in his brand of pragmatism. In one of his more well-known quotes from *Logic: The Theory of Inquiry* (1938), Dewey concluded: "Inquiry is the controlled or directed transformation of an indeterminate situation into one that is so determinate in its constituent distinctions and relations as to convert the elements of the original situation into a unified whole" (cited in Martindale, 1960, p. 302). In contrast to James, who stressed morals and religion, Dewey viewed science as being essential to the philosophy of pragmatism, because it seemed to him to be the most efficient of all instruments.

Mead did not try to resolve the different emphases of James's and Dewey's pragmatism. Instead, he borrowed from both and therefore provided an excellent overview of this philosophy. According to Mead, thinking and reflection were instrumental problem-solving activities, which served to facilitate and guide action. Thought and action were both parts of a broader dialectical process. When action was thwarted, thinking and reflection arose to test the alternative ways of resuming the action. From the point of view of Mead's pragmatic philosophy, knowledge thus was an active process of discovery that helped solve concrete problems and overcome those obstacles that blocked them. When it was possible to resume a course of action that helped to achieve a purpose, knowledge had proved itself adequate.[3]

Finally, the school of behaviorism, which developed mainly in the field of psychology during the 1920s, is mentioned here, not because of its positive contribution to symbolic interactionism but because it was almost universally and unequivocally criticized by the early symbolic interactionists. As such, it represented something of a competing and, perhaps for a time, a more widely accepted paradigm, which was directed against the work of such scholars as Wundt, James, Dewey, Mead, and Cooley. In terms of its philosophical and theoretical origins it was not a revolutionary or even a new paradigm. Instead, it represented a throwback or return to the Social Contract theorists, the Empiricists, and to Newton's mechanistic model. Some of the better known behaviorists of this period included Ivan Pavlov and John B. Watson, both of whom were trained in animal physiology and psychology.

Watson probably more than anyone else was representative of the early behaviorist tradition. For him, behaviorism was simply the study of the experience of the individual from the point of view of objective, observable conduct.

---

[3]Pragmatism, as conceived here, overlooks one crucial aspect of social life — the power element. Those who exercise complete and total power and control over others are more likely to resume their purposive action unhindered by the opposition. History is replete with such examples. This, of course, raises the question of whether we are really talking about knowledge per se. It also raises another question. Is knowledge nothing more than power?

Introspection, perception, desire, purpose, emotions, and even thinking were re-nounced as concepts of "the old psychology" that were untestable and unobservable. Historically, behaviorism was very strongly influenced by instinct theory and animal psychology. In animal psychology, the concept of introspec-tion obviously was inappropriate. The experimenter could not appeal to the animal's introspection, but instead had to study the animal in terms of its ex-ternal conduct. Once this behavioristic standpoint was taken for the lower ani-mals, it was then also carried over to human beings. The meaning of any human action therefore became what the observing scientist said it was and nothing else. Meaning and intention were discarded. As Mead (1934) stated so well, "John B. Watson's attitude was that of the Queen in *Alice in Wonderland* – 'off with their heads!' – there were no such things. There was no imagery, and no conscious-ness" (p. 2-3). Strongly embracing the tradition of the natural and physical sciences, Watson's overall approach was delineated in his perennial question of whether or not human behavior could be explained in terms of stimulus and response. His answer was in the affirmative. Hence, the conditioned reflex furnished the behaviorists with a disarmingly simple framework for explaining all cognitive activity and gave promise of controlling, manipulating, and ultimately transforming human life. Mead, James, Cooley, and Dewey all attacked this posi-tion in a series of different articles and lectures both prior to and during this period.

All of the diverse traditions, schools, ideas, and even several of the key in-dividuals mentioned above found their way to the new University of Chicago (Faris, 1967). Endowed by John D. Rockefeller and his Standard Oil fortune, the new university opened in 1892 under the leadership of William Harper Rainey, its president, who was formerly a Yale professor of Greek and Hebrew. From the beginning, it was meant to be a spectacular success, and it was. Harper proceeded with vigorous leadership, inventiveness, and boldness. In many ways, he challenged traditional academia: recruiting distinguished professors from other universities at about twice their former salaries; hiring women in the facul-ty at equal rank and salary; starting the quarter system and the full summer session; instituting university extension services; and getting faculty and students involved in the affairs of the rapidly growing new city.

Harper's efforts were a smashing success. The faculty he originally recruited was universally recognized as being outstanding, including among its membership eight professors who had been former college presidents themselves. In what was then a combined department of philosophy and psychology, John Dewey be-came chairman. G. H. Mead and James Tufts were both immediately recruited, thus creating a department in which the new pragmatic philosophy flourished. In sociology, Albion Small, who had studied in Berlin and Leipzig and received his doctorate in history from Johns Hopkins, became chairman. He recruited George E. Vincent, Charles Henderson, and W. I. Thomas as his original colleagues in the department. All of the members had studied the classics, several of them going to Europe, as was fashionable then, and they hoped to combine their book learning with empirical studies in the vast urban laboratory of Chicago. Enthusiasm ran extremely high. During this early period and especially later in the period from 1920 to 1932, the sociology department was the best one in the country and perhaps even the world. Robert E. Park, Ernest W. Burgess, Ellsworth Faris, William F. Ogburn, Louis Wirth and others joined the faculty during this time. Students in the department included such well-known figures as Walter Reckless, Ruth Shonle Cavan, Herbert Blumer, Everett Hughes, Robert Redfield, Howard P. Becker, Samuel Stouffer, John Dollard, Robert E. L. Faris, and E. Franklin Frazier.

Throughout this period, the Chicago sociologists, philosophers, and, to a lesser extent, psychologists were forging what they thought was a much firmer view of reality in their social psychology. Dewey was a prolific writer, but Mead had not published a single book by the time he died. Indeed, his work became nationally known only when it was published posthumously by his students. Therefore, much of the early symbolic interactionist perspective was articulated only in Mead's lectures and informally among the graduate students in sociology, philosophy, and psychology at Chicago. Two other sociologists, however, often are associated with those who helped to develop the perspective and make it better known. The first of these was the sociologist Charles H. Cooley of the University of Michigan, the former colleague and close intellectual companion of Mead, Dewey, and Tufts. The second was W. I. Thomas, who was also at Chicago.

Cooley (1864-1929), much like Mead, was heavily influenced by the work of Kant, William James, and James Mark Baldwin. He was also very deeply impressed by the writings of historians and literary men. At heart he was very much an idealist and an "armchair sociologist." Still, Cooley's writings on the social and reflective nature of the self have found their way directly or indirectly into most texts in sociology and social psychology, as have the many concepts he coined or made popular, for example, the looking-glass self, the primary group, and social process.

Throughout his two major works, *Human Nature and the Social Order* (1902) and *Social Organization* (1909), one can clearly see the emphasis on the mental as society's essence. In these works and others, Cooley suggested that social organization was nothing more than a great web of communication and interaction that included all human beings. Society was located in the mind; each person had a different society composed of its own people, events, places and images. In the words of Angell (1968):

> Cooley was mainly trying to emphasize what is now called the phenomenological position: that it is not what people are but what we think they are that determines our reaction to them. In large part interactions take place according to the interpretations that the parties have of each other, and these interpretations are mental facts. One of his favorite statements was that sociologists have to "imagine imaginations." By this

he meant that they were not qualified to study the social world unless they could project themselves into people's minds and interpret the world as those people did (p. 5).

William Isaac Thomas (1863-1947), one of the original members of the sociology department at Chicago, viewed social psychology primarily as the study of individual mental processes for most of his career. His theoretical approach was in this sense much closer to the work of Floyd Allport than it was to that of Dewey, Mead, and Cooley. Thomas never completely abandoned his emphasis on biological instincts and individualism, but later in his career he seemed to be moving more toward the perspective advocated by Dewey, Mead, and Cooley. They laid the groundwork for his well-known concept of "the definition of the situation." Here Thomas meant that if a person defined a situation as real, it was real in its consequences. Thus, the individual's interpretation of an event or object was more important than its physical and objective properties. Finally, Thomas and Znaniecki's classic, *The Polish Peasant in Europe and America* (1918), became a model for those students and colleagues at Chicago and elsewhere who wanted to engage in concrete, large-scale studies of the subjective aspects of human life. As such, Thomas and Znaniecki's work was instrumental in providing an alternative style of social research to that of the behaviorists in psychology. A whole series of grounded studies of this type came out of the University of Chicago in the years that followed.

All of those individuals mentioned so far have thus figured prominently in the development of the symbolic interaction perspective. Nevertheless, as important as all of these contributions were, it was still left to George H. Mead to bring the various related concepts and perspectives together. He did this by developing a coherent theoretical perspective that linked the emergence of the human mind, the social self, and the organization of society to the basic process of social interaction.

Mead's Synthesis: Mind, Self, and Society

Although Mead expressed himself best in lectures and in conversation, he also did manage to publish many papers in the field of social psychology. As previously mentioned, at the time of his death in 1931, however, he had not published a single book. In the words of Charles W. Morris, a philosophy student of Mead's: "That he was not the writer of a system is due to the fact that he was always engaged in building one. His thought was too rich in internal development to allow him to set down his ideas in ordered array" (quoted in Mead, 1934, p. vii). In light of the current age of "academic credentials," there is another little known (or expected) fact about Mead's career: he never received a doctoral degree.

Following his death, many of the students who had been so impressed with the quality of his work were successful in publishing four posthumous volumes based upon his lectures, class notes, and writings. These included the following:

The Philosophy of the Present (1932), *Mind, Self, and Society* (1934), *Movements of Thought in the Nineteenth Century* (1936), and *The Philosophy of the Act* (1938). Since our major concern here is Mead's contribution to social psychology, we will concentrate exclusively upon the book that most fully spells out this position, *Mind, Self, and Society*. In the other material we have covered thus far in this section, we hope to have pointed out the breadth and scope of Mead's thought, the major influences upon him, and his underlying assumptions about the social world. These wider philosophical concerns are spelled out in more detail in the other three books. For example, Mead's conceptions of the nature of time and history are elaborated upon in *The Philosophy of the Present*. His exposition on pragmatism can be found in *The Philosophy of the Act*. Finally, his account of the major nineteenth century schools of thought is presented in *Movements of Thought in the Nineteenth Century*.

We have already discussed the traditional bifurcation of nature in philosophy prior to Kant, into mind on the one hand and the objective, physical world on the other. Mead continued in the tradition of Kant, by insisting that these views were extreme and defective and could not be applied successfully to the study of human affairs. Thus, his life's work can be viewed as an effort to overcome this dichotomy. We would concur with Zeitlin (1973), who states, "In Mead's view, the individual as a sensitive, active, social being contributes to the constitution of his effective environment as truly as the environment (natural and social) conditions his sensitivity and action" (p. 220). Following logically from this, Mead argued that there could be no self, no consciousness of self, and no communication apart from society. Society, in its turn, had to be understood as a structure that emerged in an ongoing process of communicative social interactions among individuals who were mutually oriented toward one another. We will begin our analysis, as did Mead, with the mind.

To begin, Mead (1934) believed that there were unique features of the human mind that distinguished it from the minds of animals. These consisted of its capacity to: (a) use symbols to designate objects in the environment; (b) mentally rehearse alternative forms of action toward these objects; and (c) consciously turn off inappropriate lines of action and select the proper or "expected" course of action. Mead used the illustration of two dogs fighting to make this point. Each dog's gesture served as a stimulus for the other's response, which in turn became another new stimulus. Mead referred to this as a "conversation of gestures" and suggested that gestures of this type were not very significant, since they carried no meaning. Although it was possible for men to engage in the same kinds of gestures (for example, when boxing or fencing), Mead felt that this type of action constituted a relatively small proportion of their overall interactions. Man could engage in this kind of activity but he could also shake his fist in anger, thus displaying his hostile attitude to the other. In this case, however, there was an *idea* behind the gesture. Therefore, when a gesture carried a specific meaning that aroused the same meaning in the other individual, Mead said we then had a "significant symbol" (p. 45). Human language and communication is conducted by means of these symbols.

A substantial proportion of Mead's analysis focused not on how the mature mind functioned, but on how this capacity first evolved in humans, since, according to his perspective, if infants didn't develop minds it would be impossible for either the self or society to exist. For Mead, the infant's mind developed in a selective process of give-and-take between the infant and those upon whom he depended for his survival. In this process, the initially wide repertoire of random gestures put forth by the infant were narrowed down as some of them brought more favorable reactions from the parents or guardians. This selection of gestures could occur either as a result of conscious coaching by the parents, or by trial and error. Eventually, however, certain gestures would come to have common meanings for the infant and parents alike. When this had occurred, the gestures came to denote the same objects and carried similar dispositions for the interacting parties involved. These common meanings increased the efficiency of interaction among the individuals, since they allowed for more precise communication of desires and wants as well as intended courses of action. In this same way, common meanings increased the capacity of individuals to adjust and adapt to one another. This ability to interpret and act upon conventional gestures with common meanings represented a very significant step in the development of mind, self, and society. By virtue of being capable of perceiving and interpreting gestures, humans also developed the ability to "take the role of the other." Thus, they could assume the perspective of those with whom they must cooperate for survival. By being able to put oneself in another person's place or to "take the role of the other," the covert rehearsal of future courses of action also increased efficiency, and the probability of cooperative interaction was enhanced.

Mead's account of the genesis of consciousness and the self through the gradually developing ability in childhood to take on the role of others and to visualize performance from the viewpoint of others was certainly one of his greatest achievements. Just as individuals could symbolically designate other actors in the environment, so too could they symbolically represent themselves as objects. The interpretation of gestures thus not only helped to facilitate human interaction and cooperation, but also served as the basis for self-assessment and evaluation. This capacity of the individual to view himself or herself as the object of evaluation in interaction was dependent upon the processes of the mind. According to Mead, what was significant about this process was that, as individuals matured, all of the transitory self-images derived from specific others eventually became crystallized into a more or less stabilized self-conception of oneself. When these self-conceptions had developed, then the actions of individuals could be seen as taking on consistency and form in fairly coherent patterns.

Three stages in the development of the self were accentuated. Each of the stages represented not only a change in the kinds of transitory self-images the individual could receive from role-taking but also an increased tendency on the part of the individual to develop a more stabilized self-conception. Mead termed the initial stage of role-taking play. In play, infants are capable of assuming the perspective of only a very limited number of players, usually only one or two others. For example, a child will run away when chased. Although the child has learned through imagination to put himself or herself in the position of the other, the child is still at this point incapable of relating in his mind the various roles others play with one another outside of this particular sphere of activity. Hence, the child can understand the relationship of mother or father with himself or herself, but cannot understand that the mother is not the father's mother also.

Later, due to biological maturation and increased practice at role-taking, the more mature child becomes capable of taking the role of several others engaged in organized activities. Mead called this second stage the game. This stage designated the capacity of individuals to keep in mind all of the roles of the other players and make assessments about their potential responses to one another. Moreover, such games had to be distinguished from more simple games like Jacks or Hide-and-seek. In these simple games, only two types of role partners are involved; the actors do not modify each other's play; hence, they do not have to anticipate the other partner's response. Mead frequently illustrated the game stage by giving the example of baseball, in which all the players must be able to symbolically assume the role of all others on the team in order to effectively participate.

The final stage in the development of the self occurs when the individual can take the role of the generalized other, the attitude of the whole community or even society in general. At this stage, Mead felt individuals were capable of assuming the overall perspective of a community or the general beliefs, values, and norms of their various spheres of interaction. The mature self therefore develops when the "generalized other" has become internalized to the extent that both the community and the broader society exercise social control over individual members.

Zeitlin (1973) summarizes the overall significance of the self well:

> The self is both subject and object; it is an object to itself. This is what fundamentally differentiates man from other animals; for the ability to become an object to oneself means that one can achieve *self*-consciousness, not just consciousness. And self-consciousness means that one can adopt an objective and impersonal attitude toward oneself and the situation in which one acts. Man's capacity for intelligent and rational action rests squarely on this uniquely human ability to look upon oneself *objectively* (p. 225).

There is, however, one other complex part of Mead's theory of the self that needs some amplification. Mead attempted to clarify his views regarding the social foundation of the self and that particular part of his theory that implied the individual's self eventually became little more than a reflection of the broader organized network of social norms, values, and attitudes. He did this by introducing a distinction between the "I" and the "me" (pp. 173-222). Both terms related to social experience. But the "I" represented the response of the individual to the attitude of the others; the "me" was the organized set of attitudes of others that the individual assumed. In Mead's words, "The attitudes of the others constitute the organized 'me,' and then one reacts toward that as an 'I'" (p. 175). As a "me," the individual views himself or herself as an object. The individual reacts or responds toward the self in terms of the attitudes others have toward that self. Self-appraisal is the result of what the individual assumes to be the appraisal by others. Hence, the "me" reflects the laws and mores of the broader community. The "I," however, represented "the answer which the individual makes to the attitude which others take toward him when he assumes an attitude toward them . . . it gives the sense of freedom, of initiative" (p. 177). The "I" and the "me" are thus different. Again, quoting Mead, "the "I" is something that is never calculable . . . it is always something different from what the situation itself calls for" (p. 178). The self as a whole thus is a compound of both the stabilized reflections of the generalized other found in the "me" and the incalculable, spontaneous activities of the "I." As such, it is always an open self.

Finally, society (or institutions, as Mead often phrased it) represented the constructed patterns of coordinated activity that were maintained by and changed through symbolic interaction among and within actors. Organized and patterned interaction among diverse individuals was dependent upon the mind because, without the capacities of mind to take on roles and rehearse alternative lines of activity, individuals could not coordinate their activities. The ability of the individual to evaluate himself or herself from the perspective of the generalized other was crucial here. Nevertheless, while Mead's theory was virtually concerned with how society and its institutions were maintained and perpetuated by the mind and the self, these same concepts also allowed him to view society as constantly being in flux and rife with potential change. Role taking and imaginative rehearsal therefore represented the ongoing social processes of the mind, which always had the potential to create change. The "I," in particular, represented this possibility for spontaneous and unpredictable actions that could alter existing patterns of interaction and, accordingly, the basic organization of society itself. Thus, Mead rejects any reification of society, and the individual, interacting in conjunction with others, ultimately plays the dominant role in shaping the future.

Efforts by Blumer and Others to Popularize and Further Develop the Perspective

Since Mead's death, numerous scholars have adopted the perspective of symbolic interactionism and attempted with varying degrees of success to pass it on to their students and colleagues alike. Among the more prominent symbolic interactionists today are Anselm L. Strauss, Fred Davis, Erving Goffman, Howard S. Becker, Gregory Stone, Harvey Farberman, Norman Denzin, Alfred Lindesmith, and Sheldon Stryker, all of whom are sociologists. In terms of specific schools, Chicago, Minnesota, Iowa, and Berkeley have all had fairly active groups of symbolic interactionists. However, one figure, Herbert Blumer, has unquestionably been the foremost living disciple and interpreter of Mead's work.

In the years following Mead's death, both Ellsworth Faris and Herbert Blumer helped to transmit his ideas to many hundreds of students at the University of Chicago through their annual lectures. Faris, however, retired from the University of Chicago in 1939 and, for a time at least, Blumer took on this task almost singlehandedly. A member of the sociology department from 1927 to 1952, Blumer left a strong impact on many of his students. More importantly, he succeeded Mead as intellectual leader of the symbolic interaction perspective, coining the term itself only in 1937, and became increasingly involved in organizational activities, which gave him more leverage to disseminate the perspective to a wider audience (Mullins, 1973, p. 80). Following World War II, a number of graduate students conducted and completed research for dissertations in sociology at Chicago utilizing this perspective and, upon graduation, assumed positions at other universities. Thus, a wider network developed and spread. In 1952, Blumer himself accepted a position in the sociology department of the University of California at Berkeley. He continues to teach there today. Shortly thereafter, Erving Goffman also accepted a position there. Soon a number of symbolic interactionists began to graduate from Berkeley.

Blumer has been very important to the development of symbolic interactionism for a number of reasons.[4] First, he was the first person, following Mead, to provide a systematic and programatic statement on symbolic interactionism (1937). Second, he made Mead's work much more well known and tried to make explicit parts of the perspective, which had earlier only been implied either in Mead's writings or lectures. Finally, Blumer was an important figure in conveying a particular methodological stance for the social scientist, a stance which was, and continues to be, quite critical of the highly positivistic methods that subsequently seem to have taken over the predominant position in social research. More important than the methodological stance, however, was the particular conception of social psychological theory that Mead, Blumer, and others have presented to us. In the section that follows, we will attempt to comparatively examine this aspect, albeit quite briefly.

Variations of the Perspective

During the last 25 years or so, symbolic interactionism has branched out into at least two different perspectives (Kuhn, 1964; Meltzer and Petras, 1970; Mullins, 1973; Reynolds and Meltzer, 1973; Vaughan and Reynolds, 1968). Although

[4]There are varying opinions of Blumer's contributions to the overall perspective. In *The Structure of Sociological Theory* (1974), Jonathan H. Turner suggests that Blumer's methodological stance has actually hindered the development of the perspective. Zeitlin, in *Rethinking Sociology* (1973), takes Blumer to task for diverting, and defusing the original dialectical, historical, and structural emphases in Mead's work. There are a variety of other critical comments, but these seem to be the most common type.

most writers have tended to emphasize the differences in methodological approaches between the two, there are also different epistemological assumptions involved here.[5] The two major spokesmen of these perspectives have been Herbert G. Blumer and the late Manford H. Kuhn. Blumer, who has been discussed earlier, developed the most well-known variety of the perspective at Chicago and the University of California at Berkeley. It is known simply as the Chicago School. The other perspective, the Iowa School, developed somewhat later in the works of Kuhn and his students at the University of Iowa. Only the major differences between the two perspectives will be noted here.[6]

In many ways, the Chicago and Iowa schools reflect fundamental differences of opinion as to the very nature and scope of the social sciences. Those from the Chicago School emphasize the need for a special methodology for the study of human behavior, given the distinctively different character of the social and physical worlds. Hence, the importance of grounded, participant observation methods, natural case studies, historical research, and the use of sensitizing concepts, which will hopefully help to make systems of shared meanings more understandable. Furthermore, from this perspective the researcher becomes an integral part of the research process and plays an active role in discovering the meaning of reality, in all of its contextual variations. For this reason, many symbolic interactionists have recently become increasingly interested in the study of phenomenology and ethnomethodology. The major reason for utilizing the above methodological techniques is, to be certain, related to the particular epistemological stance taken by most of the Chicagoans. For them, the nature and form of social life is always going through a process of change. The individual is given more freedom to act and/or react and, correspondingly, some leeway is given to the unpredictable or indeterminate dimensions of human behavior. Therefore, the performance of social roles is viewed as a dynamic and creative process. Roles are tentative social constructions of particular slices of reality. This emphasis also leads the Chicago School to consider the nonsymbolic conversational gestures in human conduct as well, for example, the whole burgeoning area of body language and nonverbal communication.

The Iowa School, on the other hand, is much more tough-minded and positivistic in its stance. For most of the Iowans, there is little need for different methodological strategies and techniques in the social sciences. Perhaps responding to the criticisms regarding looseness and vagueness wagered against the

---

[5]The term epistemology refers to the study or theory of the origin, nature, methods, and limits of knowledge.

[6]These two schools are, of course, ideal types. Reynolds and Meltzer have recently suggested that "the majority of present-day interactionists are, methodologically speaking, 'middle-of-the-roaders.'" By this, they simply mean that most researchers combine both of these techniques in their work. See Larry T. Reynolds and Bernard.N. Meltzer, "The Origins of Divergent Methodological Stances in Symbolic Interactionism," *The Sociological Quarterly, 14,* 2, (Spring, 1973), p. 199.

Chicagoans by the positivists, the Iowa School has been largely preoccupied with the operationalization of key terms used by symbolic interactionists. The Twenty Statements Test (Kuhn and McPartland, 1954) is an example of one paper-and-pencil measuring instrument used by the group to empirically investigate self-attitudes. In contrast to the sensitizing concepts of the Chicagoans, the Iowans prefer definitive concepts and follow the logic of scientific verification. The Iowa approach assigns to the researcher a detached, objective, passive role in the collection of data. And, in terms of their epistemological position, the Iowans downplay the indeterminate or unpredictable aspects of human behavior and stress the determinacy of individual behavior. Finally, in contrast to the dynamic, creative, and tentative nature of the process of role performances portrayed in the Chicago School, the Iowa School views role performances more as a set of internalized self-attitudes, which provide fairly well-determined patterns of role-playing for the individual. Implicit in this epistemological stance is a tendency to view society itself in more static terms, or, as some critics have pointed out, to simply ignore society and those events occurring at a macrolevel.

In the examples that follow, there are works representing the diversity one encounters in the symbolic interaction perspective. The section on participant observation and the labeling perspective illustrates the general approach taken by the Chicagoans. The sections on grid analysis and multidimensional scaling come closer to the Iowa School. Midway between the two are the sections on content analysis and personal structure analysis.

A NOTE ON METHODS

Before presenting some of the research and theory stemming from the symbolic interaction perspective, there are a couple of preliminary points we need to make. First, in any field of science, theory is to a large extent bound by available methods. Questions can be asked, but they often cannot be pursued, elaborated upon, and refined because techniques or methods have not been developed that would allow one to investigate these questions. Galileo's discovery of four of the moons of Jupiter, for example, had to await the invention of the telescope. The implications of the moons being there could not be pursued until their presence was established. Similarly, the early symbolic interactionists raised questions and issues for which there were only limited methodological resources available. Hence, it was a long time before people began to sharpen and focus the questions, before empirical evidence that spoke to the questions began to accumulate. As we shall see below, there are questions implied by the symbolic interaction perspective that are still extremely difficult to investigate, questions for which currently available research methods are only minimally adequate. Hopefully, it will also become clear that progress is being made. Questions that could not be investigated 50 years ago are being pursued vigorously, partly because new research methods have been developed and made available.

A second preliminary point concerns the common theme tying together the various theoretical and methodological issues presented below. That theme is a concern for understanding the constructions or interpretations that individuals place on their own experience. This is a deceptively simple statement. Hidden away are the implications that:

1. "Reality" is susceptible to different interpretations.
2. "Reality" is less important to the individual than is his or her interpretation of reality.
3. In order to understand the perceptions of another we cannot rely entirely on an analysis of the external stimulus situation.

As Kelly (1963) puts it:

> The universe is real; it is happening all the time; it is integral; and it is open to piecemeal interpretation. Different men construe it in different ways. Since it owes no prior allegiance to any one man's construction system, it is always open to reconstruction. . . . Since man is always faced with constructive alternatives, which he may explore if he wishes, he need not continue indefinitely to be the absolute victim either of his past history or of his present circumstances. . . . The construction systems are also real, though they may be biased in their representation (p. 43).

More than beauty resides in the eye of the beholder.

There are several research techniques available that can help us get a picture of what reality looks like to someone else. The particular technique that we choose will, in part, determine how we interpret the reality of the other. Even so, we should never lose sight of the fact, noted almost half a century ago by Thomas and Thomas (1928), that the most important element in any situation is how the subject views the situation. The early symbolic interactionists placed considerable emphasis upon this idea, and it follows that for many years the favored methodology of symbolic interactionists has been a method calling for total immersion in situations. It was, and is, believed by many that only through such immersion can one hope to understand the complexities and ambiguities of the situational definitions imposed and manipulated by individuals.

PARTICIPANT OBSERVATION AND LABELING

The generic name for this particular methodological approach, an approach calling for total immersion in the ongoing events and situations surrounding people, is participant observation. After defining and describing participant observation, we shall make our description more concrete with illustrations from the labeling approach to deviance, one of the most important substantive areas within the symbolic interaction perspective and an area that has been to a large extent dependent upon participant observation as a source of data.

Participant Observation

Like most things, there is a little more to participant observation than the name implies. Participation in and observation of an event are not sufficient. As Pearsall (1970) has pointed out, this method means different things to different people.

> At one extreme, the term "participant observer" refers to a master role assumed for purposes of getting data from live subjects by whatever methods and techniques appropriate to a particular research design. . . . At the other extreme, the term is limited to informally conducted but systematically recorded observations. . . . Between the extremes . . . participant observation perhaps most commonly refers to research aimed at maximal knowledge of the beliefs and behavior of human beings in their natural settings interpreted in terms of some general theory or combination of theories (p. 341)

There are several aspects to the method, then, which are not contained in the name. A particularly important one is the systematic recording of observations. Another aspect, not usually thought of, is referred to in the phrase "aimed at maximal knowledge." Thus the participant observer cannot be satisfied with simply observing. Rather, it is incumbent upon the participant observer to seek all knowledge relevant to his or her particular purpose.

As an example, suppose one were interested in doomsday cults, cults that predict the world will end on a certain day. To study such groups by participant observation, it would not be sufficient simply to attend group meetings and record what occurred. Rather, one would have to gather all the information available: biographical information about each of the group members; historical accounts of the group's activities; information about group members who had drifted away and why they left. Such data can be obtained in various ways, by informal interviews, by use of informants, by going through old newspapers and other archives. The gathering of all pertinent information through such diverse techniques helps the participant observer guard against bias, against seeing only what is expected, and it is a form of triangulation of measurement.

Definition

Given these various aspects of participant observation, let us commit ourselves to a definition. *Participant observation* is that method in which the researcher enters into the routine of the people or situation under study for some length of time, observing and systematically recording things that happen, informally or formally interviewing all who might have information pertinent to the events under study, and gathering auxiliary information relevant to his or her purpose. The researcher may assume any of a number of roles, varying from complete openness about why he or she is there to complete secrecy and assumption of a disguise.

The advantages of participant observation over other research methods all re-volve around the completeness or range of information gathered. Becker and Geer (1970) even go so far as to state that "participant observation can thus pro-vide us with a yardstick against which to measure the completeness of data gathered in other ways" (p. 133). That is a slight overstatement and, as Trow (1970) points out, it assumes that all "events" could be studied by participant observation, which is just not so. For appropriately selected problems, however, participant observation can be beneficial in at least the following ways.

First, there are many things that people are unwilling or unable to discuss with others. Participant observation provides a way of obtaining information about some of these topics. Becker (1963), himself a jazz musician, was able to learn about the values, habits, and prestige hierarchies among dance musicians by intimately participating in that particular subculture. Much of the information obtained by Becker could never have been obtained by or revealed to oustiders, or "squares." A second advantage of participant observation has to do with language. Many groups develop certain idiosyncratic terms and phrases to refer to aspects of their environment. The participant observer, as Becker and Geer (1970) note, can learn the meanings of such words and phrases ("crock," "taking care of business," "looking for Mr. G.") with great precision. A third advantage of participant observation is that it enhances awareness of the existence of vary-ing perspectives within the group or situation under study. From the symbolic interaction perspective, this is of the utmost importance.

There are many examples of participant observation that could be used to il-lustrate our definition. We shall begin by briefly describing a recent study that has received a great deal of notoriety and publicity. This particular study also addresses one of the central substantive issues within the symbolic interaction approach.

Participant Observation in Psychiatric Wards

In the past few years, a great deal of controversy has arisen over the question of whether or not "mental illness" really exists. Thomas Szasz, one of the most outspoken critics of the concept, points out that "Psychiatrists have traditional-ly regarded mental illness as a problem apart from and independent of the social context in which it occurred" (1961, p. 52). This, of course, is totally inimical to the symbolic interaction perspective, in which social and mental events can-not be considered separately from their context. The apparent reason for the neglect of the social context was that the concept of mental illness developed by analogy with physical or bodily illness, in which it usually seemed reasonable to treat diseases without regard to the social situation of the victim. Szasz argues that the result of this pseudomedical analogy has been to locate mental illness in the victim when, in fact, what we are usually talking about when we say that

someone is "mentally ill" is that the person in question has interpersonal problems, problems in his or her social relationships — problems, in short, in living.

Concurrent with the line of reasoning advanced by Szasz and others (cf.,
Scheff, 1966), there has developed a large and growing body of data questioning
the reliability and usefulness of psychiatric diagnosis (e.g., Chapman and Chapman, 1967). As if this were not enough to give one pause, anthropological field
reports have repeatedly made the point that behaviors defined as deviant or insane in one culture are frequently looked upon with equanimity in another.

Thus, as Rosenhan (1973) points out, "The view has grown that psychological categorization of mental illness is useless at best and downright harmful,
misleading, and pejorative at worst. Psychiatric diagnoses, in this view, are *in
the minds of the observers* and not valid summaries of characteristics displayed
by the observed" (p. 251, emphases added). If this is true, a consequence would
be that normal or sane people who take up residence in a psychiatric ward and
act "normally" would go undetected. On the other hand, "If the sanity of such
pseudo-patients were always detected, there would be prima facie evidence that
a sane individual can be distinguished from the insane context in which he is
found. Normality (and presumably abnormality) is distinct enough that it can be
recognized wherever it occurs, for it is carried within the person" (p. 251).

To check on which of these alternatives occurred, Rosenhan and seven coworkers became participant observers by gaining secret admission to the psychiatric wards of twelve different hospitals. Each pseudo-patient gained admission
by claiming to hear voices saying such things as "empty" and "hollow," a symp-
tom chosen because of its similarity to the self-questioning that occurs when
people wonder about the meaningfulness of their lives. The only other alteration
for the participant observers was that they employed pseudonyms and, in several
cases, gave false occupations to protect their true identity.

As soon as they had been admitted, all pseudo-patients began to behave
normally; they stopped simulating any symptoms. "That their behavior was in
no way disruptive is confirmed by nursing reports. . . . These reports uniformly
indicate that the patients were 'friendly,' 'cooperative,' and 'exhibited no abnormal indications'" (p. 252). Each pseudo-patient had been told upon entry
that he would be discharged when he convinced the staff that he was sane. They
stayed an average of 19 days — at least one stayed as long as 52 days — but not
one of the pseudo-patients was ever detected. Not one was ever deemed sane by
the staff.

During the course of their stays, the pseudo-patients took notes and systematically recorded what went on in the wards: the number and types of drugs
given (remember, these were people with *no* bodily or "mental" problems, but
they were administered over 2,000 pills!); the amount of time that staff spent on
the ward; the behaviors of their fellow patients. One of the things that became
clear from the notes is that:

Once a person is designated abnormal (most of the pseudo-patients were diagnosed as schizophrenic on entry), all of his other behaviors and characteristics are colored by that label. . . . One psychiatrist pointed to a group of patients who were sitting outside the cafeteria entrance half an hour before lunchtime. To a group of young residents, he indicated that such behavior was characteristic of the oral-acquisitive nature of the syndrome (p. 253).

It apparently never occured to the psychiatrist that life in a mental ward is incredibly dull and that there is not much to look forward to other than mealtime.

Aside from the reinterpretation of normal behaviors so that they would fit into what the staff "knew" about the pseudo-patients, the pseudo-patients quickly began to experience depersonalization. Several of the intake physical exams were given in semi-public rooms; staff would often discuss a patient within his hearing range; staff would avoid eye-contact with patients and fail to acknowledge their questions; morning attendants often woke patients with "Come on, you mother-fuckers, out of bed!" (p. 256). All of these behaviors by the staff have the effect of defining the situation in a particular way, a way which includes the pseudo-patients only as "mental cases" — not as persons. Had the pseudo-patients expressed their indignation at such treatment and demanded the normal respect due any other person, this in itself would be interpreted as further evidence of their "craziness." As Rosenhan notes, "The hospital itself imposes a special environment in which the meanings of behavior can be easily misunderstood" (p. 257).

We chose the Rosenhan study to illustrate participant observation for several reasons. It is, in itself, an important study bearing on the social definition of "mental illness" and — contrary to the typical participant observation study — has aroused a small storm of angry comments both pro and con.[7]

Another reason for selecting the Rosenhan example is that the study makes explicit one of the most severe obstacles to participant observation. That is, such studies typically require an enormous investment in time and effort for what some would argue is a rather meager yield. Consider what was involved in the Rosenhan study. For an average of 19 days, participant observers lived in 12 different hospitals. Assuming no overlap, that is slightly more than 7½ months of 24-hour-a-day, 7-day-a-week living in a psychiatric ward. Further, the majority of the participant observers in this study were professional people who had numerous obligations in addition to the study and whose time was money, both figuratively and literally. With such prodigious amounts of time, money, and effort needed, it should come as no surprise that "The most persistent difficulty in the scientific study of deviant behavior is a lack of solid data, a paucity of facts and information on which to base our theories. There are simply not

---

[7]Within days after the publication of Rosenhan's study, a local (Lexington, Ky.) psychiatrist had organized a symposium, to which our university community was invited, for purposes of publicly defending psychiatry and denouncing Rosenhan's methodology and conclusions.

enough studies that provide us with facts about the lives of deviants *as they live them*" (Becker, 1963, p. 165).

The problem is a real one, and it is likely to get worse as grant funds dwindle and pressure on young academicians to produce continues. Long-term participant observation of subcultures is a risky and difficult undertaking. As a partial solution to this problem, many researchers have placed reliance on what we referred to above as auxiliary information. That is, building on a somewhat limited core of active participant observation, a case is developed for the researcher's hypothesis or perspective by employing diverse bits and pieces of knowledge obtained from various and sundry sources. The prime example of someone who uses this approach is Erving Goffman.

Erving Goffman

Goffman appears to be one of the few social psychologists who is widely read and quoted both by sociologists and psychologists. Making excellent use of library materials, personal documents, metaphors, and an exuberant capacity to report his own experiences as a participant observer, Goffman presents a plethora of ideas. From his doctoral dissertation on communication among Shetland Islanders to his most recent work, subtitled *The Organization of Experience,* Goffman has been obsessed with the details, nuances, and subtleties of social intercourse and impression management (e.g., Goffman, 1959, 1961, 1963a, 1963b, 1967, 1969, 1971, 1974).

The metaphor with which Goffman is most closely identified is "All the world's a stage." Individuals and/or "teams" of individuals are conceived of as staging "performances," in virtually all of their day-to-day activities. These performances are geared to specific "audiences" and are intended to project particular definitions of both the situation and the performer's self. Each performer attempts to control or manage the available information about themselves and the situation to insure that the audience perceives the intended message. Goffman relentlessly pursues the dramaturgical metaphor in *The Presentation of Self in Everyday Life* and interprets much of our daily experience with theatrical concepts such as: settings, appearance, performances, front region, back region, communication out of character, and audience.

Much of the focus of Goffman's work can be summarized by understanding his distinction between an impression that one "gives" — the conscious attempts by the person to convey or project a particular body of information about oneself or the situation — and an impression that one "gives off" — the not-so-conscious cues and nuances that may destroy the definition of the situation that one wishes to maintain. For example, the projected definition of being dispassionate and objective and taking part in an intellectual discussion may fall apart when one's voice breaks or a particularly cutting remark escapes. The consequences of such inadvertently given-off impressions are severe. As Goffman (1959) puts it,

> Given the fact that the individual effectively projects a definition of the situation when he enters the presence of others, we can assume that events may occur within the interaction which contradict, discredit, or otherwise throw doubt upon this projection. When these disruptive events occur, the interaction itself may come to a confused and embarrassed halt. Some of the assumptions upon which the responses of the participants had been predicated become untenable, and the participants find themselves lodged in an interaction for which the situation has been wrongly defined and is now no longer defined. . . . Society is organized on the principle that any individual who possesses certain social characteristics has a moral right to expect that others will value and treat him in an appropriate way. Connected with this principle is a second, namely, that an individual who implicitly or explicitly signifies that he has certain social characteristics ought in fact to be what he claims he is (p. 12).

The most important thread running through Goffman's work, then, is the concept of "information management." The individual is seen as attempting to control the information about his or herself to which his audience has access.

Complications arise due to the fact that every performer plays multiple roles and cannot be onstage for a particular audience at all times. Goffman's distinction between "front" and "back" regions takes this into account. The front region is simply the place or setting in which a particular performance is given and the back region is a place, relative to a particular performance, where the situational or self definition fostered by the performance does not have to be maintained. Goffman (1959) illustrates the discrepancy between behavior in front and back regions with data from his study of the Shetland Islands as well as auxiliary information culled from various sources. In the dining room of the Shetland Hotel, British middle-class standards of decorum and cleanliness were maintained by the staff, whereas

> . . . in the scullery wing of the kitchen region, mold would sometimes form on soup yet to be used. Over the kitchen stove, wet socks would be dried on the steaming kettle. . . . Tea, when guests had asked for it newly infused, would be brewed in a pot encrusted at the bottom with tea leaves that were weeks old. . . . Another interesting example of backstage . . . is found in radio and television. Thus an announcer may hold the sponsor's product up at arm's length in front of the camera while he holds his nose with his other hand, his face being out of the picture (p. 117-119).

Such interspersing of his own observations with anecdotes and excerpts from literature, biographies, and other sources is characteristic of the way Goffman develops his points and supports the arguments for his perspective on reality. This approach is best exemplified in *Stigma* (1963a), an investigation into the techniques utilized by stigmatized individuals to structure their interpersonal relationships.

In *Stigma,* as in most of Goffman's work, the key question is the nature of the relationship between the individual and society. How does the individual maintain and project a particular identity in the face of the multiple roles that must be enacted and the varying expectations that others thrust upon him or her while he or she is enacting roles. If "all the world's a stage," is the self merely a sequence of different costumes behind which there is little or no substance? As Rosenberg (1975) has recently pointed out, Goffman is not nearly so cynical as this question and some of his critics imply.

> For Goffman . . . the term "self" does not refer to any actual being who resides either inside or outside our situations; it refers, rather, to a *sense* we have of ourselves as somehow continuing through all the roles we play. More specifically, it refers to the principle of continuity itself as we recognize it in the deeds we have done and program it into our future actions. What we are capable of doing tells us who we are, and, conversely, we use our sense of who we are to determine what we will be capable of doing. . . . Fourteen years ago Goffman expressed this relationship perfectly in *Asylums:* "An important implication of being a good friend or a loyal brother is that one *is* the sort of person who can be a good friend or loyal brother" (p. 26).

Such a view of the relationships between self and others is, of course, a direct descendent of the thinking of James and Mead, which we mentioned earlier. And it is precisely the line of argument employed by Bem (1965, 1967) in his analysis of self-perception.[8] We define ourselves by observing the "deeds we have done" and abstracting various continuities or imposing an organization on diverse deeds, whereby they become meaningful. One of the most interesting and provocative lines of research within the symbolic interaction perspective has sprung from the application of a similar line of reasoning to our perceptions of others.

Deviance and Labeling

According to Schur (1971), "Human behavior is deviant *to the extent that* it comes to be viewed as involving a *personally discreditable* departure from a group's normative expectations, *and* it *elicits* interpersonal or collective reactions that serve to 'isolate,' 'treat,' 'correct,' or 'punish' individuals engaged in such behavior" (p. 24). The key to this perspective on deviance, a perspective we shall refer to as the labeling perspective, is the *reaction* of society and not simply the action of the deviating individual. That the action of the deviating individual is not all there is to deviance can be illustrated in a number of ways.

Hollander (1958), for example, introduced the concept of "idiosyncrasy credit" to account for the fact that, in many groups, a double standard seems to operate. That is, newcomers or initiates into the group often are expected to toe the line and conform rigidly to the group's expectations, while old-timers appear much more lackadaisical in their adherence to group norms. Hollander's agrument is that old-timers have built up credit by their proven support of the group in the past and are allowed minor deviations. It is important to note that the notion of idiosyncrasy credit implies that groups have a sliding definition of deviance which is, in part, a function of other characteristics of the deviating

---

[8]It is interesting to note that Bem makes only a passing one-sentence reference to Mead in these papers and does not cite Goffman or James at all.

individual. Consider the treatment of teenagers who get caught engaging in acts of petty vandalism. They are much more likely to be formally arrested if they happen to be lower-class blacks than if they are middle-class whites (Turk, 1969).

Once an individual has been arrested, he becomes someone "with a record," and any future violations are apt to be more harshly punished. This latter point is worthy of note from the labeling perspective. Once society has defined someone as a deviate, there frequently follows a downhill "career" (Goffman, 1961) in which society's reaction compounds, elaborates, and reinforces whatever impulses led the individual to commit the initial deviant action.

The Theoretical Stance

In a book now considered to be at least a small classic by many interested in the study of deviance, Lemert (1951) was one of the first to touch upon the problem of labeling. The idea of labeling occurred in his distinction between primary deviation and secondary deviation. The concept of secondary deviation was developed primarily to distinguish between *original* and *effective* causes of deviant attributes and action associated with physical defects and incapacity, crime, prostitution, alcoholism, drug addiction, and mental disorders. Whereas primary deviation is that "deviation which is not invidiously symbolized by the person and which is integrated into the socially acceptable role of this person" (Lemert, 1951, p. 448), secondary deviation refers to "a special class of socially defined responses which people make to problems created by the societal reaction to their deviation" (Lemert, 1967, p. 40).

The problems involved here are essentially moral problems revolving around stigmatization, punishment, segregation, and social control. The general effect of these problems is to differentiate the symbolic and interactional environment to which the person responds, so that continued socialization and integration into society are categorically affected. As such, these problems "become central facts of existence for those experiencing them, altering psychic structure, producing specialized organization of social roles and self-regulating attitudes" (Lemert, 1967, p. 40-41). The secondary deviant's very existence becomes organized around his deviancy.

Of special importance in Lemert's work is the strong emphasis he places on the role played by the forces of social control in the process by which a person or group becomes "deviant." He demonstrates the ongoing processes of action and reaction, response and counterresponse in a diversity of actors and activities. Here, then, we see a very crucial aspect of labeling theory. Certain types of deviance revolve mainly around struggles of varying intensities in which the forces of social control try to impose rather definite systems of meaning, moral philosophies, and political ideologies upon individuals who make it obvious that they prefer to think and act differently regarding certain matters.

Other spokesmen for the labeling perspective on deviance have highlighted additional aspects of the processes involved. Becker (1963), for instance, goes somewhat further than Lemert by stating that "social groups create deviance by making the rules whose infraction constitutes deviance, and by applying those rules to particular people and labeling them as outsiders" (p. 9). Moreover, it becomes even clearer that "deviance is *not* a quality of the act the person commits, but rather a consequence of the application by others of rules and sanctions to an offender" (p. 9). Similarly, Schur (1971) argues that there are three basic response processes involved in the making of deviants: stereotyping, retrospective interpretation, and negotiation. Stereotyping "reflects the needs of participants in complex interactions to order their expectations so that they can predict the actions of others; at least to an extent sufficient for coherent organization of their own behavior" (p. 41). The second response, retrospective interpretation, involves a process by which others reinterpret all of the newly-labeled deviant's past behaviors so that salient aspects of his past become consistent with the new label. It is crucial for the others' peace of mind that a murderer, say, have been a bad apple all along. That way he or she is less threatening; they are different. The final process is one of negotiation between the deviant and the others who are attempting to apply and enforce the label. The outcomes of these processes involve the role engulfment of individuals in deviant careers and the secondary expansion of deviance problems of society.

To summarize, the keys to the labeling approach are: 1) The idea that particular "types" or "categories" of people are *expected by others* to display certain additional characteristics and/or to be consistently deviant; 2) Once we have discovered that another is a certain "type," we react to them in ways that push them into secondary deviance, thereby confirming our initial expectations. With this overview, let us take a look at some additional work derived from the perspective.

Additional Evidence

As we mentioned earlier, the methodological foundation for the labeling perspective has been participant observation, and Rosenhan's (1973) study was used as an example of participant observation designed to gather some evidence pertinent to the labeling approach to mental illness. Goffman's (for example, 1959, 1963a) combinations of participant observation with literary cullings and the use of metaphor, and autobiographical accounts of experiences are further examples of the types of evidence employed by proponents of the labeling approach. We could continue to illustrate aspects of labeling with such evidence, but it might be better to shift our methodological focus slightly. We do not want to leave the impression that the labeling perspective is limited to, or bound by, the types of methodological approaches described above.

Given the importance of preexisting expectations and stereotypes in society's edging of individuals into secondary deviance, two questions arise. First, is there any evidence that one's expectations for another's behavior actually influence the other's behavior? Second, if it is true that we do somehow induce others to behave as expected, what are the mechanisms and processes involved? Evidence bearing on both of these questions is fully discussed in the section titled "Developing Conceptions of Others" on page 115. Hence, we would only like to add a few comments here.

For several decades, there has been a rising tide of experimental and quasi-experimental studies (Campbell and Stanley, 1966) on the importance of expectations in interpersonal behavior. Much of this research has been carried out or stimulated, either directly or indirectly, by Robert Rosenthal (e.g., 1966, 1968). Although people had long been aware of the importance of expectations in perception, one of the more important findings from Rosenthal's research was that, even in apparently well-controlled laboratory settings, experimenters who expected their subjects to respond in certain ways were more likely to obtain those responses than were experimenters who had no such prior expectations.

There have now been well over 100 studies demonstrating the operation of such a self-fulfilling prophecy in laboratories, offices, classrooms, and factory settings. It would, of course, be impractical to review these studies here. It is important to note, however, that in spite of occasional telling methodological critiques of some of the research (cf., Barber and Silver, 1968), the evidence is overwhelming that our expectations about the behavior of others do influence that behavior. It is also interesting to note that the proponents of the labeling approach to deviance have not, apparently, recognized the importance of this line of research for their own perspective. In any event, as Rosenthal (1973) points out, "As the evidence continues to accumulate showing that one person's expectation of another person's behavior can come to serve as a self-fulfilling prophecy, it becomes less and less useful to conduct studies that do nothing but increase still further the very high probability that such effects do occur" (p. 24). Even some of Rosenthal's erstwhile critics now agree that "the question for future research is not whether there are expectancy effects, but how they operate" (Baker and Crist, 1971, p. 64).

Although not quite as voluminous, the literature on the latter question continues to grow. How do expectations get communicated? How do we let others know what *we* believe their "place" to be? It is really very simple. As Berne (1961) points out, "a great deal of linguistic, social, and cultural structure revolves around the question of mere recognition: special pronouns, inflections, gestures, postures, gifts, and offerings are designed to exhibit recognition of status and person" (p. 85).

As an example, consider one facet of this process by which we "recognize" another, the manner in which we address them. Ervin-Tripp (1969) points out that, in our culture, there are certain widely understood "rules" for how we should address people in different circumstances. When one of the parties to an interaction wants to define the other and the situation in a certain way, it can be done, in part, by the form of address. Consider a young, attractive well-dressed professional woman carrying an attaché case along a street in a business district. The accepted manner for a stranger to address her might be something like "Excuse me, Ms., I . . ." Other forms of address, especially those beginning with exclamations or a reference to her physical atrractiveness, would be viewed as attempts to redefine her from a professional woman into a sexual object. By her style of dress and her attaché case, the professional woman is projecting a certain image and definition of herself. Watzlawick, Beavin, and Jackson (1967) suggest that "person P may offer the other, O, a definition of self. P may do this in one or another of many possible ways, but whatever and however he may communicate on the content level, the prototype of his metacommunication will be 'This is how I see myself'" (p. 84).

The other, of course, may or may not accept the projected image: "'What's your name, boy?' 'Dr. Poussaint. I'm a physician . . .' 'What's your first name, boy?'" (Poussaint, 1967, p. 53, as quoted in Ervin-Tripp, 1969, p. 97-98.) As Ervin-Tripp points out there was no problem of communication in this interchange. Both parties were acutely aware of what was going on. "Both were familiar with an address system which contained a selector for race available to both black and white for insult, condescension, or deference, as needed. Only because they shared these norms could the policeman's act have its unequivocal impact" (p. 98).

There are other ways in which expectations get communicated and situations defined in ways that increase the probability that the expectations will be fulfilled. A line of research stemming from Rosenthal's work has been the attempt to identify aspects of teacher-pupil interaction and how that interaction differs as a function of whether or not the teacher expects the pupil to be "bright" or "dull." Chaikin, Sigler, and Derlega (1974), for example, assigned undergraduates the task of teaching a brief lesson on home and family safety to a 12-year-old. Some of the teachers were led to believe that the pupil was very bright, others were given no information about the pupil, and still others were led to believe that the pupil was somewhat slow. During the actual teaching session, the teachers' faces and body movements were recorded simultaneously on a split screen video tape. The video tapes were then rated on a number of nonverbal indices. Teachers who had been led to believe that their pupil was very bright were found to lean forward more during the interaction, to look their pupils in the eye more, to nod their heads up and down more, and to smile more than did those who either had no prior expectancy about their pupils or who expected them to be somewhat slow. Unfortunately, the Chaikin et al. design did not allow for assessment of what effect these behaviors had on the pupils, since the roles of pupils were played by confederates. It seems plausible, however, that such nonverbal mediators may actually make the learning task more enjoyable and interesting for pupils with the consequence that they do, indeed, learn more. Thus, the teachers' expectations would be communicated to the pupils in a manner that increased the probability that those expectations would be fulfilled. This is an area of research in which many interesting and exciting ideas are being actively pursued. The Chaikin et al. study is simply an example.

A related line of experimental research concerns our reactions to others with various physical stigma and/or deformities. Somewhat paradoxically, it appears that the tendency to treat such stigmatized individuals with kid gloves, and to do more for them than we would for "normal" others, has detrimental effects. Apparently, as part of our sympathy with their plight and as a consequence of our expectations that they are not really complete people, we are somewhat hesitant to give them negative feedback even when it is appropriate. The consequences, of course, are that their learning is impaired and we eventually confirm our expectations that they cannot "handle" things. There is some evidence that even in nonlearning situations, the interaction between stigmatized and normal individuals is inhibited, stilted, and overcontrolled (Kleck, Ono, and Hastorf, 1966). Thus, the stigmatized are less likely to be exposed to the range of verbal and nonverbal cues to which normals are exposed and the conseuqneces for the development of their interpersonal skills are obvious.

If our expectations about the behaviors of others are of such importance to the symbolic interaction perspective in general and labeling theory in particular, it should follow that an important area of investigation for the symbolic interaction perspective is the study of how conceptions of others develop. That is the substantive topic we shall take up next. Before doing so, however, we will describe another research method, a method which has been widely employed in the study of how conceptions of others develop.

CONTENT ANALYSIS AND DEVELOPING
CONCEPTIONS OF OTHERS

We have seen that one of the more important concepts employed by the early symbolic interactionists was the notion of significant others. This concept has led into several lines of research we will not have room to discuss in this chapter, for example, research on social comparison processes (Festinger, 1954) and reference groups. A prior concern, however, is the question of how children develop their conceptions of others. From the symbolic interaction perspective, this is one of the crucial questions about socialization. Unfortunately, it is also a question that has been difficult to investigate. Part of the problem is that young children do not yet speak quite the same language as do older children or adults.

Content Analysis

Holsti (1969) makes the point that content analysis is a particularly useful technique for research problems in which the subject's *own language* is crucial. The assumption is that an individual's language reflects the way "reality" is broken up and categorized by that individual. Much of the social psychological research on person perception, for example, has required subjects to check those adjectives on a list that seem to be descriptive of certain stimulus persons or to rate others on a set of rating scales. From the symbolic interaction perspective, one of the major problems with such procedures, which restrict subjects to a fixed format and/or a preselected vocabulary, is that they may fail to provide the subjects with categories that are relevant or meaningful with respect to their particular perceptions. Accordingly, a number of writers (e.g., Hastorf, Richardson, and Dornbusch, 1958) have advocated the use of free-response formats, in which subjects are allowed to describe others with terms of their own choosing. Content analysis can be employed with such free response protocols.

Definition

What does content analysis involve? As Holsti (1969, p. 5) notes, many are surprised that since learning to read they have been constantly performing informal versions of content analysis. The specific definition that we endorse comes from Stone, Dunphy, Smith, and Ogilvie (1966). "Content analysis [is] a research technique for making inferences by systematically and objectively identifying specified characteristics within text" (p. 5). The text or texts within which one attempts to identify certain characteristics are not, of course, randomly determined.

Selection of Texts

As in any research method, the question with which one begins is crucial, because it guides the entire process. In content analysis, the first things determined by the question are the texts to be compared. If we were interested in the extent to which newspaper editorial support for a political candidate is reflected in biased news coverage, our texts would be to some extent determined. We would look at editorials and news stories about candidates but not, for example, television political commercials or the candidate's own campaign literature. Given that we would look at newspaper editorials and news stories, there would be a sampling problem. We could not possibly look at all newspaper editorials and news items about all political candidates at all times and in all places. The next step, then, would be to set up some rules for sampling. We might decide to look only at presidential candidates in the 1960, 1964, 1968, and 1972 elections and use editorials and news items from ten daily papers with circulations of 100,000 or more. We also have to decide a time period within which to sample. The point is that, given even a relatively clear-cut research question, a series of important sampling decisions remain to be made in the process of selecting the texts to be compared.

Originally, content analysis was employed primarily with preexisting documents, reflecting its beginnings in journalism and political science. As we shall see in the section on developing conceptions of others, an increasingly common use of content analysis among social psychologists is to employ it on text material that subjects have specifically generated for the investigator.

Specification of Coding Categories

However the texts are selected, once they have been selected, the key process of content analysis has to be done: specification of the coding categories and rules for deriving indices. The object is to come up with a set of categories into which the content of the text can be coded. Holsti (1969) points out that "without reference to a specific research question, it is impossible to discuss substantive aspects of content analysis categories beyond giving illustrations" (p. 95). He does note the following general principles of category construction, however. Categories should: (a) reflect the purposes of the research; (b) be exhaustive; (c) be mutually exclusive; (d) be independent; and (e) be derived from a single classification principle. The first of these criteria is obvious. That the categories be exhaustive and mutually exclusive mean, respectively, that there must be a category into which each datum or relevant item can be placed and that each item should only be capable of being placed in one category. Independence means that assignment of one item to a given category should not affect the assignment of other items. Use of a single classification principle means that the categories cannot mix conceptually different levels of analysis.

In content analysis, we are usually interested in patterns of category occurrence as a function of some other variable. As we shall see in the following section, a question of particular interest from a symbolic interaction point of view is how conceptions of others differ as a function of children's ages. Content analysis is the chief technique that has been used to explore this question.

Coding into Categories

Once the texts have been selected and/or generated and our categories defined, the texts are read and the frequency of category appearance is recorded. This process must be checked for reliability and the usual technique is to have two or more coders independently code the same portions of the text. If their agreement about the relative frequency of occurrence of the various categories is high, we have some faith that the coding scheme and categories are well defined. What we conclude or what we infer from any given content analysis depends, of course, on the research question with which we started, the texts we decided to sample, the category system we constructed, and how the text fits into the categories.

At the beginning of this section, we asserted that content analysis can be a valuable research tool in helping us understand how people categorize and perceive "reality." That, of course, was our reason for describing it. We now turn to a substantive area of some import to the symbolic interaction perspective on social psychology, an area in which content analysis has indeed proven useful.

Developing Conceptions of Others

The general theoretical orientation that seems to have dominated this area of interest is a mixture of the ideas of Gardner Murphy, Heinz Werner, Jean Piaget, and Jerome Bruner. Recognizing that there are major differences among the theoretical orientations of these four (cf., Anglin, 1973), they share, nevertheless, a common view in which cognitive development is believed to proceed through various stages characterized by increasing degrees of both differentiation and integration. Gollin (1960), in elaborating on Werner's (1937, 1948) and Murphy's (1947) writings, makes the point that cognitive integration means different things at different levels of development. "Diffuse wholeness at the first level of development is different from the more and more differentiated wholeness exhibited at the second level in the maturation phenomena, and differs again from the integrated wholeness which appears when the differentiated functions achieve a stable, articulated interdependence" (p. 159).

An early study in the realm of the development of person concepts, which offers some tentative evidence on this view of cognitive development, was carried out by Hartley, Rosenbaum, and Schwartz (1948). Eighty-six boys and girls between the ages of three and ten were interviewed and asked questions such as: "What is Daddy (Mommy)?"; "What are you?"; "What does it take to be Jewish?" The responses were categorized in order to explore the ways in which the children identified themselves and others. Of interest here is that, among the younger age groups, almost *no* children spontaneously attributed personal characteristics to others. Rather, they responded in terms of global role categories. In the older age groups, there was an increasing tendency to attribute distinguishing or differentiating personality characteristics to significant others.

It appears, then, that some evidence exists for increasing differentiation of person perception with increasing age. From the symbolic interactionist perspective, it is important to know if there is any evidence for greater integration of these increasingly differentiated perceptions of others. That is, we have been arguing that individuals construct interpretations of reality. It should follow that, when dealing with perception of others or "person concepts," at some point the child begins to "put together" or "associate" or "expect" certain combinations of characteristics to co-occur. Gollin (1958) conducted a rather stringent test of the hypothesis derived from this question. He presented a five-scene silent motion picture about an eleven year old boy to three groups of boys and girls who differed in age (group averages were 10.7 years, 13.6 years, and 16.6 years). In one of the movie scenes, the actor was simply shown; in two scenes, he was shown engaging in socially approved behavior; and in two scenes, he was engaging in socially disapproved behavior. As anticipated, with increasing age there was a dramatic increase in the percentage of subjects who were able to integrate both the "good" and "bad" behavior into their descriptions of the boy. Though by no means definitive, the Gollin study hints at the beginnings of some sort of hierarchic organization imposed *by the perceiver* on the personality characteristics perceived in others.

One of the major problems in trying to look at how children organize their perceptions of others is how to avoid predetermining the outcome. As Dubin and Dubin (1965) rather pessimistically note in their review of children's social perception, "When technologies measuring intrapersonal factors are employed in research such factors . . . appear in the results . . ., when relations are measured the variables discovered are relations . . ., when the responses are limited to role categories the results are in terms of roles" (p. 817). The most common way in which investigators have attempted to circumvent this problem is the use of an open-ended, unstructured interview ("Tell me about _____") coupled with some sort of content analysis of the responses.

An example of this approach is a study by Yarrow and Campbell (1963). In that study, 267 boys and girls were interviewed shortly after their arrival at a summer camp and again after two weeks at camp. At each interview, campers were asked to choose one child from his or her cabin mates about whom most was known and to tell all about him/her. On the average, children gave 11 units of description and some gave as many as 27. The descriptions were coded according to the characteristics of personality that were present, such as aggressive behavior or affiliative behavior. It was found that if a child used a particular characteristic in the first interview he or she was significantly more likely to employ it in the second interview than were children who had not used it initially. It is important to note that this was true even if a *different* child was being described in the second interview. As Yarrow and Campbell (1963) note, "Such intraindividual thematic emphasis suggests that each child develops a perceptual framework that for him has general applicability" (p. 61).

In an elaboration of the above study, Dornbusch, Hastorf, Richardson, Muzzy, and Vreeland (1965) addressed themselves to the question of the relative contributions of perceiver and perceived in person perception. Again, information was solicited from boys and girls in summer camps. Each child was interviewed twice and in each interview was asked to describe *two* other children who shared his or her tent. A set of 69 content-analysis categories was developed and the descriptions reliably coded into these categories. Without exception, there was greater category overlap when one child was describing two other children than when two children were describing the same other child. This finding held up even when the two descriptions from a given child were elicited a week apart.

To return to the Yarrow and Campbell study for a moment, there was another finding which is of particular interest here. In addition to the interviews, Yarrow and Campbell set up an observational sampling system to record the *actual* behavior of the campers. As might have been anticipated from the symbolic interaction perspective, but somewhat contrary to the anticipations of common sense, the observational data indicated that, in a child's picture of another child, the salience of a given characteristic did *not* correspond to the actual frequency of that characteristic in the behavior of the perceived child. Finding such a discrepancy between behavior of others and perceptions of others is a relatively common occurrence. D'Andrade (1973), for example, has recently demonstrated that observers' and participants' memories for what occurred in a group interaction are systematically biased by a tendency to recall similar behaviors as having been performed by the same person when, in fact, they were not.

The preceding studies offer some support for the idea that, quite early in life, people begin to place constructions on their perceptions of others. Apparent contradictions may be "handled" by some sort of hierarchical integration, descriptive categories into which behaviors are coded are more a function of the perceiver than the perceived, and systematic distortions occur in perception of and memory for the behavior of others.

There is another facet of the developing conceptions of "what's out there," which we have not mentioned yet, one on which there has been relatively little research. At some point in life, children begin to realize that other people have intentions and purposes and that in order to understand another you can not focus only on their overt behavior. You have to try to figure out what the behavior was intended to accomplish. This, of course, is a very useful strategy for simplifying the universe. Rather than trying to keep track of millions of behaviors that another might perform, you only need to know what his or her intentions are and all the behaviors can be interpreted in terms of a few underlying purposes. In a study of this sort of developmental change, Rappoport and Fritzler (1969) employed animated cartoon sequences to study the extent to which children focused on the overt behavior of depicted geometrical objects or on underlying "intentions" of the objects. First grade subjects responded predominantly in terms of perceptually salient movements of the objects, whereas sixth graders responded in terms of attributed intentions.

In a related but somewhat less artificial study, Peevers and Secord (1973) analyzed open-ended person descriptions of both liked and disliked peers from five groups of subjects: preschoolers, third graders, seventh graders, eleventh graders, and college students. The descriptions were coded in terms of their level of descriptiveness, the extent of personal involvement of the describer, the evaluative consistency of the description, and the depth of the description. Although fewer items overall were used to describe disliked peers, dispositional items were much more common in the descriptions of disliked peers. It appears that attribution of a negative dispositional quality is more likely to be taken as a sufficient explanation of "all there is" to that person than is attribution of a positive dispositional quality. Another finding of interest was a trend toward increasing use of "deeper levels" of description with increasing age, a finding we mentioned in conjunction with the Hartley, et al. (1948) study. Finally, descriptions of others which were egocentrically phrased were much more common among younger subjects.

An earlier study by Rockway (1969) reported a similar result concerning egocentricity. Rockway employed a "programmed case," in which a subject must decide at a number of choice points which one of three behavioral descriptions is true or real for the person being described in the case. After each choice, the subject was asked to explain his choice and then was given immediate feedback as to whether he was right or not, based on data from the actual case history. A response was called egocentric if the choice was justified in terms of what the subject himself would have done. Using boys from the sixth, ninth, and twelfth grades, egocentric responses decreased from early to middle adolescence but, surprisingly, showed a slight increase in late adolescence (twelfth-grade subjects). Rockway (1969) interprets the latter finding as a kind of "enlightened egocentricity which differs from a blanket assumption by younger individuals that one's own reactions are necessarily relevant data. Older adolescents may focus on their own past reactions to predict an object person's behavior only where it appears logical to assume that self and others are in some way alike" (p. 5).

Signell (1966) reports a finding that seems to be congruent with this interpretation. She employed a modification of Kelly's (1955) Role Construct Repertory Test to elicit descriptions of persons from children 9 to 16 years old and found that, as they increase in age, children seem to increase the complexity of the person concepts they employ. Hence, while younger subjects might base a prediction such as that requested by Rockway on whether or not the person in the case was "like me," older subjects might base the prediction on whether or not the person was "like me in terms of how he responded to X." Apparently, as the self-concept becomes more differentiated people become aware that they behave differently and, to some extent, actually have different characteristics in different situations. When they are secure, they are likely to be kind to others; when insecure, they are likely to be tense and even cruel. Such relationships as they become aware of in their own life are in all probability incorporated into their interpersonal expectations. As the study by Rockway suggests, among adults, these incorporations will be applied to others selectively, that is, "only when it appears logical to assume that self and others *are in some way alike*" (p. 5). This is one of the basic suppositions of social comparison theory (Festinger, 1954).

The idea that perceptions of others are tied to one's own self-concept and/or life situation is underscored by Olshan (1970). Olshan used children in the third, sixth, and ninth grades as subjects and employed a sentence-completion task to determine the traits most frequently used in person perception at each of these levels. ("My Mother is _____"; "A Fireman is _____.") Once these traits had been obtained, subjects at each grade level were asked to sort a number of traits into piles, each pile corresponding to a different type of person. Using a rather sophisticated scaling procedure, which we describe briefly on page 126, Olshan was able to determine the organizational structure underlying the ways in which subjects sorted the traits. Of importance here is that, as Rosenberg and Sedlak (1972) point out, the sortings were interpretable in psychologically meaningful ways in terms of the stage of life of the subjects: "While *adult-child* is a highly significant dimension underlying third graders' personality perceptions, this dimension is no longer salient with the beginning of adolescence. On the other hand, preadolescents do not perceive sex as a dimension, whereas adolescents do" (p. 290). Such findings make sense in terms of the life of the subjects. They also emphasize that as one's life situation changes, salient interpersonal expectations also change and one organizes those expectations in terms of current preoccupations and social interactions.

There is no reason to expect that such shifts and reorganizations stop at any particular point in life, even though most of the studies cited in this section have dealt only with children. As an example, Friendly and Glucksberg (1970) reasoned that novices in a particular culture often lack an understanding of the way full-fledged members of the culture view things. Full-fledged members of a culture often seem to make discriminations and differentiations that are lost on newcomers. An example is the old standby about Eskimos being able to discriminate (and having words for) a large number of different kinds of snow. But more than this, Friendly and Glucksberg were also interested in whether experience in a particular culture or subculture led to changed perceptions about the associations or relations among objects.

With the aid of undergraduate informants, Friendly and Glucksberg selected 20 trait names that were peculiar to the Princeton undergraduate culture (for example, "Ivy Type," "Meatball," "Lunch") and asked one group of freshmen (novices in the culture) and one group of seniors (old hands) to sort these traits along with 40 additional personality characteristics. The structures underlying the perceived relationships were then obtained separately for the two groups. For the freshmen, two dimensions were adequate to account for the variations that they perceived among the 60 terms. Seniors, on the other hand, perceived these same two variations, but also a third. The latter variation had to do with socially approved behavior for Princetonians, a discrimination that the freshmen did not yet make.

Thus, it again appears that the ways in which people organize their interpersonal perceptions are related to their situations in life. As Kelly (1955) argued and as Friendly and Glucksberg (1970) have empirically demonstrated, we are continually reconstruing, reorganizing, and placing alternative constructions on our perceptions of others. This process does not stop at some point in late childhood, but continues throughout life.

A majority of the studies that were mentioned in this section employed some form of content analysis. From a symbolic-interaction perspective, one of the limitations of content analysis, as it is usually employed, is that the investigator defines the categories into which content is to be coded. What is really needed is some sort of research method or tool that would allow whatever structure inherent in the data itself to emerge. What attempts have been made to find a "purer" method? In approaching this question, we will continue to focus on the substantive topic of how individuals conceptualize others.

CONCEPTIONS OF OTHERS AND THE
SEARCH FOR A METHOD

According to MacLeod (1947), "The phenomonological method in social psychology, as in the psychology of perception . . . is the attempt to view phenomena in their entirety and without prejudice, to distinguish the essential from the nonessential, to let the phenomena themselves dictate the conceptual framework and the further course of the inquiry" (p. 207-208). In practice, the phenomenological method is extremely difficult. How, for example, is one to distinguish the essential from the nonessential? How are we to view anything without prejudice?

Early Studies

Many researchers who have been attracted to the phenomenological approach in the area of person perception have usually taken the first step of asking subjects for "free," "open-ended," or "unconstrained" descriptions of others. This has usually been done as a substitute or accompaniment to rating the others on a series of standard scales. Asch (1946), for example, in his classic series of studies on impression formation, asked subjects to write out brief descriptions of persons who had been described to them with short lists of traits. Asch used these sketches to illustrate some of the characteristics of how subjects organized their impressions and reinterpreted certain specific traits of the stimulus person, like "intelligent," in light of whether the stimulus person was also "warm" or "cold." While Asch used the sketches effectively to buttress his arguments about the gestalt or holistic quality of the impressions formed, the sketches were not themselves used for any purpose other than plausible illustration.

Kelley (1950), in his follow-up of the Asch study, also asked subjects to write out free descriptions of an instructor who had just presented a brief lecture-discussion and who had previously been described as warm or cold. Again, however, the free descriptions were not themselves subjected to detailed analysis, but were simply read to glean some "impressions" of how the subjects organized their perceptions of the instructor. If this were the best that this line of research had to offer, we could quickly go on to the next topic. Things began to pick up during the fifties, however, as researchers began to push the free-response approach.

Spreading Recognition of the Problem

Between 1954 and 1958, such eminent social psychologists as Allport, Bruner, Hastorf, and Tagiuri all published persuasive arguments that the study of person perception and impression formation would be greatly enriched by the study of how people *spontaneously* categorize others. At the heart of their arguments was a theme which should be familiar by now: to "understand" another, we need to know how he perceives and interprets his world. In order to obtain this understanding it is necessary to avoid putting words into the subjects' mouths or asking them to make inferences from traits they seldom if ever employ in thinking about others or asking them to sort into categories a group of traits that they do not ordinarily employ. All of these, and related procedures, may distort the resulting picture of the subjects' conceptual structures.

Suppose, for example, that someone thinks of others in terms of how practical, friendly, honest, and hard-working they are. If you then ask that person to infer whether a practical person is likely to be polite or blunt, they will have to fall back on something other than their own cognitive framework to make the judgment, because they have never associated being practical with either politeness or bluntness. What might occur is that they would fall back on the meanings of the terms (c.f., D'Andrade, 1965) and reason that "politeness is sort of a superficial friendliness and practical people are friendly so, I guess a practical person would be polite." In short, the response would reflect the descriptive similarity (Peabody, 1967) between the presented scale and one facet of the person's conceptual framework, but it would be false to take the response as indicating that in the person's naive expectations, before being asked to make the inference, there was a relationship between another's being practical and their politeness.

A study of particular pertinence here is one by Allport (1958). One of the things that concerned Allport was the artificiality of giving subjects long series of bipolar scales defined by traits that they may or may not have used to think about the personalities of others and asking them to make ratings on those scales. He reports a study in which 93 students were asked "to think of some one individual of your sex whom you know well . . . [and] describe him or her by writing in each space provided a word, a phrase, or a sentence that expressed fairly well . . . some essential characteristic of this person" (p. 254). Ninety percent of the subjects found ten spaces to be completely sufficient and, on the average, the subjects felt that seven "essential" characteristics could capture their beliefs and impressions of the person described. One might begin to wonder what the results of studies really mean when subjects are asked to rate their acquaintances on hundreds of scales. "Perhaps what we need is fewer units than we now use, but units more relevant to individual structural patterns" (Allport, 1958, p. 253).

Partly as a result of the urgings by Bruner and Tagiuri (1954), Hastorf et al. (1958), Tagiuri (1958), and Allport (1958), people began to study "the perceptual categories that are actually employed by, and thus relevant to, the perceiver under consideration" (Hastorf et al., 1958, p. 55). Sarbin (1954), for example, had selected students in a classroom to stand for ten seconds while their classmates wrote down the first three words that came to mind about the person standing. Females were significantly more likely to think of words which represented inferred qualities or traits such as "aggressive," "warm," "hostile," and "logical," while males were more likely to think of purely descriptive terms like "tall," "girl," and "gray clothes."

One question that might occur when we give subjects so much freedom to select the terms they will use in describing others is the extent to which the terms employed are reflections of their own cognitive structures or are simply reflections of what the stimulus person is really like. That is, students in a classroom would presumably have some knowledge of their fellows. Hence, when John stands up, one may think of "athlete" *and* "intelligent," even though one believes that most athletes are unintelligent. It will be recalled that, on page 116, we mentioned several studies that bear on this issue. Dornbusch, *et al.* (1965), for example, found that content analysis of the descriptions of others given by children revealed greater category overlap when one child was describing two others than when two children were describing the same other child.

Although many other researchers have attempted to utilize free response data to come to grips with the manner in which individuals structure and categorize their worlds, the main reason that this approach has not received more emphasis is the difficulty in handling the data. Substantive advances have been hindered by the lack of adequate methods. What do you do with an open-ended description once you have it? As we have seen, content analysis provides a partial answer to this question and content analysis can be quite useful under certain circumstances. As we have also seen, for our purposes, content analysis suffers from definite limitations. First, content analysis must stand or fall by its categories and these categories are usually imposed by the investigator and are, to some extent, arbitrary. Different investigators might construct different categories. Secondly, content analysis usually gives us only minimal information about the interrelationships of various categories. As we said earlier, what is really needed are research methods or tools that allow whatever structure inherent in the data to emerge.

Searching for an Unbiased Method

There have been several attempts to develop techniques for investigating the conceptual links and relationships underlying language and thought in as unbiased a manner as possible. We will discuss three such techniques.

Personal Structure Analysis

In an early attempt to analyze such free response data as that contained in diaries and letters, Baldwin (1942) employed a technique that he termed "personal structure analysis." The technique was based on two assumptions, involving frequency and contiguity of units. The more often a given item appeared in the material to be analyzed, the more important it was assumed to be and the repeated appearance of two items in close proximity was taken as evidence that they were perceived to be related.

Baldwin employed his technique to analyze a series of letters from an elderly lady named Jenny in which she wrote about many things that concerned her, but mainly about her son (Ross), his friends, and their relationships to her. Baldwin prepared a long list of categories; the categories had to be prepared anew for each individual to be analyzed and were based on prior knowledge of what the material contained. Defining an incident as a small temporal segment of the letters in which Jenny was writing about one general topic, two items or categories were said to be contiguous if they both appeared in the incident. The more often two categories appeared contiguously, the more closely related they were taken to be, in Jenny's view of things.

Once the relationships among categories had been determined, Baldwin was able to represent these cooccurrences graphically. Figure 2.1 is taken from Baldwin (1942, p. 175) and illustrates the type of interrelations among categories that Baldwin was able to depict. In the figure, a line connecting two categories means that they were significantly related in the letters. Otherwise the location of the categories in the diagram is arbitrary.

Baldwin's technique was a valuable start, but, as a general tool for investigating the manner in which an individual orders and interprets "reality," it has serious problems. For one thing it is extremely time consuming and requires a large amount of material (oral or written) from a subject. Another problem is that, while it allows us to depict internal relations within an "ideational cluster" (see Figure 2.1), we are unable to determine relations among the various clusters. To know the relationships among clusters is, of course, crucial because such relationships define the meanings of the clusters. A technique that overcomes these problems, while at the same time allowing an individual to reveal the structure of his or her own view of the world, was developed in the early 1950s by George Kelly.

George Kelly and Grid Methods

Kelly was a practicing psychotherapist who developed a theoretical perspective, which he called the psychology of personal constructs. The basic philosophical position underlying Kelly's perspective was "constructive alternativism"

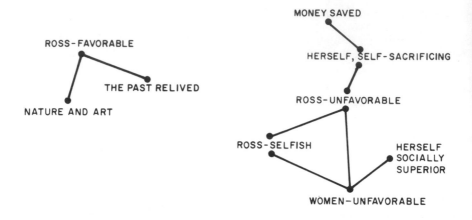

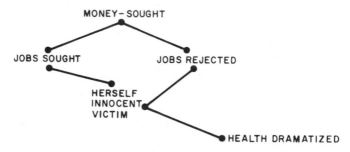

FIGURE 2.1.   Principal Ideational Cluster in Jenny's Life. (From Baldwin, 1942, p. 175. Copyright 1942 by the American Psychological Association. Reprinted by permission.)

and is essentially the same as the position taken by symbolic interactionists. Constructive alternativism is the position that

> ... whatever nature may be, or howsoever the quest for truth will turn out in the end, the events we face today are subject to as great a variety of constructions as our wits will enable us to contrive. . . . Events do not tell us what to do, nor do they carry their meanings engraved on their backs for us to discover. For better or worse, we ourselves create the only meanings they will ever convey during our lifetime" (Kelly, 1966, as cited in Bannister and Mair, 1968, p. 6-7).

Kelly assumed that, in the attempt to bring some order to the events surrounding them, each person developed their own idiosyncratic, hierarchically organized system of personal constructs. A construct is simply a dichotomous abstraction that the person has made of the similarities and differences among events in the onrushing stream of stimuli surrounding them. The key, of course, is that different people make different abstractions from the same events. To say that a person's system of constructs is hierarchically organized means that some constructs are more important than others and that the interrelationships between constructs are of central concern. "A single construct by itself would allow no predictions, since it is along the line of interrelationships between constructs that predictions are made. Only when constructs are interrelated and organized into some kind of system can they form the bases for consistent or useful anticipations" (Bannister and Mair, 1968, p. 15). If we know that someone construes others in terms of a "like me-not like me" construct, we need to know how the perception that another is "not like me" relates to other aspects of the person's construct system. What is that perception likely to imply?

In the attempt to understand the constructions that people place on reality, Kelly (1955) devised a methodology that is both simple and general. The method has been used primarily in relation to an individual's perceptions of other persons, but is certainly not limited to such an "interpersonal world." Rather it can be used to measure perceptual relationships among any sorts of events, situations, persons, or concepts that exist in a person's "psychological space." In practice, administration of Kelly's methodology begins with a list of "objects" that may be persons, situations, or whatever, and that may have been generated by the investigator or by the subject. The point is to understand how the subject perceives the interrelations among these objects, that is, what constructs he or she imposes on the objects to make sense of their similarities and differences. The procedure consists of successive selections by the experimenter of triads of the objects, each selection being followed by a request for the subject to indicate how two of the objects are alike in some way and different from the third.

For example, a person might be asked to consider three people, for instance, his or her father, mother, and boss. The person would then be asked to think of some way in which any two of them seem to be alike and different from the third. The person might reply that his or her father and boss were gentle, while the mother was harsh. They might then be asked to apply this gentle-harsh distinction to a number of others such as their brother or sister, their spouse, an old flame, a neighbor, and others. This particular distinction might not apply to some of these figures, but it would apply to others. Kelly points out that by extending this gentle-harsh dichotomy the person is, in effect, providing a definition of what the gentle-harsh distinction means to them.

In a similar manner, other triads of figures would be picked, such as sister, ex-flame, and boss, and the person would be asked how any two of them were alike and different from the third. Eventually, one would have elicited from the person a list of the dichotomous constructs with which he or she organized their perceptions of their interpersonal world, as well as indications of the particular people to which the various constructs applied.

An example of the type of matrix that results from such a procedure is given in Figure 2.2. It is important to realize that the objects among which relations are to be determined do not have to be people; they can be important experiences in the person's life, life plans or values to which the person subscribes, almost anything. The method is potentially a very general one for understanding how an individual construes his or her world. Further, once a matrix such as that in Figure 2.2 has been obtained, a number of statistical techniques are available with which one might determine the degree of overlap of the various constructs employed, the similarity of the various objects and whether particular constructs subsume others, whether there is an hierarchical ordering of the constructs.

Kelly's methodology has proven itself useful in both clinical and research settings (see Bonarius, 1965, for a review). The psychological basis for both Kelly's theoretical perspective and his method is the perception of similarities and differences among objects. Remember, a construct is simply a dichotomous abstraction that a person has made of the similarities and differences among events that surround him or her. Knowing what a person perceives as similar is, in a very real sense, the key to understanding that person's construction of reality. In the last 15 years, some sophisticated mathematical techniques have been developed for the treatment of perceived similarity indices, which promise to be of major importance for the symbolic interaction perspective in social psychology. We will briefly describe one class of these techniques.

Multidimensional Scaling

Multidimensional scaling is a particularly useful technique whenever we want to discover the structure or organization underlying a matrix of similarity indices. As Shepard (1964) points out,

> Behavioral scientists, as well as physical scientists, often collect large arrays of data. But highly developed theoretical models, which have proved so useful in the physical sciences, are still largely lacking in the behavioral sciences. Since less structure can be imposed upon the data from outside, then, a greater demand is placed upon the behavioral scientist to proceed, in a purely inductive way, to discover what structure may already exist in the data themselves (p. 51).

Suppose we were interested in how an individual construes or interprets a particular set of objects; the "objects" could be other people, situations, ethnic groups, values, personality traits, almost anything. Another way of stating our intention would be to say that we were interested in how the individual structures his or her perception of the objects. Our first step would be to obtain from the individual some indication of how similar he or she perceived each pair of the objects to be, some sort of perceived proximity index. According to Fillenbaum and Rapoport (1971),

> Proximity data include almost any measure of similarity, substitutability, co-occurrence, and association between every two stimulus objects . . . under study. In psychological experiments, proximity measures have been obtained traditionally by asking subjects which of two pairs of stimulus objects are more similar (or dissimilar),

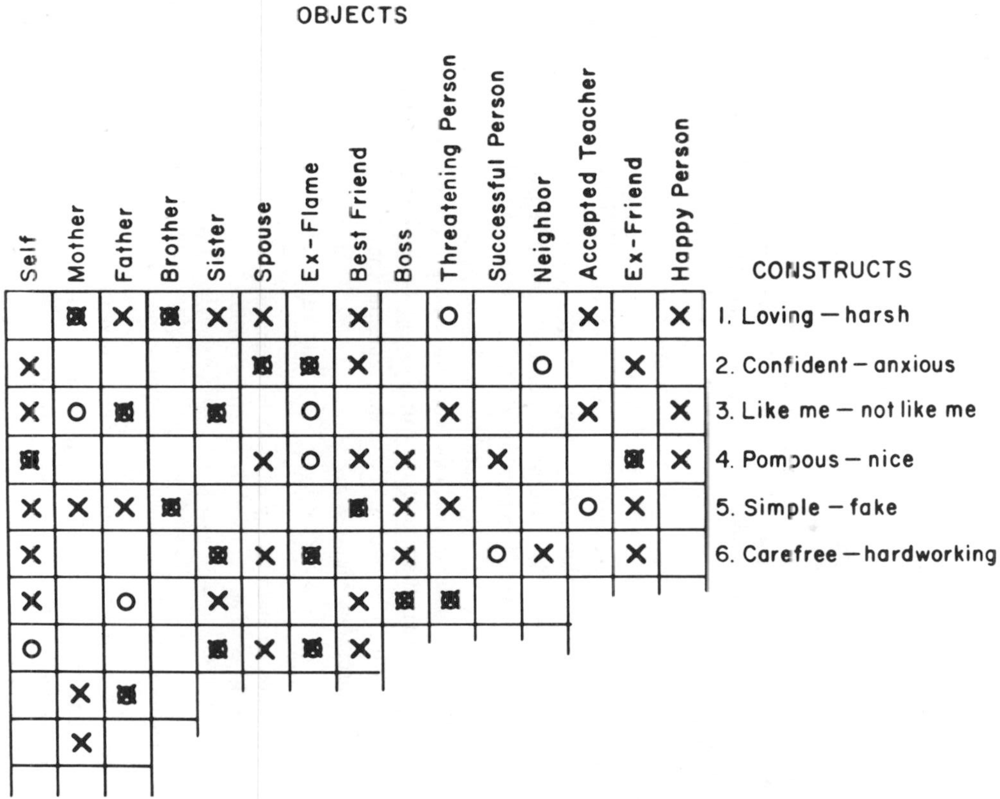

OBJECTS

CONSTRUCTS

Object	1. Loving — harsh	2. Confident — anxious	3. Like me — not like me	4. Pompous — nice	5. Simple — fake	6. Carefree — hardworking
Self	X	X	⊠	X	X	O
Mother	⊠	O	X		X	X
Father	X	⊠	X	O	⊠	
Brother	⊠				⊠	
Sister	X		⊠	⊠	X	⊠
Spouse	X	⊠	X	X	X	
Ex-Flame		⊠	O	O	⊠	⊠
Best Friend	X	X	X	⊠	X	X
Boss			X	X	X	⊠
Threatening Person	O		X	X	⊠	
Successful Person			X	O		
Neighbor		O		X		
Accepted Teacher	X		X	O		
Ex-Friend		X		⊠	X	X
Happy Person	X		X	X		

FIGURE 2.2. Hypothetical example of Kelly's Grid Method with persons important in the subject's life as "objects." Circles indicate the triad of persons within each row used to elicit the construct at the right of the row. Xs within a row indicate which of the persons are described by the first pole of the construct. Blanks indicate persons seen as characterized by the contrast pole.

127

by asking them to rate each pair of stimulus objects according to the strength of similarity between its elements or by rank ordering some or all pairs of stimulus objects with respect to similarity, dissimilarity, substitutability, co-occurrence (p. 9).

However the proximity measures between objects are obtained, once they have been obtained we may then employ multidimensional scaling to generate spatial configurations of the objects such that the order of distances between the objects in the spatial configurations corresponds to the proximity measures between the objects. To put this a little more precisely,

We are given, for every two "objects" (i and j) in some set of n, a datum, s_{ij}, representing the similarity, substitutability, affinity, association, interaction, correlation, or, in general, "proximity" between them. We seek, simply, that configuration of n points in the (Euclidean) space of smallest possible dimension such that, to an acceptable degree of approximation, the resulting interpoint distances d_{ij} are monotonically related to the given proximity data in the sense that $d_{ij} \langle d_{ki}$ whenever $s_{ij} \rangle s_{ki}$ (Shepard, 1972, p. 7-8).

By representing the n objects in a space of, say, two or three dimensions, we are better able to understand and interpret the important variations among the n objects. An example might help clarify this. Jones, Sensenig, and Ashmore (1974) asked subjects to sort 36 values into categories on the basis of what they believed about which values "go together." For each possible pair of values, a proximity measure was derived, based on the number of times the two values were put into the same category. There are 630 such proximity measures. By employing one of the several available versions of multidimensional scaling (Kruskal, 1964a, 1964b), these 630 measures could be represented in a two-dimensional space, which is much more understandable than the 36 x 36 matrix of proximity measures. See Figure 2.3.[9]

It is important to note, as Shepard (1972) points out, that

. . . a representation obtained by any of these multidimensional methods should not be regarded merely as an end in itself. The primary purpose of such a representation is to enable the investigator to gain a better understanding of the total pattern of interrelations in his data and, hence, to decide what further observations, experiments, or modifications of theory will most advance the science as a whole (p. 3).

We realize that we have not described personal structure analysis, grid methods, or multidimensional scaling in detail sufficient to allow one to use these methods; that was not our purpose. Our purpose was to call attention to a growing armamentarium of methods available to the researcher interested in understanding how an individual construes and interprets and organizes reality. We were led into this brief discussion of methods by pointing out the growing recognition of the need for such methods within the field of person perception.

[9]For information on how the two interpretive axes, self-society and active-passive, were obtained and why they appear where they do, see Rosenberg and Sedlak, 1972.

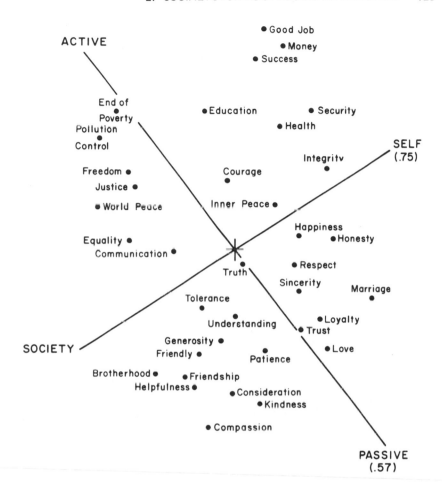

FIGURE 2.3.   Two dimensional configuration of 36 Values.

RETROSPECT AND CRITIQUES

Lindesmith and Strauss (1968) point out that "the symbolic interactionist view as it was formulated by George H. Mead and other founding fathers was not so much a body of specific testable theory as it was a general orientation or image of man" (p. 11). That image, as we have tried to illustrate, is one that views the self as both an active and reactive information-processing agent engaged in the attempt to impose some order on and to extract some meaning from the "booming, buzzing confusion" that surrounds us all.

A Note About Topics Omitted

In our attempt to illustrate some of the implications of the symbolic interaction "image" of mankind, we have, of necessity, been selective. We have covered some topics — participant observation, labeling theory, and deviance — that might be considered a part of the symbolic interaction mainstream. Other topics and literature discussed have seldom appeared in textbooks written within the symbolic interaction perspective. Still other topics, of course, simply had to be omitted. The fact that we have omitted some topics and included others says nothing about the relative importance or interest of the two categories.

Further, the fact that we have not discussed research that has employed the manipulative laboratory experiment should not be taken to mean that the symbolic interaction perspective is unamenable to such research. Festinger's (1954) theory of social comparison processes, Bem's (1965) model of self-perception, and Schachter's (1964) research on labeling internal bodily states, for example, all flow rather directly from the symbolic interaction perspective as formulated by James, Mead, and others. Much valuable research on these three theoretical models has, of course, been conducted in laboratory experiments.

Criticisms of the Perspective

There are a number of different kinds of criticisms that have been made of symbolic interaction as a perspective and of the methods often employed by symbolic interactionists.

Consider, for example, the Rosenhan (1973) study, which we discussed earlier. One might raise serious questions about the extent to which preconceptions and biases of the participant observers themselves influenced what they "chose" to see and report. Perhaps in some instances the staff had already decided that the participant observers were indeed sane, but chose to wait a little longer before informing others of their decision just to be sure.

The point here is not limited to the Rosenhan study, of course, but is a general one, which is a recurring source of concern with respect to the interpretation of participant observation studies. To the extent that participant observers embrace one particular view of a situation, for example, the inmates' view of a mental hospital or the workers' view of a union-management confrontation, they are likely to give short shrift to other perspectives on the same situation. The result may be a lack of critical observation, a failure to verify interpretations by the use of additional data sources such as records and observations of others, and a general tendency to ignore or dismiss evidence that appears to contradict or question the adopted view.

Even if the participant observer is scrupulously fair and gives equal weight and attention to all perspectives on and interpretations of a given situation, there is another problem. At best, participant observation studies capture only a limited slice of reality, a "snapshot" of some group or organization at a particular point in time. There is usually very little historical or longitudinal emphasis. This, of course, is related to one of the most frequently voiced criticisms of symbolic interaction, that little attention is paid to how the larger structural features of society influence and, perhaps, predetermine some of the micro-processes on which participant observers focus their attention. It is impossible to investigate or even theorize about the effects of such structural features if one's data base is confined to the here-and-now. In the here-and-now, of course, structural features are a constant, and one cannot determine whether or not changes in those features would have any effect.

There are further criticisms of particular aspects of the symbolic interaction perspective. Consider the case of labeling theory. Since labeling "theory" became so labeled, critics have argued that: (a) it is not really a theory; (b) it does not explain the source of deviance; (c) it does not explain why some people do "deviant" things and others do not; (d) many of the leading proponents were only studying things to which they had easy access; (e) the labeling perspective on deviance was undermining the establishment; (f) the perspective was supporting the status quo; and (g) in short, the "theory" did not explain everything about deviance. Most of these criticisms have little merit, as Becker (1971) has recently pointed out. No one but the critics of labeling theory ever claimed it was a "theory," for example, and there is nothing about the labeling approach that precludes explanations for why some people do deviant things and others do not; that simply is not the focus of the approach. However, it is important to note that, even if some of these critiques have merit, symbolic interaction as a whole would be little effected. If it were to turn out that the weight of the evidence indicated that the labeling approach did not account for what is known about "mental illness" or juvenile delinquency very well, the symbolic interaction perspective could still be useful, as a way of understanding how language develops, for example. As we pointed out above, the perspective is a "general orientation or image of man." There may be some areas in which this "image" is not particularly useful. There are other areas, however, in which it is.

As we have already mentioned, there is, unfortunately, something missing from this image of man. As Reynolds and Reynolds (1973) point out, "Critics of either the general perspective or of certain of its practitioners have argued that either interactionism or at least several prominent interactionists have a narrow, individualized conception of social life which, in turn, leads to an ignoring of society's larger features and master institutions" (p. 85). If it is true, as we suggested earlier, that the position of an individual within a given social structure is an important determinant of the manner in which reality will be defined *by* and *for* that individual, it should be important to look systematically at the influence of different types of social structures and organizations on this process.

For example, the political, economic, and religious institutions of a society clearly influence the conception of reality an individual develops. In a society dominated by the profit motive and a corresponding economic system, an interpersonal norm of equity is much more likely to play a role in individual conceptions of reality and to govern interpersonal relations than in a society with a different economic organization. Similarly, in an autocratic political system, micro-analyses of group processes are likely to reveal different sorts of relationships to authority figures than those that would be displayed in truly democratic societies, in which an egalitarian respect for the opinions of others has been instilled as a part of each person's conception of reality. In short, the symbolic-interaction perspective pays little attention to the influence of the norms and power relations within societies, which may influence the nature of the micro-processes and interpersonal relations that are the focus of most work in symbolic interaction.

The result of this lack of attention to political, economic, religious, and other overriding structural frameworks within which interpersonal processes play themselves out is an extreme relativism. Pushed to its limits, symbolic interactionism often seems to imply that there are *no* absolutes. Whatever meaning we abstract from reality is taken to be ephemeral; in other times and places, one might abstract totally different meanings from the same events. The point here, of course, is that by taking into account the larger structural features of the societies in which these events are embedded, we may very well discover that these events are only superficially similar and that, in contrast to the apparent relativism, there is in fact a deterministic relationship between the events and their contexts.

REFERENCES

Allport, G. W. What units shall we employ? In G. Lindzey (Ed.), *Assessment of human motives*. New York: Rinehart, 1958.

Angell, R. C. Introduction. In A. J. Reiss, Jr. (Ed.), *Cooley and sociological analysis*. Ann Arbor: University of Michigan Press, 1968.

Anglin, J. M. (Ed.). *Beyond the information given*. New York: Norton, 1973.

Asch, S. E. Forming impressions of personality. *Journal of Abnormal and Social Psychology*, 1946, *41*, 258-290.

Baker, J. P., & Crist, J. L. Teacher expectancies: A review of the literature. In J. D. Elashoff & R. E. Snow (Eds.), *Pygmalion reconsidered*. Worthington, Ohio: C. H. Jones, 1971.

Baldwin, A. L. Personal structure analysis: A statistical method for investigating the single personality. *Journal of Abnormal and Social Psychology*, 1942, *37*, 163-183.

Bannister, D., & Mair, J. M. M. *The evaluation of personal constructs*. New York: Academic Press, 1968.

Barber, T. X., & Silver, M. J. Fact, fiction, and the experimenter bias effect. *Psychological Bulletin Monograph*, 1968, *70*, (6, Pt. 2).

Becker, H. S. *Outsiders*. Glencoe, Ill.: The Free Press, 1963.

Becker, H. S. *Labeling theory reconsidered*. Paper presented to the Annual Meeting of the British Sociological Association, April, 1971.

Becker, H. S., & Geer, B. Participant observation and interviewing: A comparison. In W. J. Filstead (Ed.), *Qualitative methodology: Firsthand involvement with the social world.* Chicago: Markham, 1970.

Bem, D. J. An experimental analysis of self-persuasion. *Journal of Experimental Social Psychology*, 1965, *1*, 199-218.

Bem, D. J. Self-perception: An alternative interpretation of cognitive dissonance phenomena. *Psychological Review*, 1967, *74*, 183-200.

Berger, P. L., & Luckmann, T. *The social construction of reality.* New York: Doubleday Anchor, 1966.

Berne, E. *Transactional analysis in psychotherapy.* New York: Grove Press, 1961.

Blumer, H. Social psychology. In E. P. Schmidt (Ed.), *Man and society.* New York: Prentice-Hall, 1937.

Bonarius, J. C. J. Research in the personal construct theory of George A. Kelly. In B. A. Maher (Ed.), *Progress in experimental personality research* (Vol. 2). New York: Academic Press, 1965.

Boring, E. G. *A history of experimental psychology.* New York: Appleton-Century, 1950.

Bruner, J. S., & Tagiuri, R. The perception of people. In G. Lindzey (Ed.), *Handbook of social psychology* (Vol. 2). Cambridge, Mass.: Addison Wesley, 1954.

Bryson, G. *Man and society: The scottish inquiry of the eighteenth century.* Princeton, New Jersey: Princeton University Press, 1945.

Campbell, D. T., & Stanley, J. C. *Experimental and quasi-experimental designs for research.* Chicago: Rand-McNally, 1966.

Chaikin, A. L., Sigler, E., & Derlega, V. J. Nonverbal mediators of teacher expectancy effects. *Journal of Personality and Social Psychology*, 1974, *30*, 144-149.

Chapman, L., & Chapman, J. Genesis of popular but erroneous psycho-diagnostic observations. *Journal of Abnormal Psychology*, 1967, *72*, 192-204.

Coser, L. A. *Masters of sociological thought: Ideas in historical and social context.* New York: Harcourt, Brace, Jovanovich, Inc., 1971.

D'Andrade, R. G. Trait psychology and componential analysis. *American Anthopologist*, 1965, *67*, 215-228.

D'Andrade, R. G. Memory and the assessment of behavior. In H. M. Blalock (Ed.), *Measurement in the social sciences: Theories and strategies.* Chicago: Aldine, 1973.

Denzin, N. K. Symbolic interactionism and ethnomethodology: A proposed synthesis. *American Sociological Review*, 1969, *34*, 922-934.

Dornbusch, S. M., Hastorf, A. H., Richardson, S. A., Muzzy, R. E., & Vreeland, R. S. The perceiver and the perceived: Their relative influence on the categories of interpersonal perception. *Journal of Personality and Social Psychology*, 1965, *1*, 434-440.

Dubin, R., & Dubin, E. R. Children's social perception: A review of research. *Child Development*, 1965, *36*, 809-838.

Ervin-Tripp, S. M. Sociolinguistics. In L. Berkowitz (Ed.), *Advances in experimental social psychology* (Vol. 4). New York: Academic Press, 1969.

Faris, R. E. *Chicago sociology, 1920-1932.* San Francisco: Chandler, 1967.

Festinger, L. A theory of social comparison processes. *Human Relations*, 1954, *7*, 117-140.

Fillenbaum, S., & Rapoport, A. *Structures in the subjective lexicon.* New York: Academic Press, 1971.

Freud, S. *Psychopathology of everyday life.* In A. A. Brill (Ed.), *The basic writings of Sigmund Freud,* New York: Modern Library, 1938.

Friendly, M. L., & Glucksberg, S. On the description of subcultural lexicons: A multidimensional approach. *Journal of Personality and Social Psychology*, 1970, *14*, 55-65.

Goffman, E. *The presentation of self in everyday life.* New York: Doubleday, 1959.

Goffman, E. *Asylums.* New York: Doubleday Anchor, 1961.

Goffman, E. *Stigma: Notes on the management of spoiled identity.* Englewood Cliffs, N.J.: Prentice-Hall, 1963. (a)

Goffman, E. *Behavior in public places.* New York: The Free Press, 1963. (b)

Goffman, E. *Interaction ritual: Essays on face-to-face behavior.* Garden City, New York: Doubleday Anchor, 1967.

Goffman, E. *Strategic interaction.* Philadelphia: University of Pennsylvania Press, 1969.

Goffman, E. *Relations in public.* New York: Harper-Colophon, 1971.

Goffman, E. *Frame analysis: An essay on the organization of experience.* Cambridge, Mass.: Harvard University Press, 1974.

Gollin, E. S. Organizational characteristics of social judgment: A developmental investigation. *Journal of Personality,* 1958, *26,* 139-154.

Gollin, E. S. Cognitive dispositions and the formation of impressions of personality. In J. G. Peatman & E. L. Hartley (Eds.), *Festschrift for Gardner Murphy.* New York: Harper, 1960.

Gouldner, A. W. The sociologist as partisan: Sociology and welfare state. *American Sociologist,* 1968, *3,* 103-116.

Hartley, E. L., Rosenbaum, M., & Schwartz, S. Children's use of ethnic frames of reference. *Journal of Psychology,* 1948, *26,* 367-386.

Hastorf, A. H., Richardson, S. A., & Dornbusch, S. M. The problem of relevance in the study of person perception. In R. Tagiuri & L. Petrullo (Eds.), *Person perception and interpersonal behavior.* Stanford: Stanford University Press, 1958.

Hollander, E. P. Conformity, status, and idiosyncrasy credit. *Psychological Review,* 1958, *65,* 117-127.

Holsti, O. R. *Content analysis for the social sciences and humanities.* Reading, Mass.: Addison-Wesley, 1969.

Jones, R., & Cooper, J. Mediation of experimenter effects. *Journal of Personality and Social Psychology,* 1971, *20,* 70-74.

Jones, R. A., Sensenig, J., & Ashmore, R. D. *Systems of values and their multidimensional representation.* Unpublished manuscript, University of Kentucky, 1974.

Kelley, H. H. The warm-cold variable in first impressions of persons. *Journal of Personality,* 1950, *18,* 431-439.

Kelly, G. A. *The psychology of personal constructs.* New York: Norton, 1955.

Kelly, G. A. *A theory of personality: The psychology of personal constructs.* New York: Norton, 1963.

Kleck, R., Ono, H., & Hastorf, A. The effects of physical deviance upon face-to-face interaction. *Human Relations,* 1966, *19,* 425-436.

Kruskal, J. B. Multidimensional scaling by optimizing goodness of fit to a nonmetric hypothesis. *Psychometrika,* 1964, *29,* 1-28. (a)

Kruskal, J. B. Nonmetric multidimensional scaling: A numerical method. *Psychometrika,* 1964, *29,* 115-130. (b)

Kuhn, M. H. Major trends in symbolic interaction theory in the past 25 years. *Sociological Quarterly,* 1964, *5,* 61-84.

Kuhn, M. H., & McPartland, T. S. An empirical investigation of self attitudes. *American Sociological Review,* 1954, *19,* 68-76.

Lemert, E. M. *Social pathology.* New York: McGraw-Hill, 1951.

Lemert, E. M. *Human deviance, social problems and social control.* Englewood Cliffs, N.J.: Prentice-Hall, 1967.

Lichtman, R. Symbolic interactionism and social reality: Some marxist queries. *Berkeley Journal of Sociology*, 1970, *15*, 75-94.

Lindesmith, A. R., & Strauss, A. L. *Social psychology* (3rd ed.). New York: Holt, Rinehart, and Winston, 1968.

MacLeod, R. B. The phenomenological approach to social psychology. *Psychological Review*, 1947, *54*, 193-210.

Manis, J. G., & Meltzer, B. N. (Eds.). *Symbolic interaction*. Boston: Allyn and Bacon, 1967.

Martindale, D. *The nature and types of sociological theory*. Boston: Houghton MIfflin Company, 1960.

Mead, G. H. *Mind, self, and society*. Chicago: University of Chicago Press, 1934.

Meltzer, B., & Petras, J. The Chicago and Iowa schools of symbolic interactionism. In T. Shibutani (Ed.), *Human nature and collective behavior*. Englewood Cliffs: Prentice-Hall, 1970, p. 3-17.

Mullins, N. C. *Theory and theory groups in contemporary American sociology*. New York: Harper and Row, 1973.

Murphy, G. *Personality: A biosocial approach to origins and structure*. New York: Harper, 1947.

Olshan, K. The multidimensional structure of person perception in children. Unpublished doctoral dissertation, Rutgers University, 1970.

Peabody, D. Trait inferences: Evaluative and descriptive aspects. *Journal of Personality and Social Psychology Monograph*, 1967, *7* (4, Whole No. 644).

Pearsall, M. Participant observation as role and method in behavioral research. In W. J. Filstead (Ed.), *Qualitative methodology: Firsthand involvement with the social world*. Chicago: Markham, 1970.

Peevers, B., & Secord, P. F. Developmental changes in attribution of descriptive concepts to persons. *Journal of Personality and Social Psychology*, 1973, *27*, 120-128.

Petras, J. W., & Meltzer, B. Theoretical and ideological variations in contemporary interactionism. *Catalyst*, 1973, *7*, 1-8.

Rappoport, L., & Fritzler, D. Developmental response to quantity changes in artificial social objects. *Child Development*, 1969, *40*, 1145-1154.

Reynolds, L. T., & Meltzer, B. N. The origins of divergent methodological stances in symbolic interactionism. *Sociological Quarterly*, 1973, *14*, 189-199.

Reynolds, J. M., & Reynolds, L. T. Interactionism, complicity and the astructural bias. *Catalyst*, 1973, *7*, 76-85.

Rockway, A. Cognitive factors in adolescent person perception development. Unpublished manuscript, University of Miami, 1969.

Rosenberg, P. Review of *Frame Analysis by Erving Goffman. The New York Times Book Review*, February 16, 1975, 21-26.

Rosenberg, S., & Cohen, B. D. Referential processes of speakers and listeners. *Psychological Review*, 1966, *73*, 208-231.

Rosenberg, S., & Sedlak, A. Structural representations of implicit personality theory. In L. Berkowitz (Ed.), *Advances in experimental social psychology* (Vol. 6). New York: Academic Press, 1972.

Rosenhan, D. L. On being sane in insane places. *Science*, 1973, *178*, 250-258.

Rosenthal, R. *Experimenter effects in behavioral research*. New York: Appleton-Century, 1966.

Rosenthal, R. On the social psychology of the self-fulfilling prophecy: Further evidence for Pygmalion effects and their mediating mechanisms. *Module 53*. New York: MSS Modulor Publications, 1973.

Rosenthal, R., & Jacobson, L. *Pygmalion in the classroom.* New York: Holt, Rinehart, and Winston, 1968.

Sarbin, T. R. Role theory. In G. Lindzey (Ed.), *Handbook of social psychology* (Vol. 1). Reading, Mass.: Addison-Wesley, 1954.

Schachter, S. The interaction of cognitive and physiological determinants of emotional state. In L. Berkowitz (Ed.), *Advances in experimental social psychology* (Vol. 1). New York: Academic Press, 1964.

Scheff, T. J. *Being mentally ill.* Chicago: Aldine, 1966.

Schneider, L. (Ed.) *The scottish moralists: On human nature and society.* Chicago: The University of Chicago Press, 1967.

Schur, E. M. *Labeling deviant behavior.* New York: Harper & Row, 1971.

Shepard, R. N. Extracting latent structure from behavioral data. *Proceedings of the symposium on digital computing.* Holmdel: Bell Telephone Labs, 1964.

Shepard, R. N. Introduction. In R. N. Shepard, A. K. Romney & S. B. Nerlove (Eds.), *Multidimensional scaling: Theory and applications in the behavioral sciences* (Vol. 1). New York: Seminar Press, 1972.

Signell, K. Cognitive complexity in person perception and nation perception: A developmental approach. *Journal of Personality, 1966, 34,* 517-537.

Stone, G. P., & Farberman, H. A. (Eds.). *Social psychology through symbolic interaction.* Waltham, Mass.: Ginn-Blaisdell, 1970.

Stone, P. J., Dunphy, D. C., Smith, M. S., & Ogilvie, D. M. *The general inquirer: A computer approach to content analysis.* Cambridge, Mass.: The M.I.T. Press, 1966.

Strauss, A. (Ed.). *George Herbert Mead: On social psychology.* Chicago: The University of Chicago Press, 1964.

Szasz, T. *The myth of mental illness.* New York: Dell, 1961.

Tagiuri, R. Introduction. In R. Tagiuri & L. Petrullo (Eds.), *Person perception and interpersonal behavior.* Stanford, Calif.: Stanford University Press, 1958.

Thomas, W. I., & Thomas, D. S. *The child in America.* New York: Knopf, 1928.

Trow, M. Comment on participant observation and interviewing: A comparison. In W. J. Filstead (Ed.), *Qualitative methodology: Firsthand involvement with the social world.* Chicago: Markham, 1970.

Turk, A. T. *Criminality and legal order.* Chicago: Rand McNally, 1969.

Turner, J. H. *The structure of sociological theory.* Homewood, Illinois: Dorsey, 1974.

Vaughan, T. R., & Reynolds, L. T. The sociology of symbolic interactionism. *American Sociologist, 1968, 3,* 208-214.

Watzlawick, P., Beavin, J. H., & Jackson, D. C. *Pragmatics of human communication.* New York: Norton, 1967.

Werner, H. Process and achievement: A basic problem of education and developmental psychology. *Harvard Education Review, 1937, 7,* 353-368.

Werner, H. *Comparative psychology of mental development.* Chicago: Follett Press, 1948.

Yarrow, M., & Campbell, J. Person perception in children. *Merrill-Palmer Quarterly of Behavior and Development, 1963, 9,* 57-73.

Zeitlin, I. M. *Ideology and the development of sociological theory.* Englewood Cliffs, N.J.: Prentice-Hall, 1968.

Zeitlin, I. M. *Rethinking sociology: A critique of contemporary theory.* New York: Appleton-Century-Crofts, 1973.

3

Social Psychology From a
Social-Developmental Perspective

David R. Shaffer

University of Georgia

INTRODUCTION

The assimilation of the child into the prevailing sociocultural milieu is a significant and remarkable process. The neonatal human is an undifferentiated organism who is generally perceived as cute, cuddly, and lovable by his parents, but is essentially an unknowing, dependent, demanding, and often unreasonable little creature. He is not equipped at birth with a set of social or cultural attitudes. He possesses no interpersonal skills. He speaks no language. He evidences no sense of morality, sex-role identity, achievement, competence, etc. It is easy to understand how John Locke (1690) could describe the infant as tabula rasa — a blank slate, who is therefore receptive to any and all kinds of learning.

Irvin Child (1954) has noted that, despite the wide range of experiences and the large number of behavioral possibilities open to the young child, he/she is "led to develop actual behavior which is confined within a much narrower range — the range of what is customary and acceptable according to the standards of his group" (p. 655). In one setting the child will speak English, in another Chinese; in one setting he will learn that his governors are elected, in another he will expect leaders to inherit their role; in one setting he will eat pork, in another he will turn away in disgust; in one setting he will greet friends with a handshake, in another with a bodily embrace; in one setting he will prefer rock music, in another country music; in one setting he will defy his parents, in another he will be silent and obedient to parental commands. Clearly, the child develops in a manner and direction prescribed by his culture, his community, and his family.

The process through which a child acquires the behaviors, beliefs, standards, and values deemed significant and appropriate by his social grouping is called socialization. The socialization of children serves numerous functions. First, socialization serves to regulate behavior. Laws against rape, theft, murder, and other crimes do not prevent their occurrence on a large scale. Prevention of antisocial acts and the resulting sense of social control is largely a result of the standards of morality — right and wrong — that the child acquires as a result of his interactions with parents, siblings, peers, teachers, and other members of his society. Second, socialization helps to insure personal growth and development by providing the child with the opportunity to acquire the knowledge, skills, motives, and aspirations that will enable him to function effectively within his community. Finally, socialization serves to perpetuate the social order, as socialized children become socialized adults who, in their role as parents, will impart their social knowledge to their own offspring.

The significance of socialization for all human beings makes its investigation a logical point of convergence for scientists interested in the study of man. Social scientists of different persuasions have focused their attention on slightly differing aspects of the socialization process. Sociologists have concerned themselves with the similarities evidenced among children in their adjustment to the group and its institutions. The sociological perspective is nicely illustrated by Elkin (1960), who notes that

> ... although it is true that no two individuals are alike, and that each person has a singular heredity, distinctive experiences, and a unique personality development, socialization focuses not on such individualizing patterns and processes but on similarities and those aspects of development which concern the learning of, and adaptation to, the culture and society (p. 5).

Anthropologists are also interested in the products or common outcomes of socialization, but they have focused their attention upon variations in the content of socialization across cultures and the effects of these cultural variations upon social-personality development. Students of social-personality development will long be indebted to the significant anthropological research of investigators such as Mead (1939, 1949), Sapir, (1949), Whiting (1961), and Whiting and Child (1953), who have demonstrated that the content of socialization, that is, what the child acquires, depends upon the structure of his social grouping and the personalities therein.

Psychological explorations of social and personality development have focused upon the processes as well as the products of socialization. A psychological perspective on socialization envisions each person as the product of his social experience which, of course, varies both within and across cultures and social groupings. Similarities among the socialized products of a particular group are anticipated to the extent that members of that group share common perceptions of what constitutes preferred and/or acceptable behavior, beliefs, motives, etc. Yet psychologists have consistently emphasized that each individual encounters a unique social milieu in the course of development and, therefore, should not be expected to emerge as a carbon copy of his or her parents, siblings, or the child next door. Individual personalities are an integral component of a psychological model of socialization and are treated as something other than anomalies in the socialization process.

The underpinnings of socialization, that is, the process or mechanisms by which a child acquires socially approved beliefs, behaviors, and motives, are of central interest to psychologists concerned with social and personality development. Psychologists have generally argued that all children assimilate their social experience in a similar fashion, despite the fact that the content of their social experience varies considerably across families, communities, and cultures. For example, French children and English children are thought to acquire language through the same processes even though their native tongues differ considerably in content. This chapter will follow a psychological perspective on social and personality development, emphasizing the common processes that are thought to underlie the child's acquisition of a social identity.

Three theoretical perspectives on social development are examined in the pages that follow: the psychoanalytic perspective, the social learning perspective, and the cognitive-developmental perspective. Each of these theories advances its own constructs and terminology. Each has its own range and focus of convenience. The psychoanalytic perspective originates from Sigmund Freud's clinical studies of emotionally disturbed adults. Freud was convinced that the course of early emotional development laid the foundations of the adult personality. His emphasis on emotional development has led proponents of a psychoanalytic perspective to consider parental child rearing practices and their effects upon the quality of the parent-child relationship as the underpinnings of social-personality development.

Advocates of a social learning perspective emphasize that, to an overwhelming extent, human behavior is learned. Socializing agents are said to steer the child toward "acceptable" patterns of behavior by reinforcing him/her for approved behaviors and by punishing the child and/or by withholding reinforcement should he/she emit undesirable behaviors. The more radical proponents of a social learning perspective (Bijou & Baer, 1961; Gewirtz, 1969) consider most organismic variables (emotions, sentiments, cognitions, etc.) to be excess theoretical baggage that are unnecessary to predict or explain the socialization process. Of central importance to the radical behaviorists is a functional analysis of the relationships between discrete response and stimulus events. The only organismic variables considered important in determining the child's response to various social stimuli are his past reinforcement history and his level of satiation on the reinforcer that is offered in an attempt to influence his behavior.

The cognitive-developmental perspective on socialization originates from the extensive efforts of Jean Piaget (e.g., 1932, 1950), a theorist who was primarily concerned with the course of intellectual development rather than the nature of socialization. The development of cognition is said to involve much more than a gradual acquisition of knowledge. Piaget views intellectual development as a recurring epigenesis in which new cognitive structures appear as transformations of their predecessors. Kohlberg (1966, 1969) argues that social and personality development is likewise an epigenetic phenomenon. The assumption is that the child's existing cognitive structures mediate his social experience and are therefore important in determining what the child can or will attend to and assimilate as a result of his interactions with others.

It will become apparent that none of the three theories to be reviewed presents a totally adequate account of social and personality development. As we shall see, each theory has its definite strengths and weaknesses. By and large, there are relatively few issues on which the three theories confront each other directly (although instances of confrontation are stressed in the chapter). Thus, the theories are largely concerned with nonoverlapping aspects of development rather than with the generation of competing explanations of the same phenomena.

The reader might suppose that a synthesis of the psychoanalytic, social learning, and cognitive-developmental perspectives would provide some promise of a comprehensive theory of social and personality development. The author shares this feeling, although to date, controversy among the proponents of these three theories has outweighted any sentiment for integration. The problems encountered by the would-be integrative theorist are formidable. First, he or she would have to establish some common, neutral language so that the processes, mechanisms, and events described by theories stressing emotions (psychoanalysis), learning (social learning theory), and cognition (cognitive-developmental theory) might reasonably be compared and then assimilated into an integrative framework. Second, and seemingly of major importance, the integrative theorist must effect a reconciliation of certain philosophical differences among proponents of the three approaches regarding the nature of man and his development. These philosophical differences are examined in the following section.

Philosophical Perspectives on Social and Personality Development

In addition to their focus upon different aspects of the socialization process, theories of social and personality development differ on three very basic philosophical issues:

1. The question of whether man should be viewed as inherently good or inherently bad;
2. the question of whether man should be considered an active or a passive agent in his socialization; and
3. the question of whether the course of human development should be considered continuous or discontinuous, additive or epigenetic.

Early Perspectives

History has witnessed the emergence of three philosophical perspectives on socialization: the doctrine of original sin, the doctrine of tabula rasa, and the doctrine of innate purity. These differing perspectives result from the diverse positions taken by early philosophers on the questions of man's inherent nature and man's role in determining the course of his social development. The character of each of these three philosophical perspectives requires further explication, as each serves as the philosophical underpinning of a major theory of social and personality development.

Perhaps the best known proponent of the doctrine of original sin is the seventeenth-century British philosopher, Thomas Hobbes. In his classic work, *Leviathan*, Hobbes (1651) portrays humanity in an extremely uncomplimentary fashion by advancing the thesis that man's basic striving is ego enhancement, a goal most easily accomplished by the attainment of power and mastery over others. Since a social order is unthinkable in the absence of checks on man's pre-programmed, insatiable egoism, children were said to have imposed upon them a social contract that bought them protection from other power-hungry persons, while rechanneling their own egoism into socially acceptable outlets. (For example, they learn to coexist peacefully with their fellow man while yielding to, and enhancing, the common power of the group, the state, etc.). Clearly, Hobbes viewed children as inherently negative creatures who are passively molded into social entities by the more powerful elements of society.

The tabula rasa perspective on socialization advanced by Hobbes's contemporary, John Locke, assumes that the child is neither inherently good nor inherently bad but, rather, a remarkably malleable organism who is molded into socially desirable or socially undesirable patterns of behavior by his experiences and rewards and punishments provided by the environment. Locke believed that if man had one most basic inherent quality, it was rationality: "The great principle and foundation of all Virtue and Worth is placed in this; that a man is able to deny himself his own desires, cross his own inclinations, and purely follow what reason directs as best, although the appetite lean the other way" (Locke, as cited in Kessen, 1965, p. 59). The tabula rasa approach suggests that the purpose of socialization is impulse control; the denial of satisfaction when our desires are unreasonable.[1] To achieve this worthy and necessary goal, Locke advised parents to begin instructing their children in self-denial "from their very cradles."

Both the original sin and the tabula rasa philosophies view socialization as the habit training of a passive child that is undertaken primarily to prevent the expression of socially undesirable behavior. Eighteenth-century philosophers Jean Jacques Rousseau and Immanuel Kant have advanced a radically different perspective on socialization known as the doctrine of innate purity. Both men have testified to man's inherent goodness by arguing that children possess an innate morality that, Rousseau believed, is often misdirected by the demands and experiences imposed upon children by society. In addition, both men believed the

---

[1] These impulses or desires are biological needs or learned motives that are totally self-serving and distasteful or annoying to others if expressed. Thus, the tabula rasa perspective does not deny that man may have innate drives; it simply fails to characterize these drives with an evaluative label.

child to be *actively* involved in determining the course of his development. Kant attributed to the child a set of innate perceptual-logical structures through which he actively created, ordered, interpreted, and responded to impressions received through the senses. Rousseau also argued that the child actively engages his world, fitting

> ... his abilities to the world in play and in the solving of problems, not as a passive recipient of the tutor's instruction ... but as a busy, testing, motivated, explorer. Knowledge is not an intervention of adults poured into willing or unwilling vessels; it is a joint construction of the child in nature and the natural world ... The active searching child, setting his own problems, stands in contrast to the receptive one, even the one equipped with curiosity, on whom society fixes its stamp (Rousseau, as cited in Kessen, 1965, p. 75).

Thus, the picture of social development emanating from a doctrine of innate purity is that of a "noble savage" who actively engages his environment and, in the process, develops in a healthy direction if not unduly thwarted by the demands and restrictions of society.

These three early perspectives on socialization might be expected to promote strikingly different theories of social and personality development, each with its own unique emphasis. This has, indeed, been the case as will become apparent upon an examination of the philosophical underpinnings of psychonalytic, social learning, and cognitive-developmental theories.

The Philosophy of Psychoanalysis

The doctrine of original sin would seem to provide the philosophical bedrock of Freud's original version of psychoanalytic theory. In the Hobbesian tradition, Freud popularized the view of man as a "seething cauldron" who is relentlessly pursued by the necessity of gratifying innate sexual and aggressive urges (instincts). According to Freud, the function of socialization is to prevent the child from expressing primitive, selfish, and destructive urges by displacing his instinctual energies away from their natural outlets into socially acceptable channels. Man is viewed as a passive agent in the sense that his developmental course and outcome depend largely upon the emotional climate produced by parents in their attempts at child rearing.

More recent extensions of the psychoanalytic framework (Erikson, 1950, 1963, 1972; Hartmann, 1958; Hartmann, Kris, & Lowenstein, 1949) have shifted the philosophical perspective of psychoanalysis in the direction advocated by the innate purists. The neoanalytic ego psychologists advance the notion that man is a curious, manipulating, exploring animal whose lifelong attempts at adapting to and mastering his environment are not easily explained as some "displacement" or other manifestation of libidinal or aggressive drives. Hartmann describes inborn ego energies, independent of those originating from primitive sexual or aggressive instincts, that provide the impetus for the child's adaptation to his environment. In his description of psychosocial development,

Erikson (1950, 1959, 1963, 1972) stresses the creative and adaptive abilities of the child mediated by the ego. Erikson views ego development as a lengthy and arduous series of psychosocial crises, each of which provides experiences that are conducive to personal growth. Thus, the ego psychologists view the child as the product of his active interaction with the environment. They clearly stress the positive and adaptive aspects of man's nature rather than viewing man as a slave to primitive and undesirable instinctual urges.

The Philosophy of Social Learning Theory

Descended from the Lockean tabula rasa perspective on socialization are a number of theoretical approaches known collectively as social learning theory. While the insights of better than a dozen theorists are labeled as social learning theories, it was John B. Watson who provided the seminal influence in this regard. Watson viewed the neonate as an undifferentiated but malleable behavior potential who developed in accordance with the kinds of learning experiences provided by the environment. Watson's strong advocacy that learning principles rather than organismic characteristics (genetic codes, instincts, etc.) are the key processes in social and personality development is nicely illustrated by the following statement.

> Give me a dozen healthy infants, well formed, and my own specified world to bring them up in, and I'll guarantee to take any one at random and train him to become any type of specialist I might select — doctor, lawyer, merchant, chief, and yes, even beggar man and thief, regardless of his talents, peculiarities, tendencies, abilities, vocations, and race of his ancestors" (Watson, as cited in Allport, 1937, p. 103).

Contemporary social learning theories can be grouped into three principal categories: The neo-Hullian approach (Dollard & Miller, 1950; Mowrer, 1950; Nowlis, 1952; Scars, 1944, 1951a; Sears, Maccoby, & Levin, 1957; Sears, Whiting, Nowlis, & Sears, 1953); the Skinnerian approach (Bijou & Baer, 1961; Gewirtz, 1969; Krasner & Ullmann, 1965; Ullmann & Krasner, 1965); and the Bandurian approach (Bandura, 1962, 1965, 1969, 1971; Bandura & Walters, 1959, 1963; Walters & Brown, 1964; Walters & Parke, 1964). The neo-Hullian and Skinnerian approaches have retained a tabula rasa perspective, wherein man is viewed as a passive recipient of environmental influence. The Bandurians have criticized these traditional behavioristic models for their failure to recognize that children largely determine the course of their social development. That is, children are viewed as active, thinking organisms capable of self-instruction, self-reinforcement, and many other forms of internal regulation and control of their behavior. While the neo-Hullians and Skinnerians describe one's behavioral development as the product of his environment and its affective consequences, the Bandurians argue that there exists a reciprocal interaction between behavioral and environmental events. The environment is not viewed as a fixed, omnipotent entity that determines behavior. Rather, the child's behavior is also assumed to affect his environment, and the resulting environment, in turn affects his behavior. Thus, the Bandurians are set apart from neo-Hullian and Skinnerian theorists by their claim that the child is an active agent who, in part, determines the character of his own socializing environment.

The Philosophy of the Cognitive-Developmentalists

The model of man advanced by cognitive-developmental theorists (Kohlberg, 1963, 1966, 1969; Piaget, 1932, 1950, 1951, 1952b, 1954, 1960; Werner, 1957) comes closest among contemporary perspectives on socialization to the philosophy of the innate purists. While they do not attribute innate goodness or an innate moral sense to man, Piaget, Kohlberg, and Werner all stress the positive and adaptive aspects of development, while rejecting the notions that man is primarily motivated by irrational or unconscious forces and/or is totally under the control of external stimuli. Piaget argues that man is an active biological entity who comes equipped with a need to adapt to (cope with) his environment. Development is conceptualized as a continual process of adaptation, with the developing child demonstrating and fulfilling his increasing adaptive potential as his cognitive construction of the world becomes increasingly differentiated.

The cognitive-developmentalists describe adaptation as the product of the *interaction* between the child's evolving cognitive structures and the environment. Adaptation proceeds toward equilibrium, that is, toward a greater balance or reciprocity between the child's action on his (perceived) environment and the actions of the environment upon the child. The environment provides the impetus for the reorganization of cognitive structures. However, this reorganization is actively undertaken by the child when he is prepared for this undertaking, and is not "shaped" by external agents. As adaptation proceeds through cognitive reorganization, the child's conceptions of the self, the environment, and their interrelationship are also reorganized. Thus, cognitive development and social-personality development represent a fundamental unity. The child's interpretation of and/or response to parental teachings and demands, peer pressures, social models, and other social events should clearly depend upon his cognitive constructions of these events. In a word, man does not mirror experience, he creates it, and in the process he changes himself (Langer, 1969).

The Continuity-Discontinuity Controversy

Theories of social and personality development have differed rather dramatically on the issue of whether development is best described as (a) a continuous or additive process without sudden or sharp behavioral reorganization; or (b) a step-wise progression through an orderly sequence of stages, each of which is characterized by a distinctive behavioral structure. It would seem that the layman, for whatever reason, favors the stage approach as evidenced by his willingness to speak of periods such as the "toddler stage," the "four-year-old stage," the "obstinate stage," the "adolescent stage," the "change of life," etc. These lay characterizations are unsatisfactory to the developmental-stage theorist, for they possess only descriptive rather than explanatory significance. That is, the layman's stages may adequately describe a set of of observations without offering any insight as to the etiology of the phenomena they describe.

The term stage, as used in a developmental-stage theory, ranks among the most misunderstood concepts in psychology. Those who advocate an epigenetic perspective on human development define a stage in terms of a complicated set of characteristics, behaviors, motives, or cognitions that occur together and, thus, can be conveniently grouped. In order to possess any explanatory significance, a developmental-stage theory must contain two essential features. First, the theory must transcend the descriptive by postulating some rationale for binding the elements of a stage together into an organized whole. Second, the theory should provide a set of transition rules outlining the processes by which the developing child moves on from one stage to another.

We shall discuss two theoretical approaches — psychoanalytic theory and cognitive-developmental theory — that clearly qualify as stage theories. Both of these theoretical systems include a series of complex, unified behavioral patterns that represent the components of an orderly sequence of development. In Piagetian cognitive-developmental theory, for example, the child's intellectual development is said to progress through a systematic and invariant set of stages. Each stage is defined by the specific cognitive characteristics displayed by the child, and every successive stage in the sequence represents a reorganization of previous stages into an organized whole that is qualitatively different from its predecessor. Freudian psychoanalytic theory is similar to cognitive-developmental theory in its description of a fixed sequence of (psychosexual) stages, each of which is characterized by complex motives, behaviors, and critical emotional developments that represent a unified whole with distinctive influences upon the developing personality.

Social learning theorists have criticized stage theories on a number of grounds. First, they argue that stage theories place far too much emphasis upon variation within the individual from stage to stage and upon the similarity among individuals at similar stages of development, while completely ignoring the vast behavioral differences among individuals resulting from biogenetic, socioeconomic, and cultural influences. Their argument is that children at any single age (or stage) differ greatly among themselves in the reinforcement histories and the social models they have encountered and, therefore, should differ considerably in their overt patterns of behavior. Second, the social-learning camp argues (with some degree of justification) that the transition rules of stage progression are not explicit in contemporary stage theories. Bandura (1971), Bandura and Walters (1963), and Gewirtz (1969) view the learning process as qualitatively equivalent at every point along the developmental continuum. Their belief in the continuity of development remains unshaken by a rather extensive body of research literature (e.g., Kendler, 1963; Kendler & Kendler, 1962; Wallach, 1963; White, 1963,

1965) suggesting that qualitative changes in the learning process do occur at various points throughout the course of childhood. Their counterargument is that learning only *appears* to be a discontinuous process; experimenters who compare subjects of different ages do not detect the gradual changes that are continuously occurring. As a consequence, they mistakenly assume that dramatic changes in behavior over an interval of six months to a year constitute evidence of discontinuous development.[2]

Any attempt by those advocating one side of the continuity-discontinuity issue to impose their views on those favoring the opposing side seems unwise for one very compelling reason: continuity theorists and discontinuity theorists emphasize nonoverlapping aspects of development. As aptly noted by Zigler and Child (1973), social learning theorists concern themselves with social behaviors observable at many developmental levels, and varying widely among individuals at each level, whereas stage theorists focus upon developmental commonalities that characterize narrowly delimited periods of the life cycle. It is perhaps a bit premature to choose between continuity and discontinuity at this point in time. We need not assume that *all* aspects or systems of development are continuous or discontinuous. In fact, it is possible that within the limited and generally nonoverlapping range and foci of convenience of their models, both the social learning theorists and the stage theorists are correct in their views on the continuity-discontinuity issue. This prospect highlights the need for a conceptual integration of these approaches before a comprehensive theory of social and personality development is to be realized.

Table 3.1 summarizes the philosophical underpinnings of the theories selected for coverage in the following sections of the chapter.

PSYCHOANALYTIC THEORY

Sigmund Freud is the founder of psychoanalysis, a term that refers simultaneously to (a) a method of behavioral investigation; (b) a set of therapeutic procedures; and (c) a theory of social and personality development. In this section, we shall be concerned with the theoretical aspects of psychoanalysis as originally outlined by Freud, and as reformulated by one of Freud's disciples, Erik Erikson.

Origins of Psychoanalytic Theory

As Freud was a trained neurologist, it is perhaps not surprising that he specialized in the treatment of nervous disorders. This particular branch of medicine was

---

[2]This counterargument would seem to be contradicted by research (e.g., Kendler, 1963; Smedslund, 1961; Turiel, 1966) demonstrating that attempts to teach children at one stage of functioning to operate at a level characteristic of a higher stage are generally unsuccessful.

TABLE 3.1

Summary of the Philosophical Perspectives of Representative
Theories of Social and Personality Development

Theoretical system	Philosophical dimensions						
	Active-passive man		Good-bad man			Continuity-discontinuity of development	
	Active	Passive	Good	Bad	Tabula rasa	Continuous	Discontinuous
Psychoanalysis							
Freud		x		x			x
Erikson and the Neo-Freudian Ego Psychologists	x		?				x
Social learning theory							
Neo-Hullians		x			x	x	
Skinnerians		x			x	x	
Bandurians[a]	x	x			x	x	
Cognitive-developmental theory							
Piaget, Kohlberg and Werner	x		?				x

[a]Bandura's position on the active-passive dimension is best described as follows: man is viewed as a product of an environment that he has a hand in creating.

not refined in the late nineteenth century when Freud began his practice. There was simply very little that could be done for emotionally disturbed persons. One technique that was receiving much attention as a treatment for hysteria was the hypnotic therapy of Jean Charcot. Although Freud had spent some time under Charcot's tutelage and was generally enthused about the use of hypnosis for treating nervous disorders, the real impetus for his eventual development of psychoanalysis derived from the work of a friend and colleague, Dr. Josef Breuer. Breuer, who initially used hypnosis to treat hysterical symptoms, discovered that if patients could be encouraged to discuss the origin of their symptoms, the symptoms would often disappear. Intrigued by this phenomenon, Breuer encouraged patients to expound upon their disorders in a technique he called the talking cure.

Freud and Breuer collaborated for a period of three years, during which they attempted to perfect a therapy consisting of a combination of hypnosis and the talking cure. However, Freud eventually abandoned hypnosis altogether in favor of other methods which allowed him to probe the minds of his patients to reveal the underlying causes of their pathologies. On the basis of his analyses of himself and of a number of his patients, Freud developed the rudiments of his psychoanalytic theory of personality.

The Methods of Psychoanalysis

Psychoanalytic theory is not the product of an experimental science. It is not a deductive theory that begins with well defined concepts and postulates from which hypotheses are derived and tested. Indeed, Freud did not perform any well-controlled experiments. He did not quantify his data, analyze them for statistical significance, or even describe them with so much as a table. Nor did Freud ever employ objective diagnostic instruments to collect the data from which he fashioned his theories. Rather, Freud's analytic theory of social and personality development derives from data consisting primarily of the verbalizations, fantasies, and actions of his mentally disturbed patients. Freud's principal methods of data collection were his free association technique and his method of dream analysis. Recall that Breuer's talking cure required patients to discuss the origins of their nervous symptoms in the hope that the symptoms would disappear. The free association technique extends far beyond the scope of the talking cure by requiring patients to discuss anything that comes to mind without hesitation, restraint, or any attempt to organize the utterance in a logical, coherent fashion. The therapist's role is to listen to the patient without intervening himself, except to ask proding or directing questions should the patient's narration begin to wane. Freud discovered that patients undergoing free association would often start with their current problems and work backwards, recalling many of the significant events of their lives, eventually concluding with a discourse about rather vivid memories of early childhood experiences. Freud further noted that each statement in the patient's reconstruction of his life was related in a meaningful way to its predecessor. Thus, the patient's life history as reflected in his own words provided Freud with the data he needed to formulate his theory of personality development.

Dream analysis is a corollary of the free association technique. Many of Freud's patients would spontaneously mention their dreams during therapy, and Freud would encourage them to verbalize their associations to these dreams. Freud's careful analyses of the content of his own dreams and those of his patients led him to infer that dreams represent the pure, unbridled "wishful thinking" of the most primitive of thought processes, and as such, were a particularly rich source of information about the development of the personality.

Freud anticipated many of the difficulties he would encounter in convincing the scientific community that his psychoanalytic methods could provide substantiating evidence for his theories. In his defense, it must be noted that Freud cautioned other psychoanalysts to be objective and analyze their clinical data for internal consistency prior to making any inferences about the relationship of data to theory. Specifically, Freud'a method required that "inferences made from one part of the material [be] checked against evidence appearing in other parts, so that the final conclusions drawn from a case were based upon an interlocking network of facts and inferences" (Hall and Lindsey, 1957, p. 56). Psychoanalysts remind us that unlike psychological experiments, where a subject is observed for an hour or less, in clinical situations, the patient is often observed many hours a week for as long as two to three years. Thus, the analytic method allows the therapist the rather unique opportunity to test his hypotheses repeatedly before arriving at a final conclusion. For this reason, psychoanalytic theorists consider data obtained by other methods as auxiliary evidence that cannot, in itself, either prove or refute conclusions drawn from the comprehensive therapeutic method.

The Organizational Dynamics of the Personality

Freud's model of man is psychodynamic in character. The human organism is viewed as a complex energy system that derives energy from food and expends this energy in the service of physiological and psychological life functions. Energy derived from food is said to take many forms — mechanical, chemical, electrical, etc. — that are capable of being transformed from one form into another. The energy that performs the work of the personality (thinking, perceiving, remembering, etc.) is called psychic energy.

Freud (1915, 1923, 1930) assumed that the infant was born with little more than a number of programmed reflexes and instinctual appetites. Freud defined an instinct as a mechanism that imparts direction to psychological processes. The hunger instinct, for example, directs the psychological processes of perceiving, remembering, and thinking about food and/or food getting. Thus, an instinct functions like a river bed, directing the flow of psychic energy along a particular cognitive and/or behavioral course.

Every instinct is characterized by its source, impetus, aim, and object. The source of an instinct is some somatic or physiological need that releases bodily energy to excite the instinct. The impetus of an instinct refers to its strength or excitatory potential. The aim of an instinct is the removal of the bodily need state that activated it in the first place. The object is that which the instinct seeks in accomplishing its aim (for example, eating food is the object of the hunger instinct; copulation is the object of the sex instinct).

Freud posited two major classes of instincts that are presumably operative throughout the life cycle: Eros, the life (self-preservative) instincts, and Thanatos. the death (self-destructive or aggressive) instincts. Eros is a life-giving, constructive set of forces. Its energy seeks to promote life-giving activity such as sex and food-getting. The aim of Thanatos (tensionlessness, a return to the constancy of the inorganic) is contradictory to that of Eros; thus, the life and death instincts may often produce conflicting behaviors. For example, love, a derivative of Eros, often neutralizes hate, a derivative of Thanatos. Despite their conflicting aims, Eros and Thanatos often complement one another by expending psychic energy in certain behaviors that serve both (for example, sleep brings a tension relief and a revitalization of life functions), a process Freud called instinctual fusion.

Freud believed the total personality to consist of three major processes: the id, the ego, and the superego. At birth, the neonate could be described as man the id, for the ego and the superego are as yet undeveloped. In the mature healthy personality, the three processes are clearly differentiated and tend to work together, allowing the individual to invest his psychic energy in activities that will satisfy his basic needs and desires. An understanding of the functioning of the mature personality necessitates a discussion of the origin and dynamics of each of its three components.

The Id: Legislator of the Personality

The id is the seat of all the instincts and, thus, the original reservoir of psychic energy. Its sole purpose is to provide for the discharge of energy used in gratifying bodily needs. The id was said to fulfill the primordial life function that Freud called the pleasure principle. The goal of the pleasure principle is the reduction of tension. Since the reduction of tension associated with bodily need states is a pleasurable experience, we can say that the pleasure principle represents the seeking of pleasure through the avoidance of pain or discomfort.

The id cannot tolerate discomfort and will seek immediate gratification whenever tension or discomfort is experienced. It its earliest form, the id often succeeds at producing immediate relief from many discomforts by triggering reflexes to shut out or dispel noxious stimuli (for example, sneezing expels foreign particles from the nose; the bladder opens when the pressure upon it reaches a certain intensity). Nevertheless, the id often experiences frustration since relatively few tensions can be reduced through the activation of a reflex. For example, no reflex will dispel hunger contractions. The child must be fed by an outside agent or die.

The frustrations of the id provide the impetus for its further development by stimulating the investment of psychic energy in other activities when reflexes prove ineffective at reducing tension. Thus in the process of being fed, the child sees, smells, feels, and tastes food, the breast, etc., and these experiences are stored as images in memory. Over repeated feedings, the child associates these memories of food and the feeding situation with the reduction of hunger, and when he is hungry on future occasions, he will attempt to reproduce food-related images or perceptions as a means of reducing tension. The id's attempt to reduce tension by reproducing images of the desired object is termed the primary process.

Primary-process thinking is not very adaptive and is, in fact, quite irrational. The id considers the memory image of an instinctual object to be equivalent to the object itself. For example, the image of a breast to suck is seen by the id as the functional equivalent of the real thing. Clearly, instinctual needs are not often gratified by the "wishful thinking" of the primary processes. The child must develop a secondary process through which he learns to delay attempts at gratification long enough to recognize and discriminate realistic goal objects from their images or memory traces. Freud believed that the id retained its impulsive, hedonistic, irrational character throughout life and, thus, remained incapable of functioning at a level higher than the primary process.

The Ego: Executive of the Personality

The failure of the id to relieve tension through wish fulfillment ultimately stimulates the development of a second personality process, the ego. As the executive of the personality, the ego has two primary functions: (a) to distinguish between the mental images of an instinctual object (for example, the object-cathexes of the id) and the instinctual object itself; and (b) to postpone the discharge of psychic energy by the id until the actual object of the instinct is produced or discovered. Because the ego is primarily concerned with producing realistic means of need satisfaction, it is said to serve the reality principle.

Freud (1923) believed that the ego originally has no energy of its own and cannot even be said to exist until psychic energy has been diverted from the id into a number of latent processes (memory, discrimination, logical reason) that comprise its structure. Unfortunately, Freud is not at all explicit as to how instinctual energy is displaced from the id to the ego. He just assumed that this displacement occurs. The energy displaced from the id is said to activate the latent cognitive processes of the ego, which operate according to the secondary process. The secondary process produces realistic methods of reducing tension by means of a course of action developed through thought and reason.

When the ego attempts to produce reality, it is said to be reality testing. If initial tests do not work, that is, the need is not satisfied by the object discovered or produced, a new course of action is planned and tested. Eventually, the secondary process produces the objects or situations that satisfy a variety of instinctual needs: children learn to discriminate their thumbs from the mother's breast when hungry; they learn to turn to their mothers or other familiar caretakers rather than to strange persons or inanimate objects in order to quell their fears. During the search for realistic means of tension reduction, the ego has been investing a portion of its available energy to block the tendency of the id to seek immediate gratification through wish fulfillment. The forces that block the unrealistic object cathexes of the id are called anti-cathexes. Without investing energy in anti-cathexes, the ego could not control the impulsive character of the id long enough to learn to discriminate the subjective world of id-based mental imagery from objective reality. In sum, the ego is both servant and master to the id. It

> . . . is like a man on horseback, who has to hold in check the superior strength of the horse; with this difference, that the rider seeks to do so with his own strength while the ego uses borrowed forces. The illustration may be carried further, often a rider, if he is not to be parted from his horse, is obliged to guide it where it wants to go; so in the same way the ego constantly carries into action the wishes of the id as if they were its own (Freud, 1923, p. 30).

The successes of the developing ego at satisfying very basic instinctual urges allows it to siphon progressively more of the psychic energy stored in the id. This displaced energy is used to further develop the psychological processes of perception, learning, discrimination, memory, and reason, which, in turn, allow the individual to become more familiar with his environment, and better able to function within it. In the normal course of personality development, the ego becomes so efficient at reducing normal instinctual urges that it is able to draw away from the id a substantial portion of the total reservoir of psychic energy. Energy in excess of that needed for anti-cathexes and need satisfaction is often channeled into ego interests or is used to effect an integration of the three systems of the mature personality. An ego interest is an interest in stimuli or activities that do not directly satisfy basic instinctual urges, but are associated with objects or activities that do. Painting nudes, listening to certain kinds of music, or reading racy novels may become ego interests that are sex-related, although they do not actually reduce sexual tensions. The ego's investment of energy in effecting a synthesis of the personality is discussed below.

The Superego: Judicial Branch of the Personality

The superego, often referred to as the moral or judicial branch of the personality, is the final system to be developed. The superego originates from the ego as the child gradually assimilates the moral code of his parents along with the traditional values and attitudes of their culture. The superego serves the ideal rather than the actual or the real; it strives for perfection rather than for pleasure or reality.

The early experience of the helpless child insures that parents will be among the first of his object-cathexes. The child is said to cathect his parents as a result of their benevolence in satisfying his instinctual needs. In addition to their role as benevolent caretakers, parents also serve as instructors and disciplinary agents who convey their standards of virtue and evil, right and wrong, acceptable and unacceptable by rewarding the child for "good" behavior and punishing him for "bad" behavior. Rewards are defined as treatments that decrease tension (praise, a smile, a cookie, granting of a privilege, etc.), while punishments are acts or stimuli that increase tension (a spanking, denying the child a pleasurable activity or a desirable object, disapproval, etc.). The desire to maintain parental approval, secure rewards, and avoid parental punishment is said to motivate the child to identify with parental standards and, thus, to make his behavior consistent with parental teachings and prohibitions. The superego is formed as the child invests psychic energy (drawn from the ego) in the introjection (internalization) of these parental standards and attitudes. The child's conception of what his parents consider good and virtuous becomes his ego-ideal. His conception of parental standards of evil or immoral becomes his conscience. These opposite poles of the same moral dimension are the components of the mature superego.

Once developed, the superego controls the child's behavior in much the same fashion as his parents previously did; that is, by administering rewards and punishments to the agent responsible for emitted behaviors, the ego. If the child's thoughts and actions are consistent with his ego-ideal, the ego is rewarded. For example,, the ego-ideal communicates to the ego that virtuous conduct deserves a treat such as a good meal, a movie, etc., or it may bestow feelings of pride and heightened self-esteem. Conversely, the conscience punishes the ego for moral transgressions by producing feelings of guilt, shame, or inferiority, and/or misfortunes such as accidents, illnesses, or the loss of treasured possessions.

The development of a stable superego is of obvious significance to society. Without this internal regulation of behavior, the child would consistently manifest his sexual and aggressive instincts in ways that could endanger the structure and basic institutions of the social order. In essence, the formation of a mature sense of morality and the assimilation of related cultural ideals is perhaps the biggest hurdle faced in socializing a child. Once the child has internalized these moral and cultural standards, society is protected from the horrors of his id and can generally expect him to remain a moral, law-abiding constituent.

Despite its noble, idealistic character, the superego is said to be as irrational as its major adversary, the id. In striving toward the ideal, the superego attempts to persuade the ego to adopt moralistic rather than realistic or adaptive goals. Unlike the rational ego, the superego does not merely postpone instinctual gratification; it attempts to deny the instincts. The superego, like the id, demonstrates its inability to distinguish subjective from objective when punishing the ego for merely thinking immoral thoughts. Thought and deed are one and the same in the eyes of the conscience. Finally, the superego is often manipulated by the id to serve rather than restrain the instincts. For example, the righteous movie censor may pride himself for protecting others against smut while actually serving the sexual impulses of the id through his work.

In sum, Freud depicts the personality as a system of checks and balances between the driving forces (cathexes) and the restraining forces (anti-cathexes). Recall that the id, energized by the instincts, is the primary driving force. Its message is *go*. The ego serves a restraining function by delaying the id until realistic solutions to instinctual needs are produced or discovered. Its message is *wait*. The superego, on the other hand, may frustrate the id and tie the ego in moral knots by saying *no*. It should be emphasized that Freud conceived of the id, ego, and superego as personality processes rather than structural entities. They are thought to share a fixed amount of psychic energy, and the person's overall conduct is determined by the distribution of energy across these three processes. If the bulk of the energy is controlled by the superego, the person will be rigidly moralistic with an underdeveloped id and ego. If the bulk of the energy is controlled by the ego, the result is the realist, or the instrumental pragmatist. The impulsive personality results when the id has retained the majority of available energy leaving the ego and superego underdeveloped. Ordinarily, the id, ego, and superego do not incapacitate or cancel one another. A smoothly functioning personality is one having a fairly equitable distribution of energy among the three processes, with the ego retaining a slightly larger share in order to effect realistic compromises between id impulses and superego compulsions and to prevent the permanent accumulation of vast amounts of psychic energy by any one of the three systems.

Psychosexual Development

Freud (1930,1960) advanced the thesis that personality and social development is largely based upon the maturation of the sex instincts. Sexual maturation was said to follow a predetermined epigenetic course characterized by the gradual shift in the investment of libido (the psychic energy of the sex instincts) from one sexually excitable (erogenous) bodily zone to another. The principal erogenous zones in the order of their developmental significance are the mouth, the anus, and the genitals. Each stage of personality and social development is the consequence of the investment of libidinal energy into a particular erogenous zone. The concentration of energy activates the zone's modes of functioning, which, in turn, determine the kinds of adaptive activity the child undertakes and place constraints upon the types of social interaction that are likely to occur during that particular period of the life cycle.

Oral Stage

During the first year of life, the primary erogenous zone is the infant's mouth, which derives sensual pleasure through sucking, swallowing, or taking in materials necessary for sustenance (food, water, oxygen, etc.). This incorporation, or taking-in, is the precursory form of introjection, the mechanism whereby the child later internalizes attributes and ideals of significant others. The child who is not getting enough food or love early in life may retain incorporation as his primary mode of oral functioning, a consequence that is said to be the precursor of the personality trait of acquisitiveness.[3] Acquisitiveness was felt to manifest itself later in life as a greed or lust for whatever the person is seeking, be it love, fame, power, or money.

Holding on, biting, spitting out, and closing up are four additional modes of oral functioning that may become dominant, fixate, and serve as prototypes of certain adult personality characteristics. The development of clinging or holding on as a dominant mode of oral functioning is likely to occur if a mother weans her child too abruptly or if she withholds the breast as part of her attempt to control the child's conduct. Since food giving becomes associated with the mother's giving of love and withholding of food with rejection and disapproval, the child becomes anxious when the breast is withheld. Anxiety resulting from a loss of the breast (and love) causes the child to cling to the mother and become overly dependent upon her for both need satisfaction and affection. This clinging dependence upon the mother is believed to generalize to other people and, thus, serves as the precursor of the overly dependent adult personality, that is, the oral-dependent personality.

Biting is seen by Freud as an oral-aggressive mode that is the prototype for many forms of direct and displaced aggression. The child who adopts biting as a primary mode of oral functioning may develop into a sarcastic, cynical adult, who will likely choose an occupation through which he or she can rip others apart orally (law, politics, editorial work, etc.). When the oral-aggressive personality feels guilty, the conscience is likely to suggest biting of the lips and/or the tongue as a form of self-punishment.

Spitting out and closing up are less frequently adopted as primary modes of oral functioning. These particular oral modes may be transformed in many possible ways depending upon the satisfactions they bring and/or the responses of others (primarily parents) to them. The spitting-out type of oral personality commonly becomes overly guarded, disdainful, and contemptuous as an adult.

---

[3]Freud (1930) mentioned two ways in which early modes of pyschosexual functioning may influence or determine certain aspects of the adult personality. First, if the child should experience substantial anxiety or frustration during any psychosexual stage, he/she may adopt a mode of functioning that alleviates these discomforts and then fixate at this level of functioning in order to forestall a repetition of discomforting experiences. Fixation may result in a total arrest of psychosexual development, or it may be incomplete, in which case further development is impaired by the individual's frequent and continued use of the fixated mode of functioning. Second, if the frustrations or anxieties associated with any stage of psychosexual development are too severe to overcome, the individual may regress, that is, retreat to earlier, less stressful levels of functioning and subsequently organize his/her personality around these earlier functional modes.

Closing up as a primary oral mode is believed to be the prototype of the socially cautious, introverted personality.

Anal Stage

The elimination of waste from the alimentary canal is a reflexive activity during the first year of life. In the second or third year, the child develops the musculature necessary for sphincter control and begins to use the bowel movement as a means of reducing the tension caused by the accumulation of feces in the lower intestine. Since the voluntary bowel movement produces pleasure through the reduction of tension, libido begins to move from the oral to the anal region. The concentration of libido into the anal erogenous zone is hastened by the attention and significance parents give to anal events when they begin to toilet train their child.

Ordinarily, toilet training is the first time that the child has any prolonged experience with external authority and disciplinary agents. Since toilet training represents a major conflict between an instinctual cathexis (the wish to defecate) and an external barrier, its consequences were believed to have profound effects upon subsequent social and personality development.

Freud (Freud, 1930; Hall, 1954) described the etiology of three modes of anal functioning and the possible effects of each on the adult personality. Overly strict and punitive toilet training may engender hostility in the child, leading him to retaliate against his parents by intentionally soiling himself. As he grows older, the child who adopts this explusive mode of anal functioning will likely attempt to get even with frustrating authority figures by being cruel, disorderly, irresponsible, wasteful, and/or extravagant. Parental pleading coupled with their use of extravagant praise for successful bowel movements is thought to lead the child to consider the elimination of his feces as the creation of a significant gift. Later in life, the child who adopts a gift-giving style of anal functioning may attempt a creative occupation (art, music, etc.) or may become overly generous and charitable in his attempts to please others (the philanthropist type). Finally, strict toilet training coupled with parental emphasis upon the value of feces may cause the child to become anxious about losing a valuable commodity when he defecates. The child's response is likely to be a retention of his feces, an act that produces sensual pressures on the walls of the rectum and is thus, pleasurable in itself. If this anal-retentive mode becomes primary, fixates, and generalizes, the child will likely become obstinate, stingy, hoarding, and economical as an adult.

The Phallic Stage

When the child is about four years old, libido begins to concentrate in his/her genital region. This libidinal shift from the anal to the genital erogenous zone is primarily the result of a biological maturation of the genitals, which, for the first time, have developed sufficiently to be an important source of sensual stimulation. With the maturation of the genitals comes an increased interest in genital functioning, increased genital manipulation, and the development of an intense sexual longing for the parent of the opposite sex.

The course of the phallic stage is somewhat different for boys and girls. The emergence of genital libido causes the boy to cathect his mother as a sex object and view his father as a rival for her affection, a situation known as the Oedipus complex. The development of the Oedipus complex creates a perceived danger for the male child. When he discovers that girls lack penises, he develops a fear that his father will punish his incestuous desires and rivaling conduct by removing his penis. As a result of this intense castration anxiety, the boy begins to resolve his Oedipus complex by repressing (forcing out of conscious awareness) his incestuous desires and by imitating or identifying with his father. This latter process, called identification with the aggressor, is the means by which the boy incorporates the proper attitudes and conduct expected of a male in his culture. In the course of switching his primary cathexis to the father through identification, the child lessens his chances of castration and obtains some vicarious satisfaction of his now repressed incestuous wishes. Finally, the child's resolution of his Oedipal conflict completes the development of his superego, since he has deferred to his father's authority by repressing a socially disapproved motive (incest), and adopted his father's moral standards as a consequence of paternal identification.

As is the case with the boy, the girl's primary parental cathexis is for her benevolent caretaker, the mother. However, when the girl discovers that she lacks a penis, she feels castrated, blames her mother for this castration, and her cathexis for the mother is weakened. She now envies her father for possessing a penis, and this penis envy results in a transfer of her affections to the father in the hope that she may share with him the valued organ she lacks. Clearly, the female Oedipal conflict, the Electra complex, is analogous to that of the male, as the girl comes to view her mother as a rival for her father's affection. However, the girl does not resolve the Electra complex by first fearing castration and then identifying with her mother; she already feels castrated and attributes the act to the mother. Instead, Freud (1924, 1925) suggested that the Electra complex may finally just wear off as the girl comes to realize the impossibility of ever possessing her father. Since the occurrence of any subsequent identification with the mother is not based on an intense fear or threat, Freud reasoned that females were less well identified than males with the same-sex parent and, thus, less likely to acquire either a proper sex-role identity or a strong internalized morality (superego).

Freud's reasoning would seem to require some revision to account for the observation that most women eventually adopt a feminine sex-role preference. Anna Freud (1946) has suggested that, during the Electra conflict, the father provides the impetus for the girl's eventual identification with her mother by encouraging his daughter to look and act feminine. In the course of acting feminine to win the father's love, the girl is said to become aware of the similarity between her own conduct and that of her mother. Her recognition of the basic similarity between herself and her mother is believed to strengthen the vestiges of the girl's pre-phallic cathexis for the mother, resulting in her eventual identification with the mother and the adoption of a feminine sex-role preference.

The Latency Period

Between the ages of six, when the Oedipus or Electra complex is resolved, and twelve, when puberty results in increased genital excitation, the sex instincts appear to be relatively quiescent. This latency period derives its name from the fact that libido is now latent rather than concentrated in a particular erogenous zone or directed at external sex objects. The relatively long latency period was thought to occur for two reasons. First, the repression of the traumatic events of the phallic period is so great that the child either consciously or unconsciously rejects all things involving sex. Second, available libido is sublimated: that is, channeled into socially acceptable activities such as school or vigorous play that require virtually all of the child's available physical and psychic energy. At puberty, the child's repression of all things sexual begins to crumble as he or she enters the genital stage of psychosexual development.

The Genital Stage

The onset of puberty is accompanied by a maturation of the sex organs, the production of sex hormones, and not surprisingly, a revitalization of the sex instincts. For the first time, the goal of the sex instincts is reproduction. Libido is openly expressed toward members of the opposite sex. The genital stage is a period of sexual socialization, heterosexual group activities, vocational training, courting, and marriage, activities that prepare the person to undertake the responsibility of satisfying the sex instincts through reproduction. The genital stage is the longest of Freud's stages of psychosexual development lasting from the teens until senility, at which time the person often regresses back to pregenital activities and behaviors.

Freud was careful to note that pregenital activities are not completely overlaid by genital activities. The cathexes of the oral, anal, and phallic stages become fused with genital activities to further the satisfaction of the sex instincts. For example, kissing, caressing, and other forms of lovemaking employed in the act of mating derive their primary impetus from pregenital impulses; yet they are aimed at producing sexual union and reproduction. As previously noted, displacements and other transformations of pregenital modes of functioning may also be instrumental in the shaping of the adult personality.

Erikson's Theory of Psychosocial Development

Erik Erikson's (1950, 1959, 1963, 1972) elaboration and extension of the Freudian developmental scheme serves as a good example of a *neo-Freudian* theory of social and personality development. As implied by his designated status as a neo-Freudian, Erikson builds solidly upon Freudian psychoanalytic theory in constructing his own approach. He accepts the basic Freudian premise that libidinal energy is present at birth and is at the core of all human functioning. Like Freud, Erikson believes that libidinal energy is shared among three basic personality processes: the id, the ego, and the superego. Erikson also assumes that development follows a maturational ground plan. The child is said to pass through a series of crises or stages, several of which are related though certainly not identical to the Freudian psychosexual stages.

Despite the basic similarities between the Freudian and Eriksonian perspectives, Erikson's views on social-personality development differ from those of Freud in three important aspects (Maier, 1969). First, Erikson places a much greater emphasis than did Freud upon the role played by the ego during the course of development. While Freud concentrates largely upon the action of irrational, instinctual components of the personality as the chief "maker" of man, Erikson stresses ego development and the activities undertaken by the rational ego as primary determinants of one's personality, or personal identity. Second, Erikson emphasizes the broad sociocultural context in which development occurs. The mother-father-child matrix is expanded to place the developing child within the context of the family and its broader sociocultural heritage. Thus, Erikson's emphasis upon societal influences qualifies his approach as a theory of psychosocial rather than psychosexual development. Third, Erikson focuses upon the adaptive consequences of successful resolutions of developmental crises, whereas Freud was primarily concerned with pathologies resulting from their unsuccessful resolutions. The psychosocial crisis characterizing each stage of the Eriksonian framework provides the scenario for the development of a particular ego quality that must emerge if the person's sense of identity is to develop properly. Thus, Eriksonian crises are to be viewed as contributors to normalcy rather than as forebearers of pathology.

Erikson's contention that man continues to develop beyond the point of sexual maturity led him to formulate an eight-stage developmental scheme extending from infancy to old age. Particularly noteworthy as elaborations or extensions of the Freudian developmental scheme are Erikson's separation of adolescence and young adulthood into two distinct developmental periods and his detailing of the psychosocial consequences of aging. Table 2 provides a comparison of Erikson's psychosocial and Freud's psychosexual stages of social and personality development. An overview of Erikson's eight-stage developmental model appears below.

Stage 1: Basic Trust vs. Mistrust

According to Erikson, the cornerstone of all later development occurs in the first psychosocial stage, as the child develops a sense of trust or mistrust of himself and his environment. The child is said to develop a trust of his environment if his parents, particularly the mother, are warm, prompt, and consistent in

TABLE 3.2

A Comparison of Erikson's and Freud's Theories
of Social and Personality Development

Chronological age	Psychosexual stage	Significant persons	Psychosocial crisis (stage)
Infancy (0-1 approx.)	Oral	Mother	Trust vs. mistrust
1-3 years	Anal	Parents	Autonomy vs. shame and doubt
3-5½ years	Phallic	Family	Initiative vs. guilt
5½-12 years	Latency	Neighborhood, teacher, school	Industry vs. inferiority
12-17	Adolescence (early genital stage)	Peer groups outgroups	Identity vs. role confusion
17-22	Genital	Friends, opposite sex partners	Intimacy vs. isolation
Adulthood		Wife, children	Generativity vs. stagnation
Maturity (old age)		Self, mankind	Ego integrity vs. despair

satisfying his bodily needs. Erikson believes that the emotional quality of the care-taker-child relationship is the primary determinant of the strength of the child's sense of trust. Parental smiling, tender handling, vocalization, and demonstrations of attention are considered just as important to the establishment and mainten-ance of the child's trusting attitudes as the basic caretaking activities (for exam-ple, feeding) themselves. As the child learns to trust his environment, he also develops a sense of self-trust. That is, in the course of interacting with his care-takers, the child actively participates in feeding, reciprocal vocalization, play, etc. and, thus, learns to trust his own reactions to be effective and reliable at achiev-ing desired ends. The development of trust is viewed by Erikson as a prerequisite for the healthy resolution of subsequent psychosocial crises.

Mistrust develops when infants receive maternal care that is roughly opposite to that described above. If maternal care is not overly harsh, the child may re-flect little more than a mild fear of close mutual-trust relationships. However, extremely harsh and inconsistent care may have immediate pathological conse-quences (for example, schizophrenia, solitary depression).

Stage 2: Autonomy vs. Shame and Doubt

Between the ages of one and three, the child faces a conflict as to whether or not he should assert his will. During this developmental phase, he gains the nec-essary muscular control to grasp, hold, and manipulate objects, to crawl, walk, etc.

As the child exercises his musculature and derives pleasure from his newly acquired ability to explore and manipulate his environment, he attempts to establish a sense of personal autonomy, a feeling that he can make things happen and that he is no longer totally dependent upon others. However, the child's strivings for autonomy are often inhibited by parents who begin to train him to control his assertiveness with the aim of instilling a sense of self-control and socially desirable conduct. Toilet training nicely exemplifies the child's "battle for autonomy." If parental toilet training practices are strict and severe, the child is unable to assert his will, and may experience shame and/or self-doubt over his failure to meet strict parental expectations. Tolerant, supportive toilet training allows the child to gradually acquire a proper control of his anal functioning, an achievement that generates feelings of self-pride and autonomy rather than shame and doubt. Thus, a sensitive and supportive imposition of rules by parents fosters the sense of autonomy that is necessary for establishment of an independent identity.

Stage 3: Initiative vs. Guilt

Having achieved some autonomy, the three-to-five-year-old faces a conflict between initiative and guilt. The child's environment now challenges him to be purposeful and master many tasks. He must assume responsibility for his own care and hygiene, his toys, his pets, etc. In essence, the child realizes that he is expected to satisfy most of his own needs. At this stage, the child initiates many purposeful actions, some of which will conflict with the needs and wishes of others. These conflicts often produce guilt feelings which, if sufficiently intense, may serve to restrict the child's future initiative due to his fear of intruding upon the autonomy of others.

Like Freud, Erikson views the Oedipal conflict as the most important single event of this developmental period. As a result of an initiative to "make like" or take the role of the same-sex parent, the child develops a strong attraction for the opposite-sex parent. The desire to displace the same-sex parent in the heart of the opposite-sex parent produces intense guilt feelings which the child normally overcomes by substituting other love objects for the opposite-sex parent, and introjecting the characteristics, attitudes, and moral standards of the same-sex parent through the process of identification. The resolution of Oedipal conflicts allows the child to retain a basic sense of initiative without experiencing guilt, as he/she is now morally responsible and can derive pleasure from the satisfactory performance of socially approved roles, functions, and activities.

Stage 4: Industry vs. Inferiority

With the successful resolution of the Oedipal conflict, the child turns away from the familial context to find an identity among his school-age peers. During this period that coincides with the Freudian latency stage, libido is rerouted to effect the acquisition of "technological tools" or skills (reading, writing, cooperation with others in constructive activities, etc.) that are important criteria for acceptance. The psychosocial crisis that arises during this stage of ego development centers on the problem of whether or not the child will become acceptably industrious or productive in his own eyes and the eyes of others. A failure to acquire the proper technological skills will lead the child to feel relatively unproductive and inferior vis-à-vis his peers. As a consequence, he may either become alienated and reject his culture, or he may passively conform to the dictates of those who adequately represent it. The acquisition of a basic sense of industry or competence is viewed as essential to insure the continuing development of ego autonomy and a mature personal identity.

Stage 5: Identity vs. Role Confusion

The physiological upheaval known as puberty forces the teenager to reevaluate his identity. Maturation of the reproductive system introduces physical and physiological events such as the appearance of body hair, pimples, rapidly changing bodily dimensions, physical awkwardness, genital sensations, and sexual urges, all of which must be incorporated into the ego structure. The teenager must reevaluate his/her identity vis-à-vis members of the opposite sex. Society consistently reminds the teenager of his/her impending adulthood, a fact that necessitates an appraisal of many different values, ideologies, and occupations as part of an attempt to select an identity with which to embrace the responsibilities of adulthood. Finding the answer to the question "Who am I to be?" is the crisis faced by teenagers during the adolescent phase of development.

Teenagers may experience role confusion if they cannot establish a proper sexual identity and/or the promise of a suitable career. While all adolescents experience a bit of role confusion, some find it extremely difficult to establish a stable identity. Faddish conformity and/or overidentification with folk heroes are viewed by Erikson as defenses against prolonged and intense role confusion. Adolescent love is, for Erikson, a largely asexual attempt by the confused adolescent to project his emerging identity onto another in the hope that it will be sharpened and stabilized. A failure to establish a strong personal identity during adolescence may result in general feelings of purposelessness and a subsequent inability to invest oneself in activities (for example, occupational training, intimate relationships) characteristic of adulthood.

Stage 6: Intimacy vs. Isolation

The establishment of a strong personal identity readies the young adult for social and sexual intimacy with a member of the opposite sex. The primary psychosocial function of this stage is "to lose and find oneself in another" (Erikson, 1963). The social interactions of the young adult center around the selection of partners in friendship, sex, and love.

True intimacy, unlike adolescent love, requires a genuine, concrete commitment to another in which each partner must sacrifice or compromise his or her own desires to effect a sense of shared identity. The major crisis or choice faced by the the young adult is to either achieve gratification and personal growth through intimacy with others, or to withdraw and thereby isolate oneself from intimate contacts. Persons with weak adolescent identities may be ambivalent about intimacy; that is, they desire its advantages, but they are unable to effectively compromise their already fragile identities to establish a shared identity with another. Erikson views the achievement of a sense of intimacy with others as a necessary prerequisite for the adoption of a normal adult identity.

Stage 7: Generativity vs. Stagnation

The successful establishment of intimacy and genital adjustment eventually leads to an expansion of ego interests that Erikson termed the generative phase of development. The adult now invests libido in generative activities such as establishing a sense of divided labor and a shared household, producing children, and taking an interest in the adjustment, training, and guidance of a new generation. Adults who reject responsibility for the care and guidance of the next generation may experience a sense of personal impoverishment or stagnation during middle age. At this point, the adult may feel generally apathetic; life may seem meaningless. In some cases, the stagnated adult may desperately attempt a kind of pseudo-generativity such as engaging in childish forms of self-indulgence and thereby defining oneself as a child who needs guidance, adopting an exaggerated self-concern like that of the hypochondriac, or selecting a mate much younger than oneself in order to have somebody young to advise and look after. The sense of purposelessness that accompanies stagnation makes life's final crisis — impending disintegration and death — very difficult to accept.

Stage 8: Ego Integrity vs. Despair

Erikson contrasts ego integrity with despair as the two perspectives that the aged may assume in response to the inevitability of their death. The individual who has not adequately resolved prior psychosocial crises is likely to experience despair; that is, a sense of purposelessness, a dissatisfaction with the course of one's life, a desire to put off death in order to continue the search for dignity. One who experiences despair truly fears death because death represents the conclusion of a nonproductive, unintegrated, incomplete life cycle.

In contrast, ego integrity consists of a sense of dignity, a feeling of satisfaction with one's life, a feeling of having contributed to the continuance and development of mankind. The adult who has satisfactorily resolved prior psychosocial crises and achieved satisfaction from having children and helping them grow is likely to develop the integrity to view his life as "something that had to be and that, by necessity, permitted no substitutions" (Erikson, 1963). A sense of ego integrity allows one to fearlessly accept death as nothing more than the end of a productive and meaningful life cycle.

Applications of Psychoanalytic Theory to Selected Topics

Common to all theories of social and personality development is a concern with topics such as dependency and its development, sexuality and sex-role development, and morality and moral development. Psychoanalytic theory assigns considerable importance to these attributes by providing elaborate theoretical explanations of their origins. Brief summaries of the psychoanalytic positions on the three topics and examples of research performed to test these positions appear in the following paragraphs.

Dependency

Freud believed that dependent attitudes and behaviors originate from conflicts experienced by the child during the oral stage. Recall that the infant is said to cathect his mother because he equates her food giving activities with the giving of love. Should the benevolent mother subsequently wean her children too a-bruptly and/or withhold the breast as a form of punishment, the child experiences anxiety: he feels that he has lost his food supply and his mother's love. This early association between oral deprivation and perceived rejection may induce the child to cling to or remain near the mother at all times. Under these circumstances, the child obeys the mother's commands and refrains from activities that may displease her as part of his attempt to recapture and maintain her affection. In sum, the child learns that passive-obedient behavior is reinforcing. This passive dependence upon the mother may then generalize to other persons and indeed, to the world at large. The corporation yes-man is the classic example of the oral-dependent personality. Freud became convinced that the oral stage was the true locus of dependent attitudes when he discovered that patients with repressed oral conflicts often adopted exaggerated or unusual oral behaviors (for example, compulsive eating and drinking) to combat depression and feelings of rejection. Erikson agrees that oral conflicts contribute to dependency. However, he argues that the child's failure to develop the ego qualities of autonomy, initiative, industry, and identity also contribute substantially to the dependent personality.

Research attempting to demonstrate relationships between oral socialization practices and dependency in children has provided, at best, mixed inconclusive support for psychoanalytic assertions. For example, parental adoption of a rigid feeding schedule (where, despite the child's protests, food is withheld until an appointed feeding time) is related to high dependency in school-age girls (Sears et al., 1953; Smith, 1958), but to low dependency in school-age boys (Sears, Maccoby & Levin, 1957). To complicate matters, Sears, Rau, and Alpert (1965),

Sewell (1952), and Sewell and Mussen (1952) found *no* relationship between rigidity of feeding during infancy and later dependency. Consistent with psychoanalytic assertions, Sears et al. (1953), and Sears et al. (1965) reported positive relationships between severity of weaning and dependency in school age children, and Whiting and Child (1953), in a cross-cultural study, report a positive correlation between societal weaning severity and anxiety about oral activities in adult life. However, Sears et al. (1957) found no relationship between severity of weaning and dependency, and Sears et al. (1965) reported an inverse relationship between weaning severity and proximity seeking in children. Thus, support for the psychoanalytic explanation of dependency is spotty and inconsistent. The inconsistencies in this line of research likely result from a host of methodological problems that are described elsewhere in some detail (Maccoby and Masters, 1970; Zigler and Child, 1973).

Sexuality and Sex-Role Development

Freud, Erikson, and indeed most psychoanalysts hold a similar view of human sexuality and sex-role development. Sexuality is not taught or shaped. It is an innate attribute, manifest at birth in the form of instincts or life forces that help to insure the organism's survival. Freud's theory of infantile sexuality was nothing less than revolutionary at the time of its publication during the Victorian era. One of Freud's major contributions was his demonstration that the puritanical attitudes of his day fostered the development of many sexual conflicts which, when repressed, often develop into full-blown neuroses and/or other personality dysfunctions.

Freud believed that everyone was constitutionally bisexual, inheriting, in differing proportions, the biological attributes of both males and females. What, then, is responsible for the child's adoption of a sex-role appropriate for his/her biological sex? Freud's answer: the sexual conflicts of the Oedipal period. Recall that males are said to incorporate masculine attitudes, attributes, and behaviors by identifying with their fathers (the aggressor) in the course of resolving the Oedipal conflict. The expression of feminine attributes and/or homosexuality in males may result if fathers are not threatening enough to foster identification, if the father is an inappropriate masculine model, if the father is largely absent from the home, if the bisexual male child has inherited a strong feminine constitution, or if some combination of these factors are operating. Girls are said to have a harder time developing an appropriately feminine sex-role because their identifications with their mothers are not motivated by a sense of fear or anxiety arising from the Oedipal situation. Instead, girls are said to identify with the mother for two reasons: (a) the mother retains some attractiveness from having played benevolent caretaker to the girl during infancy; and (b) the father reinforces femininity in his daughter, an act that enhances the attractiveness of an appropriate feminine model — the mother. Like males, females are constitutionally bisexual and may adopt masculine behaviors, tomboyism, or a lesbian orientation if they fail to identify with their mothers and/or overidentify with their fathers, if their mothers are inadequate feminine models, or if they have inherited relatively strong masculine constitutional attributes.

Research reflecting upon the psychoanalytic explanation of sex-role development has provided mostly nonsupportive results. For example, in homes where the father-son relationship was rated as stressful, Bronson (1959) found a negative correlation between the masculinity of fathers and sons. Other researchers (Mussen and Distler, 1959, 1960; Mussen and Rutherford, 1963; Payne and Mussen, 1956) report that boys show a stronger identification with their fathers and heightened masculinity if the father is nurturant rather than threatening or punitive. Lazowick (1955) and Sutton-Smith and Rosenberg (1970) found an inverse relationship between anxiety and appropriate sex-role development in males. All of these results are inconsistent with the psychoanalytic assertion that male sex-role development results from the male child's fear-induced identification with an aggressor. In addition, studies focusing upon sex-role development of hermaphrodites (Hampson, 1965; Money, 1965a, 1965b) and males from fathers-absent homes (reviewed in Biller, 1970) suggest that the critical period for the development of basic sex-role orientations occurs prior to the time the Oedipal conflict is said to occur.

The neoanalytic explanation of female sex-role development (A. Freud, 1946) has received some support. Apparently, five-year-old girls do show a preference for the father over the mother (cf. McCandless, 1967), and fathers do contribute to the sex-role development of their daughters by reinforcing feminine attitudes and behaviors (Hetherington, 1972; Mussen and Rutherford, 1963). While these results are consistent with analytic assertions, they are subject to a variety of alternative interpretations (Mischel, 1970).

Moral Development

Psychoanalytic theorists generally agree that moral development proceeds along the following course. The young child experiences many frustrations, some of which result from parental attempts to impose rules and regulations that have the effect of restricting and controlling his behavior. These frustrations contribute to the development of hostility toward parents. The child now faces quite a dilemma. He would like to get even with his parents, but if he attempts to retaliate, he faces the possibility of losing his parents' love. Due to this anxiety over a possible loss of love, the child is said to repress his hostility toward his parents and seek parental affection or approval by introjecting their standards and moral prohibitions through the process of identification. This identification creates the superego. which has the capacity to punish the child whenever he violates a moral principle or is tempted to do so. Recall that Freud believed that Oedipal conflicts provide the major impetus for the child's development of a sense of morality.[4] Erikson also recognizes the importance of Oedipal conflicts, but he argues much more forcefully than does Freud that it is the child's experiences with disciplinary agents during the anal (autonomy vs. shame) phase that forms the bedrock of a sense of social propriety upon which the superego develops.

The psychoanalytic account of morality and moral development has proven quite heuristic. Many testable hypotheses derive from the analytic assertion that anxiety over loss of love is an important dynamic underlying moral (superego) development. This assertion implies that children who experience predominantly love-oriented punishments, where parental withholding of affection generates anxiety over loss of love, should identify more strongly with parents and develop stronger superegos than would children who experience predominantly power-assertive punishments, where parents withhold objects, privileges, or use physical punishments, all of which may generate hostility rather than anxiety over a love loss. In addition, we might predict, as did Freud, that males, who experience more intense Oedipal anxieties than females, should be more motivated than females to identify with the same-sex parent and incorporate that parent's moral standards into a strong superego. The literature provides little support for the latter hypothesis. However, several researchers (e.g., Bandura and Walters, 1959; Glueck and Glueck, 1950; MacKinnon, 1938; Sears et al., 1957) report data consistent with the former hypothesis. Hoffman and Saltzstein (1967) argue that previous research demonstrating a positive relationship between love-oriented discipline and moral behavior must be qualified. In a study designed to overcome many methodological deficiencies of its predecessors, Hoffman and Saltzstein found that love-oriented punishment is associated with the development of a strong moral orientation *only* if parents also provide their child with an explanation of the consequences of his misbehavior as part of their disciplinary strategy. An excellent review of the literature pertinent to the psychoanalytic model of moral development appears in Hoffman (1970).

Criticisms of the Psychoanalytic Approach

Three frequent criticisms of the methods and/or content of psychoanalysis are especially noteworthy. First, psychoanalysis deals directly with neurotic patients and the development of pathological behavior and, consequently, data reflecting upon the "normal" or "healthy" course of social-personality development are meager at best. Thus, one must seriously question the generalizability of the

---

[4] Although Freud conceded that anxiety over a possible love loss is an important contributor to early superego development, he believed that his fear-induced "identification with the aggressor" played the more prominent role in the development of the mature superego. Hoffman (1970) notes that most of Freud's followers have rejected this position in favor of the argument that moral development is fostered to the extent that parental discipline arouses anxiety over a loss of love rather than fear of an aggressor.

psychoanalytic model beyond the abnormal populace upon which it is based.

Second, proponents of the experimental method note quite correctly that psychoanalytic concepts and assertions are rarely defined in a manner that is subject to experimental verification. How, for example, might one objectively measure the relative strength of the id, ego, and superego in order to verify or refute Freud's model of the organizational dynamics of personality? We simply cannot measure these constructs with the objective instruments currently available, and thus, much of psychoanalytic theory remains untestable through any method other than psychoanalysis.

This brings us to the third major criticism. Despite Freud's attempts to be objective, the data obtained through psychoanalytic methods are hopelessly confounded with the therapist's technique and/or interpretive biases. That is, psychoanalysts "confirm" their theoretical expectations by selectively probing and differentially reinforcing their patient's verbal reports, thereby producing protocols or case studies that may amount to little more than theoretically inspired self-fulfilling prophesies.

Many advocates of psychoanalytic theory have responded to criticisms of the therapeutic method by adopting auxiliary methodologies to test analytic assertions (Langer, 1969). One alternative is the play therapy used by Erikson (1951) and Klein (1959) with children. Play therapy is a projective technique through which the child is assumed to act out, during play, the psychosocial and/or psychosexual conflicts that psychoanalytic theory expects him to encounter at his age or stage or development. Other researchers (e.g., Barry, Bacon & Child, 1957; Kardiner, 1939, 1945; Malinowski, 1927; Whiting, 1941, 1961; Whiting & Child, 1953) favor the cross-cultural comparison as an alternative methodology. This technique seeks to test the analytic assertion that cross-cultural differences in parental handling of various psychosocial or psychosexual conflicts results in the development of culture-specific behavioral patterns and/or distinctive cultural personalities. A third alternative, the experimental-correlational method, has been used by many researchers seeking support for analytic assertions that various early childhood experiences are related to the structure of the adult personality. Finally, some psychoanalysts have employed the biographical analysis, the intent of which is to demonstrate that the personality attributes of famous persons can be understood from post hoc analyses of their childhoods.

Langer (1969) correctly notes that none of these alternatives are without their obvious methodological flaws. Even more damaging, from Langer's perspective, is the fact that these methods have not been successful at extending or modifying psychoanalytic theory. The latter point is a weakness of theory, not methodology. For example, the developmental component of psychoanalytic theory represents a little more than an a posteriori descriptive interpretation of one's developmental history and has demonstrated little or no a priori predictive capability. Loevinger (1966) has noted the difficulties in extending a developmental theory that "has not yet been conceived in terms of a model that lends itself well to any measurement. There is indeed a postulated sequence of stages and undoubtedly there is some influence on later stages of the outcome of earlier stages, but there is no clear model for the nature of this influence" (p. 197).

In sum, psychoanalytic theory represents an important first attempt to explain the complexities of social and personality development. It has proven extremely heuristic in terms of stimulating a voluminous literature, the results of which have often contributed to the development of competing theories. The problems with analytic theory qua theory make it obvious that the analytic model must be revised substantially in order to remain a viable explanation of social and personality development.

SOCIAL LEARNING THEORY

The social learning perspective is the product of numerous attempts to explain the complexities of social and personality development by means of general principles from learning theory. Just as there are many theories of learning, so are there many social learning theories. These differing theories are all placed into one category because they all make two very basic assumptions: (a) to an overwhelming extent, human behavior is learned; and (b) man learns, and thus develops, in accordance with his experiences and the dictates of his environment. One implication of a social learning perspective is that individual differences, both within and across cultures, are reflections of the differing environmental conditions and experiences that people encounter.

We have previously noted that social learning theorists can be divided into three major groups: the neo-Hullians, the Skinnerians, and the Bandurians. The neo-Hullians are primarily concerned with explaining psychoanalytic phenomena in terms of Hullian learning principles. Their approach depicts behavior as motivated by primary and secondary drives and shaped by its effectiveness at reducing these drives. The Skinnerians dispense with the drive concept and all other organismic characteristics as excess theoretical baggage. Human behavior is analyzed in terms of the external stimulus events that evoke it and the reinforcing stimuli that alter, shape, and maintain it. The Bandurians criticize both the neo-Hullian and the radical behaviorist (Skinnerian) approaches for underemphasizing the role of cognition in human development, and have stressed the role of symbolic and vicarious processes in their theory of social learning and personality development.

Neo-Hullian and Bandurian social learning theories are examined in this chapter. The neo-Hullian approach nicely illustrates Freud's rather dramatic influence upon those early learning theorists who were interested in formulating an objective, testable theory of social-personality development. The Bandurian approach is more congruent with the current cognitive Zeitgeist in general psychology.

From Bandura's perspective, traditional social learning (that is, neo-Hullian and Skinnerian) explanations of human functioning and development are more adequately characterized as incomplete rather than inaccurate. Bandura argues that man is "neither driven by inner forces nor buffeted helplessly by environmental forces" (Bandura, 1971, p. 2). Rather, man, the thinking, self-regulating animal, is viewed as an active contributor to the very environment that influences his further development. The omission of the radical behaviorist or Skinnerian perspective is dictated solely by space considerations, and certainly does not imply that model's lack of importance. Many significant aspects of the radical behaviorist approach are compared to those of the Bandurian approach in subsequent sections of the chapter. The reader who seeks a greater familiarity with the radical behaviorist model of social learning is referred to Gewirtz's (1969) excellent summary.

Research Methods of Social Learning Theorists

Rather than focusing upon subjective and/or mentalistic phenomena such as impressions, cognitions, and the unconscious, social learning theorists have generally followed Watson's behavioristic imperative by adopting the child's overt behavior as their basic unit of analysis. The task of the social learning theorist is to demonstrate the longitudinal causality of social behavior; that is, how social learning experiences occurring earlier in one's developmental history are catalogued and subsequently influence or determine one's responses to environmental stimuli later in life. A basic assumption of the social learning approach is that the learning history of every individual creates a set of behavior potentials (habits) that, when considered collectively, represent that individual's personality.

The search for antecedent causes of overt behavior has led proponents of social learning theory to adopt the experimental method as a preferred research strategy. Three common types of social learning experiments are described below.

The Nondevelopmental Laboratory Experiment

Social learning theorists are often interested in determining the cause(s) of behaviors that are characteristic of most or all individuals at a given developmental level. The search for these causes proceeds roughly as follows: subjects of a specified age or level of development are exposed to treatments (environmental stimuli, motivating circumstances) that are believed to determine the strength and/or frequency of the behavior in question. The behavioral effects of these experimental treatments are compared to effects observed in a set of control conditions where subjects are treated exactly the same as their experimental counterparts except that they are not exposed to the hypothesized causal agent. A positive result is one where the experimental treatment produces the behavior and the control treatment does not. Such an outcome implies that the experimental treatment is one cause of the behavior under investigation. However, a single experiment of this kind does not rule out other antecedent conditions or treatments which might conceivably produce a similar behavioral effect. Bandura, Ross, and Ross (1963) and Weisberg (1963) clearly exemplify the nondevelopmental social-learning experiment.

The Cross-sectional Experiment

The cross-sectional experiment attempts to isolate processes underlying developmental changes in behavior by observing whether certain hypothesized causes are operating or have similar effects upon the behavior of children of different ages. A clear-cut example of a cross-sectional research program is reported by Kendler (1963). Kendler hypothesized that young preschool children do not use language as a conceptual tool and, hence, should perform poorly when compared to older, school-age children on any problem where verbal mediation is an aid to its solution. To test his hypothesis, Kendler asked children of different ages to work on a task where the use of verbal mediators would lead to a specific mode of problem solving. Kendler noted that older (presumably mediating) children operated as if they were using verbal mediators in attacking the problem, whereas younger children did not. Kendler's original hypothesis received further support from the subsequent observation that presenting the hypothesized "cause" (verbal mediators) increased the likelihood that the younger children would choose the mediating strategy, but did not appreciably affect the performance of older (mediating) children. Thus, Kendler concluded that the development of verbal mediating responses underlies certain developmental changes in concept formation and/or problem-solving strategies.

The Longitudinal Experiment

Cross-sectional experiments convey little information about development if the hypothesized causes of developmental changes in behavior have the same effects upon children at widely varying age levels. As an alternative to the cross-sectional design, the longitudinal experiment assesses the long-term developmental effects of certain experimental treatments by exposing children to those treatments and repeatedly testing these children as they grow older. Typically, different groups of children are exposed to different treatments, and the long-term as well as the short-term behavioral effects of these treatments are recorded. If different treatments have distinct developmental effects, the researcher should observe his experimental groups to manifest different patterns of behavior over time. Experiments by Hicks (1965) and Rheingold and Bayley 1959) are well-known examples of the longitudinal experiment.

The correlational experiment, mentioned earlier as an alternative to traditional psychoanalytic methods, is often employed by social learning theorists to determine if particular stimuli or events occurring earlier in life are related to the strength and/or frequency of contemporary behaviors. The now classic Fels long-itudinal study (Kagan & Moss, 1962) illustrates this research approach. In the Fels study, the behaviors of 91 children and their parents were observed over a 14-year period. Information concerning the adult personality of each child in the sample was also available. Both parental and child behaviors were rated along a number of dimensions, and these dimensional ratings were subjected to correla-tional analyses. A number of parental behaviors were in fact correlated with behaviors shown by the children at adulthood. For example, maternal restrictive-ness in the first ten years of the child's life was positively correlated with adult passivity and dependence for females, but was generally unrelated to indices of adult dependence in males.

Extreme caution is required in interpreting the results of a correlational ex-periment. A significant correlation between maternal restrictiveness and adult dependency in female offspring does not mean that maternal restrictiveness causes female children to be dependent as adults. A strong relationship between any two variables may be caused by a third factor. For example, Fridays and Mondays are clearly related to one another, but this relationship is caused by our method of sequencing the days of the week.[5] Despite its inability to specify causal links between variables, the correlational method is valuable for demon-strating interesting relationships that can be subjected to a causal analysis through experimentation.

Neo-Hullian Social Learning Theory

The genesis of neo-Hullian social learning theory can be traced to 1936, the year that a group of social scientists began an interdisciplinary seminar in the Institute of Human Relations at Yale University. The most notable participants in this seminar were Clark Hull, Neal Miller, John Dollard, O. H. Mowrer, and Robert Sears, although a large number of additional young faculty members and graduate students took part in the seminar and contributed to the development of the neo-Hullian perspective.

The reader who expects a detailed chronological account of the course of so-cial and personality development may well be disappointed with the neo-Hullian model. The early Yale group advanced the thesis that the essential features of social-personality development could easily be described by a very few principles from Hull's learning theory. Thus, neo-Hullian theory is not a developmental model; that is, it postulates no critical periods or distinct stages of development. Neo-Hullians argue that social learning obeys exactly the same empirical laws at

[5] It should be noted that age, which is often analyzed as an independent variable in devel-opmental studies, is really nothing more than a correlational variable. That is, age per se is not a process variable; it produces no developmental effects. However, factors correlated with age (for example, maturation, experience) may well underlie many changes in behavior that occur as the child grows older.

all points along the developmental continuum. One's social-personality development is simply viewed as a reflection of his cumulative social learning experiences.

Dollard and Miller (e.g., Dollard & Miller, 1950; Miller & Dollard, 1941) and one of their colleagues, Robert Sears (Sears, 1944, 1951a; Sears et al., 1957; Sears et al., 1965), provide the most comprehensive accounts of neo-Hullian social learning theory. The influence of Freud upon these theorists was enormous. Both Dollard and Miller were trained in psychoanalysis, and they, along with Sears, were primarily concerned with translating psychoanalytic phenomena and theory into Hullian stimulus-response terminology. Sears (1944) reflected upon the nature of their endeavors and the challenges they faced by stating:

> It seems doubtful whether the sheer testing of psychoanalytic theory is an appropriate task for experimental psychology. Its general method is estimable but its available techniques are clumsy. Instead of trying to ride on the tail of a kite that was never meant to carry such a load, experimentalists would probably be wise to get all the hunches, intuitions, and experience possible from psychoanalysis and then for themselves, start the laborious task of constructing a systematic psychology of personality but a system based on behavioral rather than experiential data (p. 329).

This unique impetus has resulted in the development of a theory whose descriptions of many social-developmental phenomena appear remarkably similar to the descriptions advanced by psychoanalytic theory. The following discussion represents a brief overview of the major principles of neo-Hullian social learning theory.

Structural Components of the Personality

The one structural concept used by neo-Hullians to describe relatively stable personality attributes is habit. A habit is defined as a learned association between a stimulus (cue) and a response. One's personality consists of the sum total of his learned habits. The development of specific habits is not emphasized in the neo-Hullian scheme. Rather, the neo-Hullians have primarily concerned themselves with the process of habit formation, that is, learning.

Personality Dynamics

The neo-Hullians argue that drives are the principal sources of motivation. Dollard and Miller (1950) define a drive as any stimulus strong enough to impel an organism into action. Learning consists of developing efficient strategies (habitual responses) through which drives may be reduced. While any sufficiently intense stimulus can serve as a drive, a certain class of stimuli, the primary drives, are the impetus of most behavior. Among the primary drives are hunger, thirst, respiration, sex, cold, and pain.

At the core of the neo-Hullian model is the concept of secondary or acquired drive. Secondary drives are learned; they are said to result whenever a particular stimulus or class of stimuli is repeatedly associated with a primary drive. For example, a child may develop a fear (secondary drive) of his parents if contacts with them are consistently painful. That is, the association between parents and pain stimuli produces a fear of parents that may then motivate the child to avoid his parents as a means of fear reduction. Both Dollard and Miller (1950) and Sears (1944) argue that the typical child develops many secondary drives that instigate and direct much of his subsequent social behavior. We shall have more to say about secondary drives and the behavior they energize a little later.

Social Learning

Neo-Hullians consider the concepts of drive, cue, response, and reinforcement to be of central importance to the learning process. As we have noted, drives produce activity. Cues are stimuli that guide the organism's activity. That is, "cues determine when [the organism] will respond, where he will respond, and which response he will make " (Dollard, & Miller, 1950, p. 32). While any stimulus might serve to cue a response, the cue value (that is, the directive influence) of a particular stimulus depends upon its distinctiveness. The distinctiveness of a cue is a function of its intensity and/or uniqueness. Dollard and Miller note that complex patterns of stimuli may serve a cueing function. In fact, they argue that the most distinctive cues are often unique combinations or patterns of stimuli — for example, a spoken word is an auditory cue composed of a unique pattern of phonemes.

In order to establish an association between a cue and a response, the response must occur. An important feature of the child's social learning is that he produce the "correct" or "socially appropriate" response to a given cue. Dollard and Miller assume that the child has an initial hierarchy of responses to any given situation. Often, the most probable responses in the child's initial hierarchy may be effective at reducing drive, but may not be the kind of responses that are condoned by socialization agents. For example, masturbation may reduce the child's sex drive, but may also bring disapproval from parents. Thus, social learning can be conceptualized as the changes that occur in the child's hierarchical order of responses as a function of his experiences. His resultant hierarchy is structured so that the most probable responses to a given cue or situation are those that are both effective at reducing whatever drive is aroused and condoned by significant others in his environment.

Implicit in the preceding statement is the neo-Hullian concept of reinforcement. A reinforcer is an event that strengthens the connection between a particular cue and a response made to that cue. Responses that are reinforced become more probable, or habitual; those that are continually not reinforced become less probable. The weakening of a response tendency as a function of its nonreinforcement is called extinction.

Neo-Hullians contend that the reinforcement of a response occurs only when there is a significant reduction in the drive stimuli impinging upon the organism

at the time of the response. A corollary assertion is that a response must be reinforced in order to be learned. Responses may be reinforced through the reduction of either primary or secondary drive stimuli, and Dollard and Miller argue
that many of the reinforcements experienced by human beings result from a reduction of secondary drive stimuli. Secondary drive stimuli are reduced by secondary reinforcers — events or stimuli that have been repeatedly associated with
the events that reduce primary drives. Money is a common secondary reinforcer.
Originally, money does not have the capacity to reinforce anything. But as the
child associates money with the purchase of goods that reduce a variety of primary drives, he comes to view money as a valued commodity. That is, the child
acquires a drive or motive for money, and any behavior energized by this acquired drive may be strengthened by the presentation of money. Dollard and Miller
propose that many of our everyday behaviors (work, efforts to please others,
etc.) are motivated by learned drives for significant sources of secondary reinforcement such as money or love. We will have more to say about acquired drives
and secondary reinforcers when we examine neo-Hullian explanations of selected
social-developmental phenomena.

One of the more remarkable features of social-personality development is the
rapidity at which it occurs. In the course of the first few years of life, the child is
exposed to a multitude of situations or cues that provide the opportunity for
learning many diverse behaviors. However, the child soon shows a remarkable
regularity in his interpersonal behavior, sex-role behavior, and moral conduct.
Given that no two cues or stimulus situations are ever precisely the same, one
might wonder how the neo-Hullians would explain the rapidity with which children form these general habits.

Dollard and Miller (1950) explain the rapidity of social development by making reference to two concepts: the cue-producing response and generalization. A
cue-producing response is a self-generated act that cues or mediates other responses. Language labeling is a cue-producing response. If the child labels an object as "hot," this act may mediate his avoidance of the object in the future.

Since no two cues are exactly alike, learning to adjust to one's environment
would be difficult if habits learned in one situation did not generalize to other
similar situations. Generalization of habits across cues is enhanced when the
child labels two slightly different cues or situations as similar or equivalent. For
example, the label "meal" can serve as a cue-producing response that directs the
child to demonstrate the table manners he has learned at home, regardless of
where he may now be dining. Thus habit generalization, aided by cue-producing
responses, accounts for the rapid evolution of very broad, general habits from
one's diverse experiential history.

The environment often demands that children inhibit generalization and learn
to respond differentially to similar cues. This process of cue discrimination is accomplished when responses to only a few of a group of similar cues are reinforced. For example, children may initially surmise that all clear liquids will
reduce thirst. Since few clear liquids accomplish this purpose, the child will

eventually learn to discriminate thirst-quenching clear liquids (water, creme soda) from those clear liquids that do not quench thirst (paint thinner, cleaning solvent). A failure to make the above discrimination could have rather disastrous consequences if the child were to drink paint thinner. Thus, parents often accelerate the discrimination process by introducing the child to verbal labels which, once learned, serve as cue-producing responses that mediate his discriminations.

Dollard and Miller (1950) argue that man's multifaceted use of language distinguishes his learning capabilities from those of infrahuman species. Man alone uses verbal labels to mediate very complex generalizations and discriminations that lower species find difficult or impossible. Words serve to bind time for man, permitting him to reinforce present behavior by making symbolic reference to future consequences. Reasoning, itself, is viewed as a substitution of internal cue-producing responses (for example, thoughts) for overt acts. Dollard and Miller view the reasoning process as a much more efficient mode of problem solving than the trial and error learning of infrahuman species. In addition, one man today can learn what others took centuries to discover, simply because the accomplishments of his predecessors have been recorded in the written language.

Our focus upon Dollard and Miller's social learning theory has neglected the important theoretical efforts of Robert Sears. In view of Sears' close association both with Hull and with Dollard and Miller, it is perhaps not surprising that his own social learning theory is generally quite compatible with the Dollard and Miller model. However, Sears is much more concerned than are Dollard and Miller with formulating and testing a truly systematic alternative explanation of psychoanalytic phenomena, particularly psychosexual development. While much of the empirical support for Dollard and Miller's theory derives from animal studies conducted under tightly controlled laboratory conditions, Sears has consistently studied the social learning of human beings, both in the laboratory and in natural settings.

The differences between Sears' approach and that of other neo-Hullians are outlined in Sears' (1951a) presidential address to the American Psychological Association. In this statement, Sears argues that an individual must be judged by his actions or overt behaviors. While he clearly recognizes that perception, cognition, and other internal processes may partially account for action, Sears contends that actions, rather than internal processes, represent the very developmental products that we hope to explain. This emphasis on overt behavior and deemphasis of internal mediators suggests that Sears was influenced by the radical behaviorists, a conclusion that is strengthened by his frequent use of radical behavioristic terminology in some of his later work (e.g., Sears 1961; Sears et al. 1965).

Sears' (1951a, 1951b) theoretical statements advance a second important view: the theorist who is truly interested in social learning and social-personality development simply must be prepared to focus upon social behavior, that is, behavioral sequences involving the interaction of two or more individuals. Sears sharply criticizes students of behavior for emphasizing the actions of a single individual without placing these actions into their appropriate social context. He proceeds to argue that the vast majority of human behavior — and, indeed, all social learning — occurs within the dyadic behavioral unit, where the response of one individual serves as the stimulus (cue) for the other. Sears believes that the behavior of socialization agents influences the child's behavior, and at the same time, the child's behavior has an influence upon the subsequent behavior of socialization agents. Thus, Sears considers the child much more active in determining the course of his development than do other neo-Hullians, although his position on the activity-passivity dimension is weak compared to that of the Bandurians to whom we will now turn.

Bandurian Social Learning Theory

The social learning theory of Bandura and his associates (Bandura, 1969, 1971; Bandura & Walters, 1959, 1963; Walters & Brown, 1964; Walters & Parke, 1964) is in many ways similar to the neo-Hullian and the radical behaviorist models. All three approaches contend that one's social learning history determines his personality. All three approaches view the concepts of cue, response, and reinforcement as important theoretical elements. But despite these obvious topological similarities, Bandura's explanation of social learning is quite different from the explanations advanced by the neo-Hullians and the radical behaviorists.

Like the radical behaviorists, Bandurians reject the neo-Hullian assertion that human behavior is motivated by primary and secondary drives. Proponents of both approaches view drives as circular motivational labels (for example, a person is driven to explore by an exploratory drive that we know is operative because he explores), and advocate avoiding this circularity by focusing upon the organism's responses and the stimuli that determine or control these responses. In their zealous attempt to eschew all inner determinants, the radical behaviorists argue that external stimuli (cues, reinforcing stimuli) evoke and/or control human behavior. This assertion is rejected by the Bandurians because it neglects man's cognitive capabilities and the role played by cognition in determining human behavior. We will discover that Bandura places much more emphasis on symbolic and/or vicarious determinants of social learning, and less emphasis on the role played by directly experienced response consequences, than either the neo-Hullians or the radical behaviorists.

Both the neo-Hullians and the radical behaviorists argue that reinforcement is necessary for learning. Accordingly, the child's social behavior can be viewed as the product of directly experienced response consequences. Bandura (1971) advances the counterargument that "all learning phenomena resulting from direct experience can occur on a vicarious basis through observation of other people's behavior and its consequences for them" (p. 2). The assumptions implicit in this statement are that the child need not receive reinforcement or even respond in order to learn from observing the actions of others. Seeking to support his assertions, Bandura (1965) had three groups of children watch a film of an adult who displayed novel aggressive responses toward an inflatable Bobo doll. One group saw the model rewarded for aggression, one group saw the model punished, and the final group observed that the model received no consequences for his aggressive actions. In a later free-play session, children imitated the rewarded model most and the punished model least. However, children in all three experimental groups were easily able to reproduce the adult model's behavior when they were subsequently offered attractive incentives for correct imitation in a final testing session. Clearly, the children had learned the novel aggressive responses by observation, as no child had actually responded himself prior to the free-play session. Directly experienced reinforcement did determine the childrens' willingness to perform, but not their ability to perform. Thus, the Bandurians argue that contiguity, the temporal association of cues and responses, is necessary for learning, and that reinforcement affects performance.

Bandura believes that the vast majority of human behavior is learned by example. There are several reasons for the pervasive impact of observational learning on social-personality development. First, observational learning is much more efficient than trial and error processes. Parents soon learn that they may once model, either verbally or behaviorally, a behavior they are trying to instill and be successful, whereas they would have to spend considerably more time and effort if they were to differentially reinforce the child's unguided actions. Second, some complex behaviors may well be produced only through the influence of models. For example, if children were not exposed to speaking models, it would be impossible for them to acquire the spoken language. That is, it seems implausible that parents could ever shape words, not to mention grammatical speech, by differentially reinforcing the child's random vocalizations. Indeed, psycholinguists (cf. McNeill, 1970) have determined that parents do not "shape" grammatical speech. However, Bandura and Harris (1966), Liebert, Odom, Hill, and Huff (1969), and Rosenthal and Whitebook (1970) have all demonstrated that children lacking certain grammatical knowledge will change their syntactic constructions in accordance with modeled rules. Finally, observational learning enables the child to acquire many novel responses in a variety of settings where his models are not especially intent upon teaching him anything in particular. Thus, the child is constantly learning by observing the actions of others, and it is not at all surprising to the Bandurians that his social-personality development proceeds so very rapidly.

Mechanisms of Observational Learning

It would be highly inappropriate to create the impression that the neo-Hullians and the radical behaviorists fail to see the importance of modeling influences on social-personality development. Both Miller and Dollard (1941) and Skinner (1953) recognize that a very large percentage of the child's behavior is learned through the influence of example. However, their explanations of observational learning require that the modeled response be performed (imitated) by the observer and positively reinforced before it will be learned. These explanations, of course, cannot explain Bandura's (1965) results or, indeed, any instance of delayed imitation where: (a) the observer does not imitate the modeled response in the setting in which it occurred; (b) reinforcements are not forthcoming to the model or the observer; and (c) the acquired responses are not displayed until days or weeks have elapsed. Phenomena such as delayed imitation suggest to Bandura (1971) that observational learning occurs through symbolic (cognitive) processes during exposure to modeled activities and before the observer's imitative responses have been performed or reinforced.

Bandura (1969, 1971) suggests that observational learning is largely mediated by four interrelated subprocesses.

Attentional Processes

Observational learning cannot occur unless the observer carefully attends to the model's behavior. Among the many variables that are thought to influence the observer's attention to modeled sequences are: characteristics of the model, such as his or her attractiveness, nurturance, competence, social power, etc.; characteristics of the observer, such as his or her self-esteem, similarity to the model, socioeconomic status; and various factors such as intrinsic interest of the modeled behavior and instructions to pay attention.

Retention Processes

An observer must somehow commit the model's behavior to memory if he is to reproduce that behavior at a later time when the model is no longer present to serve as a guide. Bandura (1969, 1971) posits two symbolic representational systems that aid the observer to retain the important elements of a model's behavior. First, attention to modeling stimuli produces retrievable images of modeled behavior in the observer's imaginal representational system. These images are primarily visual in character, but auditory, kinesthetic, and/or other sensory images may also aid the observer in coding the modeled sequence. Second, observers commonly make use of a verbal representational system, whereby observed behavior is translated into summary (verbal) labels that describe the observations made. This latter system is very efficient, in that complicated behavior sequences that are difficult to code or retain imaginally (for example, the model's sequential actions in opening a combination safe) may easily be retained when imaginal information is summarized verbally (for example, combination equals L29 R15 L47). Once formed, imaginal and verbal codes serve as guides for the future reproduction of modeled behavior. Evidence is rapidly accumulating to demonstrate that symbolic coding of observed responses does enhance the observational learning and retention of both children (Bandura, Grusec, & Menlove,

1966; Coates & Hartup, 1969) and adults (Bandura & Jeffery, 1973; Gerst, 1971).

Motoric Reproduction Processes

This third component of observational learning refers to the processes through which symbolic representations guide overt behavior. The rate at which the model's behavior can be acquired depends, in part, upon the observer's ability to execute all of the component responses. If the observer has all the components in his behavioral repertoire, he may easily combine them into new patterns to emulate the model's behavior, whereas if they are lacking, imitation of the modeled sequence is either not possible or, at best, incomplete. For example, a child may have acquired and retained symbolic representations of the behavioral sequence necessary for dunking a basketball, but if he is too short to reach over the rim of the basket, he will never emulate the actions of a Wilt Chamberlain.

Often, observers find it exceedingly difficult to skillfully reproduce modeled activities that have been learned through observation. For example, the novice golfer may have adequately represented and retained all facets of the Jack Nicklaus swing, and may have all the necessary components in his behavioral repertoire, but still fail to reproduce the Nicklaus swing, or at least its results. Our golfer's problem is that he cannot directly observe his own swing to determine if it matches his symbolic model of Nicklaus' swing; instead, he must depend upon proprioceptive cues and/or the verbal reports of fellow players or other onlookers. The golfer will likely refine his swing somewhat through self-corrective adjustments that are made largely on the basis of performance-based feedback. Indeed, Bandura argues that most observers acquire only rough approximations of a modeled sequence through observation. These approximations are subsequently refined through self-corrective adjustments made on the basis of feedback from motoric reproduction.

Reinforcement (Motivational Processes)

A person might well acquire, retain, and rehearse all of the elements necessary for executing modeled behavior, but may choose not to perform that behavior if it is likely to yield negative outcomes. When positively reinforced, observational learning that was previously not expressed is readily performed (*cf.* Bandura, 1965). Thus, Bandura believes that the primary function of both direct and vicarious reinforcement is to regulate the performance of learned behavior.

Bandura concedes that reinforcement may play a small part in the observer's acquisition of modeled responses. That is, one's anticipation of being reinforced for correct imitation may well control what he attends to and/or how actively he codes and mentally rehearses what he has observed.

Active Man: Self-control through Self-reinforcement

An adequate theory of social behavior must explain not only the acquisition of behavioral patterns, but also the means by which they are regulated and maintained. Bandura (1971) recognizes that much of human behavior is controlled by external discriminative stimuli, that is, real or anticipated response consequences. However, he notes that the common notion that behavior is regulated by its consequences has often been interpreted to mean that man's actions are totally controlled by environmental influences. Bandura proposes that much of man's behavior is self-regulated by self-produced consequences (for example, self-reinforcement).

The artist who sculpts a bust from clay does not require the presence of an outsider to differentially reinforce his every move until an acceptable product is created. Rather, the artist possesses his own standards of acceptable work and will engage in his own self-corrective actions until his bust satisfies those standards. The result of his self-scrutinizing may often be a product that far exceeds the requirements of what would be perfectly acceptable to others. Indeed, I once knew an artist who, in his own words, had never created a "finished" product because he was never satisfied with anything he had produced. Although the artist made a substantial amount of money through the sale of his work, his failure to match his own standards of acceptable art was a major impetus for his eventual selection of another occupation. This particular self-monitoring or self-reinforcing system is only one of many that easily serves the function of example. Bandura argues that people similarly set self-standards in most areas of human functioning and respond to their own behavior either positively or negatively in accordance with these self-imposed behavioral demands.

Development of Self-reinforcing Systems

Self-reinforcement contingencies are thought to be acquired through differential reinforcement and/or modeling. People often learn to evaluate their own behavior on the basis of how others evaluate it. For example, parents may praise their child or provide him with some material reward for every grade on his report card that is at least "B" or above. As a result of this differential reinforcement, the child may well adopt the grade "B" as an acceptable standard of performance and respond to his subsequent academic performance in self-approving or self-critical ways depending upon its departure from this acquired performance standard. In addition, the results of several experiments (reviewed in Bandura, 1971) suggest that people do learn standards of self-reinforcement or self-punishment displayed by exemplary models, and will subsequently evaluate their own performances relative to these standards.

Bandura describes self-esteem as the discrepancy between a person's behavior and the standards that person has selected as indices of good or acceptable performance. When his behavior consistently falls short of his self-imposed standards, the person evaluates himself negatively and is low in self-esteem. When his performance consistently meets or exceeds his standards, the person evaluates himself positively or holds himself in high esteem. Thus, one's self-esteem is dependent upon more than one's behavior per se, or the reactions of others to that behavior. Rather, it depends upon one's behavior vis-à-vis one's *own* performance expectancies. Bandura notes that many very competent people who have achieved substantially or made it in the eyes of others may hold themselves in low regard because they have failed to satisfy unrealistically high standards of self-evaluation. In fact, the tendency to adopt harsh self-reinforcement standards that are difficult if not impossible to satisfy is one of the defining characteristics of neurotic and psychotic depression (Loeb, Beck, Diggory, & Tuthill, 1967).

Maintenance of Self-reinforcement Contingencies

Both research (e.g., Bandura & Perloff, 1967) and common observation suggest that people will often deny themselves rewards over which they have complete control if their behavior does not meet or exceed their standards of acceptable performance. At this point, it seems necessary to ask why, in the absence of external surveillance, will people deny themselves reward and/or punish themselves for failing to satisfy these self-imposed and self-regulated behavioral demands? Bandura discusses three explanations of this intriguing phenomenon.

The conditioned relief hypothesis (Aronfreed, 1964) assumes that people punish themselves for unacceptable behavior because punishment has acquired anxiety relief value through prior conditioning experiences. That is, when parents discipline their children, they often voice their criticisms at or near the conclusion of the child's punishment. In the process, criticism becomes a conditioned stimulus that signifies the end of punishment and the anxiety associated with punishment. Accordingly, people may learn to criticize themselves for their own unacceptable or transgressive behavior, since self-critical responses may now serve as a conditioned stimulus for anxiety reduction.

The self-generated distress hypothesis assumes that the performance of punishable behavior creates anticipatory fears of detection that persist until the transgressor is reprimanded. Punishment is said to terminate this self-generated distress and may even serve to restore the favor of others (for example, by taking his punishment, the transgressor has redeemed himself). Self-punishment may serve similar functions by eliminating the person's distress or anxiety about detection and by serving as an atonement for his unacceptable actions.

Bandura believes that periodic external reinforcements are largely responsible for sustaining self-reinforcement contingencies. He argues that adherence to high standards of self-reinforcement is actively encouraged by praise, honors, and social recognition, while adherence to minimal standards is likely to bring criticism from others. Bandura notes that the act of belittling oneself for failing to meet high standards may actually produce the kind of external reinforcement necessary to maintain those standards. That is, by criticizing oneself, the person may be successful at persuading others to elaborate upon his good qualities and to assure him that his persistent efforts to achieve most worthy goals will ultimately end in success.

The Role of the Child in his Socialization

Bandura contends that children are actively involved in determining the course of their social-personality development. Observational learning requires the observer to actively attend to, code, and mentally rehearse the behavior exhibited by models. The self-regulation of behavior through self-produced consequences obviously implies that man is actively involved in his own behavioral development. Indeed, Bandura (1971) argues that all psychological functioning can be characterized as a continuous reciprocal interaction between behavior and its controlling circumstances. According to this notion, the environment is said to affect the organism's behavior which, in turn, affects the environment. Thus, the behaving child is said to be actively involved in creating the very environment that influences his development.

Bandura (1971) cites a study by Sidman (1966) to illustrate the reciprocal interaction between behavior and the environment. Sidman created a situation in which animals could delay indefinitely the onset of painful shocks by pressing a bar that forestalled the shock for a set period of time. Animals who quickly learned to make bar presses within successive delay intervals created for themselves an environment that was low in its punitiveness. Other animals who were slow to acquire the coping mechanism experienced a highly punitive environment. Note that the potential environment is identical for all animals, but that the actual environment and its effects depend upon their behavior. Bandura argues that children, like Sidman's animals, are not controlled by a fixed, omnipotent environment. Rather, ". . . people play an active role in controlling their own [environmental] reinforcement contingencies through their characteristic modes of response" (Bandura, 1971, p. 40).

Applications of Social Learning Theory to Selected Topics

Dependency

Neo-Hullians view dependency as one of the many secondary drives that the child learns during the socialization process. Dependent habits are said to be established by the presence and behavior of need-gratifying adults. Initially, the child smiles at his mother, clings to her, and remains in her close proximity in order to insure that his biological needs (hunger, thirst, etc.) are gratified. Because of her repeated association with primary drive reduction, the mother and her nurturant acts assume the characteristics of secondary reinforcers. The child thus acquires a need to maintain contact with the mother and to receive her nurturance — a dependency need — and will become anxious when deprived of these significant sources of secondary reinforcement. These dependency needs eventually generalize to other targets when other people become significant sources of social reinforcement (Charlesworth & Hartup, 1967).

Sears, Whiting, Nowlis, and Sears (1953) argue more specifically that the dependency drive emerges when social rewards and/or nurturant acts expected of the mother are withheld. Such a state of affairs produces a conflict between the child's prior expectancies of nurturance and his emerging expectancies of nonnurturance. Sears (1961) depicts the dependency drive as ". . . the need to regain control of the parental resources that provide the child with many forms of gratification, especially the expression of love." The strength of the child's dependency drive is determined by the intensity of the conflict between nurturant and nonnurturant expectancies. The literature (reviewed in Hartup, 1963, and Walters & Parke, 1964) does suggest that children who have been deprived or frustrated in their efforts to obtain nurturance show heightened dependency needs and an increased susceptibility to social influence.

Bandurians (Bandura & Walters, 1963; Walters & Parke, 1964) are especially critical of the neo-Hullian characterization of dependency as an acquired drive for nurturance, attention, or social reinforcement. Rather than label dependency as a specific motivational system, Walters and Parke (1964) define it as a class of behavior that is instrumental in obtaining help, approval, reassurance, or other forms of nurturance from others. Dependent behaviors are said to be learned in the same way that other behaviors are learned (that is, through differential reinforcement of the child's overt behavior and/or modeling), and are exhibited whenever the child experiences or anticipates a loss of parental nurturance.

Recall that Sears posited a learned drive for dependence from evidence that suggests that frustrating the child's attempts to obtain nurturance from others leads to greater attention-seeking (that is, dependency). Walters and Parke's (1964) explanation of this phenomenon requires no mention of a learned dependency drive. Rather, they contend that parents who are inconsistent in either their withholding of nurturance or their punishment of dependent behavior are, by virtue of their inconsistencies, partially reinforcing dependent behavior. Since partial reinforcement makes behavior extremely resistant to extinction (Skinner, 1953), Walters and Parke suggest that parents who intermittently reinforce dependence will produce highly dependent children. Support for this latter hypothesis derives from studies that have investigated the origins of dependency in dogs (e.g., Fisher, 1955; Scott, 1958) as well as humans (Gewirtz & Baer, 1958; Hartup, 1958; Sears et al., 1957).

Sexuality

Sex is certainly not the primary impetus of social-personality development according to the neo-Hullian perspective. Rather, neo-Hullians view human sexuality as nothing more than an important class of behavior that is motivated by a primary (sex) drive and shaped by social learning. Dollard and Miller (1950) and Sears et al. (1965) accept the Oedipus complex as a genuine developmental phenomenon, although they believe that this conflict originates from parental punishment of the child's sexual responses, for example, masturbation, as opposed to the child's incestuous desires for the opposite-sex parent. Parental punishment of the child's sexual responses attaches fear to those responses. The child now faces a conflict between the need to reduce sexual urges via sexual behavior and the need to reduce acquired fear by avoiding sexual behavior. In neo-Hullian terminology, sexual behavior becomes the object of an approach-avoidance conflict (cf. Miller, 1948). Since the avoidance gradient is steeper than the approach gradient in such a conflict, the child's sexual thoughts, urges, and behaviors are likely to be inhibited. Severe sexual conflicts may prevent the child from ever learning "normal" sexual behaviors unless the fear associated with sexual functioning is weakened or overcome. Thus, neo-Hullians are easily able to explain why Freud would often discover sexual conflicts at the core of personality dysfunctions.

Bandura and Walters (1963) deemphasize the role of a biological sex drive in their explanation of human sexuality. Rather, they are primarily concerned with demonstrating how parental inhibitions and sexual anxieties are passed along to children through modeling or direct tuition. Unlike the neo-Hullians who have reinterpreted Freud's views of childhood sexuality, Bandura and Walters largely reject these views and treat sex as just another class of behavior acquired through direct experience or observational learning. In any given situation, a person's performance of learned sexual responses is said to depend upon the rewards and punishments anticipated should he/she emit those responses.

Sex-role Development

Neo-Hullian theorists (Mowrer, 1950, 1960; Sears, 1957; Sears et al., 1965) contend that children acquire culturally approved sex-role attitudes and behaviors through the process of identification. Although identification has been defined in a number of ways (cf. Winch, 1962), the neo-Hullians describe it as a motive to emulate the behavior of another person. Mowrer (1960) and Sears (1957) specifically argue that the child's initial (anaclitic) identification occurs when he (she) becomes dependent upon the mother for nurturance. The mother (or primary caretaker) is the person who gratifies the primary biological and social needs of the young child. In the process, the child associates her presence with reinforcing consequences, and the mother *and her behaviors* become sources of secondary reinforcement. Thus, the child is motivated to obey the mother in order to retain her nurturance, and to emulate her behavior in her absence (sex-role behaviors included) in order to provide himself or herself with positively valenced secondary reinforcers. Consistent with the neo-Hullian model of identification are a number of studies (e.g., Bandura & Huston, 1961; Mussen, 1961; Mussen & Distler, 1959, 1960; Mussen & Rutherford, 1963; Payne & Mussen, 1956; P. S. Sears, 1953) demonstrating that children more readily imitate the behavior of warm, nurturant models as opposed to those who are cold and rejecting.

One problem with this model of sex-role socialization is its inability to explain how a boy might eventually acquire an appropriately masculine sex-role orientation through his anaclitic identification with his mother. That is, it does not account for a boy's identification with his father. Sears et al. (1965) address this problem by positing a second kind of identification, defensive identification, which occurs when ". . . the already established anaclitic identification produces an internalization of punitive and restrictive and qualities of a threatening [same-sex] parent" (p. 7). The logic of this process remains unclear to this writer. While it seems reasonable to argue that a strong anaclitic bond could conceivably mediate the daughter's further identification with a mother who begins to punish dependency, sexuality, etc. (that is, the daughter obeys the mother and emulates her behavior in order to regain her nurturance), it is not at all clear how the mother-son anaclitic bond mediates the son's identification with a punitive, threatening father. Indeed, Mussen and Distler (1960) report that a mother's warmth or nurturance is unrelated to her son's masculinity, a finding that suggests the anaclitic bond may not be related to a boy's identification with his father. In fact, the validity of a theory of sex-role socialization based on defensive identification must be questioned in view of a substantial body of literature (e.g., Bronson, 1959; Mussen, 1961; Mussen & Distler, 1959, 1960; Mussen & Rutherford, 1963; P. S. Sears, 1953) indicating a positive relationship between *paternal* nurturance and the masculinity of male children.

Bandurians (Bandura, 1969; Bandura & Walters, 1963) argue that one need not posit a motive to emulate the behavior of others, that is, identification, in order to explain sex-role socialization. What others call identification is nothing more than observational learning in the Bandurian scheme. Bandura contends that a child learns culturally approved sex-role attitudes and behaviors by direct tuition and by observing the behavior of numerous same-sex models. As the child grows older and is increasingly exposed to peers, same-sex teachers, media personalities, etc., his or her sex-role behavior might be expected to become progressively less similar to that of the same-sex parent. Indeed, Brim (1958), Rosenberg and Sutton-Smith (1968), and Sutton-Smith and Rosenberg (1970) report that the number of siblings in the family and their distribution by age and sex affect the patterning of sex-typing among all family members. The main point of these studies is that even the child's familial sex-role socialization is not based solely on the same-sex parent, but is also influenced by other children *of both sexes* and the total familial environment.

Moral Development

Social learning theorists maintain that the child acquires a conscience, or a set of internalized standards against which he or she judges the appropriateness of conduct, in roughly the same way that he or she acquires a culturally appropriate sex-role. The neo-Hullians, for example, view moral development as a product of the child's general identification with his or her parents. As the child becomes dependent upon parents for nurturance, he imitates more and more of his parents' behaviors and codes of conduct in order to forestall a loss of parental love (Sears, 1957). According to this view, parents must be nurturant to their child before he/she will become dependent upon them and incorporate their moral standards. Parents who are low in nurturance or those who primarily use power-assertive (physical) disciplinary techniques are thought to produce hostile children who show weak parental identification and, thus, develop weak consciences. Indeed, the literature (reviewed in Hoffman, 1963, 1970) is generally consistent with this latter assertion. Sears et al. (1957) argue that the most effective mode of moral socialization involves a combination of high parental nurturance and the adoption of love-withdrawal as a principal disciplinary strategy.

Bandurians (Bandura, 1969; Bandura & Walters, 1963) counterargue that the neo-Hullian concept of identification is not needed to explain the child's acquisition and use of moral standards. According to the Bandurian perspective, the internalized standards that comprise the conscience are merely examples of self-reinforcement contingencies that have been acquired through direct tuition or observational learning. Once established, these self-imposed, self-regulated moral standards are maintained by their ability to prevent anxiety, guilt, or punishment (*cf.* Aronfreed, 1964; Bandura, 1971), and by the external reinforcements that others – parents, peers, teachers, the church – provide for their continued use.

A perusal of the literature suggests that neither the neo-Hullian nor the Bandurian explanation of moral development is totally satisfactory. Studies of the effects of observing a model's behavior on childrens' subsequent resistance to temptation (Stein, 1967; Walters, Leat, & Mezei, 1963; Walters & Parke, 1964), inhibition of aggression (Bandura, 1965; Bandura, Ross, & Ross, 1963). adoption of self-imposed standards resulting in self-denial (Bandura & Kupers, 1964; Bandura & Whalen, 1966; Mischel & Liebert, 1966), and delay of gratification (Bandura & Mischel, 1965; Mischel, 1965) have failed to support the assertion that modeling plays a major role in the development of internalized behavioral controls. These experiments suggest that, while observing the actions of models can easily disinhibit previously inhibited behaviors, the reverse is only occasionally true. That is, internal controls are not often *firmly established* by observing the exemplary behavior of models, but they are often weakened by observing models' transgressions (cf. Hoffman, 1970, for an extended discussion of this point). These findings tend to discredit any theory that asserts that identification or any other imitative learning is the major process by which internal moral controls are established.[6]

One reason that the child may not readily acquire internalized behavioral controls through observation or identification is that significant components of these internal controls are perhaps not often modeled by parents and other socialization agents. It is obviously true that certain moral attributes are enacted (for example, helping others in need) or verbalized (for example, moral rules such as the golden rule) for the child. However, other significant aspects of a model's conscience such as guilt, temptation, self-denial, and self-criticism may never be verbalized, and are not easily discernible from the model's overt behavior. Thus, processes in addition to identification or modeling may well be necessary for the socialization of morality (cf. Hoffman, 1970; Kohlberg, 1969).

Social learning theory is currently the majority position in the study of social-personality development. It has stimulated the bulk of the domestic socialization research for the past two decades, and has replaced psychoanalysis as a major interpretive framework for cross-cultural studies of social-personality development. There is one additional perspective on social-personality development, the cognitive-developmental approach, which has recently attracted many proponents. We shall now focus our attention upon this theoretical position.

COGNITIVE-DEVELOPMENTAL THEORY

If I had written this chapter in 1960, the odds are good that it would have included only a passing reference to cognitive-developmental theory. In the short span of 15 years, the cognitive-developmental perspective has progressed from a position of relative obscurity to the point where it is currently hailed as the "new look" at social-personality development. This new look derives from the efforts of a number of cognitive theorists (e.g., Baldwin, 1906; Bruner, 1964; Bruner, Oliver, & Greenfield, 1966; Dewey, 1930; Kohlberg, 1966, 1969; Loevinger, 1966; Werner, 1957), although the major contributor has to be Jean Piaget, a Swiss scholar, who for the past 50-plus years has engaged himself in a program of research aimed at providing an understanding of the processes and products of cognitive development.

---

[6]Hoffman's (1963, 1970) review of the effects of various parental disciplinary strategies upon the subsequent moral development of children also tends to discredit neo-Hullian assertions. Contrary to the expectations of Sears, Maccoby, and Levin (1957), nurturant parents who use love-withdrawal as their principal disciplinary strategy *do not* produce children who have especially well-established consciences or moral controls.

The cognitive-developmental perspective on socialization is not so much a well articulated theory of social-personality development as it is a model of psychological functioning that has obvious implications for social-personality development. Cognitive-developmentalists view man as a constructivist; that is, an organism who responds to his environment in terms of his own understanding (or construction) of its essential features. A person's construction of reality, or the characteristics of his environment, is said to depend upon the cognitive operational systems (structures) currently available at that point in his developmental history. It is a fallacy, according to the cognitive-developmentalists, to assume that environmental stimuli are interpreted by everyone as if they possess a fundamental reality. Kessen (1966) notes that "the child who is confronted by a stable reality that can be described adequately in the language of contemporary physics is a child very different from the one who is seen facing phenomenal disorder from which he must construct a coherent view of reality" (pp. 58-59). Piaget adds:

> Knowledge is not a copy of reality. To know an object, to know an event, is not simply to look at it and make a mental copy, or image, of it. To know is to modify, to transform the object, and to understand the way the object is constructed. An operation is thus the essence of knowledge; it is an interiorized action which modifies the object of knowledge (Piaget, as cited in Jennings, 1967).

The obvious implication of a constructivist view of man is that one's interpretations of and responses to social stimuli are mediated by his constructions (conceptualizations) of those stimuli at that particular point in his developmental history. Psychologists favoring a cognitive-developmental perspective on socialization contend that a child's social-personality development is underlaid by his changing cognitive constructions of the social environment. Thus, one must understand the processes and products of cognitive development before he may fully comprehend the course of social-personality development. We will now turn to Piaget's theory of intellectual development as a prerequisite for both of these ends.

Origins of Piagetian Cognitive-Developmental Theory

As an adolescent and throughout the course of his formal academic training, Piaget maintained an active interest in biology and epistemology, a branch of philosophy concerned with the study of knowledge. One of the major reasons that Piaget chose zoology as a graduate major at Neuchatel, where he earned his doctoral degree in 1918, was his belief that a biological orientation would prove an invaluable addition to his philosophical analysis of epistemological questions. Piaget's early attempts to integrate these two interests were unsuccessful because he realized that "Between biology and the study of knowledge I needed something other than philosophy. I believe it was at that moment that I discovered a need that could be satisfied only by psychology" (Piaget, 1952a, p. 240).

After completing his doctoral studies, Piaget went to Zurich to pursue the study of psychology. In the short span of one year in Zurich, he worked in two psychological laboratories and in Bleuler's psychiatric clinic. Piaget then journeyed to Paris where he spent two years at the Sorbonne studying abnormal psychology, logic, epistemology, and philosophy of science. While studying at the Sorbonne, he was offered a position with Dr. Theopile Simon in the Binet laboratory in Paris. His decision to accept this position standardizing French versions of English reasoning tests ultimately shaped the direction of his career.

Standardizing an intelligence test is in many ways a tedious process. The examiner must present members of a sample with a preestablished sequence of precisely worded questions according to a set procedure from which he may not deviate. This testing method is said to insure that variations in subjects' performance on the test are due to individual differences in intelligence as opposed to variations in either the tester's methods or the questions asked of subjects. The subject's intellectual capacity is defined in terms of the number and types of questions he or she answers correctly.

Piaget soon discovered that he was more interested in a subject's *incorrect* answers to questions. At first, he was intrigued by his finding that the same kinds of wrong answers were recurrent among children of about the same age. Piaget then began to question children further about their wrong answers using the clinical method that he had learned and practiced while working in Bleuler's laboratory. He discovered that children produce different kinds of common wrong answers at different ages and concluded from these observations that intelligence was something other than a linear continuum. That is, older children were not simply more intelligent than younger children; their thought was qualitatively different from that of younger children. Piaget soon realized that his calling was to investigate the different modes of thought used by children of different ages and, if possible, to account for the way in which a child progresses from one mode of thought to another. In a word, Piaget developed an interest in cognitive development that provided the impetus for his research and theorizing of the next forty years.

Research Methods of the Cognitive-Developmentalists

Piaget's methods vary considerably in accordance with the age of his subjects and the types of behavior being studied.[7] At times, he has favored a naturalistic-observational method, where he and his coworkers make detailed observations of ongoing behavior and its antecedents and consequences without intervening

[7]This brief overview of Piagetian methods focuses only upon the naturalistic-observational and the clinical-experimental methods used by Piaget in his work on intellectual development. We have purposely omitted yet other methods that Piaget uses to investigate other phenomena, for example, perceptual development. The reader is referred to Flavell (1963) for a more comprehensive description of Piagetian methodology.

themselves to elicit or direct this behavior. For example, much of the data reported in Piaget's (1951, 1952b, 1954) three volumes on intellectual growth in infancy and early childhood is based upon his careful observations of the behavior of his own three children. Of course, Piaget's observational methods are subject to many criticisms. He did not make use of any standard research instruments to collect his data nor did he use another observer to check the reliability of his observations. The use of his own three children as research subjects leaves Piaget open to the criticisms that: (a) his status as a parent may have biased his observations; and (b) his observations and the theory they helped to generate may not be generalizable beyond the small and very select sample on which they were based. Experimentalists further criticize the observational method for its inability to specify cause and effect relationships with any certainty. Despite the fact that the discoveries he made using the observational technique have been replicated by independent observers (cf. Decarie, 1965), Piaget was well aware of the shortcomings of this method and has relied mainly upon other quasi-experimental techniques in the majority of his research endeavors.

The most common of Piaget's "experimental" techniques is his clinical method.[8] In a typical Piagetian experiment, the child is presented with a test stimulus, or question of some sort, to which he is asked to make a response. When the child has responded, the experimenter, in response to the child's behavior, will introduce a variation of the original test stimulus and/or ask another question which he hopes will clarify the cognitive structures and processes underlying the child's original response. Each successive response made by the child largely determines what the experimenter will ask or do next. This clinical-experimental method is clearly different from a standard experimental method because *no two children ever receive exactly the same experimental treatment.* Piaget (1929) hastened to note the biases, oversights, and lack of controls that could conceivably result from his use of a clinical-experimental methodology. However, he argues that the discovery and explication of the many cognitive structures and stages characterizing the child's intellectual development absolutely requires a flexible methodology where the experimenter can follow the child's thought without deforming it by suggestion or imposing his own views upon the child. The clinical method, which adopts the child's language and keeps questions at a level accessible to the child, seemed appropriate to Piaget for the scientific task that he had set out to accomplish.

The vast majority of the data from which Piaget fashioned his theory of cognitive development were generated by his clinical-experimental studies of children's thought. The data of a Piagetian clinical-experiment consist of protocol records of experimenter-child interactions. The following is a sample data protocol describing the interaction between an experimenter and a seven-year-old

---

[8]The clinical method derives its name from its similarity to the procedures employed by therapists to extract information from clinical patients (Piaget, 1929).

child named Pie in an experiment designed to test children's understanding of the concepts of mass and weight:

E: You see these two little balls here. Is there just as much dough in this
    one as in this one?
Pie: Yes.
E: Now watch. (the experimenter changes one of them into the shape of a
    sausage).
Pie: The sausage has more dough.
E: And if I roll it up into a ball again?
Pie: Then I think there will be the same amount. (The clay is rolled into a ball once
    more and the other ball is molded into the shape of a disc).
E: There's still as much dough? (in the disc)
Pie: There is more dough in the ball.
    (Piaget and Inhelder, cited in Flavell, 1963).

Piaget's published studies generally include primary data such as the above protocol in the text of the article. These protocols are generally preceded, accompanied, and followed by a substantial amount of discussion and theoretical interpretation. By presenting a number of children of differing ages with a wide variety of intellectual problems, Piaget was able to observe different modes of cognitive functioning that are age-related and indicative, in his opinion, of qualitatively distinct stages of cognitive development. In most of his published studies, Piaget discusses the characteristics of each cognitive stage that he has identified, and then illustrates his own reasoning by presenting data protocols descriptive of each of these stages.

Piaget makes no attempt to quantify his data and, thus, one will search in vain for a statistical analysis of his results. There are two major reasons for Piaget's decision to avoid a statistical presentation of his data. First, he contends that it makes little sense to quantify along a linear dimension a series of cognitive structures that are qualitatively different from one another. Second, Piaget has stated:". . . I am always very suspicious (of the use) of statistics on our results. Not that I dislike statistics; I worked on biometrics enthusiastically when I was a zoologist, but to make statistical tables on children when each was questioned differently appears to me very much open to criticism as regards the results of the dispersion" (cited in Flavell, 1963, p. 31).

One might argue that the clinical methodology is deficient in a number of ways. First, Piaget's decisions to conduct unstandardized interviews and to shun statistical description of his data make it difficult for other researchers to replicate his studies, especially in view of the fact that his writings contain only portions of selected clinical interviews for the reader's examination. An unstandardized procedure also raises the possibility that the clinical examiner's pre-existing hypotheses or theoretical biases may determine the question asked, stimuli presented, and/or answers suggested to a subject of a given age. This brings us to an epistemological concern that is worthy of note: Piaget's theory of cognitive development was largely formulated from the very data that he uses to support it. Thus, an acceptance of the theory from this clinical data alone requires the reader to accept, largely on faith, Piaget's skills as a clinical examiner, an objective observer, a synthesizer, and a theoretician. Fortunately, Piaget's cognitive-developmental theory and the models descended from it (e.g., Bruner, 1964 ; Kohlberg, 1966, 1969) have received additional support from the efforts of many other investigators (e.g., Bruner et al., 1966; Kohlberg & Zigler, 1967; Rest, Turiel, & Kohlberg, 1969; Sigel, Roeper, & Hooper, 1966; Smedslund, 1961; Turiel, 1966) who have adopted more traditional experimental methods to test cognitive-developmental assertions.

The Piagetian Theoretical Framework-Basic Concepts

Piaget offers several definitions of intelligence, all of which reflect his strong biological orientation. For example, he has described intelligence as "a system of living and acting operations" (Piaget, 1950, p. 7) that represents "a particular mode of biological adaptation" (Piaget, 1952b, pp. 3-4). Thus, intelligence is viewed as a purely biological function which produces an effective interchange between the individual and his environment. Piaget (1950) adds that intelligence "is the form of equilibrium toward which all the structures . . . tend" (p. 6). This latter statement is extremely rich in its theoretical connotations. It implies that one's intellectual functioning tends toward a harmonious or balanced relationship between his psychological (cognitive) structures and his environment. It is the environment that produces disequilibrium or imbalance which, in turn, stimulates the individual to undertake certain mental activities (described below) in an attempt to restore equilibrium. Thus, the Piagetian model of intelligence is a "balance" model which implies that disequilibrium between cognitive structures and environmental demands is a primary determinant of cognitive functioning and intellectual growth. Note that, for Piaget, intelligence is an extremely complex, multifaceted construct. Indeed, he argues that intelligence consists of three interrelated components: content, structure, and function.

Intellectual Content.

The content of intelligence refers to the external behavior from which we infer cognitive activity. Thus, when one of Piaget's subjects states that the sun is alive because it moves across the sky, or that a rule cannot be altered or violated because of its parental origin, we witness the "evidence" that (a) cognitive functioning has occurred; and (b) this cognition has an underlying base or structure. Although much of Piaget's early work (Piaget, 1929, 1930) focuses upon the content of the child's intellect, he considers these efforts to be of minor significance for an understanding of intelligence. That is, studies of intellectual content cannot explain why thought assumes the form that it does. For this reason,

Piaget devoted most of his attention to the study of intellectual structure and function.

Cognitive Structures

Cognitive structures are the organizational components of intellect that are created through (and, hence, are indissoluble from) cognitive functioning and inferred from the intellectual content that they determine. The neonate has no cognitive structures, although he does come equipped with innate hereditary structures or reflexes that aid him in his interaction with the environment. No training is required for reflexes to operate. The sucking reflex is elicited whenever an object touches the infant's lips; the crying reflex is elicited by biological need states such as hunger; the grasping reflex is elicited whenever an object comes in contact with the infant's hand. Aside from their adaptive significance, these automatic behavioral responses provide the substrate for the development of the child's first psychological structures. Piaget's observations of neonates suggest that, after the first few days of life, reflexes are modified by experience to become very different structures from those provided by heredity. That is, reflexes become elementary psychological structures upon which further intellectual activities are based. We shall have much more to say about the characteristics of psychological structures after we have discussed the processes through which these structures are created, and are subsequently modified.

Intellectual Functions

The most important biological endowment related to intelligence is not the organism's inborn structural capabilities (for example, reflexes) but rather, a set of two inherited functional invariants: organization and adaptation. Piaget argues that these two functional characteristics are at the very core of intelligence, since it is through these functional modes that psychological structures are created, arranged, and altered. These invariant functions are said to be characteristic of not only intelligence, but all biological life systems. This isomorphism reflects Piaget's assertion that intelligence is a highly developed extension of more primitive biological activities whose most general characteristics or functional invariants it shares. Our analysis of the functional invariants will include a description of their essential characteristics and a discussion of their interrelatedness.

Organization refers to the tendency of all species to systematize their structures, be they physical, physiological, or psychological, into an integrated framework. For example, man possesses a number of structures (the mouth, a trachea, lungs, etc.) that are organized into an efficient respiratory system. Psychological structures are similarly organized into coherent systems. For example, the very young infant may have a gazing structure and a grasping structure that are initially unrelated to one another but are gradually organized into a higher-order psychological structure that allows visually-directed grasping. Although psychological structures take different forms at different levels or stages of development, organization is stage-independent. That is, the organism is always in the process of organizing whatever psychological structures are available into higher-order systems or structures.

Adaptation refers to the organism's innate tendency to adapt to or cope with the demands of its environment. It is said to occur "whenever a given organism-environment interchange has the effect of modifying the organism in such a way that further interchanges, favorable to its preservation, are enhanced" (Piaget, as cited in Flavell, 1963, p. 45). Adaptation is divisible into two complementary processes: assimilation and accommodation.

Assimilation refers to the process of changing or reconstructing environmental elements in such a way that they can be incorporated into the structures of the organism. At a physiological level, the organism must change the structure of foodstuffs, first physically by chewing, then biochemically via the digestive process, in order to incorporate these nutrients into the tissue structures of the body. At a psychological level, an infant exposed to a new toy such as a beach ball may initially attempt to assimilate this object into his grasping structure in much the same way rattles, rubber animals, and other small toys have been assimilated previously. In a sense, the child is attempting to transform the beach ball into something that he is familiar with, that is, something to be grasped.

In the process of assimilating environmental stimuli or events, the organism also accommodates i.e., adjusts its structures to meet the demands or structures of environmental elements. For example, the feeding organism must adjust itself to food; it must open its mouth, decide upon a means such as chewing or sucking to get food to the stomach or some analogous structure, and secrete the proper digestive substances to break down that particular food stuff in order that the food be taken into its tissue structures. The infant may have to alter his grasping structure somewhat (for example, using two hands instead of one) in order to incorporate the beach ball into that structure. Although Piaget distinguishes between assimilation and accommodation on conceptual grounds, he believes that they are indissociable components of any adaptive act. Every assimilation of an object to the organism involves an accommodation of the organism to that object.[9]

Cognitive development is said to occur because the organism is continually extending its existing cognitive structures to novel aspects of its milieu. During the process of assimilating new environmental stimuli, the organism must modify its structures, or accommodate, in order to achieve a state of equilibrium be-

[9]This statement does not imply that assimilation and accommodation occur equally (are exactly balanced) for every act, within any cognitive stage, or across stages. Indeed, some acts (for example, fantasy or symbolic play) show a relative preponderance of the assimilative mode, whereas other acts (for example, imitation) are primarily accommodating in character. Piaget (1952a, 1954) stresses that there are no examples of "pure" assimilatory or "pure" accommodatory acts; *all* intellectual acts involve both in varying proportions.

tween those structures and the environment. But equilibrium is, at best, only momentarily achieved since the organism's extension of its structures to novel environmental stimuli occurs continually. Even in the absence of novel environmental stimulation, the organism is engaged in reorganizing its available cognitive structures into higher-order structural systems. Thus, Piaget contends that two kinds of changes — internal reorganization of structures and structural change induced by attempts to deal with novel environmental events — make possible a progressively greater understanding of the nature of one's world. The functional invariants adaptation and organization operate in reciprocal fashion: assimilatory operations induce new accommodations; and accommodatory changes stimulate structural reorganization and further assimilatory activity. In short, the activities of the functional invariants represent the dynamics of cognitive growth in the Piagetian theoretical system.[10]

Types of Cognitive Structures

Piaget's investigations of intellectual development have centered upon the structural aspects of intelligence. His most specific concerns have been: (a) the study of the different types of intellectual organizations, that is, structures, that emerge during the course of development; and (b) the relationships among these successive intellectual organizations. We shall see that Piaget describes the course of intellectual development as a series of stages, where each stage is characterized by a distinct type and/or patterning of cognitive structures.

The first kind of psychological structure to emerge is the simple behavioral schema of the infancy period. For much of the first two years of life, the infant's "thought" or knowledge is limited to that which he can represent by his overt actions. A schema may be defined as a psychological structure that refers to a class of similar action sequences in which the behavioral elements of the sequence are bound into an organized whole. Thumb-sucking, for example, is a behavioral schema that refers to the child's tendency to voluntarily place his hand to his mouth, separate his thumb from his other fingers, open his mouth, place his thumb therein, and suck. While schemas are named for the behavior to which they refer, they also represent the child's underlying disposition to behave. Thus, a thumb-sucking schema refers to the organization of the behavioral components of thumb-sucking and to the adaptive significance of this behavioral pattern. Piaget (1952b) contends that thumb-sucking is adaptive — hence, intrinsically rewarding to the child — because it serves to exercise the reflexive sucking schema which must be exercised to function properly.

[10]Specifically, Piaget (1952b, 1959) argues that human beings have an intrinsic need to cognize. Cognitive structures created by intellectual functioning must perpetuate themselves by additional functioning. Structures are said to have an intrinsic tendency to assimilate environmental "nutriment" for sustenance. Structures also tend toward equilibrium with the environment through accommodatory and/or organizational functions. Thus, the motive for cognitive functioning is indigenous to the child according to Piaget.

During the second year of life, the child has developed to the point where he can acquire new knowledge about objects and events prior to his having acted upon them. That is, the child becomes capable of representing objects, events, or actions internally through the formation of mental symbols, and may then use mental symbolism to direct his subsequent problem-solving and/or imitative behavior. Consider Piaget's (1951) description of the behavior of his 16-month-old daughter in the following passage:

> Jacqueline had a visit from a little boy of (18 months of age) . . . who, in the course of the afternoon got into a terrible temper. He screamed as he tried to get out of the playpen and pushed it backward, stamping his feet. Jacqueline stood watching him in amazement, never having witnessed such a scene before. The next day, she herself screamed in her playpen and tried to move it, stamping her foot several times in succession (p. 63).

Clearly Jacqueline was imitating the actions of an absent model, even though she did not perform those actions at the time that they were modeled. This deferred imitation is possible because Jacqueline had represented the actions of the model in some internal symbolic form that preserved the original scene thus allowing its later re-creation.

According to Piaget (1951), symbolism evolves from the internalization of behavioral schemas. We have stated that the child initially comes to know objects and their properties through his actions on those objects. For example, the infant may represent a rattle by a shaking motion of his arm, an act which is the behavioral equivalent of the older child's symbolic representation of a rattle. Toward the end of the infancy period, the child's representative actions are internalized; he now makes very slight, almost imperceptible muscular responses which symbolize the rattle. Thus, the very first mental symbols are descended from action schemas and are not necessarily visual in character, although vision is certainly a component of many action schemas. Eventually, visual and covert muscular responses are organized to produce the symbolic images necessary for the performance of activities such as deferred imitation. The rapid development of the symbolic function over the course of early childhood enables the child to cognize at new levels. At this point, for example, he is not restricted to acting upon his present environment because he can now easily evoke the past and use his representations of past and/or present happenings to anticipate the future.

The psychological structures of older children (age seven and above) are primarily operational structures. A cognitive operation is defined as an internal mental activity that is an integral part of an organized network of related mental activities. The cognitive operations used by the child to represent (that is, structure) and act upon his environment are many in number. As a general rule of thumb, Piaget (1950) suggests that all of the logical operations involved in mathematics (for example, addition, subtraction, multiplication, division, equivalence, relations such as greater than and less than) belong to, but do not exhaust, the universe of internal intellectual operations performed upon objects and events by the operational child.

An operational structure consists of some combination of cognitive operations that are bound into an organized whole. The existence of one specific operational structure can be inferred from the child's ability to place objects into hierarchical classes. When presented with a set of red, yellow, and blue beads mixed together, the operational child is easily able to group these beads into nonoverlapping classes based on color. The inclusion of similarly colored objects into a class is one example of a cognitive operation. The operational child realizes that he may combine these color classes to form a supraordinate class consisting of beads in general. He is also capable of reversing the process, by logical subtraction, to once again conceive of the beads as forming three color classes. Piaget contends that the formation of hierarchical classes of objects is the intellectual content of a cognitive structure called classification. Classification is composed of the operations of inclusion, addition, and subtraction bound into an organized whole. The child may not be aware that he has this kind of a structure or that he uses this combination of operations when he constructs hierarchical classes. However, the classification structure described above seems to Piaget to adequately describe the basic mental activities underlying the child's classification behavior.

Stages of Cognitive Development

Piaget's theory divides intellectual development into four major periods or stages: the sensorimotor stage (0-1 years); the preoperational stage (2-7 years); the concrete operational stage (7-11 years); and the formal operational stage (11 years and above). Piaget (1960) characterized these cognitive stages and the developmental sequence they define as follows:

1. Stages imply qualitative differences in the thought and/or problem solving strategies of children at different ages.

2. These different modes of thought form an invariant development sequence. Cultural and other environmental influences may hasten or retard the child's progression through the stages, but they do not alter the sequence of stage progression.

3. Each of these sequential modes of thought forms a structured whole. That is, a child's stage-response to some intellectual task, question, or puzzle is not a simple function of his familiarity with that or similar problems. Rather, it depends upon and reflects his underlying thought-organization, or cognitive structuring tendencies.

4. Cognitive stages are hierarchical integrations. The stage sequence is a sequence of increasingly differentiated and integrated structures, all of which serve the common adaptive function. Higher stage structures are said to be a reorganization of lower structures into a new and more complex level of intellectual

operation. For example, formal operational thought includes all of the structural features of concrete operations and its predecessors, but these structures are now at a new level of organization.

If cognitive stages that meet the Piagetian description do, in fact, exist, the implications for social-personality development seem obvious. A stage sequence implies that the child's basic modes of organizing his experience cannot be the direct result of adult teaching, or they would be copies of adult thought from the very beginning. In contrast to the perspective of social learning theorists who view development as a product of learning, the cognitive developmentalists argue that learning is dependent upon cognitive development. That is, the behavioral ramifications of environmental experience depend upon the child's construction (that is, representation and interpretation) of that experience, which, in turn, depends upon the cognitive structuring tendencies available to him at that point in his developmental history. Thus, the cognitive-developmentalists stress that the child's stage-related structural modes determine *what* the child learns from his interactions with others as well as *how* this learning occurs (Kohlberg, 1969).

We will now briefly describe each of Piaget's four stages of cognitive development and conclude this portion of the chapter with a discussion of the applications of cognitive-developmental theory to selected social-developmental phenomena.

The Sensorimotor Stage (0-1 years)

The dominant cognitive structure of the sensorimotor stage is the behavioral or action schema. The child comes to "know" the limits and the characteristics of objects, including his own body, by acting upon them. The responses a child makes toward objects define the meaning of those objects for him.

A number of significant developments occur during the sensorimotor period. At first, the infant's behavior is radically egocentric; his earliest schemes are centered on his own body. At about 3 to 4 months of age, the child extends his actions to objects in the external environment. His conception of his environment is still quite egocentric, in that he fails to recognize that external objects exist independent of his own constructions or perceptions of them (i.e., external objects are viewed as extensions of himself). As the child's action schemas gradually assimilate more and more environmental stimuli and are accommodated (and reorganized) to more adequately represent those stimuli, objects are dissociated from the self; they are viewed as having a permanence, as taking up space and existing independent of his construction of them. The development of object permanence coincides with the development of a self-concept. That is, the realization of the separateness of objects from the self necessarily implies the conception of oneself as an entity that has substance, takes up space, and occupies a position relative to other objects. Finally, the child develops a symbolic representational capability which makes possible behaviors such as deferred imitation and invention (the ability to imagine the outcome of one's acts before they are performed). The advent of symbolism marks the child's passage into the preoperational stage where his symbolic capability becomes the most important instrument of thought.

Preoperational Stage (2-7 years)

Piaget divides the preoperational stage into two principal substages: preconceptual thought, from 2 to 4 years of age; and intuitive thought, from 4-7 years of age. During the preconceptual period, the child is rapidly extending his symbolic capabilities. For example, he begins to use words to signify objects and events, and he comes to discriminate signifiers (words and images) from the objects and events they signify. Despite this discrimination capability, the child may often use a word to transform one object (for example, an old stick) into another (for example, a gun). This symbolic play illustrates a tendency of the preconceptual child to use symbols as a means of assimilating the world to his own desires.

The reasoning of the preconceptual child is rather primitive from an adult's perspective. The child possesses only preconcepts that result from his transductive reasoning, (reasoning from the particular to the particular). For example, the child will likely regard every bird he sees as a sighting of "bird." He does not yet realize that each bird is a member of a class of birds, sharing similar characteristics with other birds, as well as distinguishing features that make it an individual.

The thought and speech of the preconceptual child are unquestionably egocentric, centered upon the child's own perspective. The child is not effective at telling stories or explaining things to others because he makes no attempt to adapt his speech to the needs or interests of his listeners. Instead, he relates only those parts of a story that were interesting to him. If a male child of this age who has two brothers is asked "How many brothers are there in your family?" he will very likely say "two." In sum, the preconceptual child cannot assume the role or the perspective of another; he operates strictly from his own point of view.

Intuitive thought is an extension of the preconceptual mode in which the child demonstrates a greater proficiency for constructing and utilizing complex representations, thoughts, and images. The child's thought is called intuitive because his comprehension of objects and events is centered upon their single most salient perceptual feature, that is, the way they appear to him. Intuitive thought is clearly exemplified in Piaget's well-known conservation experiments (cf. Piaget, 1952b; Flavell, 1963). One such experiment initially requires the child to judge the equivalence of the volumes of water in two tall thin containers, a task that children in the intuitive stage find quite simple. Then the water of one of the tall thin containers is emptied into a short broad container. The intuitive child now asserts that the remaining tall thin receptable contains more water than the short broad one. Apparently, his thinking about volume and its defining characteristics is centered upon one salient perceptual feature, the heights of the columns of water in the two containers. Piaget and his associates suggest that the child fails to conserve (that is, to recognize that certain properties of a stimulus remain invariant despite a change in its appearance) because his thought is not yet characterized by certain very basic cognitive operations. First, the child is incapable of mentally reversing the transformation of the target stimulus; he does not yet realize that the water in the short broad container would attain its former "height" if he were to pour it back into the tall thin container. Second, the child does not realize that increases in the width of a column of water can *compensate* for decreases in its height to preserve its absolute quantity. Compensation requires the child to "decenter", that is, he must attend simultaneously to both the height and width of a container when making judgements about its volume. The acquisition of basic cognitive operations such as reversible thought and compensation allows the child to solve conservation problems and marks his passage into the stage of concrete operations.

The Concrete Operational Stage (7-11 Years)

The concrete operational period is characterized by the child's acquisition of cognitive operations, and his organization of these operations into operational structures. We have already described two such operational groupings or structures: classification and conservation. In addition, the concrete operator can now think in relational terms, can arrange stimuli according to their positions along a quantifiable dimension (serialization), can make mental representations of a complex sequence of actions, and can understand the cardinal properties of number and think in numerical terms. All of these operational structures represent advances beyond the "centered" thought of the preoperational period. In sum, the concrete operator progresses to the point where he is able to think logically and understand relationships between specific objects and events in his environment. However, he is not yet capable of reasoning at a level that transcends his concrete experiences.

The Formal Operational Stage (11 Years and Above)

During the preadolescent period, the child enters the stage of formal operations. His concrete experiences are now viewed as the observable portion of an imaginable totality. In other words, the formal operator is capable of transcending the concrete to reason in terms of hypothetical propositions that may not even come close to approximating reality.

When faced with a problem, the formal operator is able to apply the hypothetical-deductive method to generate and systematically evaluate all of the possible solutions to that problem. One may compare and contrast the reasoning of formal and concrete operators by examining children's responses to the following problem:

> ... the child is given four similar flasks containing colorless, odorless liquids which are perceptually identical. We number them (1)..., (2)..., (3)..., (4)...; we add a bottle (with a dropper) which we call g... [Mixing] $1 + 3 + g$ will yield a yellow color ... The experimenter presents to the subject two glasses, one containing $1 + 3$, the other containing 2. In front of the subject, he pours several drops of g in each of the two glasses and notes the different reactions. Then the subject is asked simply to reproduce the yellow color, using flasks 1, 2, 3, 4, and g as he wishes (Inhelder & Piaget, 1958, pp. 108-109).

Children at the concrete operational stage attack this problem by doing exactly what they saw the experimenter do; they pour g into each one of the four flasks and, thus, fail to produce the yellow color. Concrete operators have to be prodded to transcend their visual experience and mix three chemicals. Their higher-order combinations are unsystematic, and should they produce the yellow color, they are unable to replicate it.

The older, formal operator initially attacks this problem in the same way as the concrete operator, but he subsequently proceeds to test every possible combination of three or more chemicals when the binary combinations ($1 + g$, $2 + g$, $3 + g$, $4 + g$) fail to solve the problem. Moreover, he systematically generates these higher-order combinations, testing first $1 + 2 + g$ and proceeding through $1 + 3 + g$, $1 + 4 + g$, $2 + 3 + g$, etc., until he has tested all possible combinations and arrived at the one correct solution to the problem. The verbalizations that accompany the formal operator's problem-solving behavior contain many if-then propositional statements indicative of hypothetical-deductive reasoning. These statements are not found in the protocols of concrete operational children.

In sum, formal operational thought can be characterized as rational, systematic, and abstract. The adolescent may now combine or otherwise operate upon his operational structures to propose and explore hypothetical propositions, no matter how far removed thay may be from concrete reality. The ability to operate upon his operations allows the formal operator to think about his thinking. Piaget sees it as no accident that adolescents suddenly begin to think about themselves, their present and future roles in life, their beliefs and attitudes, and the way things "ought to be" as opposed to the way things are. A preoccupation with thought and its products is one of the defining characteristics of the formal operational cognitive style.

Piaget's descriptions of the course and content of intellectual development are apparently quite generalizable. For example, the invariant sequence of cognitive stages that characterizes the intellectual growth of Piaget's Swiss subjects also describes the intellectual development of American, Arab, British, Chinese, Indian, and West African children (cf. Kohlberg, 1969; Zigler & Child, 1973). Cultural factors affect the age at which children attain the various stage-related modes of cognitive functioning, but the structure and sequence of these cognitive stages do appear to transcend cultural influences.

Applications of Cognitive-developmental Theory to Selected Topics

An extension of Piaget's cognitive-developmental theory to problems of social-personality development requires some additional assumptions about the relationship of cognition to social-emotional phenomena. Kohlberg's (1969) cognitive-developmental approach to socialization rests upon the following assumptions:

1. Affective (emotional) development parallels cognitive development.

2. Social-personality development is best described as a restructuring of the self-concept and the perceived relationship of the self to others.

3. Social cognition (that is, thought about the self vis-à-vis others) involves reciprocal role-taking; developmental changes in the social self reflect parallel changes in the child's conceptions of others in his social environment.

4. The direction of social-personality development is toward an equilibrium or *reciprocity* between the child's actions and the actions of others toward the child. The child progresses toward the establishment of a stable identity across transformations in the various role relationships he encounters and must himself assume. The establishment of a stable identity is the "social" analogue of logical and physical conservations.

In sum, Kohlberg argues that social development proceeds through a sequence of qualitatively distinct stages. The specific content of each social-developmental stage is said to depend upon the interaction of the child's cognitive structuring tendencies with the kinds of social experiences he encounters. Thus, the cognitive-developmental approach to socialization differs from other stage-sequential approaches (for example, psychoanalytic and neopsychoanalytic models) in its emphasis upon cognitive transformations as the underpinnings of stage-sequential social development. Kohlberg (1969) defends this emphasis by stating:

> On the logical side, our approach is cognitively based because any description of the shape or pattern of a structure of social responses necessarily entails some cognitive dimensions. Description of the organization of the child's social responses entails a description of the way in which he perceives, or conceives, the social world and the way in which he conceives himself (p. 372).

Kohlberg does not deny the importance of social learning as a mechanism of social-personality development. Quite the contrary, Kohlberg argues that if the child failed to assimilate social experience or to accommodate himself to that experience, then social-personality development would not occur. From the cognitive-developmental perspective, the important qualification is that the child's cognitive structures determine how he perceives his social experiences and, hence, what he may learn from his interactions with others.

We shall conclude this section with a brief overview of the cognitive-developmental explanations of dependency, sex-role development, and moral development.

Dependency

In common with both the psychoanalytic and social learning perspectives, cognitive-developmental theory posits a relationship between a child's dependency upon adults and his tendencies to identify with (or imitate) adult models. Recall that both psychoanalytic theory and neo-Hullian social learning theory assume a developmental sequence in which: (a) the child's dependency upon an adult for nurturance motivates him/her to prevent punishment or a loss of nurturance by (b) identifying with the adult, which (c) causes the child to internalize the adult's behaviors and behavioral standards (sex-role standards, moral standards, etc.). In sum, an emotional dependency upon caretaking adults, usually parents, is said to motivate an imitation of, and an eventual identification with those adults.

Kohlberg's (1969) cognitive analysis of the origins of dependency and identification turns the above sequence completely around. The young child is said to be *intrinsically motivated* to imitate the interesting or seemingly competent actions of older models. This intrinsic motive to imitate is best understood as a need to adapt to (Piaget, 1952b) or master (White, 1959) the environment. The 2 to 3 year old feels no sense of incompetence in imitating others. By imitating, the child is demonstrating his newly acquired competence to the model rather than simply seeking the model's approval. During the period from 3 to 6 years of age, the child's cognitive developments include a differentiation of the perspectives of the self and others — he is decentering — and an ability to make comparative judgements of competence — the child realizes that he is not as competent as adults or older siblings. The child's competence motivation now directs the imitation of adult models who share certain social identities with him (for example, sex or kinship) and who are unquestionably more competent than he. The child becomes dependent upon the social reinforcements (or approval) given by these competent models because social reinforcers have information value, (the rewards are perceived as indicating that the child's imitative responses are "correct" or in accordance with a standard held by a person more competent than himself). To recapitulate, Kohlberg is arguing that imitation of older, more competent models leads to dependency rather than the converse. The child's need for approval is viewed as the consequence rather than the cause of imitative behavior.

Kohlberg cites the results of Bandura's studies on the imitation of self-reinforcement standards (e.g., Bandura et al., 1967) to illustrate that social reinforcement has an informational rather than a "pellet" effect upon imitative behaviors. In these studies, children generally imitate the behavior of a model who denies himself readily available physical rewards when he performs "unacceptably" in an experimental game. However, the children's imitation of the model's self-reinforcement standards is partly contingent upon their perceptions that the model is socially reinforced for his self-denial. Since the children's own self-denial in these studies occurs in the absence of social agents, it doesn't make sense to Kohlberg that the children were imitating the model's self-denial, and thus denying themselves physical rewards, in anticipation of receiving social reinforcement. Rather, Kohlberg argues that the social reinforcement received by the model defined for the child the "legitimate" standards of self-reinforcement, so that the child came to imitate these standards in order to "play the game" in a way that competent others agree that it should be played.

Sex-role Development

Kohlberg's (1966, 1969) cognitive-developmental analysis of sex-role socialization is strikingly different from explanations advanced by psychoanalytic and social learning theories. Recall that both the psychoanalytic and the social learning approaches contend that a boy identifies with his father and a girl with her mother because the same-sex parent is (or becomes) the child's major source of rewards and punishment. One important product of this identification (or habitual imitation) of the same-sex parent is the child's sex-typed identity, including an incorporation of the attitudes and behaviors considered appropriate for his/her sex.

Kohlberg's contention is that a child's sex-typed (gender) identity is a cognitive judgement about reality that precedes his/her identification of same-sex adult models. The child is said to recognize his/her sex by attending to physical, morphological, and behavioral similarities between the self and the same-sex parent. Between 3 and 7 years of age, children conserve their gender identities; for example, they no longer believe that mommie will grow up to be a daddy or that little boys can become mommies if they want to. By the age of 3 to 4, the child can tell an observer which sex he or she is and shows a preference for activities appropriate for his or her sex. This preference for sex-typed activities stimulates the girl to identify with her mother and, thus, acquire the constellation of attitudes and behaviors considered appropriate in her culture for a member of her sex. A boy who has sex-typed himself switches his orientation from his nurturant mother to his father, who is now viewed as an appropriate model for masculine activities and becomes the major source of social reinforcement for the boy.[11] In sum, Kohlberg argues that the child's conceptualization of his (her)

---

[11]Kohlberg's explanation of the developmental shift in the boy's orientation to his parents is attractive simply because it does not rely upon the boy's experience of castration anxiety or his defensive identification with a hostile aggressive father to account for this shift. There is little if any doubt that a shift in parental preference from mother to father occurs among preschool boys, but as we have previously noted, the literature consistently indicates that a defensive identification with hostile, punitive fathers is almost certainly *not* the mechanism by which this shift occurs.

gender identity is *cause* rather than *consequence* of an identification with same-sex adult models.

The results of a semi-longitudinal study of boys aged 4 to 8 (Kohlberg & Zigler, 1967) are generally consistent with the cognitive-developmental analysis of sex-role development. In this study, boys showed a clear preference for sex-typed objects and activities on projective tests of masculinity-femininity (that is, on Brown's (1956) IT Scale and the Sears et al. (1965) Pictures Test) by age 4. Boys showed a preference for imitating male as opposed to female models (in doll play and on other imitative tasks) by the age of 5. Finally, boys showed a clear preference for males as agents of social reinforcements and nurturance by the age of 6. The speed at which the boys moved through this sequence was positively correlated with intelligence. For example, bright 4-year-olds, whose mental ages were about 6, displayed male preferences on the sex typing, imitation, and dependency tests, whereas average boys did not display the male dependency preference until age 6. Regardless of the speed at which the boys passed the three experimental tests, they progressed through the sequence in the same order, that is, sex-typing first, imitation next, and dependency last. This invariant sequence is clearly inconsistent with psychoanalytic and social learning explanations of sex-role development and provides, in Kohlberg's opinion, strong support for the cognitive-developmental analysis of sex-role socialization. While a number of additional studies (e.g., Epstein & Liverant, 1963; C. Smith as cited in Kohlberg, 1966) provide results consistent with Kohlberg's model of sex-role development, other data can be interpreted as nonsupportive (cf. Thompson & Bentler, 1973; Wolf, 1973).

Moral Development

The cognitive-developmental approach to moral development focuses upon the cognitive structures underlying moral judgements of children of different ages. The basic assumption of the cognitive-developmentalists is that moral development is underlaid by cognitive development. Morality is said to progress through an invariant stage sequence in which each stage is an integrated (nonadditive) whole that evolves from but is qualitatively different than its predecessor. We shall briefly consider two cognitive-developmental models of moral development, Piaget's (1932) model and Kohlberg's (1966; 1969) extension of the Piagetian scheme.

Piaget (1932) contends that a mature morality includes both a respect for the rules of social order and a sense of equal justice (a concern for reciprocity and equality among individuals under the socially defined rules of order). Piaget began his study of moral development by playing marbles with children and thereby observing the attitudes of different aged youngsters toward the origins, legitimacy, and violability of the rules of the game. Once he had established developmental stages in the meaning of the rules of a marble game, Piaget broadened his focus to study the child's changing conceptions of the goodness or badness of various acts and the justice (punishments) considered appropriate for various transgressions. These latter interests were pursued by asking different aged children to listen to stories describing various transgressions, and then to judge: (a) which among the transgressions was the naughtiest; and (b) how the transgressions should (or would) be punished.

Employing these research strategies, Piaget developed a descriptive model of moral development consisting of a pre-moral level and two moral stages. The pre-moral 3 to 5-year-old is not bound by (or at least does not abide by) the rules of a game, although he knows of the existence of these rules and insists that he obeys them. During the first moral stage — referred to as the stage of moral realism or heteronomous morality — the child understands and rigidly obeys rules because their onmipotent origin (adults) renders them sacred and unalterable. The 6 to 10-year-old heteronomous child judges any deviation from the established rule as wrong, and the "badness" of an act depends upon the magnitude of its consequences rather than the actor's intentions. For example, a child who accidentally breaks 15 cups while doing something he is allowed to do is judged naughtier than a child who breaks 1 cup while performing an act of deception or disobedience. The heteronomous child favors expiatory punishment, that is, punishment for its own sake with no concern for its relationship to the nature of the forbidden act. For example, the heteronomous child would favor spanking a boy who had misbehaved and broken a window, as opposed to making the boy pay for the window from his allowance. The heteronomous child believes in immanent justice, or the idea that violations of social rules are automatically punished by God or some other natural force. For example, the child who cuts himself while "shaving" believes his cut to be a punishment for doing something he is not supposed to do.

By age 10 to 11, most children have progressed into Piaget's second moral stage known as autonomous morality, or the morality of cooperation and reciprocity. The older child now realizes that rules are socially defined and hence alterable with the mutual consent of those whose behavior they regulate. Judgements pertaining to the rightness versus wrongness or goodness versus badness of an act now depend more upon the actor's intent to deceive or intent to violate social rules as opposed to the objective consequences of the act itself. The autonomous child rejects expiatory punishment in favor of reciprocal punishment, which shapes punitive consequences to the "crime" so that the rule breaker will understand the implications of his misdeed. For instance, the autonomous child would favor having the boy in the previous example pay for the broken window as opposed to making him submit to a spanking. Finally, the older, autonomous child no longer believes in immanent justice because he has learned from his experiences that transgressions often go unpunished. As he comes to view rules as the product of cooperative agreement with others, the autonomous child developes a sense of distributive or equitable justice. For example, in a transgression committed by a group of offenders, punishments given to individual members of the offending group should be scaled to their levels of involvement in the transgression.

In sum, Piaget contends that the child progresses from heteronomous morality, where moral judgements are rigid, concrete, and absolute, to an autonomous morality, where there are flexible cooperative, reciprocal overtones to the child's moral reasoning. The younger child is said to exhibit his brand of moral absolutism because of two cognitive defects: (a) egocentrism — his inability to recognize or assume the perspective of others; and (b) realism — his tendency to equate subjective phenomena with external, objective events. During the course of middle childhood, the child increasingly interacts with peers on the playground and in the classroom. These interactions sensitize the child to the fact that other children have ideas different from his own about the way games should be played, conduct should be governed, etc. Additionally, children of this age often form their own clubs or their own governmental structure within the classroom. They must often compromise their views in order to play cooperatively on the playground. In short, the child comes to realize that he can and often must participate in the formation of behavioral rules independent of any adult influence. This realization is thought to: (a) increase the child's self-respect; (b) lessen his unilateral respect for adults; and (c) illustrate that rules are the products of cooperation with others and are alterable by mutual consent of the group. In sum, social interaction helps the child to overcome his absolutistic and egocentric conception of rules which, in turn, enables him to pass into the stage of autonomous morality.

While a number of investigations provide data that are generally consistent with Piaget's model of moral development (e.g., Abel, 1941; Gesell, Ilg, & Ames, 1956; Liu, 1950; Strauss, 1954), other studies suggest that Piaget's two-stage moral sequence is too simplistic (Isaacs, 1966; Kohlberg, 1963, 1964; Lerner, 1937a, 1937b). Kohlberg (1963, 1964) has presented boys aged 10 to 16 with moral dilemmas that ask the subject to choose between a legal rule or social norm on one hand and a human need on the other. Kohlberg's careful analyses of his subjects' responses to these moral dilemmas led him to conclude that moral development is far from complete when the child reaches age 10 or 11 — Piaget's autonomous stage. Rather, Kohlberg argues that moral development continues throughout the adolescent period, progressing through an invariant sequence of three moral levels, each of which is comprised of two qualitatively distinct moral stages.[12] Table 3 presents the basic themes and defining characteristics of the component levels and stages of the Kohlberg moral-developmental scheme.

---

[12]Kohlberg does not maintain that every individual eventually achieves the most advanced levels of moral reasoning. Fixation (arrested development) may occur at any stage and is especially likely to occur if the individual is not exposed to persons or experiences that might force a reevaluation or reorganization of his current moral concepts.

TABLE 3.3

Kohlberg's Stage-Sequential Model of Moral Development

Level 1 — Preconventional level

Stage 1: Punishment and obedience orientation. Acts are judged as good or bad on the basis of their physical consequences. Avoiding punishment and deference to those more powerful than themselves are the reasons children obey rules.

Stage 2: Naive hedonism. Right acts are those that satisfy one's own needs. Human exchanges occur, but the reciprocity is pragmatic, i.e., "You scratch my back and I'll scratch yours."

Level 2 — Conventional (conforming) morality

Stage 3: Good boy-nice girl orientation. Good behavior is defined as behavior that pleases others. The emphasis is upon approval seeking and conforming to other's expectations as a means to this end.

Stage 4: Law and order orientation. The focus is upon authority and social rules. Moral behavior consists of doing one's duty, showing respect for authority, and obeying the laws or rules of social order so that the social order may be maintained.

Level 3 — Postconventional (principled) morality

Stage 5: Morality of contract and democratically accepted law. Right and wrong are defined in terms of laws or rules that express the will of the majority or maximize social welfare. There is an awareness of the arbitrariness and/or unjust nature of law vis-à-vis individual needs, but when individual needs conflict with the law, the law must prevail because of its functional value to society in general.

Stage 6: Morality of individual principles of conscience. Right and wrong are defined not by laws or rules of social order, but by one's own conscience, i.e., self-chosen ethical principles. These principles are universal principles of justice (e.g., the equality of human rights, respect for the dignity of human beings as individual persons). Laws and social contracts are normally consistent with these principles, but if they are inconsistent, one acts in accordance with the principles. Deviation from "principled" morality results in self-condemnation.

Kohlberg's (1964) data indicate that, at any given age, there is considerable overlap among subjects in the use of his six moral stages. However, the frequencies of the more primitive stages of moral reasoning decline sharply with age, and the frequencies of the more mature forms of reasoning increase with age. Kohlberg (1969) reports that, while the child's rate of progression through the six moral stages may be affected by cultural factors, children in Taiwan, Malaya, Mexico, Turkey, and the United States all show the same sequence of moral development. Kohlberg cites this cross-cultural data as support for his notion that moral stages are qualitatively distinct "structured wholes" that comprise an invariant developmental sequence.

If Kohlberg's moral stages are truly nonadditive — each stage representing a qualitative reorganization of its predecessor rather than simply being more of the same — and form an invariant sequence, then two critical predictions can be derived. The nonadditivity assumption leads to the prediction that children exposed to moral reasoning of a stage level different from their own will prefer reasoning that is one stage above as opposed to one stage below their current level. Lower-level reasoning should be rejected because the child's current moral concepts have replaced their more simplistic predecessors, and going back to an earlier level of moral reasoning represents a difficult regressive restructuring of cognitive processes. The invariant sequence assumption leads to the prediction that subjects will prefer moral reasoning one stage above their own (i.e., reasoning that they are capable of assimilating into their current cognitive structures) as opposed to reasoning two stages above their own (reasoning too discrepant with existing structures to be assimilated).

Research reflecting on these two hypotheses provides mixed support for Kohlberg's stage-sequential assertions. Rest et al. (1969) found that children exposed to statements of differing moral levels preferred those above as compared to those below their own level. Turiel (1966) found that subjects exposed to models were more likely to adopt the modeled moral reasoning if the model's reasoning was one stage above as opposed to two stages above the subject's own. These experiments provide some support for the invariant sequence assumption. However, Turiel's (1966) experiment does not conclusively demonstrate that subjects favored moral reasoning that was one stage above as opposed to reasoning one stage below their own. Evidently, subjects can and do regress to earlier levels of moral reasoning when exposed to models who use that reasoning (Bandura & MacDonald, 1963; Cowan, Langer, Heavenrich, & Nathanson, 1969), and this "moral regression"not only generalizes to other moral dilemmas, but has remained stable for as long as three months (LeFurgy & Woloshin, 1969). These latter results call into question the cognitive-developmental assumptions that moral stages are nonadditive structured wholes that form a truly invariant and irreversible developmental sequence (cf. Kurtines & Grief, 1974, for an extended discussion of these and other data and their implications for Kohlberg's model of moral development).

EPILOGUE

I have described three theoretical perspectives on socialization that clearly differ amongst themselves in their underlying philosophies, their methods of research, and the aspects of development they emphasize. I have referred to research indicating that, while each of the three perspectives has received some empirical support, not one of the three provides a totally adequate explanation of social-personality development. Although the reader may have developed a preference for one of the three approaches, judgements concerning their relative adequacy are hampered by the fact that these three perspectives are really complementary in their focus rather than competing explanations of identical phenomena. It is my contention that each perspective has contributed substantially to our understanding of social-personality development.

I shall not attempt to combine the three approaches into a comprehensive theory of socialization. In my opinion, such an attempt presupposes a more extensive knowledge of the interdependence of emotion, cognition, and behavior than is currently available. However, I will attempt to demonstrate how a knowledge of all three theoretical perspectives and the research they have generated provides a more comprehensive understanding of social-developmental phenomena than is possible from a knowledge of any one perspective considered alone. The illustration will focus upon moral development.

Recall that psychoanalytic, social learning, and cognitive-developmental theories agree that the morality of middle childhood derives largely from the morality of parents. Psychoanalytic and neo-Hullian theorists argue that the child internalizes his parents' moral attributes through the process of identification, and his degree of moral internalization (that is, the strength of his conscience) is said to depend largely upon the emotional climate of the parent-child relationship. Bandura suggests that children attend to and imitate the attributes of nurturant and/or prestigious models. Since parents are generally nurturant and prestigious in the eyes of a child, Bandura suggests that the child will come to emulate many of their attributes and behaviors, moral attributes included. Piaget also asserts that the morality of middle childhood is largely based upon rules and guidelines laid down by parents. Children of age 6 to 10 consider parental rules to be sacred and unalterable; they demonstrate an uncritical acceptance of external (adult) authority.

Only the cognitive-developmentalists have studied the course of moral development beyond the middle childhood era, and, as I have noted, they stress the cognitive aspects of morality (moral reasoning). Kohlberg and his associates present a substantial amount of data which indicate that moral reasoning continues to develop well into the adolescent period, progressing through a stage sequence that is related to the course of cognitive development. While the cognitive-developmental focus has contributed substantially to our understanding of the development of moral reasoning, it tells us very little about the development of affective and behavioral aspects of morality. We might reasonably wonder whether these affective and/or behavioral components are related to moral reasoning and, thus, progress through a similar stage-sequential course of development.

Kohlberg (1969) presents data consistent with his notion that the affective components of one's moral structure (for example, anxiety over others' detection of one's transgression, shame, guilt as a self-judgement about one's own behavior) develop in parallel with moral reasoning. However, other research (e.g., Grinder, 1964; Nelson, Grinder, & Challas, 1968) indicates that a child's level of moral reasoning does not accurately predict his/her moral behavior. Thus, it is apparent that a focus upon the cognitive aspects of morality simply cannot tell us all that we may wish to know about moral development.

The finding that moral judgements are not always related to moral behavior implies that these two aspects of morality may evolve along differing developmental paths. Freud (1960) argues that the child's superego is a reflection of parental commands and exhortations rather than parental behavior. The social learning literature suggests that this is really an overstatement. It seems probable that the child's continued interactions with parents and other typical agents of socialization (for example, siblings, relatives, peers, teachers) results in the development of at least two moral systems: (a) a knowledge of what others say is right and wrong, which the child constructs from others' moral commands and exhortations; and (b) a set of behavioral tendencies based upon the consequences of moral or immoral acts that the child emits himself or observes of others in his environment. The degree of correspondence between the child's cognitive and behavioral moralities probably depends upon the correspondence between what models say and do. If a model's moral exhortations are inconsistent with his behavior, it is likely that the child-observer will reproduce either the model's moral reasoning (or at least his understanding of the model's reasoning) or the model's behavior, depending upon which he is later asked to demonstrate. Mischel and Liebert (1966) report that children did not do as the model said when they were exposed to a model who advocated one rule but deviated from that rule behaviorally. When placed in an analogous situation, the children followed the model's behavioral example. A number of additional modeling experiments (e.g., Bryan & Walbek, 1970a, 1970b; Walbek, 1969) concur in suggesting that a model's moral behavior has a stronger influence upon a child's own moral behavior than do the model's verbal exhortations. It must be noted that the dependent measures in these experiments were always behavioral in character. We can only speculate that had the child-observers been asked how they ought to behave, they may well have responded with their interpretations of the model's verbal exhortations.

Although moral behavior may not always be related to moral reasoning, these aspects of morality are certainly not orthogonal. Studies deriving from the social learning perspective (e.g., Walbek, 1969), and the cognitive-developmental perspective (e.g., Kohlberg, 1969; Krebs, 1968) indicate that certain "moral" behaviors (for example, generosity, fairness to others) increase with age. These increases are particularly interesting because they appear to accompany age-related changes in the child's moral reasoning as outlined by Kohlberg (that is, children are moving from a hedonistic orientation to a good boy-nice girl morality). In addition, Midlarsky and Bryan (1972) report that a model's moral reasoning does have a significant impact upon the subsequent moral behavior of child-observers if that reasoning emphasizes the consequences of moral behavior for others in a conceptual language that the child can easily assimilate.

The psychoanalytic focus upon the child-rearing antecedents of morality has stimulated research that contributes substantially to an understanding of moral development. Recall that psychoanalytic theorists view the child's anxiety over a a loss of parental love as the principal dynamic underlying his attachment to parents and his eventual internalization of their moral standards. This assertion leads to the prediction that children who experience mostly love-oriented discipline from parents — where parents punish the child by withholding affection, thereby generating anxiety over a loss of love — should show a stronger identification with their parents and, thus, develop stronger superegos than would children exposed to power-assertive discipline — where parents punish the child physically or withhold desired objects or privileges, thereby generating anger or hostility. Hoffman and his associates (Hoffman, 1963; 1970; Hoffman & Saltzstein, 1967) have reviewed the child-rearing literature and concluded that neither the love-withdrawing nor the power-assertive disciplinary strategies are conducive to the development of affective, cognitive, or behavioral aspects of morality. The disciplinary strategy found to be conducive to the development of all three aspects of morality is induction, which is described as follows:

> Induction includes techniques in which the parent gives explanations or reasons for requiring the child to change his behavior. Examples are pointing out physical requirements of the situation or the harmful consequences of the child's behavior for himself or others. These techniques are . . . an attempt to persuade or convince the child that he should change his behavior in the prescribed manner. Also included are techniques which appeal to conformity-inducing agents that already exist within the child. Examples are appeals to the child's pride, strivings for mastery and to be "grown up," and concern for others (Hoffman, 1970, p. 286).

Hoffman found that parents who stressed the needs of others as part of their inductive disciplinary strategies produced children showing the highest degree of moral maturity. This particular kind of inductive strategy is called other- oriented induction. Other-oriented induction is accomplished by:

> . . . directly pointing out the nature of the consequence (e.g., if you throw snow on their wall, they will have to clean it up all over again; pulling the leash like that can hurt the dog's neck; that hurts my feelings); pointing out the relevant needs or desires of others (e.g., he is afraid of the dark, so please turn the lights back on); or explaining the motives underlying the other person's behavior toward the child (e.g., don't yell at him. He was only trying to help.) (Hoffman, 1970, p. 286).

What processes underlie the effectiveness of induction as a contributor to moral maturity? First, inductive discipline communicates to the child not only that his behavior was wrong, but also the reasons why his behavior was inappropriate. When inductive discipline is other-oriented, parents are providing their child with the kinds of experience conducive to the development of empathy and reciprocal role-playing, two cognitive abilities that Piaget and Kohlberg consider prerequisites for the development of mature forms of moral reasoning. Second, an inductive strategy allows parents to discuss internal affective components of a mature morality (for example, shame or guilt) that are not easily communicated to a child made very emotional (for example, angry, hostile, or anxious) by power-assertive or love-oriented discipline, and are not easily discernible to the child from his observations of others' transgressive behaviors (a parent who has transgressed does not often project his shame, guilt, or self-criticism so that a child may readily observe these affective consequences of transgression). Finally, parents who use inductive discipline are likely to illustrate or explain to the child how he should have behaved in the situation where he has transgressed and why he should have behaved that way. Thus, induction is an effective contributor to moral maturity because it clearly illustrates and often integrates affective, cognitive, and behavioral aspects of morality so that they may be readily assimilated by the child. Further, these inductive explanations occur in a nonpunitive context, so that the child is not so emotionally aroused that he fails to attend to parental exhortations and illustrations or is not motivated to do so.[13]

In sum, the psychoanalytic emphasis upon social-emotional determinants of morality, the cognitive-developmental emphasis upon the cognitive underpinnings of moral reasoning, and the social learning emphasis upon the determinants of moral behavior have all contributed to our knowledge of moral development, each in its own particular way.[14] Clearly, there is much more to be learned and many issues and controversies to be resolved concerning moral development in particular and social-personality development in general. I hope that my brief overview of the three major theoretical perspectives on social-personality development will encourage the reader to delve further into this interesting area of social psychology in search of knowledge that, at present, we so clearly lack.

[13]Hoffman (1970) hastens to note that parents' disciplinary strategies are not purely inductive, love-oriented, or power assertive, but contain all three of these components in differing proportions. However, he argues that if a disciplinary strategy consists primarily of love-withdrawal or power assertion, the dominant (aversive) component may emotionally disrupt the child to the point where he is either hindered in processing or motivated to ignore the inductive component of that discipline.

[14]Although many psychoanalytic assertions about morality have not received much empirical support, it would be inappropriate to argue that psychoanalysis has failed to contribute to our understanding of moral development. Freud's moral theorizing served as the impetus for: (a) research reflecting upon child rearing correlates of moral development (cf. Hoffman, 1963, 1970; Sears, Maccoby, & Levin, 1957); (b) early research on moral attitudes and behaviors (e.g., MacKinnon, 1938; Peck & Havighurst, 1960); and (c) the development of alternative explanations of moral phenomena. Thus, the psychoanalytic contribution to an understanding of moral development, although somewhat indirect, is very substantial.

REFERENCES

Abel, T. Moral judgments among subnormals. *Journal of Abnormal and Social Psychology,* 1941, *36,* 378-392.

Allport, G. *Personality: A psychological interpretation.* New York: Holt, Rinehart, and Winston, 1937.

Aronfreed, J. The origin of self-criticism. *Psychological Review,* 1964, *71,* 193-218.

Baldwin, J. M. *Social and ethical interpretations in mental development.* New York: Macmillan, 1906.

Bandura, A. Social learning through imitation. In Marshall R. Jones (Ed.), *Nebraska Symposium on Motivation.* Lincoln: University of Nebraska Press, 1962, pp. 211-269.

Bandura, A. Influence of models' reinforcement contingencies on the acquisition of imitative responses. *Journal of Personality and Social Psychology,* 1965, *1,* 589-595.

Bandura, A. Social learning theory of identificatory processes. In D. A. Goslin (Ed.), *Handbook of socialization theory and research.* Chicago: Rand McNally, 1969.

Bandura, A. *Social learning theory.* Morristown, New Jersey: General Learning Press, 1971.

Bandura, A., Grusec, J. E., & Menlove, F. L. Observational learning as a function of symbolization and incentive set. *Child Development,* 1966, *37,* 499-506.

Bandura, A., Grusec, J. E., & Menlove, F. L. Some social determinants of self-monitoring reinforcement systems. *Journal of Personality and Social Psychology,* 1967, *5,* 449-455.

Bandura, A., & Harris, M. B. Modification of syntactic style. *Journal of Experimental Child Psychology,* 1966, *4,* 341-352.

Bandura, A., & Huston, A. C. Identification as a process of incidental learning. *Journal of Abnormal and Social Psychology,* 1961, *63,* 311-318.

Bandura, A., & Jeffery, R. Role of symbolic coding and rehearsal processes in observational learning. *Journal of Personality and Social Psychology,* 1973, *26,* 122-130.

Bandura, A., & Kupers, C. J. The transmission of patterns of self-reinforcement through modeling. *Journal of Abnormal and Social Psychology,* 1964, *69,* 1-9.

Bandura, A., & MacDonald, F. J. The influence of social reinforcement and the behavior of models in shaping children's moral judgments. *Journal of Abnormal and Social Psychology,* 1963, *67,* 274-281.

Bandura, A., & Mischel, W. Modification of self-imposed delay of reward through exposure to live and symbolic models. *Journal of Personality and Social Psychology,* 1965, *2,* 698-705.

Bandura, A., & Perloff, B. Relative efficacy of self-monitored and externally-imposed reinforcement systems. *Journal of Personality and Social Psychology,* 1967, *7,* 111-116.

Bandura, A., Ross, D., & Ross, S. A. Imitation of film-mediated aggressive models. *Journal of Abnormal and Social Psychology,* 1963, *66,* 3-11.

Bandura, A., & Walters, R. H. *Adolescent aggression.* New York: Ronald Press, 1959.

Bandura, A., & Walters, R. H. *Social learning and personality development.* New York: Holt, Rinehart, and Winston, 1963.

Bandura, A., & Whalen, C. K. The influence of antecedent reinforcement and divergent modeling cues on patterns of self-reward. *Journal of Personality and Social Psychology,* 1966, *3,* 373-382.

Barry, H., Bacon, M. K., & Child, I. L. A cross-cultural survey of some sex differences in socialization. *Journal of Abnormal and Social Psychology,* 1957, *55,* 327-332.

Bijou, S., & Baer, D. M. *Child development: A systematic and empirical theory* (Vol. 1). New York: Appleton-Century-Crofts, 1961.

Biller, H. B. Father absence and the personality development of the male child. *Developmental Psychology,* 1970, *2,* 181-201.

Brim, O. G., Jr. Family structure and sex-role learning by children: A further analysis of Helen Koch's data. *Sociometry, 1958, 21,* 1-16.

Bronson, W. C. Dimensions of ego and infantile identification. *Journal of Personality, 1959, 27,* 532-545.

Brown, D. G. Sex-role preference in young children. *Psychological Monographs, 1956, 70,* (14, Whole No. 421).

Bruner, J. S. The course of cognitive growth. *American Psychologist, 1964, 19,* 1-15.

Bruner, J. S., Oliver, R. R., & Greenfield, P. M. (Eds.). *Studies in cognitive growth.* New York: Wiley, 1966.

Bryan, J. H., & Walbek, N. Preaching and practicing generosity: Children's actions and reactions. *Child Development, 1970, 41,* 329-354. (a)

Bryan, J. H., & Walbek, N. The impact of words and deeds concerning altruism upon children. *Child Development, 1970, 41,* 447-457. (b)

Charlesworth, R., & Hartup, W. W. Positive social reinforcement in the nursery school peer group. *Child Development, 1967, 38,* 993-1002.

Child, I. L. Socialization. In G. Lindzey (Ed.), *Handbook of Social Psychology.* Reading, Mass.: Addison-Wesley, 1954.

Coates, B., & Hartup, W. W. Age and verbalization in observational learning. *Developmental Psychology, 1969, 1,* 556-562.

Cowan, P. A., Langer, J., Heavenrich, J., & Nathanson, M. Social learning and Piaget's cognitive theory of moral development. *Journal of Personality and Social Psychology, 1969, 11,* 261-274.

Decarie, T. G. *Intelligence and affectivity in early childhood.* New York: International Universities Press, 1965.

Dewey, J. Experience and conduct. In C. Murchison (Ed.), *Psychologies of 1930.* Worcester: Clark University Press, 1930.

Dollard, J., & Miller, N. E. *Personality and psychotherapy: An analysis of learning, thinking, and culture.* New York: McGraw-Hill, 1950.

Elkin, F. *The child and society.* New York: Random House, 1960.

Epstein, R., & Liverant, S. Verbal conditioning and sex-role identification in children. *Child Development, 1963, 34,* 99-106.

Erikson, E. H. Sex differences in the play configuration of preadolescents. *American Journal of Orthopsychiatry, 1951, 21,* 667-692.

Erikson, E. H. Identity and the life cycle: Selected papers. *Psychological Issues,* (Monograph), *1959, 1.* New York: International Universities Press.

Erikson, E. H. *Childhood and society.* New York: W. W. Norton, 1963. (Originally published, 1950).

Erikson, E. H. Eight ages of man. In C. S. Lavatelli and F. Stendler (Eds.), *Readings in child behavior and child development.* New York: Harcourt, Brace, Jovanovich, 1972.

Fisher, A. E. The effects of differential early treatment on the social and exploratory behavior of puppies. Unpublished doctoral dissertation, Pennsylvania State University, 1955.

Flavell, J. H. *The developmental psychology of Jean Piaget.* Princeton, N.J.: Van Nostrand, 1963.

Freud, A. *The ego and the mechanisms of defense.* New York: International Universities Press, 1946.

Freud, S. Instincts and their vicissitudes. In *Collected Papers* (Vol. 4). London: The Hogarth Press, 1946. (Originally published, 1915.)

Freud, S. *The ego and the id.* London: The Hogarth Press, 1947. (Originally published, 1923.)

Freud, S. The dissolution of the Oedipus complex. In *The complete psychological works of Sigmund Freud* (Vol. 19). London: The Hogarth Press, 1961. (Originally published, 1924.)

Freud, S. Some psychical consequences of the anatomical distinction between the sexes. In *The complete psychological works of Sigmund Freud* (Vol. 19). London: The Hogarth Press, 1961. (Originally published, 1925.)

Freud, S. *Three contributions to the theory of sex.* New York: Nervous and Mental Disease Publishing Company, 1930.

Freud, S. *A general introduction to psychoanalysis.* New York: Washington Square Press, 1960.

Gerst, M. S. Symbolic coding processes in observational learning. *Journal of Personality and Social Psychology,* 1971, *19,* 7-17.

Gesell, A., Ilg, F. L., & Ames, L. B. *Youth: The years from ten to sixteen.* New York: Harper and Row, 1956.

Gewirtz, J. L. Mechanisms of social learning: Some roles of stimulation and behavior in early human development. In D. A. Goslin (Ed.), *Handbook of socialization theory and research.* Chicago: Rand McNally, 1969.

Gewirtz, J. L., & Baer, D. M. Deprivation and satiation of social reinforcers as drive conditions. *Journal of Abnormal and Social Psychology,* 1958, *57,* 165-172.

Glueck, S., & Glueck, E. *Unraveling juvenile delinquency.* Cambridge, Mass.: Harvard University Press, 1950.

Grinder, R. Relations between behavioral and cognitive dimensions of conscience in middle childhood. *Child Development,* 1964, *35,* 881-893.

Hall, C. S. *A primer of Freudian psychology.* New York: World Publishing Company, 1954.

Hall, C. S., & Lindzey, G. *Theories of personality.* New York: Wiley, 1957.

Hampson, J. L. Determinants of psycho-sexual orientation. In F. A. Beach (Ed.), *Sex and behavior.* New York: Wiley, 1965.

Hartmann, H. *Ego psychology and the problem of adaptation.* New York: International Universities Press, 1958.

Hartmann, H., Kris, E., & Lowenstein, R. Notes on the theory of aggression. In A. Freud (Ed.), *The psychoanalytic study of the child* (Vol. 3). New York: International Universities Press, 1949.

Hartup, W. W. Nurturance and nurturance withdrawal in relation to the dependency behavior of young children. *Child Development,* 1958, *29,* 191-201.

Hartup, W. W. Dependence and independence. In H. W. Stevenson (Ed.), *Child psychology.* Chicago: University of Chicago Press, 1963.

Hetherington, E. M. Effects of father absence on personality development in adolescent daughters. *Developmental Psychology,* 1972, *7,* 313-326.

Hicks, D. J. Imitation and retention of film-mediated aggressive peer and adult models. *Journal of Personality and Social Psychology,* 1965, *2,* 97-100.

Hobbs, T. (1651). *Leviathan.* (Reprint of 1st edition. Cambridge, England: Cambridge University Press, 1904).

Hoffman, M. L. Child rearing practices and moral development: Generalizations from empirical research. *Child Development,* 1963, *34,* 295-318.

Hoffman, M. L. Moral development. In P. H. Mussen (Ed.), *Carmichael's manual of child psychology* (Vol. 2). New York: Wiley, 1970.

Hoffman, M. L., & Saltzstein, H. D. Parent discipline and the child's moral development. *Journal of Personality and Social Psychology,* 1967, *5,* 45-57.

Inhelder, B., & Piaget, J. *The growth of logical thinking from childhood to adolescence.* New York: Basic Books, 1958.

Isaacs, S. *Intellectual growth in young children.* New York: Schocken, 1966.

Jennings, F. G. Jean Piaget: Notes on learning. *Saturday Review,* May 20, 1967, pp. 81-83.

Kagan, J., & Moss, H. A. *Birth to maturity.* New York: Wiley, 1962.

Kardiner, A. *The individual and his society.* New York: Columbia University Press, 1939.

Kardiner, A. *The psychological frontiers of society*. New York: Columbia University Press, 1945.

Kendler, T. S. Development of mediating responses in children. *Monographs of the Society for Research in Child Development*, 1963, *28*, (2, Serial No. 86).

Kendler, H. H., & Kendler, T. S. Vertical and horizontal processes in problem solving. *Psychological Review*, 1962, *69*, 1-16.

Kessen, W. *The child*. New York: Wiley, 1965.

Kessen, W. Questions for a theory of cognitive development. In H. Stevenson (Ed.), Concepts of development. *Monographs of the Society for Research in Child Development*, 1966, *31* (Whole No. 103).

Klein, M. *The psychoanalysis of children*. London: Hogarth Press, 1959.

Kohlberg, L. The development of children's orientations toward a moral order: 1. Sequence in the development of moral thought. *Vita Humana*, 1963, *6*, 11-33.

Kohlberg, L. Development of moral character and ideology. In M. L. Hoffman (Ed.), *Review of child development research* (Vol. 1). New York: Russell Sage Foundation, 1964.

Kohlberg, L. A cognitive developmental analysis of children's sex-role concepts and attitudes. In E. Maccoby (Ed.), *The development of sex differences*. Stanford, Calif.: Stanford University Press, 1966.

Kohlberg, L. Stage and sequence: The cognitive-developmental approach to socialization. In D. A. Goslin (Ed.), *Handbook of Socialization Theory and Research*. Chicago: Rand McNally, 1969.

Kohlberg, L., & Zigler, E. The impact of cognitive maturity on the development of sex-role attitudes in the years four to eight. *Genetic Psychology Monographs*, 1967, *75*, 89-165.

Krasner, L., & Ullmann, L. P. *Research in behavior modification*. New York: Holt, Rinehart, and Winston, 1965.

Krebs, R. L. Some relationships between moral judgment, attention and resistance to temptation. Unpublished doctoral dissertation, University of Chicago, 1968.

Kurtines, W., & Grief, E. B. The development of moral thought: Review and evaluation of Kohlberg's approach. *Psychological Bulletin*, 1974, *81*, 453-470.

Langer, J. *Theories of development*. New York: Holt, Rinehart, and Winston, 1969.

Lazowick, L. On the nature of identification. *Journal of Abnormal and Social Psychology*, 1955, *51*, 175-183.

Le Furgy, W. G., & Woloshin, G. W. Immediate and long-term effects of experimentally induced social influence on the modification of adolescents' moral judgments. *Journal of Personality and Social Psychology*, 1969, *12*, 104-110.

Lerner, E. *Constraint areas and the moral judgment of children*. Menasha, Wisc.: Banta, 1937. (a)

Lerner, E. The problem of perspective in moral reasoning. *American Journal of Sociology*, 1937, *43*, 249-269. (b)

Liebert, R. M., Odom, R. D., Hill, J. H., & Huff, R. L. Effects of age and rule familiarity on the production of modeled language constructions. *Developmental Psychology*, 1969, *1*, 108-112.

Liu, Ching-Ho. The influence of cultural background on the moral judgment of children. Unpublished doctoral dissertation, Columbia University, 1950.

Locke, J. (1690). *Some thoughts concerning education*. Sections 38 and 40. London: Cambridge University Press, 1913.

Loeb, A., Beck, A. T., Diggory, J. C., & Tuthill, R. Expectancy level of aspiration, performance, and self-evaluation in depression. *Proceedings of the 75th Annual Convention of the American Psychological Association*, 1967, *2*, 193-194.

Loevinger, J. The meaning and measurement of ego development. *American Psychologist*, 1966, *21*, 195-206.

Maccoby, E. E., & Masters, J. C. Attachment and dependency. In P. H. Mussen (Ed.), *Carmichael's manual of child psychology* (Vol. 2). New York: Wiley, 1970.

MacKinnon, D. W. Violation and prohibitions. In H. A. Murray (Ed.), *Explorations in personality*. New York: Oxford University Press, 1938.

Maier, H. W. *Three theories of child development*. New York: Harper and Row, 1969.

Malinowski, B. Prenuptial intercourse between the sexes of the Trobriand Islands, N. W. Melanesia. *Psychoanalytic Review*, 1927, *14*, 20-36.

McCandless, B. R. *Children*. New York: Holt, Rinehart, & Winston, 1967.

McNeill, D. *The acquisition of language. The study of developmental psycholinguistics*. New York: Harper and Row, 1970.

Mead, M. *From the south seas*. New York: Morrow, 1939.

Mead, M. *Male and female*. New York: Morrow, 1949.

Midlarsky, E., & Bryan, J. H. Affect expressions and children's imitative altruism. *Journal of Experimental Research in Personality*, 1972, *6*, 195-203.

Miller, N. E. Theory and experiment relating psychoanalytic displacement to stimulus-response generalization. *Journal of Abnormal and Social Psychology*, 1948, *43*, 155-178.

Miller, N. E., & Dollard, J. *Social learning and imitation*. London: Oxford University Press, 1941.

Mischel, W. Theory and research on the antecedents of self-imposed delay of reward. In B. A. Maher (Ed.), *Progress in Experimental Personality Research* (Vol. 2). New York: Academic Press, 1965.

Mischel, W. Sex-typing and socialization. In P. H. Mussen (Ed.), *Carmichael's manual of child psychology* (Vol. 2). New York: Wiley, 1970.

Mischel, W., & Liebert, R. M. Effects of discrepancies between observed and imposed reward criteria on their acquisition and transmission. *Journal of Personality and Social Psychology*, 1966, *3*, 45-53.

Money, J. Influence of hormones on sexual behavior. *Annual Review of Medicine*, 1965, *16*, 67-82. (a)

Money, J. Psychosexual differentiation. In J. Money (Ed.), *Sex research, new developments*. New York: Holt, Rinehart, and Winston, 1965. (b)

Mowrer, O. H. *Learning theory and personality dynamics*. New York: Ronald Press, 1950.

Mowrer, O. H. *Learning theory and behavior*. New York: Wiley, 1960.

Mussen, P. H. Some antecedents and consequents of masculine sex-typing in adolescent boys. *Psychological Monographs*, 1961, *75* (2, Whole No. 506).

Mussen, P. H., & Distler, L. Masculinity, identification and father-son relationship. *Journal of Abnormal and Social Psychology*, 1959, *59*, 350-356.

Mussen, P. H., & Distler, L. Child rearing antecedents of masculine identification in kindergarten boys. *Child Development*, 1960, *31*, 89-100.

Mussen, P. H., & Rutherford, E. Parent-child relations and parental personality in relation to young children's sex-role preferences. *Child Development*, 1963, *34*, 589-607.

Nelson, E. A., Grinder, R. E., & Challas, J. H. Resistance to temptation and moral judgment: Behavioral correlates of Kohlberg's measure of moral development. Mimeographed paper, University of Wisconsin, 1968.

Nowlis, V. The search for significant concepts in a study of parent-child relationships. *American Journal of Orthopsychiatry*, 1952, *22*, 286-299.

Payne, D. E., & Mussen, P. H. Parent-child relations and father identification among adolescent boys. *Journal of Abnormal and Social Psychology*, 1956, *52*, 358-362.

Peck, R. F., & Havighurst, R. J. *The psychology of character development*. New York: Wiley, 1960.

Piaget, J. *The child's conception of the world*. New York: Harcourt, Brace, 1929.

Piaget, J. *The child's conception of physical causality.* London: Routledge & Kegan Paul, 1930.

Piaget, J. *The moral judgment of the child.* New York: Harcourt, Brace, 1932.

Piaget, J. *The psychology of intelligence.* New York: Harcourt, Brace, 1950.

Piaget, J. *Play, dreams, and imitation in childhood.* New York: Norton, 1951.

Piaget, J. Autobiography. In E. G. Boring (Ed.), *History of psychology in autobiography* (Vol. 4). Worcester, Mass.: Clark University Press, 1952. (a)

Piaget, J. *The origins of intelligence in children.* New York: International Universities Press, 1952. (b)

Piaget, J. *The construction of reality in the child.* New York: Basic Books, 1954.

Piaget, J. Peering into the mind of a child. *The UNESCO Courier,* 1959, *12,* 4-7.

Piaget, J. The general problems of the psychobiological development of the child. In J. M. Tanner & B. Inhelder (Eds.), *Discussions on child development: Proceedings of the World Health Organization study group on the psychobiological development of the child* (Vol. 4). New York: International Universities Press, 1960.

Rest, J., Turiel, E., & Kohlberg, L. Level of moral development as a determinant of preference and comprehension of moral judgments made by others. *Journal of Personality,* 1969, *37,* 225-252.

Rheingold, H. L., & Bayley, N. The later effects of an experimental modification of mothering. *Child Development,* 1959, *30,* 363-372.

Rosenberg, B. G., & Sutton-Smith, B. Family interaction effects on masculinity-femininity. *Journal of Personality and Social Psychology,* 1968, *8,* 117-120.

Rosenthal, T. L., & Whitebook, J. S. Incentives versus instructions in transmitting grammatical parameters with experimenter as model. *Behavior Research and Therapy,* 1970, *8,* 189-196.

Sapir, E. *Selected writings in language, culture, and personality.* Berkeley: University of California Press, 1949.

Scott, J. P. Critical periods in the development of social behavior in puppies. *Psychosomatic Medicine,* 1958, *20,* 42-54.

Sears, P. S. Child-rearing factors related to playing of sex-typed roles. *American Psychologist,* 1953, *8,* 431. (Abstract)

Sears, R. R. Experimental analysis of psychoanalytic phenomena. In J. M. Hunt (Ed.), *Personality and the behavior disorders* (Vol. 1). New York: Ronald Press, 1944.

Sears, R. R. A theoretical framework for personality and social behavior. *American Psychologist,* 1951, *6,* 476-483. (a)

Sears, R. R. Social behavior and personality development. In T. Parsons and E. A. Shills (Eds.), *Toward a general theory of action.* Cambridge, Mass.: Harvard University Press, 1951. (b)

Sears, R. R. Identification as a form of behavior development. In D. B. Harris (Ed.), *The concept of development.* Minneapolis: University of Minnesota Press, 1957.

Sears, R. R. *Dependency.* Unpublished manuscript, Stanford University, 1961.

Sears, R. R., Maccoby, E. E., & Levin, H. *Patterns of child rearing.* Evanston, Ill.: Row, Peterson, 1957.

Sears, R. R., Rau, L., & Alpert, R. *Identification and child rearing.* Stanford, Calif.: Stanford University Press, 1965.

Sears, R. R., Whiting, J., Nowlis, V., & Sears, P. Some child rearing antecedents of aggression and dependency in young children. *Genetic Psychology Monogrpahs,* 1953, *47,* 135-234.

Sewell, W. H. Infant training and the personality of the child. *American Journal of Sociology,* 1952, *58,* 150-159.

Sewell, W. H., & Mussen, P. H. The effects of feeding, weaning, and scheduling procedures on childhood adjustment and the formation of oral symptoms. *Child Development,* 1952, *23,* 185-191.

Sidman, M. Avoidance behavior. In W. K. Honig (Ed.), *Operant Behavior.* New York: Appleton-Century-Crofts, 1966.

Sigel, I. E., Roeper, A., & Hooper, F. H. A training procedure for acquisition of Piaget's conservation of quantity: A pilot study and its replication. *British Journal of Educational Psychology,* 1966, *36,* 301-311.

Skinner, B. F. *Science and human behavior.* New York: Macmillan, 1953.

Smedslund, J. The acquisition of conservation of substance and weight in children. *Scandinavian Journal of Psychology,* 1961, *2,* 71-84.

Smith, H. T. A comparison of interview and observation measures of mother behavior. *Journal of Abnormal and Social Psychology,* 1958, *57,* 278-282.

Stein, A. H. Imitation of resistance to temptation. *Child Development,* 1967, *38,* 157-169.

Strauss, A. The learning of social roles and rules as twin processes. *Child Development,* 1954, *25,* 192-208.

Sutton-Smith, B., & Rosenberg, B. G. *The sibling.* New York: Holt, Rinehart, & Winston, 1970.

Thompson, S. K., & Bentler, P. M. A developmental study of gender constancy and parent preference. *Archives of Sexual Behavior,* 1973, *2,* 379-385.

Turiel, E. An experimental test of the sequentiality of developmental stages in the child's moral judgment. *Journal of Personality and Social Psychology,* 1966, *3,* 611-618.

Ullmann, L. P., & Krasner, L. (Eds.). *Case studies in behavior modification.* New York: Holt, Rinehart, and Winston, 1965.

Walbek, N. Charitable cognitions and actions: A study of the concurrent elicitation of children's altruistic thoughts and deeds. Unpublished master's thesis, Northwestern University, 1969.

Wallach, M. Research on children's thinking. In *Child psychology* (Part I). Chicago: National Society for the Study of Education, 1963.

Walters, R. H., & Brown, M. A test of the high-magnitude theory of aggression. *Journal of Experimental Child Psychology,* 1964, *1,* 376-387.

Walters, R. H., Leat, M., & Mezei, L. Inhibition and disinhibition of responses through empathetic learning. *Canadian Journal of Psychology,* 1963, *17,* 235-243.

Walters, R. H., & Parke, R. D. Social motivation, dependency, and susceptibility to social influence. In L. Berkowitz (Ed.), *Advances in experimental social psychology* (Vol. 1). New York: Academic Press, 1964.

Weisberg, P. Social and nonsocial conditioning of infant vocalizations. *Child Development,* 1963, *34,* 377-388.

Werner, H. The concept of development from a comparative and organismic point of view. In D. B. Harris (Ed.), *The concept of development.* Minneapolis: University of Minnesota Press, 1957.

White, R. Motivation reconsidered: The concept of competence. *Psychological Review,* 1959, *66,* 297-333.

White, S. H. Learning. In *Child Psychology* (Part I). Chicago: National Society for the Study of Education, 1963.

White, S. H. Evidence for a hierarchical arrangement of learning processes. In L. P. Lipsitt and C. C. Spiker (Eds.), *Advances in child development and behavior* (Vol. 2). New York: Academic Press, 1965.

Whiting, J. W. M. *Becoming a Kwoma.* New Haven: Yale University Press, 1941.

Whiting, J. W. M. Socialization process and personality. In F. L. K. Hsu (Ed.), *Psychological anthropology: Approaches to culture and personality.* Homewood, Ill.: Dorsey, 1961.

Whiting, J. W. M., & Child, I. L. *Child training and personality: A cross-cultural study.* New Haven: Yale University Press, 1953.

Winch, R. F. *Identification and its familial determinants.* Indianapolis: The Bobbs-Merrill Company, Inc., 1962.

Wolf, T. M. Effects of live modeled sex-inappropriate play behavior in a naturalistic setting. *Developmental Psychology,* 1973, *9,* 120-123.

Zigler, E. F., & Child, I. L. (Eds.). *Socialization and personality development.* Reading, Mass.: Addison-Wesley, 1973.

4

Ethological Elements in Social Psychology

D. W. Rajecki
Department of Psychology, University of Wisconsin

INTRODUCTION

In 1973, the Nobel Foundation awarded a tripartite prize in the category of physiology and medicine to three behavioral scientists. The granting of this particular Nobel prize was noteworthy for at least two reasons. First, this was the only time that a prize had been awarded for work that was based on a general theory of behavior. Earlier prizes to Wagner-Jauregg in 1927 and Moniz in 1949 were for work on specific psychopathologies, and von Békésy was granted the award in 1961 for his contribution to the study of the workings of the basilar membrane. Pavlov received the prize in 1904 for his work on the physiology of digestion — not the discovery of conditioned reflex. Second, this prize had been awarded for the study of *social* behavior. Clearly, the recent recipients were interested in the social lives of their subjects as reflected in the areas of study for which they are widely known: (a) the formation and expression of social attachment; (b) territoriality and the ritualization of intraspecies aggression; and (c) nonverbal social communication. Based on their interests, the reader could be forgiven for assuming that they were social psychologists. They were not, of course. Their names were Konrad Lorenz, Nikolass Tinbergen, and Karl von Frisch, and they were ethologists.

Lorenz, Tinbergen, and von Frisch are luminaries in the scientific field termed ethology. That ethology is a legitimate and formidable scientific discipline is easily demonstrated. Like any other science, it is simultaneously a body of facts and a set of methodologies in active use, and it has unique aims and statements of purpose for its investigations. Moreover, its findings are public, reliable, and theoretically coherent. To what end is this particular scientific endeavor undertaken? Nothing more or less than the understanding of phylogenetically adaptive behavior — some would call it the study of instincts. The scope of ethology is wide and includes all species (including man), living and extinct. However, the primary focus to date has been on infrahuman species.

The theme of this chapter is that certain features of human social interaction may be illuminated by the theory, method, and findings of ethology. At the same time, it is recognized that the application of general ethological principles to human behavior requires discretion. After all, these principles were derived in part, in the respective cases of Lorenz, Tinbergen, and von Frisch, from observations of birds, fish, and insects. Certain contemporary popularizers of ethology (Desmond Morris and Robert Ardrey, among others) have already been accused by critics of advocating "ethologism" or of "zoomorphizing" humans. To zoomorphize is to explain human behavior by appealing directly to concepts derived from an analysis of animal behavior. For example, Schenken (1973) interpreted fluctuations in the political power of Winston Churchill in terms of the dynamics of social structures found in groups of free-ranging baboons. On the face of it, it would seem that the study of Winston Churchill's fortunes is better left in the hands of historians and political scientists (at least for the present). In this exposition, much simpler and more mundane human social processes and patterns will be discussed.

Only a fraction of ethology can be reviewed in these pages. Happily, the Nobel prize to three ethologists suggested a workable selection of representative topics, and the subsequent organization of this paper. A general overview of ethological theory will be followed by a somewhat detailed discussion of the possible role of instinctive behavior in three areas of social phenomena. These areas were mentioned earlier: attachment, territoriality, and communication.[1] On the other hand, the material discussed will not necessarily be that for which the prize was awarded. Indeed, much of the work to be reviewed was done by persons other than ethologists. The discussions within each of the three topic areas will be different from one another, primarily because research within the given areas has progressed along different lines, or at a different pace. Across all areas, however, the intent is to identify a phenomenon at the level of animal behavior, and then systematically extend those findings to the level of human behavior.

GENERAL OVERVIEW

The beginnings of the science of ethology have been traced by Jaynes (1969) to the debates at the French *Academie des Sciences* around 1830 between Georges Cuvier and Etienne Geoffroy-Saint-Hilaire. These men had opposing accounts for the existence of the various forms of life. Cuvier believed that God had created and recreated living beings at different times; for him, the study of comparative

---

[1]The discoveries of von Frisch on communication among bees will not be discussed here because it is not a simple matter to generalize between bee and human language. Readers interested in the bee language are referred to von Frisch's (1967) excellent book on the topic.

anatomy dealt with static relationships between immutable species. Geoffroy-Saint-Hilaire, to the contrary, was an early evolutionist.

These somewhat abstract distinctions between the two theories led to a more concrete question, and to the point of the debate: What is the proper locale for the study of the different species? Since the basic tenet of theories of evolution is that organisms adapt to their environments, Geoffroy-Saint-Hilaire argued for naturalistic observation of animals *in* their environment. On the other side, because the effect of environment was irrelevant to the creation theory, Cuvier chose to rely on laboratory work for the discovery of facts. As far as the particular debates were concerned, the proponents of the laboratory won. As Jaynes (1969) put it, "Cuvier smothered the tender, unsupported suggestions of the younger man with mountains of data" (p. 60).

Nevertheless, the position of Geoffroy-Saint-Hilaire impressed some, and a series of biologists espoused the same arguments well into the early decades of the twentieth century (see the reviews of Eibl-Eibesfeldt, 1970; Mortenson, 1975). It was not until the 1930s, however, that ethology received an impetus that changed it from the concern of a splinter group of biologists to what it is today. That impetus stemmed from the empirical and theoretical work of Lorenz and Tinbergen and their associates. Interestingly, it seems that this circle of modern ethologists were not aware of the origins of the label they had applied to themselves, nor of the earlier debates (Jaynes, 1969). Regardless, it was an appropriate selection as the aim of ethology today is the same as it was in the past, the understanding of phylogenetically adapted behavior of organisms in their natural habitat.

In 1951, Tinbergen provided the first systematic and comprehensive exposition of the distinguishing features and principles of ethology. With few exceptions, these principles remain current with ethologists, although as Hinde (1970, p. vii) points out, the term ethologist is most correctly applied to students of behavior who share certain orienting attitudes, rather than the same problems, methods, or levels of analysis (see also Crook, 1970, for a contemporary overview). The following compendium has been drawn from several ethologically writers (Eibl-Eibesfeldt, 1967, 1970; Hess, 1970a, 1970b; Hinde, 1970, 1974; Lorenz, 1937, 1950, 1965; Thorpe, 1956; Tinbergen, 1948, 1951, 1963) who appear to be in general agreement on main issues.

In the broadest sense, ethologists claim to concern themselves equally with evolution, adaptation (survival), ontogeny (development), and immediate causation and organization of behavior. Much interest has centered on the last topic in the list. Ethological theory has provisions to account for the organization of an organism's behavior through the interaction of inherited internal factors and external environmental factors. In an extreme sense, behavior can be reactive in that it is controlled, within limits, by environmental stimulation. On the other extreme, behavior can be spontaneous in that it is caused by neurophysiological activities or states that are largely independent of external stimulation. Most often, of course, behavior is a product of an interplay between these conceptually distinct causal forces.

External Stimulation and Behavior

It goes without saying that animals can sense, discriminate, and localize many types and intensities of physical changes (stimuli) in their environment. A central aim of ethology is to discover which of this variety of stimulatory events do or do not have a direct influence on behavior. It is a remarkable and unavoidable fact that certain of these stimuli automatically elicit more or less complicated and obviously functional patterns of motor responses.

For example, herring gull chicks beg for food by pecking at the parent gull's bill. In reaction, the parent regurgitates food and then holds some of the food in its bill tips. Now, the chick grasps and swallows the food. The stimulus that produces the hatchling's initial pecking response is a red spot on the lower mandible (bill) of the parent. In tests with artificial models of an adult gull's head, black, blue, or white spots elicited fewer infant pecks than did a red spot, and a model with no spot elicited the fewest pecks. Moreover, the presence of the total configuration of the head was largely immaterial to the response of the chick with little diminution in pecking seen when only an outline of the bill and red spot was presented (Tinbergen, 1967). The dynamic between the parent and offspring in the feeding behavior of young gulls also provides an example of the important fact that the behavior of one organism may be a sufficient stimulus to evoke a functionally related behavior in a second. Presumably, adult gulls would be less likely to regurgitate food in response to pecks at parts of their bodies other than the bill, although Hailman (1967) did note that on occasion an adult gull will regurgitate at the sight of a chick. This interlocking of one behavior-as-stimulus with another behavior-as-stimulus has been termed *chaining* by the ethologists, and will be discussed at some length below.

There are many examples of behavior patterns produced in a reflexlike manner by external stimulation. Lack (1943) reported that intense aggressive behavior could be elicited in male robins by the presentation of a simple bundle of red feathers. On the other hand, the presentation of a model of a robin without red breast feathers was ignored. In other varieties of song birds, most aggressive responses are elicited by the eyes and head of opponents (Smith & Hosking, 1955). These birds almost invariably attacked the head of intact models. Further, they attacked a head when it was presented by itself on a stick, and failed to attack when a decapitated model was presented. In our own laboratory, it was discovered that even day-old domestic chicks peck mostly at the eyes of other chicks, to the point of causing tissue damage (Rajecki, Ivins, & Rein, 1976).

This sort of evoked reaction to external stimulation is of course not limited to birds. In a recent book, Eibl-Eibesfeldt (1970, Chapter 5) reviews related findings from studies of a wide variety of species including beetles, butterflies, crickets, flies, frogs, grasshoppers, kids (goats), kittens, monkeys, moths, sharks, spiders, toads, and many others.

While it is obvious that a stimulus must be perceived before it can have an influence on behavior, the most important point to be made here is that not all stimuli that can be perceived are effective in the same way. This point is well illustrated in the case of a certain carnivorous water beetle *(Dytiscus marginalis)* and its prey, the tadpole. Whereas it is known that the beetle possesses adequate eyesight, this insect does not react to the sight of a tadpole moving about in a nearby transparent tube. However, when an extract of meat is dissolved in the underwater environment of the beetle, it makes movements to hunt and capture any solid object available. Thus this predatory instinct is guided by chemical and tactile stimulation rather than visual stimulation (Tinbergen, 1951).

The particular stimulus configurations that produce specific unlearned response patterns have been variously called key or sign stimuli. The existence of such elaborate and unconditioned stimulus-response links provides a simple foundation on which ethologists have built an elaborate theory of adaptedness. In Lorenz' (1937) terms, such stimuli are metaphoric keys that fit and open locks of instinctive behavior patterns. The relationship between a sign stimuli and the adapted behavior is straightforward: inasmuch as we can assume that the environment existed prior to the organism, it is incumbent on the organism to adapt to the environment. According to Lorenz, "All that the evolution of the species can do is to adapt the innate perceptory patterns as closely as possible to the preexistent sets of key stimuli" (1937, p. 248). In short, members of a species that have the capacity to correctly recognize and respond to critical features in their environment tend to survive longer than those who do not, and, as the species propagates, this ability is selected for in the genetic sense. Organisms that have the capacity tend to produce more and more viable offspring. Eventually, all members of a given species would come to share the characteristic. This selection pressure is presumed to operate also on the physical characteristics of the species itself. For example, the red spot on the lower mandible of the adult herring gull is found on all such gulls simply because it is now part of the genetic heritage of that subspecies, however many gulls had it in the dim past.

Despite the diversity of particular sign stimuli across species (or even the number of sign stimuli for different reactions *within* a species), such stimuli are held to have at least one characteristic in common. While they are very simple in configuration, they are exceedingly improbable in general. For example, the color red figures importantly in the instinctive behavior of many animal species (e.g., Lack, 1943; Tinbergen, 1967), presumably because it is so unlikely in most naturalistic settings. In some animals the presumed selection for simple yet improbable sign stimuli has produced astonishing results. The gaping mouth of a young Gouldian finch provokes a feeding response in the parent, as does the pecking of the gull chick. In the case of this finch, however, the open mouth reveals a visual sign stimulus, four brilliantly blue spots vividly set in a field of yellow and pink (Eibl-Ebesfeldt, 1970, p. 84).

Internal Mechanisms and Behavior

The fact that only certain environmental stimuli produce or elicit highly differentiated response patterns implies that some sort of internal filtering or processing takes place. To account for this processing, ethologists have advanced the concept of an innate releasing mechanism (IRM). The postulate of this sort of mechanism provides a basis for the interpretation of the effectiveness of sign stimuli. While the organism may be able to perceive a variety of stimuli, an IRM is influenced by only some of these.

Conceptually, the IRM has the status of a hypothetical construct. That is, it is defined functionally as opposed to being defined operationally. In psychology, certain hypothetical constructs have been useful in advancing both theoretical and empirical efforts. Well-known examples of hypothetical constructs in psychology are Hebb's (1949) cell assemblies and phase sequences and Sokolov's (1960) neuronal models. As noted, hypothetical constructs such as IRMs are more apparent in their function than in physical terms. Nevertheless, something like primitive or simple IRMs have been discovered in (for example) cells or cell groupings in the visual systems of frogs that have special functions as feature (brightness or edge) detectors (e.g., Lettvin, Maturana, McCulloch, & Pitts, 1959; for a general review, see Lindsay & Norman, 1972).

For certain of the early modern ethologists, it seemed reasonable that a different IRM was responsible for each different innate reaction of a species. For example, the sexual pursuit of the male grayling butterfly is hardly affected whether the female model presented is brown, black, red, green, blue, yellow, or white. Models of all these colors are avidly followed. When feeding, on the other hand, male graylings are utterly indifferent to white, black, red, or green flowers and respond only to those that are blue or yellow. This example is taken as an illustration that different reactions in the very same animal are accounted for by different IRMs, with color influencing the mechanisms differentially (Tinbergen, 1951). Currently, there is some doubt whether IRMs overlap in function, whether experience influences them in some ways, whether a theory of central nervous system activity should supplant the notion of IRM entirely, or whether it is even conceivable that an IRM actually "exists" in the absence of the stimulus that influences it (see Hinde, 1970; or Hess, 1970a, for example). To date, this incipient debate has not produced very much heat or light, and we will (on a short-term basis) accept the notion of the IRM as it stands as a useful interim explanatory concept.

It must be pointed out, however, that an IRM is not *inflexibly* linked to one kind of sensory input. That is, the same sign stimulus does not always evoke an identical response. One source of variance in reactivity is found in combinations of sign stimuli. For the male stickleback fish in the correct hormonal condition, the red belly of another male is a sufficient stimulus for aggression. Additionally, if this second male swims with a head-down posture, aggressive responses are intensified in the attacker. It is as if the IRM were able to "collect" different afferent impulses. Tinbergen (1951) has termed this sort of phenomenon *heterogeneous summation.*

A second factor influencing the reactivity of an IRM to a stimulus is the internal motivational state of the organism. Briefly, with a longer and longer period between consummatory acts (food ingestion or coition, for example), there is an increased sensitivity to the sign stimuli that produce a response appropriate to that motivational state. To put it another way, the longer the duration between consummatory acts, the more likely it is that suboptimal parts of wholes or distortions of particular sign stimuli will evoke the response in question. In fact, if the consummatory or terminating response is delayed sufficiently, activity resembling the response may occur in the *absence* of any sign stimulus.[2] This is illustrated in so-called vacuum behavior. It is known that canaries deprived of nest building materials will perform stereotyped movements with nonexistent materials and weave them into a nonexistent nest (Hinde, 1958).

Findings such as those reported by Hinde (1958) on vacuum behavior suggest that there may be something like action specific energy available in or mediated by the IRM. While Hinde himself (1960) has pointed to some difficulties in interpreting certain behavior patterns, such as the urge to sleep, in terms of action specific energy, it remains that there are some data that can be considered supportive of the notion. For example, Drees (1952, reviewed in Hess, 1970a) presented jumping spiders of the *Salticidae* family with lifelike pictures of their prey. In this way, the attack response was elicited some 30 or 40 times before the predator ceased reacting completely. After an interval of two hours, the prey model was again presented and elicited an additional 10 to 20 attacks. This decline and resurgence of attack behavior cannot be directly attributed to general fatigue factors because some of the spiders were kept in constant motion by aversive stimulation (light) during the two-hour "rest" period.

Whether energization from an IRM stems from action specific energy or excitation-inhibitory influences of the central nervous system, it can be seen that the concept of a process or structure such as an IRM represents a point of

---

[2]On the other hand, it is known that certain sign stimuli are so potent that they elicit behavior in the absence of motivation or need. This evidence sometimes takes the form of an anecdote where writers tell us of various well-fed domesticated animals that continue with hunting activities. To this list of anecdotes, the author would like to add his own. On the morning of this writing (a grey Sunday in November), the author's cat was observed to feed to satiation on Nine Lives® "Tuna in Sauce" cat food. Not 10 minutes later, the cat returned to the yard from an out of doors foray, carrying a much-agitated field mouse. The mouse, although it did not survive the episode, went unconsumed.

integration or interaction between external environmental factors and internal homeostatic or hormonal factors in the causation of behavior.

Patterns of Behavior

The basic motoric unit in an ethological analysis of behavior is the fixed action pattern (FAP). Fixed action patterns are species-specific, genetically inherited, coordinated muscular contractions. The spatiotemporal form of these contractions are independent of environmental stimulation once they have been elicited. Another characteristic of an FAP is that it appears to be in the service of the organism, so to speak, since the physical consequences of such a pattern are often advantageous. There is, however, no reason to believe that the organism is necessarily aware of any long- or short-term benefits from the act. As Eibl-Eibesfeldt put it:

> Fixed action patterns usually proceed without any indication of insight into the species-preserving function of the activity on the part of the animal, as is clearly shown by inappropriate actions. When inner readiness to act coincides with the appriate releasing stimulus situation in an animal, then a particular fixed action pattern will run its course almost automatically. Thus a dog hiding a bone in the living room shows the movement of covering it as if earth were available; in this way his behavior is genetically preprogrammed to be adaptive in nature. He will turn several times before lying down, although there is no grass to be trampled (1970, p. 16).

There are many other examples across species of fixed action patterns such as grooming, eating, and sexual postures. As Eibl-Eibesfeldt notes, however, fixed action patterns are most obvious to the observer when they occur in inappropriate circumstances. It will come as a surprise to no one that adult chickens scratch at the ground with their feet as they amble about while feeding. It was a surprise to the author, though, to observe that, while literally standing on a pile or surface of granular food, a feeding chicken or chick will also scratch, often to its own disadvantage. Apparently, the animal is scratching away at the food in an attempt to get at the food, with the result that (in laboratory cages, at least) the bulk of the grain is spilled and wasted! I learned only later that this is a serious problem for poultrymen, the solution of which is to provide the animals with special troughs for food that allow pecking but prevent scratching.

The importance of the study of FAPs for the development of ethological theory cannot be overestimated. In the first place, it is on the basis of the performance of the fixed action pattern that sign stimuli are identified and cataloged. Secondly, the existence of IRMs can only be inferred or deduced from the existence of FAPs. Thirdly, if a particular FAP can be conceived of metaphorically as an *organ* of behavior, then it can be said that the animal inherits and possesses such behavioral organs in the same way it inherits and possesses morphological structures. The conception of innate behavioral capacities as organs places the study of fixed patterns directly in the mainstream of biological thought.

Because fixed action patterns are at the core of ethological endeavor, it is of upmost importance to determine which of the myriad activities of a given species are innate and which are learned. Obviously, if a behavior pattern has been acquired through conditioning, trial-and-error learning, or shaping (in the Skinnerian sense), then there is no need to posit any innate or genetic capacity. To date, one of the most critical tests for the innateness of a behavior pattern has been the development of the deprivation experiment.

The logic behind deprivation experimentation is apparently simple: if a behavior pattern is innate, it ought to emerge — in the presence of appropriate stimulation — in the absence of any opportunity for learning or imitation. Therefore, according to this procedure, the subject in question is usually kept in some condition of isolation or constraint until the behavior under study is known to occur in another subject in a more natural state. Examples of early research will serve as illustrations. Carmichael (1928) raised tadpoles under a chronic anasthesia until control animals of the same age evidenced swimming ability. When the drug was removed the experimental animals could also swim well. Grohmann (1939, cited in Eibl-Eibesfeldt, 1970) raised pigeons under conditions where they were unable to flap their wings and observed that these birds flew as well as unfettered sibs when released. In both examples, the behavior cannot be attributed to learning or to practice, but rather to the presumed phylogenetic adaptive capacities inherent in the animal. Still, the analytic advantages of deprivation experimentation have not gone unquestioned (cf. Hinde, 1970; Lehrman, 1953; Schnierla, 1966). This is so because the very conditions of isolation, since they are by no means the natural environment, may produce anamolies in the physiology or behavior of an organism to such a degree that conclusions regarding a particular response pattern are ambiguous at best. To take an example from studies of primates reared in siolation, Riesen (1966) reported that animals kept in darkness from an early age suffered severe physical deterioration of the optic system. Obviously, this particular treatment rendered them unfit as subjects in research on responses to any visual array, be they sign stimuli or whatever. Under certain circumstances, however, data from such research can be heuristic and is sometimes compelling, as we shall see.

Fixed action patterns, as they have been sketched here, are still relatively simple units of behavior. Generally, they are considered consummatory acts because, when they occur, a purpose is served or an end is reached. Thus, an automatic aggressive response such as biting or scratching might serve to remove an intruder from a nest site. These simple units of behavior do not, however, occur in unsystematic sequences. Indeed, phenomena such as the nesting activities of birds are enormously complicated and yet are apparently well coordinated and purposive. In general, ethological theory has two provisions to account for such coordination: hierarchical organization and chaining. Both of these concepts have been illustrated through descriptions of the reproductive behavior of a small fish, the stickleback.

In the spring of the year, sticklebacks migrate to shallow waters where males select areas termed territories. Within the territory, the male builds a nest, courts females that happen by, and fights with and drives off other males. Now while these behavioral patterns appear to be diverse and discrete, they are all under the control of a hierarchical organization of reproductive drive. Each of the behavior patterns occurs in response to particular sign stimuli: migration is a reaction to increases in water temperatures; territoriality is a reaction to certain kinds of underwater vegetation, as is nest building; aggression is sparked by the color of the belly of an intruding male; and courtship is triggered by the swollen abdomen of a pregnant female. Each behavior is governed by its particular IRM, which somehow transforms the so-called reproductive drive into action specific energy. If the reproductive drive was absent, the particular consummatory acts (FAPs) would be absent also. But as the drive is present, the behavior unfolds in a systematic way: first migration, then territoriality, then aggression and courtship. Each phase is based on some necessary precondition. Thus the notion of hierarchical organization for the ethologist satisfies the basic requirement for any theorist of motivation: an account of the energization and direction of behavior.

Chaining is a factor in somewhat shorter-term (but no less complicated) behavioral episodes. As noted earlier, chaining is a phenomenon where one response serves as a stimulus for a second response, usually in a "social" interaction between two animals. This is convincingly illustrated in the courtship and mating of sticklebacks as described by Tinbergen (1951):

> Each reaction of either male or female is released by the preceding reaction of the partner. . . . The male's first reaction, the zigzag dance, is dependent of the visual stimulus from the female, in which . . . the sign stimuli 'swollen abdomen' and the special movement play a part. The female reacts to the red color of the male and to his zigzag dance by swimming right towards him. This induces the male to turn around and swim rapidly to the nest. This, in turn, entices the female to follow him, thereby stimulating the male to put his head into the entrance. His behavior now releases the female's next reaction: she enters the nest. . . . This realeases the quivering reaction in the male which induces spawning. The presence of fresh eggs in the nest makes the male fertilize them (p. 48).

In short, the total complicated event of mating in this fish can be reduced to a series of chained fixed action patterns. If one of the complementary responses is imperfect or not forthcoming (for whatever reason), the chain, in a sense, may be broken and the behavioral sequence may revert to an earlier phase. That such chains are sometimes not rigid or invariant in their sequence is explained by the fact that behavior is governed by both external stimuli and internal motivational states. This qualification does not reduce the status of chaining as an explanatory concept; it merely reiterates the statement that behavior is complex and that an analysis of behavior requires the recognition of the interaction of causal factors. This points up the fact that ethology, like other modern sciences, makes probabalistic statements about its subject matter.

Evolution of Behavior

Sign stimuli and fixed action patterns play an undisputed part in the adaptive-
ness of the members of a species to their physical environment. Reactions to the
environment are certainly critical in terms of nutrition and habitat selection.
However, some of the most dramatic instances of sign stimuli and the action patterns they instigate are observed in the interaction of two members of the same
species, especially during aggressive or sexual episodes. These behavior patterns
are so striking that they sometimes impress the uninitiated human observer as
being bizarre and inexplicable. For example, during various stages of courtship
the mallard drake makes as many as ten distinctive movements while swimming
near the female, the object of his amorous intentions (as described by Lorenz,
1958):

1. "bill shake" (from left to right);
2. "shake and stretch" (head thrust upward and forward);
3. "tail shake" (from left to right);
4. "grunt whistle" (most of abdomen raised off water, bill pointed down);
5. "up-down movement" (floating on breast, head rhythmically raised up
   and down);
6. "head up, tail up" (head and tail brought close together over back);
7. "looking toward female" (self-explanatory);
8. "nod swimming" (head rhythmically thrust downward and forward);
9. "showing the back of the head" (to the female);
10. "pull up" (head stretched over the back toward the lowered tail).

Movements 1 to 5 appear during group courtship activity when drakes and
dams segregate themselves from the larger flock and form a pair-bond. Patterns
6 through 10 appear in sequence prior to copulation. Each of these responses
serve as a sign stimulus for the female. In sequence, they prompt her to separate
from social aggregates of other ducks and render her receptive to copulation.

Such distinctive behavioral and morphological features of an animal have
been termed *releasers*. Thus releasers are a special subset of sign stimuli that are
inherent in the genetically determined physical characteristics of an organism.
Not all releasers are behavioral; in various species, visual, auditory, tactile, and
chemical sign stimuli have been identified (Tinbergen, 1948).

Even so, the bulk of social releasers do involve some sort of active display on
the part of the signalling organism, and such displays themselves can be considered fixed action patterns. These displays typically resemble certain other behavioral patterns that *do not* elicit the same (or any other) response. This distinction
has led ethologists to posit a process of the ritualization of display movements.
That is, certain fixed action patterns that were originally involved in the maintenance of the individual (for example, eating, drinking, preening) or even simpler responses such as blinking in response to a startling or noxious stimulation,

have been slightly modified through evolutionary change. These changes include variations in the frequency, rate, rhythmicity, orientation, and coordination of components of the original pattern.

Now, the signal value of the evolved releaser need not have any functional relationship to the behavior from which it was derived. To present a typical example, *somehow* the distortion of a behavior like drinking or feeding is presumed to have come to be a signal of a sexual advance on the part of a mallard drake. This is observed as "nod swimming" (see above), and it evokes a complementary sexual response in the female. While it is nowhere made clear by ethologists why or how a certain response was "chosen" by evolutionary pressures for ritualization, these theorists seem to accept the completed process rather like an article of faith. After all, something like ritualization *had* to have happened, did it not? Presumably, the IRMs sensitive to the ritualized FAPs evolved concurrently with those displays.

There is, however, certain evidence that leads to an argument by analogy for the evolution of releasers. It stems from the idea introduced earlier that units of innate behavior are akin to morphological structures or organs. Similar species do have different morphological characteristics, and these differences accrued through evolutionary selection. Therefore, ritualization probably also occurred through selection, since animals of different species within a genus do exhibit ritualized behaviors to different degrees. For example, ritualized food pecking has become part of the courtship displays of certain birds. To attract a female, the domestic cock scratches and pecks at the ground and then steps back so that the female can approach the site — and the rooster. Somewhat more elaborately, the courting Impeyan pheasant pecks and then remains bowed low with maximally spread wing and tail feathers. At the extreme, the peacock does not lower his head, but points to the ground with outspread tail feathers. Here, the female searches for the imaginary food at the locale indicated by the tail (Schenkel, 1956, 1958, cited in Eibl-Eibesfeldt, 1970).

The question whether releasers (social sign stimuli) emerged through ritualization or some other process is largely eclipsed by the importance of the fact that related species do, in fact, differ systematically in terms of innate behavior patterns. When these divergent behaviors can be established as homologies (differing biological characteristics having a common genetic basis), then the genetic basis of behavior is more firmly established (see Hess, 1970a, on this point).

Innate Social Behavior in Man

Probably most of us are willing to take it for granted that the behavior of lower animals is governed, by and large, by instinctive impulses and activities. And we are pleased, in a vague sort of way, that biologists, and especially ethologists, have taken such pains to provide us with interesting examples across a variety of

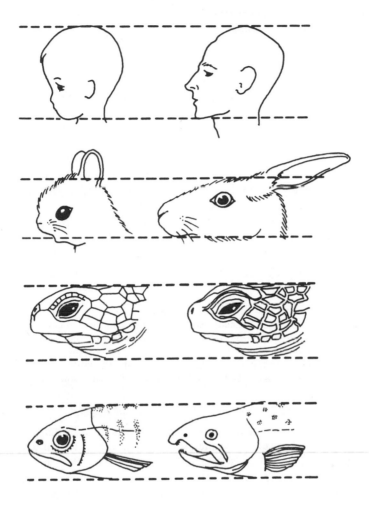

FIG. 4.1   Idealized renditions of infant (left) and adult (right) heads. The turtle is after Carr (1952, p. 345) and the fish is after Blair, Blair, Brodkorb, Cagle and Moore (1968, p. 45). (The mammals were redrawn from Lorenz (1943) by Janice Rajecki.)

organisms that this is indeed the case. But usually people want to draw the line somewhere, and usually that line is between nonhuman animals and humans.

For the modern ethologists, however, man was not meant to be excluded from the ethological study of behavior. In 1943, Lorenz published a paper in which he argued that mothers' responsiveness to their babies and peoples' reactions to infants in general were governed (released) by a number of infantile characteristics (sign stimuli). For the human child these stimuli included: (a) a head that was large in proportion to the rest of the body; (b) a prominent forehead that was large in proportion to the rest of the face; and (c) relatively large eyes located below the midline of the head. These, then, were the characteristics that activated positive emotional reactions and the behaviors that ministered to the child's needs. Indeed, Lorenz (1943) extended this analysis to include the positive affective reactions of humans to the young of a number of nonhuman vertebrates, including rabbits, dogs, and birds. Figure 4.1 illustrates the general differences between infant and adult physiognomies for certain of the species noted (as redrawn from Lorenz's original) and includes a view of an infant fish and an infant reptile.[3] According to the analysis, it is clear why the turtle and fish do not attract us. They show *none* of the three properties noted by Lorenz (1943). As a matter of fact, contemporary research has supported Lorenz's claim that the facial features termed "babyness" are attractive, at least in relation to the pictures of adult faces (Fullard & Reiling, 1976).

This matter of maternal (and perhaps fraternal) responsiveness to the sheer stimulus characteristics of the infant has also been touched on by the eminent psychologist, Harry F. Harlow. In his lectures, Harlow included a photograph of a *particularly* winsome baby monkey (see Harlow, 1971) that he termed the "elicitor of female ecstasy response" for the following reason:

> Some years ago the photograph . . . was projected on a screen at a women's college in Virginia. All 500 girls in the audience gave simultaneous gasps of ecstasy. The same test has since been conducted with many college audiences. Not only are all-male audiences completely unresponsive, but the presence of males in coeducational audiences inhibits the feminine ecstasy response. Evidently nature has not only con-structed women to produce babies, but also prepared them from the onset to be mothers (p. 6).

Well, what is evident to Harlow here may not be so evident to the rest of us. One can hear the indignant howls of liberated and enlightened individuals (women *and* men) in response to the "sexist" claim that maternal tendencies are innate. Rather, these critics would insist, women learn their place, including their alleged maternal nature, as a result of conscious or nonconscious ideologies that shape our society and its members (see the section by S. Bem and D. Bem, in D. Bem, 1970). But how could one tell which claim is the more correct? What sort of evidence would indicate whether human maternal tendencies are at least partly innate or strictly learned?

The difficulty in answering these questions is at once obvious when we con-sider the primary techniques developed by ethologists. Is it possible to apply the deprivation-experiment technique to the problem of the ontogeny of human maternal behavior? The answer is yes, of course. It certainly would be possible to rear little girls and little boys in social isolation until puberty, and then

---

[3]This particular figure is presented as much for tradition's sake as any other. It has ap-peared in many of the general treatises on ethology, including Tinbergen's (1951) book.

present them with surrogates of infants (or real infants, for that matter) to see if there were innate differences in the reactions of the sexes. But it seems unlikely in the extreme that such work will ever be realized, short of the emergence of some mad ethologist-scientist like the ghoulish Dr. Frankenstein.[4] What about another approach, that of comparing homologous behaviors across species? That would give us a clue to the innate or learned origin of motherhood. Unfortunately, the genus *Homo* has only one living species these days: *sapiens*. Therefore, this avenue is also closed to the ethologist where man is concerned.

Even this brief discussion of one aspect of infant care points up the special difficulty of discovering and studying any possible innate behavior in humans. Nevertheless, as we have seen, ethologists have tried to extend their principles to man, even if the preferred methods of study were not available. At first, they were somewhat conservative about the matter. In a seminal paper, Lorenz (1937) devoted only a dozen or so lines to the behavior of humans. Similarly, Tinbergen (1951) set aside a total of six of 210 pages in his important book to discuss the "ethological study of man." Neither early treatment went much beyond a mention of contagious yawning in humans. These days, ethologically oriented writers are more ambitious. Entire books on human ethology have appeared. Notable examples of general treatises are Hinde's *Biological Bases of Human Social Behavior* (1974) and a volume edited by White entitled *Ethology and Psychiatry* (1974). Other books containing substantial sections devoted to human behavior are the volume edited by von Cranach and Vine called *Social Communication and Movement* (1973), and Eibl-Eibesfeldt's *Ethology: the Biology of Behavior* (1970). Two volumes devoted to research on children are McGrew's *An Ethological Study of Children's Behavior* (1972), and *Ethological Studies of Child Behaviour,* edited by Blurton-Jones (1972). Several more recent books seriously consider the evolution of aspects of the behavior of man, although not all claim a strict ethological orientation, and these include a volume edited by Ekman titled *Darwin and Facial Expression: A century of research in review* (1973). Finally, two major works whose contents are certainly relevant here are Thorpe's *Animal Nature and Human Nature* (1974), and Wilson's *Sociobiology: The New Synthesis* (1975). Doubtless, more are in preparation.

It is the purpose of the balance of this chapter to explore the possibility of instinctive reactions in man and other species so that we may extend our insight into human social behavior. To predict the easy success of this or any other exploration is, of course, unwise. Perhaps the best we can hope for is that an analysis of relatively simple social phenomena might reveal that human innate (or innately human) behavior patterns do exist. But even that revelation would be something.

---

[4]Frederick II (1194-1250) once raised babies in silence (if not total isolation) to determine the possibility of a spontaneous human language. Unfortunately, all the subjects died before any data were forthcoming (Wallbank & Taylor, 1960, p. 425).

SOCIAL ATTACHMENT

The importance of early social bonding or attachment is nowhere more vividly demonstrated than in certain birds. In naturalistic settings, avian family units with precocial offspring (for example, chickens, ducks, geese) are highly mobile and do not tarry long at the nest site once hatching is completed. Since the maintenance of proximity to the parent is vital in terms of the location of food and the avoidance of predators and other dangers, it is essential that the hatchling keep up. The mobility of the parent, and the capacity of the young to accommodate to it, are aptly illustrated. from the following passage (no pun intended) from Nice (1962):

> Leopold (1951) tells of the long and dangerous trip of a baby wood duck from the place of hatching down a steep bluff and along the railroad track to the Mississippi River, which they swam across in about 20 minutes, although the distance must be close to a mile. A mother goldeneye led a newly hatched brood 1.5 kilometers through trailless country from one pond to another, while another brood swam 2140 meters in 67 minutes. On the ground they traveled from one-half to one kilometer an hour, on water up to 4.5 kilometers per hour (p. 49).

At least one study has shown the survival value of such early social bonding in the wild. Craighead and Craighead (1957) located a large number of nesting pairs of Canada geese incubating their eggs in the Flathead Valley in Montana. Prior observations indicated that these geese would migrate to the nearby Flathead Lake once their young had hatched. In order to keep track of particular goslings, the Craigheads injected certain eggs with a harmless red dye. This preparation neither influenced the hatchlings behavior nor the parents' acceptance of them. Having counted the number of red birds that hatched, Craighead and Craighead (1957) then tabulated the number that reached the shallow waters of the lake, some 2 to 10 miles distant from the nest sites. They report that the family units left the nests within 48 hours after hatching and took an average of 3 days to complete their journeys. While the Craigheads did observe first hand the corpses of several goslings due to accidents or predation, they reported that fully 80 per cent of the dyed goslings reached the brood areas alive!

The process whereby the young of such birds become attached has been termed *imprinting* by ethologists (Lorenz, 1935, 1937). Before an analysis of the process is undertaken, however, it will be helpful to describe certain conventional measures of this state of attachment or bonding (see also Sluckin, 1972, for a catalog of measures).

The most widely reported index of imprinting is the tendency of the young to approach or follow the parent, or parental surrogate, hereafter referred to as the target. This measure is obviously meaningful in view of the descriptions of the circumstances in the life of the offspring. In the current usage, this tendency to follow is considered a fixed action pattern. A second commonly used measure is the detection of one or another sort of vocal signal emitted by the bird. A large number of discrete types of vocalizations have been observed in the chick and duckling, for example, but two of these calls are of particular interest for inferring motivational states. The first of these has been termed the distress call. It is emitted when the bird is known to be cold, hungry, injured, or otherwise under stress. The other call has been labeled contentment, and it occurs when the bird is given food, returned to warmth, or otherwise comforted. These calls are easily discernable, even for the naive observer. This is so because the two calls differ in most of their physical parameters. Relative to the contentment call, the distress note is louder, longer, and is emitted at a slower rate. Further, it covers a broader range of pitch (Hz) than the contentment call, and its change in pitch over time within each emission is opposite to that of contentment (Collias & Joos, 1953; Guyomarc'h, 1962; Rajecki & Eichenbaum, 1973; Rajecki, Eichenbaum & Heilweil, 1973). These two vocalizations are also fixed action patterns, at least in the sense that they are innate.

As a measure of social attachment, observations of the vocalizations are interpreted thusly: if a bird is psychologically attached to a particular target it seems reasonable that it would be more comfortable in the presence of that target than in its absence. Therefore, the degree of attachment can be gauged by the numbers of either call when the young subject and the target are separated or reunited. This vocal measure of attachment is especially useful in cases where, for one reason or another, the subject is unable to perform the locomotor response of following. Again, as with the description of the tenacity of following behavior from field observations, there are graphic descriptions of the occurrence of distress calls in the wild, and the events that elicit them (Collias & Collias, 1956; Driver, 1960). According to Collias and Collias (1956):

> After the observer had been in the blind for about 20 minutes one duckling left the nest and the company of its nestmates. It soon began giving distress calls which promptly ceased when it climbed back into the nest and rejoined the others, a few minutes after having left. Some 45 minutes later, six of the young left the nest together and commenced feeding; this local excursion extended to a distance of at least six feet from the nest. Whenever one of the ducklings became separated from the others it gave distress calls until it had regained the company of its fellows (p. 380).

A final measure of attachment indicates not the bond itself, but consequences that stem from the bond. That is, if the presence of familiar social objects can reduce stress as indicated by a reduction in distress calls, then this presence may have an impact on all behavioral tendencies of the subject. Insofar as there are tendencies in the subject to act on the environment (to feed, play, explore, manipulate, or whatever) these tendencies might be enhanced in the company of the imprinted target. Thus, the formation or existence of an attachment has implications for the behavior of the organism toward both the object of attachment, and presumably toward everything else it encounters.

Reports of the first two of these three measures have been in the literature for over 100 years (the third measure will be discussed on page 246). Spalding

(1873) recorded his observations of the movements of newly hatched chicks and noted that one chick had "... sat complaining and motionless for six minutes, when I placed my hand on it for a few seconds. On removing my hand the chicken immediately followed it by sight backward and forward all around the table" (cited in Sluckin, 1965, p. 2). Spalding concluded that: "Chickens as soon as they are able to walk will follow any moving object. And, when guided by sight alone, they seem to have no more disposition to follow a duck, or a human being" (cited in Sluckin, 1965, p. 2). The remarkable fact here, of course, is that these birds became so easily attached to Spalding.

It was a similar observation of the attachment of certain birds to himself that prompted Lorenz (1935, 1937) to attribute certain characteristics to imprinting that, in his view, made it unique as a form of learning. According to Lorenz, the act of following the parent by a newly hatched bird was but one behavior in the class of behaviors controlled by the so-called social releasers. As noted in the introduction, the stimuli involved in a releaser impinge on an innate releasing mechanism — actually, Lorenz termed it an *innate perceptory pattern* — and, in this case, unblock the following-mother reaction. Lorenz interpreted the mistaken attachment of greylag goslings to himself by arguing that he possessed stimulus characteristics that were adequate, if not altogether appropriate, to elicit the reaction.

Furthermore, certain other observations led Lorenz to posit that imprinting could only occur in a severely delimited span of time shortly after the bird hatched. This interval has come to be called the critical period for imprinting. Lorenz estimated that this critical period in, for example, the partridge lasted only a few hours and ended even before the animal could locomote properly.

An additional characteristic attributed to imprinting by Lorenz was that it was irreversible. That is, the formation of an attachment to one object forever after precluded the formation of an attachment to any other. This notion was based on the observation that a greylag goose that had imprinted on Lorenz continued to show a preference for his human company even after it had been in constant association with a turkey hen for a number of weeks.

In sum, imprinting for Lorenz was a phenomenon that was restricted to certain birds and that was governed by innate factors. For him, identifying characteristics of the phenomenon were that: (a) it is dependent on certain social releasers; (b) it occurs only during a critical period; and (c) once it occurs, the bond that is produced is irreversible; it can neither be undone nor replaced.

Tests of Lorenz' notions were not forthcoming until after the interruption of behavioral research caused by the Second World War. From 1950 on, however, papers and books on imprinting proliferated. As an illustration of this boom, Gray published in 1963 a checklist of papers since 1951 dealing with imprinting in birds. In it, he listed over 150 papers; there have been many hundreds more since then. By now, all Lorenz' tenets have been investigated rather thoroughly and, by and large, all have been found to be seriously questionable. This literature will be reviewed point by point.

Social Releasers of Imprinting?

As noted earlier, a social releaser (or any releaser or sign stimulus) is usually simple in configuration, but otherwise improbable in the normal environment of the organism. Above all, certain responses are specific to that releaser and this specificity has arisen through natural selection and evolution. In fact, social releasers can be defined and identified in no other way but in terms of specificity. Now, regarding the variety of targets employed in the laboratory research in imprinting, it is exceedingly difficult to identify any particular visual stimulus configuration (or range of stimulus configurations) as being uniquely effective for imprinting. Imprinting, as indicated by one or another of the measures outlined, has been observed in reaction to humans (Gray & Howard, 1957); balloons, electric trains (Fabricius, 1951, 1955; Fabricius & Boyd, 1954); colored cardboard boxes (Salzen & Sluckin, 1959); light flicker (James, 1959); blinking lights (Rajecki, Eichenbaum, & Heilweil, 1973); moving horizontal lines (Smith & Hoyes, 1961); rotating discs and cards (Rajecki & Saegert, 1971; Saegert & Rajecki, 1973; Smith, 1960); animals of a different species (Baer & Gray, 1960); moving plastic milk bottles (Hoffman, 1968); and stationary three-dimensional objects (Gray, 1960) — among many other things.

It could be argued that all the stimuli listed simply fall within the restriction of a genetically determined range. However, this argument appears less than tenable in the light of the findings of an imprinting study by Melvin, Cloar, and Massingill (1967). These researchers reported that at least 7 of 18 wild bobwhite quail chicks in their sample imprinted on a live sparrow hawk. Incidentally, it may be of some significance that one chick that happened to be pounced upon by the target (the investigators tell us that they forgot to feed the hawk that day) showed a strong tendency to approach the hawk on a subsequent test!

A tentative conclusion that could be reached here is that many forms of stimulation appear adequate to produce imprinting in hatchlings. While this conclusion would be correct, it is extremely important to point out that *not all stimuli are equally effective.* It is well established that certain colors (Hess, 1956), shapes (Fantz, 1957), and patterns (Bateson, 1964) are prepotent over others in eliciting responses in the young bird. Furthermore, certain artificial visual configurations can be more attractive than a live adult of the species in question. Reese, Schotte, Bechtold and Cowley (1972) gave naive chicks a simultaneous choice between approaching a live hen or a rotating barberpole-type light. About 70 percent approached the light, whereas only 25 percent approached the hen (the balance of the animals did not choose). It may be the case, however, that the prepotency of artificial or natural stimulation could depend heavily on situational factors. Fischer (1976) found that domestic chicks showed an approach preference to maternal calls over tone bursts when targets emitting those signals were stationary, but a reverse effect when the targets in question were moving. Still other research has shown that auditory signals are more effective than visual signals in producing positive social responses in the hatchling (Fischer, 1966; Gottlieb, 1963; Gottlieb & Simner, 1969; Rajecki, 1974).

In fact, it is in the area of auditory signals that there is the only evidence for specific sensitivities in hatchlings that fits the notion of the existence of social releasers for imprinting. In a series of excellent studies, Gottlieb (1971) has demonstrated that naive domestic chicks and Peking ducklings are more responsive to the maternal vocalizations of their own species over the maternal calls of other species in simultaneous choice tests. The findings of Gottlieb are impressive, since they have also been obtained from animals hatched and reared under the strictest conditions of auditory isolation. Even where the subject is prevented from hearing its own vocalization through prenatal surgical muting such preferences are manifest (Gottlieb, 1971). Indeed, Lorenz (1937) noted that hatchlings were more inclined to follow him when he imitated the call of the adult of the species. Table 4.1 shows the typical pattern of species-specific responsiveness in various birds (after Gottlieb, 1971). Other studies have shown that prenatal birds can distinguish between feeding and distress calls of their own species (Snapp, 1969), and respond differentially to the exodus call of their own species versus some other species (Impekoven, 1973).

While the work of Gottlieb and others is important, it remains that artificial prenatal stimulation of incubating embryos also results in attachment in precocial birds (see below). Therefore, a more general conclusion regarding sign stimuli would be that the phenomenon of imprinting is not necessarily bound up in the nature of the stimulation that evokes it. However, certain types, patterns,

TABLE 4.1

Data on Species-specific Approach Preferences for Auditory Stimulation in Certain Chicks and Ducklings.[a]

Species of subjects	Test calls[b]	Percent (%) of Subjects' preferences
White rock chicks	Chicken vs. chick	92 chicken 8 chick
White rock chicks	Chicken vs. mallard duck	100 chicken 0 mallard duck
White rock chicks	Chicken vs. wood duck	82 chicken 18 wood duck
Mallard ducklings	Mallard duck vs. wood duck	95 mallard duck 5 wood duck
Mallard ducklings	Mallard duck vs. pintail duck	95 mallard duck 5 pintail duck

[a]After Gottlieb, 1971, Tables 12 and 14, with permission of the author and The University of Chicago Press. ©1971 by The University of Chicago.

[b]In the case of the chicken, mallard, pintail, and wood duck test calls, the vocalization employed is known as the exodus (maternal attraction) call.

or configurations of stimuli are more or less effective than others, regardless of whether they are inherent in the biological parent or not. The possibility of "open" sign stimuli (Mayr, 1974) will be discussed later in the chapter.

Critical Period for Imprinting?

The idea that there is a critical period for imprinting gained a great deal of plausibility from the work of Hess (Hess, 1959a, 1959b; Hess & Schaefer, 1959). The procedure employed by Hess involved rearing ducklings and chicks in darkness for various periods, and then testing them for initial approach tendency to a duck decoy that emitted a recording of a human voice. The subjects were placed in a lighted apparatus near the target and were given several minutes to respond. Although there were some species differences, the general course of responsiveness in chicks and ducklings over the various age of test was clear. The vast majority (80%) of animals that were tested around 13 to 16 hours of post-hatch age promptly approached the decoy, whereas *none* of the animals in the 1 to 4 or 29 to 32 hour age ranges did so. In general, level of responsiveness was an inverted-U function of the age of the subject.

Hess accounted for this inverted-U pattern through two processes, both under the influence of the maturation of the organism. The first factor was the improvement of locomotor capacity from the moment of hatching until 13 to 16 hours of age. This locomotor improvement accounts for the increments in responsiveness over age up to 13 to 16 hours, while the onset of fearfulness, the second factor, accounts for the decline thereafter. In this account it is clear that locomotor ability and fear responses are not the sum and substance of imprinting, but constitute two conditions limiting the critical age for imprinting. That the two conditions did in fact exist was shown by observations of changes in speed of locomotor responding with age, and the detection of distress calls.

While there is no question that the observations of Hess are accurate, there is some question about their interpretation. In the first place, if locomotion is taken as the index of a social bond and if we admit that locomotion is imperfect at certain periods in a bird's life, how are we to distinguish between the existence or nonexistence of attachment and the existence or nonexistence of an adequate motor response? The fact that a bird cannot approach a target because it cannot walk does not preclude the possibility that the target is attractive or represents a social object to the bird. It simply means that at some stages of development locomotion may be an inappropriate measure of the fixation of social objects.

In the second place, it may be unwarranted to extrapolate from initial fear reactions to an object to a presumed condition wherein the bird can never respond positively. This is so even if we agree that young birds of the sort in question do become generally more fearful over time (see Salzen, 1970). We have already seen the report of Spalding (1873) that even a chick that initially showed a negative reaction eventually became attached to his hand.

While it is true that the birds in Hess's studies were maturing prior to testing, it is also true that they were having experiences during that time as well. It may be that, as they became more accustomed to the darkness of their rearing situaation, it became more disturbing to be placed in an illuminated test situation. This might account for increased fear at later ages. This speculation need not be taken seriously, perhaps, but the experimental manipulation of experiential factors has led to some very interesting findings on the extension of the boundaries of the critical period considerably beyond what the proponents of that period claimed them to be.

Methods for extending the imprintability of precocial birds beyond the first day of life involve a restriction of their experiences. One procedure entails preventing birds from experiencing patterned light while allowing them to experience diffuse light. Moltz and Stettner (1961) hypothesized that such a technique might produce birds that would continue to be perceptually naive, and that such birds might react with less fear to an imprinting target than birds that had normal visual experience. Very shortly after their hatching, Moltz and Stettner fitted all the ducklings in their study with gogglelike head pieces. For half the subjects (the experimental group) the goggles had translucent latex lenses that did not transmit patterned light. For the remaining subjects (the control group) the lenses remained open. Four independent subgroups of each of the experimental and control groups were tested at 12, 24, 48, and 72 hours after hatching. In the experimental group the lenses were removed just prior to a test. As expected, birds in the control group (no lenses ever) became less likely to follow a green cardboard object, the older their age when tested. This was not the case, entirely, with birds deprived of patterned light prior to testing. Up to 48 hours of age, they still showed an apparently undiminished tendency to follow the object, this in stark contrast to the diminished tendency of the controls. When tested at 72 hours of age, however, subjects in neither the control nor the experimental group showed any inclination to follow.

This study by Moltz and Stettner (1961) showed that the critical period could be extended to 48 hours of age, but not to 72 hours of age. Is it the case, then, that 72 hours is the "true" end of the critical period for indiscriminant social responsiveness? Not necessarily, as a study by Macdonald (1968) demonstrated. Macdonald used a different means to limit the experience of his subjects. Beginning shortly after hatching, he gave chicks a series of injections of sodium pentobarbitol, a sleep-inducing tranquilizer. He continued to administer these injections until early in the fourth day of the chicks life. A control group received an identical series of injections of an inert substance: physiological saline. All chicks were tested for tendency to approach a stimulus array consisting of a flashing light and intermittent sound sometime during the fourth day of life (after 96 hours, that is) and retested on the fifth day. The results of those tests were quite clear: only the birds that had received injections of pentobarbitol on the days prior to testing showed any inclination to approach the target. This differential responsiveness between groups was even more in evidence during tests on the fifth day. These tests, and those of Moltz and Stettner (1961), show that the end of the critical period for imprinting does not necessarily fall near the end of the first day of life and that experiential factors must be considered influential in any analysis of such periods (see also Klopfer, 1964).

But what of the *other* extreme boundary of the period asserted by critical period enthusiasts? Does hatching really mark the onset of the critical period? Is it possible that birds could express some form of attachment as early as 4 hours after hatching and that this attachment might be the result of an experience that occurred even earlier in development?

It is noteworthy here that all the sensory systems in the chicken and duck fetus are functional well before hatching (see Gottlieb, 1968, for a review). This fact prompted Grier, Counter, and Shearer (1967) to hypothesize that the prenatal exposure of chicks to auditory signals might result in prenatal imprinting to such stimuli. In their experiment they exposed an experimental group of eggs to an intermittent 200-Hz tone from day 13 to day 18 of incubation (full incubation requires 21 days for the chicken). After that the chicks completed incubation and hatching in relative quiet and darkness. A control group of eggs was incubated in relative quiet for the entire period of incubation. Within 6 hours after hatching, subjects from both groups were tested for approach tendency to stationary speakers emitting either a 200- or 2000-Hz tone. When tested, the control subjects were indifferent in their tendency to approach and did not prefer one tone over the other. On the other hand, the experimental subjects showed a marked preference for the familiar 200-Hz signal. In addition, subsequent tests of the same subjects showed that those in the experimental group were much more inclined to follow a moving target that emitted a 200-Hz tone than were subjects from the control group.

Rajecki (1974) replicated and extended the finding of Grier et al. by exposing different groups of incubating eggs to light or sound, and then testing the newly hatched birds for distress vocalizations in the presence and absence of the two stimulus modes. In two separate experiments the results were the same: subjects gave fewer distress calls in the presence of a familiar stimulus (that is, prenatally exposed) compared to groups not exposed to that stimulus. As noted earlier, this effect was much more pronounced for sound than for light (for other work on prenatal effects, see Hess, 1973).

It is clear from these studies, taken together, that the boundaries of the critical period for imprinting (if such a period exists at all) are much wider than was originally believed, and quite labile. Further, it is clear that prior experience figures largely in the bird's responsiveness to novel imprinting targets. This would suggest, as Caldwell (1962) has argued, that certain developmental changes can be best understood not in terms of critical periods, but in terms of critical events.

Reversibility of Imprinting?

While preference for the object of initial attachment persists in simultaneous presentations of the familiar and novel object (Eiserer & Hoffman, 1974), there is a respectable amount of evidence that animals imprinted on one target will, in contrast to Lorenz' early assertion, eventually respond socially to a second target in the absence of the original (Cofoid & Honig, 1961; Hinde, Thorpe & Vince, 1956; Hoffman, Ratner, & Eiserer, 1972; Jaynes, 1956). A clear demonstration of such shifts in attachment were reported by Salzen and Meyers (1967, 1968). For the first 3 days after hatching, individual chicks were reared with either a green or blue object. At the end of the third day each was presented simultaneously with a green object and a blue object at opposite ends of a runway. In this test, over 95 percent of the subjects made more social responses (approaches) to the object of the familiar color than to the other. When the test was over, each chick was returned to its cage and was provided with a new object of alternate color to that initially exposed. Each subject was reared with the new color for an additional 3 days and then a second choice test was administered. In this test on day 6, over 86 percent of the chicks gave more social responses to the recently exposed color than to the one exposed initially. This shift in approach preference represents a clear reversal. Again the chicks were returned to their rearing situation, but with no objects present. When tested on the ninth day, the preference for the most recently exposed color persisted: some 81 percent of the chicks made most of their social responses to it. Moreover, Einsiedel (1975), using the Salzen-Meyer object-replacement procedure, demonstrated that there could be a significant shift in chicks' preference for the new object (over the old) in as little as 5 hours.

In sum, whereas imprinting is a remarkable phenomenon, it is not remarkable due to the particular features Lorenz ascribed to it. Nevertheless, it is impressive that this affiliative tendency is seen under the widest variety of experimental conditions where schedules of conventional forms of reinforcement have been ruled out. In fact, when the presentation of noxious stimulation such as electric shock (Barrett, Hoffman, Stratton, & Newby, 1971; Kovach & Hess, 1963) or loud noise (Pitz & Ross, 1961) is made contingent on approach responses, such responses are enhanced! The emergence of attachment under aversive conditions seems to rule out a reinforcement theory interpretation of imprinting (see Rajecki, 1973; for an opposing view, see Hoffman & Ratner, 1973).

To put it another way, if avian hatchlings respond to a target simply because it provides a primary (as yet unspecified) type of reinforcement, there would be little basis for predicting the animal's response to anything but the target. To the contrary, chicks and ducklings in the presence of a familiar object react to features and novelties in their environment as if the target in question was a source of reassurance. For example, ducklings imprinted on a white plastic bottle were more likely to aggress against a strange duckling when the bottle was visible to them than when it was hidden (Hoffman & Boskoff, 1972). Similarly, day-old chicks were more inclined to peck at an unfamiliar chick when a second animal of a familiar color was restrained nearby, relative to a condition where two chicks unfamiliar to the subject were involved. This enhanced tendency to peck at novel elements with a familiar object present was also in evidence when the familiar object was nothing more animate than a styrofoam block (Wilson & Rajecki, 1974).

Imprinting in Mammals

If it is possible to equate imprinting with an inherent tendency toward attachment, as opposed to equating it with a small set of exotic characteristics that have not been demonstrated, then it may be plausible to speak of imprinting in species other than precocial birds. In this sense, if attachment of the young is in evidence in the absence of, or prior to, the administration of schedules of conventional reinforcement, then we may be correct in subsuming that instance of filial behavior under the rubric of imprinting. A second criterion is that, within limits, the identity of the imprinting target is more or less irrelevant, keeping in mind that some targets are bound to be more effective than others. With this dual standard in mind, we can point to evidence for imprinting of lambs to television sets and dogs (Cairns, 1966); guinea pigs to black and white cubes, tennis balls (Sluckin, 1968; Sluckin & Fullerton, 1969), and furry objects (Harper, 1970); and dogs to human beings. In fact, the literature on the attachment of dogs to humans nicely parallels some of the findings for birds. Brodbeck (1954) found that all the cocker spaniel and beagle puppies in his study reacted positively to his presence, regardless of whether he had hand-fed them or had them fed by machine. Elliot and King (1960) underfed some of their pup subjects, but this partial starvation produced more positive responsiveness to humans than did full feeding. Finally Fisher (1955, cited in Scott & Fuller, 1965) went so far as to punish his fox terrier puppies whenever they approached him. As soon as the punishment contingency was removed, however, these pups were even more positively responsive to Fischer than were other pups he had treated with kindness.

The best-known research in nonhuman mammals is, of course, Harlow's work with rhesus monkeys (Harlow, 1971). It should be pointed out that Harlow (Harlow, Gluck, & Suomi, 1972) did not believe that the then-current analysis of imprinting generalized to the social behavior of monkeys. But neither did he believe that this analysis generalized even to the greylag gosling! If the arguments regarding Lorenz' claims have any validity, Harlow was correct. Nevertheless, certain theorists have argued for a similarity between the behavior of monkeys and the behavior of chickens and ducklings (Hoffman & Ratner, 1973). And while Harlow's work is too well known to require review here, certain of his findings will be mentioned. First, it is noteworthy that an infant rhesus monkey can become easily and strongly attached to the crudest of surrogates: a cylindrical shape covered with cloth. This intense attachment is virtually independent of whether or not the surrogate has provisions for feeding the infant. Infants who were reared with two surrogates, a bare wire form that contained a milk bottle and nipple, and a plain cloth surrogate, showed almost a total preference for clinging to the cloth mother. The appeal of the cloth surrogate has been attributed to "contact comfort."

A second point of interest is that, when infant monkeys were confronted with novel and threatening objects, those in the company of the cloth mother showed less fear and more adaptive exploration and manipulation than did infants who were alone or in the company of a wire mother (Harlow & Zimmerman, 1959).

Finally, Mason and Kenney (1974) have provided an unequivocal demonstration that the attachment of young rhesus monkeys can be shifted (or reversed) from one object to another, without particular difficulty. Mason and Kenney reared different monkeys: (a) with cloth surrogates; (b) with peers; and (c) with their natural mothers. After 1 to 7 months of such rearing, all infants were placed individually in pens with one or another kind of mongrel dog. Within hours, all monkeys had made positive social responses to their new found companions and remained attached to them thereafter. In simultaneous tests after 6 to 8 weeks of cohabitation with the dogs, the monkeys almost invariably preferred the familiar dog over other unfamiliar dogs or unfamiliar monkeys. (Tests between the familiar dog and the original object of attachment apparently were not systematically carried out). The prior social rearing experience of the various monkeys did not differentially influence their behavior during tests with the dogs.

Imprinting in Humans

For a long time, it was simply assumed that social attachment and responsiveness in human infants was an acquired characteristic based on the reduction of primary drives. As put by Dollard and Miller (1950), the first year of life is a time when the several thousand occasions the baby is cared for by the mother simply represent conditioning trials wherein the caretaker's characteristics become associated with the positive properties of food or physical care. Thus, attachment is based on the mother having taken on secondary reinforcement properties. A related analysis of the presumed role of feeding and orality has been stated by psychoanalytic theorists (e.g., A. Freud, 1946).

Recently, however, more and more writers have found reason to speculate on the possibility that the social attachments of human babies might be analogous, at least, to the attachment patterns of lower animals. For example, Gray (1958) offered the notion that the smiling response of an infant was like the initially indiscriminant following behavior of young precocial birds, but that indiscriminant smiling in babies ceases when specific attachments are known to have formed. Freedman (1966) has drawn similar parallels. In a related vein, Caldwell (1962) suggested that the visual pursuit of social objects by infants is functionally similar to following of the avian offspring. However engaging these ideas may be, data that bear on them are somewhat scanty. Nevertheless, the data that do exist are tantalizing, and should do nothing to dampen the enthusiasm of human imprinting theorists.

There are bits of evidence that stimulatory events, in the *in utero* environment of the human fetus exert some control over the neonate's behavior, not unlike the effects for prenatal imprinting in chicks. Salk (1973) has argued that most mothers, regardless of left or right handedness, carry their babies on their left side, the side in which the heart is encased. To substantiate this claim, he has assembled two main types of evidence. The first class of evidence is behavioral and was obtained from actual observations of mothers with their neonates. Side preferences were assessed by handing the child to the mother exactly at the midline of her body, and then noting on which side the mother chose to support the infant. In all, 83 percent of right-handed mothers held their child on the left side, as did 78 percent of left-handed mothers. When asked for a reason for their side preferences, right-handed mothers replied that it freed their dominant hand for other uses, while left-handed mothers claimed they carried their baby better with their dominant hand. In Salk's judgment, these reasons are probably simple rationalizations to provide a plausible account for the left side preference. The real reason for the preference resided elsewhere.

The second class of evidence for side preference is anecdotal, but certainly no less interesting. Salk (1973) tells us that, once he began his study of live mothers, he started to pay special attention to works of art or photographs that depicted an adult carrying a child. The sources were museums, galleries, anthropology texts, and art books. The assumption here was that the artist or photographer would capture reality as he found it, including side preferences. From this survey of several hundred pieces from various periods in the history of art, Salk discovered that fully 80 percent showed the child carried on the left side and that this trend held for secular as well as religious subject matter. More recent surveys of paintings and photographs are generally in line with Salk's report and show that such preferences are not restricted to women from Western cultures (Finger, 1975; Richards & Finger, 1975). However, what the latter surveys also show is that no side preferences are evident in men. Still, these two classes of evidence (behavioral and pictorial) were consistent and suggested a powerful force in determining infant-carrying preferences, at least for women.

It should be noted here that side preference is not simply a matter of cultural conditioning of how one should carry objects. Weiland (1964) reports that adults as a whole are rather indifferent regarding the side they carry grocery packages. Obviously, babies and groceries are not equivalent. Moreover, this side preference is apparently not restricted to humans. One of Salk's more casual observations is that he saw a rhesus monkey mother carry her infant on the left rather than the right side by a factor of 20 to 1.

Salk has speculated that the carrying preference may be an innate maternal response. However, the data he presents to support this notion are not compelling. These particular data show that early postnatal separation of mother and child alters (diminishes) the preference (Salk, 1973). But it seems more likely that these preferences come about through learning, and the absence of a preference may reflect a lack of learning. In most cases, mothers may have learned to carry their babies thusly because the infants are less fussy (more content) in the proximity of the adult heartbeat than in its absence. It remains, though, to demonstrate the presumed differential contentedness of infants carried on the two sides.

To do this, Salk observed infants in a nursery over the first 4 days after birth. Two groups in separate rooms were identical with one exception. One group was exposed to a continuous recording of a normal human (adult) heart beat at 72 beats per minute, while the other group heard the recording at an accelerated rate of 128 beats per minute. During the period of observation, food intake, weight change, and the amount of crying in the infants was recorded. It was found that food intake was equal across the two groups, but that the group that had heard the normal heartbeat showed a median weight gain of 40 grams, while the accelerated heartbeat showed a median weight *loss* of 20 grams. This difference in weight was attributed to the fact that there was crying in the normal-beat group during 38 percent of the observation periods, while there was crying in the accelerated-beat group 60 percent of these periods.

There is a problem of interpretation here, since Salk employed only two rates of stimulation. His data may merely indicate that the sound of a normal heartbeat is less irritating than an accelerated one. However, the fact that infants generally lose weight over the first few days of postnatal life, in conjunction with the finding that the normal-beat group gained weight, seem to partly rule out the irritation idea and to support the contention that these infants were soothed. Along these same lines, Brackbill, Adams, Crowell, and Gray (1966) found that nursery school children (average age of 34 months) fell asleep more quickly when the sound of heartbeat was played during their nap time, compared to their latency to falling asleep with no sound present. Further, Brackbill et al. also found that 2-day-old infants were less inclined to cry with the sound of a heartbeat present than under a no sound control period. Now I must point out immediately that Brackbill et al. (1966) disagree with the notion that the sound of the heart is a uniquely soothing stimulus, principally because the effect for the heart sound in their study was not statistically greater than the effects for a metronome or a lullaby, for either the older or younger children. One is not quite sure how to reconcile the findings under discussion, since Salk's data from infants were collected over a span of several days whereas the Brackbill et al. observations of neonates lasted but 15 minutes. In any event, the two sets of evidence are anything but contradictory.

Simner (1969) has also produced evidence for the continued behavioral effects of certain prenatal stimulation. Infants 3 to 4 days old were tested for rate of sucking on a nipple that was connected to a pressure transducer. In this way, a count of infant sucks could be recorded on a polygraph. After spontaneous sucking on the inserted nipple had begun, infants in various groups were exposed to intermittent auditory and visual stimulation. Some infants heard clicks and saw a light flash at 72 cycles a minute, the rate of the adult human heartbeat. Other babies were exposed with the stimulation occurring at 150 cycles a minute, the rate of the fetal heartbeat at mid-gestation. A final experimental group was exposed to the stimulation presented at a rate of 300 cycles per minute. The effects of these rates of postnatal stimulation were compared to the effects of no stimulation; a control group of infants were observed for sucking in the absence of sound and light. The main finding from Simner's study was that sucking was enhanced in the 150 cycle condition (the rate that matched the mid-gestation fetal heartbeat), but was not enhanced in the 72 or 300 cycle conditions.

The fact that Salk obtained an effect for maternal heart rate, but that Simner did not, does not necessarily represent a contradiction. Recall that Salk also did not observe differences in feeding between his treatment groups, but rather an apparent diminution in crying. It may be the case that the different rates produce different effects, with the slower rate reducing arousal and the faster rate implicated in the recruitment of behavior, although Simner is dubious about this idea. Nevertheless, the important thing here is that both researchers showed that certain experiences carried over from pre- to postnatal situations. In a very rough sense, these findings might be taken as evidence for a kind of prenatal imprinting.

On the other hand, the findings of Salk and Simner could also be taken as evidence for prenatal classical conditioning. There seems to be a deeply ingrained assumption in the psychological and psychiatric community that the prenatal environment for the fetus is the closest it will ever get to heaven-on-earth. But there seems to be no evidence for this allegedly blissful state. In fact, as I write this I wonder what my reaction would be if my heart started beating at 150 cycles a minute (the mid-gestation fetal heartbeat). Frankly, I rather doubt I would experience a state of bliss. Still, it is possible that prenatal conditions are somewhat preferable to immediately postnatal conditions, and a learned (reinforced) association between the heartbeat and the prenatal situation may account for the fact that the neonate is soothed by the heartbeat. There is evidence that the fetus can be conditioned. Spelt (1948) showed that fetal movement initially evoked by a noxious stimulus could be elicited by a neutral stimulus after the two stimuli were paired over a large number of trials.

On the face of it, it would seem virtually impossible to definitely rule out some kind of primary reinforcing event in the formation of attachment — pre- or postnatal, human or animal — at least with the evidence at hand. After all, when Harlow and Zimmerman (1959) dismissed lactation as the single most important factor in early social bonding in the rhesus monkey, they replaced feeding with contact comfort. This is to go from the mouth to the hand, which is not going very far at all. But a later finding somewhat contradicted the notion of contact comfort as the indispensable element in monkey attachment. Some monkey infants did not fare well when born to mothers who themselves had spent the early part of their lives in isolation. That is, infants who had mother-less mothers were abused by them. These mothers beat, bit, and smashed their infants, and otherwise rejected them violently (Seay, Alexander, & Harlow, 1964). Even so, the authors reported a surprising phenomenon, in that all the infants made persistent attempts to make contact. Now it would seem that these infants received as much contact *discomfort* as contact comfort from their parent, yet continued to be attracted to her. Therefore, it might be concluded that the attachment behavior of these infants was not necessarily based exclusively on contact comfort, although some might argue that the contact comfort may have outweighed the contact discomfort.

Perhaps the following is the strongest statement that can be made at this point about human attachment, whether it be called imprinting or something else. That is, there is some evidence that the reduction of primary drives (as in the view of Dollard & Miller, 1950) is *not necessarily* involved in the formation of early human social bonds. As part of a survey on socialization practices, a large number of mothers were interviewed by Schaffer and Emerson (1964). Some of the information obtained had to do with the point in their child's development when a specific attachment to a principal object occurred. Generally, this sort of specific attachment happens around the eighth month of life. Not surprisingly, many children had their mother as their principal object. On the other hand, a striking finding was that fully 22 percent of the babies in the sample formed attachments to principal objects (people) that had *never* had anything to do with the physical care or maintenance of the child. An additional 17 percent of the children in the study had as principal object persons who were not the major agents of their physical care.

Another interesting finding emerged from the Schaffer and Emerson study when they asked mothers how intensely attached their babies were, as measured by the degree of distress at separation (among some other measures). Schaffer and Emerson looked for associations between the degree of attachment and certain so-called socialization and relationship variables. As for the former, intensity of attachment did not seem to be bound up with primary drives. That is, the socialization variables of feeding rigidity during infancy, age at weaning, length of weaning period, age when toilet training began, and severity of toilet training were *not* related to intensity of attachment. To the contrary, intensity was positively related to the relationship variables of degree of maternal responsiveness, amount of maternal interaction, and personal versus impersonal means of stimulating or diverting the child. Schaffer and Emerson concluded: "Satisfaction of physical needs does not appear to be a necessary precondition to the development of attachments, the latter taking place independently and without obvious

regard to the experiences that the child encounters in physical care situations. . ."
(reprinted in Parke, 1969, p. 56).

Reinforcement contingencies aside, for the moment, the most elaborate attempt at reconciling ethological theory, the literature on imprinting, and the process of social development in children has been provided by Bowlby (1969) and Ainsworth (1969). For these writers, human "attachment" has its basis in the biological evolution of man. Presuming that early man became a distinct species in nomadic hunting and gathering societies, Bowlby and Ainsworth ascribe to human attachment the same function that imprinting has in precocial birds. Namely, species survival in terms of the protection of the offspring from environmental dangers. In their conception, attachment behavior shown by the child is but one aspect of a control system that acts to unite mother (or other adults) and offspring. A necessary and complementary aspect of such a system are reciprocal behavior patterns on the part of the mother. One such complementary maternal behavior has been termed retrieving.

This interrelated set of behavior patterns between individuals is called a control system because it resembles man-made devices that act in conjunction with feedback from the effects of previous acts. The feedback informs the child, say, whether or not a particular spatial relationship (or set goal, in the words of the theorists) to the parent is adequate under certain circumstances. For example, when a child is content, visual contact with the mother is sufficient; in times of stress or illness, physical contact may be sought by the child.

In Bowlby's (1969) view, such human attachment occurs in four phases. In Phase One, the neonate is especially sensitive to social beings in the environment and shows indiscriminant visual tracking and smiling. By Phase Two, these orientations and signals are restricted rather exclusively toward one or a few figures (as in the principal object of Schaffer and Emerson, 1964). Phase Three finds the child achieving proximity on its own initiative and ability, while in Phase Four proximity to the parent can be governed through the anticipation of the parent's movements and the control of those movements through suggestion or persuasion.

It is important to reiterate here that the forms of attachment manifest in each phase are thought to be biologically based proclivities. That is, according to this scheme, the child has an innate disposition toward attachment in an ordinary expectable environment. In order for attachment to progress or develop adequately, there need only be an object or figure with *complementary* parental behavioral tendencies.

A semi-naturalistic study by Bell and Ainsworth (1972) nicely illustrates some complementary behavioral interactions between mother and child, with specific reference to the maintenance of proximity early in the child's life. Bell and Ainsworth made their observations in the homes of 26 middle-class infant-mother pairs. The sample consisted of both girl and boy babies and primaparous and multiparous mothers. A considerable amount of time was spent gathering data, with a total of 16 hours of observation allotted to each of the subject pairs in the first quarter of the first year of life.

Of main concern was the incidence of infant crying and the maternal responses during that crying. The investigators were interested to learn under what social circumstance the infant was most likely to cry, what particular maternal responses were most likely in reaction to the crying, and which maternal responses were then most effective in comforting the child, as evidenced by the termination of the crying.

During observations begun at 1 to 3 weeks of age, infants were much more likely to initiate crying when their mothers were not close enough to touch them (or were of sight altogether) than when the mother was actually holding the child. When the mothers were close enough to touch but not hold, the child's tendency to cry was intermediate between the two extremes of proximity. When the child began crying while it was not being held, mothers tended to do any of several things that ranged from picking up the child to doing nothing at all about it. In terms of relative frequency of occurrence, the various maternal responses can be rank-ordered according to the approximate proportions they represent among all responses: (a) "picks up, holds", 40 percent of the time; (b) "vocalizes, interacts", 24 percent of the time; (c) "feeds", 13 percent of the time; and (d) "approaches, touches", 12 percent of the time. Other responses such as doing nothing at all occurred at frequencies that totalled less than 10 percent of all responses.

Some of the maternal responses were more effective than others in comforting the child. The responses can be rank-ordered for effectiveness in terms of the proportion of times each particular one was effective when it was carried out. In the first quarter of life, "picks up, holds" was effective about 90 percent of the time; "feeds" between 70 and 80 percent of the time; and "offers pacifiers, toys" about 60 percent of the time. All other maternal responses were effective less than 50 percent of the time they were carried out.

In sum, Bell and Ainsworth (1972) found that tiny babies cried more frequently when out of contact with their mothers than at other times and that the most likely maternal response was to pick up the child. The response of picking up the child showed a margin of effectiveness in terminating crying. These findings prompted Bell and Ainsworth to conclude that the behavior patterns of mothers and their infants meshed with one another and that these behaviors are "well adapted to each other." The instigation of infant crying at maternal separation, and termination of crying at reunion, presumably has survival value for the young of our species, if not now, at least during the time when we were nomadic hunters and gatherers. In that period, the quick initiation and termination of vocalizations would soon unite mother and offspring, while minimizing the possibility that the crying would alert or direct predators. In this sense, the cries of the infant and the patterns of distress vocalizations seen in other species such as chickens and ducks provide rather tempting analogies that would lead us to the inference that this socially-oriented vocalizing in humans may be innate.

Ainsworth, Bell, and Stayton (1971) have reported some additional interesting findings that bear on the propositions advanced by Bowlby (1969). In the first segment of a continuation of the work with the 26 mother-infant pairs described above, they assessed the degree of attachment of the now one-year-old children to their mothers in tests that were conducted in a so-called strange situation. Mother and child reported to a small room that contained a few pieces of furniture and some toys. In certain successive brief episodes the children were observed for their tendency to: (a) explore the room with the mother present as a safe base; (b) cry in distress at the mother's absence; and (c) to react positively to the mother's return. (Such tests are reminiscent of the "secure base" tests of monkey and chick infants mentioned earlier.)

Based on these tests Ainsworth categorized the children into three nominal types: A, B, and C. According to Ainsworth, the B-type babies (some 60 percent of the sample) were the most "normally" attached. They explored in the mothers' presence, stopped exploring and cried in her absence, and appeared happy to see her on her return. On the other hand, A-type babies appeared to be indifferent to the presence, absence, or return of the mother; they showed high levels of exploratory activity and little crying in all the three episodes. Finally, the C-type children seemed unable to use the mother as a secure base, or to find reassurance in her presence upon her return; a predominant response in all strange-situation episodes for C-types was crying.

Next, Ainsworth, et al. (1971) made further observations of mother-child interaction in the homes of these subjects. During these observations, the mothers were rated on 9-point bipolar adjective scales for sensitivity-insensitivity, acceptance-rejection, and cooperation-interference with regard to their responsiveness to the needs and demands of their children. The average ratings were clear and impressive: the mothers with children classified as B-types (normally attached) were rated as substantially more sensitive, accepting, and cooperative than were the mothers of A- or C-type children.

In terms of Bowlby's (1969) formualtion these findings can be interpreted thusly: the mothers of B-type children provided the kind of maternal behavior that is complementary to the behavior of the child in that it provided correct and adequate stimulation as feedback for the child's responses. On the other hand, mothers of A- and C-type babies were insensitive, rejecting, or interfering regarding their children (for whatever reason) and did not provide the ordinary expectable environment for the emergence of attachment.

While this argument from these data may appear circular to some, it remains that there is a certain resemblance of these findings to those from research on attachment or imprinting in infrahuman animals. Recall that the general rule for imprinting was that while the basis for the attachment did not necessarily reside in the stimulus characteristics of the object, certain objects provoked stronger attachments than others. Superficially, at least, a parallel can be drawn, for example, between stimulus characteristics of sensitive human mothers and cloth monkey-mothers that provide contact comfort. The fact that these resemblances are superficial should not be a reason for dismissing them as trivial and unimportant. Rather, it should be an instigation for more and better research in the comparative psychology of early social attachment.

Closing Thoughts on Social Attachment

By way of summing up this section, it should be pointed out that for every attempt at reducing mammalian or strictly human attachment to imprinting, there probably have been an equal number of attempts to reduce the concept of imprinting itself to one or another form of classical or operant conditioning (for notable examples, see Hoffman & Ratner, 1973; Moltz, 1960, 1963). Since articles on imprinting and related phenomena in a variety of species continue to appear at a high rate, it seems likely that this learning-imprinting debate will continue. I should like to recommend, however, that the theoretical side of this debate shift somewhat from the narrower topics such as stimulus characteristics and sensitive periods for certain species. In this regard, one could meaningfully ask: what would be some global (pan-species) characteristics of attachment if it were governed by one or the other process? What would attachment be like if it were based on an innate disposition to imprint or a tendency to conform to reinforcement contingencies? If the distinction between imprinting and learning is viewed in this light, then I thing the evidence is fairly clear that something like imprinting as a process does exist.

First, it is known that many animals persist in what can only be called attachment behavior in the absence of conventional reinforcement contingencies. Moreover, attachment develops and persists in the face of aversive consequences for the emission of attachment behavior in the case of fowl, dogs, and monkeys.

Second, if reinforcement contingencies govern the attractiveness of the attachment object (target) in question, then one would expect that more or less similar objects would also elicit more or less social behavior from the organism. This prediction derives from what is known about generalization gradients. But how could a learning theory predict that an organism might employ its target as a secure base from which to begin to cope with its universe? As we have seen, the presence or absence of a familiar target makes a great deal of difference in the tendency to explore for young fowl, monkeys, and children. In terms of positive and negative reinforcement schedules, from whence does this apparent security stem?

Finally, we can ask about the consequences of the removal of a target or an object of attachment. Most students of psychology are familiar with the pattern of events that occurs in the extinction of a positively reinforced operant response. The organism, sometimes showing mild agitation at the removal of the reinforcer, engages in the operant less and less frequently, and after a period of time stops altogether. During this period the operant is gradually supplanted by other activities. Therefore, if an object of social attachment has as its base a primary or secondary reinforcing property, then the removal of this property, or the removal of the entire object, should result in the simple extinction of the attachment behavior, and such behavior should be gradually supplanted with other activities.

Simple extinction, however, is not what occurs upon the removal of objects of attachment, at least in the case of monkey and human children (see Cairns, 1966, for a report of the contrast between the reaction of sheep to the removal of a social object and their reaction to the removal of food-stuffs). There have been a number of reports of a post-separation syndrome in the young of these species called anaclytic depression (Bowlby, 1960; Harlow, 1974; Kaufman & Rosenblum, 1967; Seay, Hansen & Harlow, 1962; Yarrow, 1964; among others). This syndrome typically proceeds through three phases. After initial separation, there is a brief period of protest, in the form of anger or distress and search activities that may last for a day or longer. This is followed by a variable period of despair, in which the monkey or child is in a state of misery and apathy. This period may or may not be followed by a kind of recovery, where the infant seems to lose interest in the original social object and begins to engage in normal activity such as social play (although at reunion monkeys may show heightened attachment reactions to the original social object).

Therefore, this post-separation syndrome in primates does not lend itself to interpretation from a strict reinforcement model of social bonding or imprinting, simply because extinction and anaclytic depression have vast topographical differences. This, in turn, causes one to question the assertion that the original attachment was necessarily a consequence of reinforcement contingencies. In our laboratories, we are currently working on studies to determine if there is anything akin to anaclytic depression in domestic chicks, as induced by the separation of mutually imprinted cagemates. Should there be positive evidence for such a depressive state in fowl, then the parallels between avian, mammalian, and human imprinting will be that much stronger (*see* Rajecki, Suomi, Scott, & Campbell, 1977).

At present, however, there seems to be sufficient reason, as outlined above, to actively and carefully pursue the possibility of imprinting in the human infant. Such an effort, I believe, would well repay students of human social behavior, whether they were ethologists, developmentalists, or social psychologists.

SOCIAL DISTANCE

Theories of social behavior are based on the fact that organisms influence one another. In order to do this, they must be in some proximity. The section on attachment elaborated one such mechanism for proximity, at least in the case of family units. However, most animal aggregations give the impression that there are forces that cause an optimal dispersion of conspecifics. The mechanisms underlying this dispersion held aside for the moment, there are certain advantages that accrue to the species, if not the individual, as a result of such spatial segregation. Carpenter (1958) noted that the spacing of animals presumably resulted in more adequate resources for individuals or small groups, reduced incidence of fighting, and reduction of the spread or rate of spread of disease, among a large catalogue of other such benefits.

Implicit in a list of benefits from dispersion are a set of corollary disadvantages in too dense populations (in addition to the unique effects of sheer overcrowding), which include, obviously, exhaustion of natural resources, increased probability of aggressive encounters, and conditions supportive of epidemics. But even further consideration suggests that too loose an aggregation would also have real disadvantages, such as fewer opportunities for mutual defense or warning or nonavailability of sexual partners. Clearly, the mechanisms that account for the appropriate dispersion of a given set of animals are important elements in the social psychology of that species. Across species, several mechanisms for the regulation of distance or access to scarce resources have been identified.

Territoriality and Dominance Hierarchy

It is a fact that animals do not wander at random within the whole of their geographic domain. Single individuals or aggregates of animals tend to be localized in definite places or areas, even though immediately adjacent areas are also ecologically suitable. The exact character of this delineation of place varies from species to species and also from place to place for a given species. Nevertheless, three features or levels of spatial segregation have been identified.

The first and broadest of these is termed the home range. This is the largest area over which an animal (or group) moves within a considerable span of time. As noted, there may be variability in the extent of the home range, depending on species or habitat. For example, Hinde (1974) has reviewed field studies of primates that show that certain lemurs restrict all their movement to an area of 0.06 square kilometers, while baboon ranges vary from 4.6 square kilometers in forests to 25 square kilometers in savannah terrain. The relatively large chimpanzee has been observed to have a range of 35 square kilometers.

A second identifiable locale in the spatial array of species has been called the core area. Core areas are located within home ranges and contain special features such as food sources and nesting sites. Animals move from one core area to another, depending on their needs.

A third sort of spatial demarcation has been given the title of territoriality, which according to Hinde's (1956) definition means primarily an area that is actively patrolled or defended. We have already seen an example of territoriality from Tinbergen's studies of the social behavior of the stickleback. These fish actively repel other males that approach the owner's nest site. Other forms of defense may include warning signals to potential intruders, for example, howling monkeys (Chivers, 1969) or signposts in the form of scent markings at territorial boundaries, for example, hyenas (Kruuk, 1972). If the intruder fails to heed signs or warnings, damaging attacks by the owner often occur, as in the case of gannets (Truslow, 1970).

The implication of all three types of spatial localization, home range, core area, and territory, however, is that certain animals in one way or another exercise some kind of control over certain areas. As noted, the exclusiveness of the control may vary, but in the broadest sense these mechanisms provide for distance between animals at the expense of some and to the benefit of others. At base it would seem that such spacing is based on proximal intolerance. We will return to this notion of intolerance shortly.

Spacing mechanisms serve to segregate conspecifics that have no apparent affiliation to one another. There is a conceptually distinct mechanism for the spatial segregation, or organization, of individuals that have clear affiliative links to each other. This mechanism is the dominance hierarchy. Animals that exist in aggregates can often be ordered on a dimension of dominance and submissiveness. The familiar term pecking order derives directly from the study of hierarchical social relationships between members of flocks of domestic fowl (Guhl, 1953, 1958; Schjelderup-Ebbe, 1935). In the case of hens, animals that give many, but receive few social pecks are considered dominant; those that give few but receive many social pecks are considered subordinate. In small groups, the resultant social order may be linear. That is, the top animal (sometimes called the alpha) can peck all those subordinate to it. In turn, the second animal (termed beta) can peck all birds but alpha, the third bird can peck at all birds but alpha and beta, and so on. Now it should be pointed out that in addition to the simple linear hierarchy described for small groups of hens, social structures of rather marked complexity have been observed and seem to depend on the size and nature of the species-specific aggregation (for example, troop, flock, pack, herd, school, or other). Unfortunately, these more complex relationships cannot be given adequate attention within the limits of this chapter.

Inherent in the concept of the dominance hierarchy is the expectation that animals in identifiable social units tend to enjoy differential privileges depending on their status. The most dominant and therefore most privileged individuals will have first options or exclusive rights over scarce resources such as food-stuffs, sex partners, and nest sites, while subordinates must content themselves as best they can. Rowell (1972) has argued that such relationships and their consequences can best be understood in terms of subordinance rather than dominance, but for all practical purposes the outcome seems the same. The general rule in the animal kingdom is that the larger animal tends to dominate the smaller. Functionally, this means that, in the overwhelming majority of species, males tend to dominate females. One interesting exception to this rule is the case of the spotted hyena where the female is larger than and clearly dominant over the male (Kruuk, 1972). The advantage of establishing either spatial arrangements or priorities for the gaining of resources based on dominance hierarchies should be clear. If a dominant animal wishes to occupy any area temporarily occupied by a subordinate, it need only make certain gestures (see the following section on communication) or approach the desired spot. The enlightened subordinate will yield or suffer the consequences.

In order to better illustrate mechanisms such as territoriality and dominance hierarchy, aspects of the social organization and structure of the rhesus monkey *(Macaca mulatta)* will be outlined. This profile is based on different troops of monkeys, at different times, and in different places. Nevertheless, it may be reasonable to expect that all rhesus troops share approximately the same features according to the following accounts.

Southwick, Beg, and Siddiqi (1965) reported the daily movements of three distinct troops of rhesus monkeys that inhabited a Hindu temple area in the city of Aligarh in northern India. The temples surrounded a large man-made pool called Achal Tank. Troop 1 (consisting of 40 members) spent their nights clustered in the main temples at the northeast corner of the tank. Troop 1b (11 members) huddled at the northwest corner. Troop 2 (34 members) lodged overnight in the South Garden at the southern side of the tank. These areas, then, were the core areas for sleeping for the three troops.

With the dawn, however, the spatial array of the troops changed markedly. Monkeys typically move off from their nighttime lodging positions in order to feed. In doing this, Troop 1 dispersed itself around the entire periphery of the tank and thereby penetrated the core sleeping areas of Troops 1b and 2. Conflict was usually avoided, however, because Troop 1b would move off in a northerly direction to a nearby bazaar, and Troop 2 pushed south deeper into a garden. This spatial rearrangement was not a matter of an amicable understanding between troops. Southwick et al. characterize the movements of 1b and 2 as retreats. After all, Troop 1 was the largest and in a real sense was the dominant troop. In any event, it was clear that Troop 1 exercised a certain control over all sides of the tank, at least during feeding hours.

It is probably the case that not all of the members of Troop 1 shared equally in the choicest sites around the tank. Kaufmann (1967) observed the spatial arrangement of the rhesus monkeys *within* a troop at the research station on Cayo Santiago in the Caribbean. Kaufmann first determined the dominance hierarchy of the males in the troop by observing which monkeys made signs that indicated threat and which monkeys gave evidence of signalling appeasement (see below). Based on these observations, males were considered to rank either high, medium, or low in the troop, or to be hangers-on called peripherals. Next, Kaufmann made other observations to assess the influence of status (rank) on preferential seating (resting) places when the troop was not enroute. The choicest places, in Kaufmann's view, were in the so-called central group, because this locale was operationally defined as the area bounded by an imaginary line drawn around all the females in the troop. On any one of a series of observations, a male could be in the central group or elsewhere.

The results of Kaufmann's study were quite clear in indicating the role of rank in spatial arrangements. The high ranking males were in the central group fully 90 percent of the time, while those that ranked medium enjoyed this privilege only 55 percent of the time. At the lower extremes, the low ranking males were in the central group during only 35 percent of all observation periods and the luckless peripherals spent a scant 14 percent of their time there.

Kaufmann's data suggest that the high ranking males would have greater access to females than any other rank-group. This might not necessarily be the case, though, since monogamy is not a characteristic of rhesus society and female rhesus in estrus are promiscuous. Data collected at Cayo Santiago earlier by Carpenter (1942) show, however, that rank does figure into mating privileges. Carpenter reported the number of different females sexually possessed by males of different rank in two independent troops. The correlations between the two factors (rank and number of sexual possessions) for the two troops were .98 and .99.

Now it is not to be thought that dominant males in rhesus troops are simply domineering, belligerent oafs that act out of sheer aggressive or sexual impulses. These males also appear to have prosocial roles, in that they actively protect subordinates from intruders (Bernstein, 1964) and serve as peacemakers by breaking up fights between the lesser citizens of their troop (Kaufmann, 1967). Still, it is tempting to caricature rhesus monkey society as based on a might-is-right principle.

The foregoing sketch of some social dynamics in rhesus monkeys will have to serve as our primary example of spatial dispersion in animals (for general treatments see Carpenter, 1958; van Kreveld, 1970; Wynne-Edwards, 1962). In the example, the mechanisms of territoriality and dominance hierarchy appeared to be conceptually and functionally distinct. The outcomes of the mechanisms are nevertheless in some ways indistinguishable. Both processes have the result that there are species-specific distances between aggregates, or between members within aggregates. In the simplest sense, there are two possible motivations for such dispersion: an intolerance of separation, or an intolerance of proximity. While both of these factors may be influential, it would seem that the most powerful would be proximal intolerance. Troops of monkeys out of contact with one another give no sign of being upset. To the contrary, troops or individuals that blunder into, or are forced into, proximity fight intensely (Southwick et al., 1965), sometimes to the extent that most of the combatants are killed or die of their injuries (K. R. L. Hall, 1964).

The notion here is that at a very basic level the complicated matters of territoriality and some aspects of dominance relations may be related to a universal *dis*inclination to get too close to other members of one's own species. This notion was apparently first suggested by Hediger in 1941 (see Hediger, 1955, p.

66) who coined the term *individual distance*. This concept has been further elaborated by E. T. Hall (1966), who suggested that individuals possess zones or concentric circles of space termed *intimate, personal, social,* and *public* distances, when arranged along a proximal-distal dimension.

One form of evidence for individual distance presented by Hediger, and re-iterated by Hall, is open to confirmation by the reader. Hediger published a photograph of a number of gulls sitting on a parapet. The fact that each gull was exactly a distance of two embankment railings from its nearest neighbor gave Hediger his idea of spacing in the first place. Apparently the same phenomenon is in evidence when large numbers of swallows perch communially. These birds typically do not disperse maximally or randomly, but rather take up positions a few inches apart. Figure 4.2 shows rather uniform spacing between some swallows which had landed on power lines in Madison, Wisconsin. It is interesting to point out, at least for heuristic reasons, that the distance between any two birds is apparently not based on clearance for wing span. If wing span was the determining factor, one might expect the distance to be doubled to make way for the two wings of adjacent animals.

Human Social Distance

Since the late 1950s, a great deal of research has been devoted to considerations of spatial factors in human social interaction. It hardly requires stating that this work was *not* directed toward the discovery of human territoriality or dominance relations. Without making any claims for an ethological interpretation, human territoriality and dominance patterns are sometimes too painfully obvious. Rather, ideas developed that there was some sort of envelope of greater or lesser extent surrounding human individuals and that the penetration or invasion of this envelope by other persons had emotional, motivational or behavioral consequences for the individual. Reaction to such a penetration was, in fact, aversive. In this sense the literature on human proximal intolerance is meaningfully linked to the findings on animal spacing mechanisms mediated by proximal intolerance, while keeping species-specific distinctions well in mind. An example of human social distancing is shown in Figure 4.3, in a photograph also taken in Madison, Wisconsin. It may be worthwhile noting that, in relation to the point made about the wing span of swallows in Figure 4.2, the distance between humans is not necessarily determined by arm length, since accommodation of the sum of the arm lengths of two people would require double the distancing seen in the photo.

The endeavor here is not to provide a representative review of the research on interpersonal distancing. Because of page limitations, that would not be possible; and besides, able reviews are fairly abundant (Altman & Lett, 1969; Argyle & Kendon, 1967; Duke & Nowicki, 1972; Edney, 1974; Leibman, 1970; Lett, Clark, & Altman, 1969; Patterson, 1968; Sommer, 1967, 1969). Rather, we will examine only a handful of selected studies that are judged to bear on the general

FIG. 4.2 Photograph showing interindividual distance in a flock of swallows perched on power lines. (Courtesy of Bruce M. Fritz and *The Capital Times*, Madison, Wisconsin.)

FIG. 4.3 Photograph showing interindividual distance in a small group of pedestrians. (Courtesy of Richard D. Barnes.)

theme of this chapter. That is, what is the evidence that allows us to decide whether proximal intolerance, and its consequences, is a learned or innate disposition?

Many variables have been tested in the growing research effort devoted to interpersonal distance. These include age, personality, setting, social history, and the identities of the people in interaction, among other factors. However, since status, or rank, has been shown to be such a powerful factor in the spacing dynamics of animals, studies on humans that manipulate status are of special interest to us. Two of these researches will be reviewed in some detail, while certain others will be mentioned in passing. The two studies were done by Felipe and Sommer (1966) and Barash (1973). These research efforts are noteworthy for the following reasons: (a) data was collected in naturalistic settings; (b) the subjects were not told that they were in a study and, therefore, their reactions can be considered spontaneous; and (c) the variety of measures obtained are all behavioral.

Felipe and Sommer (1966) conducted their experiment (Study 1) at a mental institution. The subjects were male patients. In order to qualify as a subject in the study, the person would have to be sitting alone on one of many benches in an outdoor recreational area of the hospital. Further, the subject could not be occupied in a clearly defined activity such as reading or playing cards. After a subject had been located he was assigned to one of two experimental conditions or to a third control condition.

In the control condition, the subject was allowed to remain in relative isolation. The information provided by the subjects in the control group was the length of time (for up to 20 minutes) they remained seated in the absence of experimental interruption. In contrast, the first of the two experimental conditions provided an intrusion by a relatively low-status person. Here the experimenter (Sommer) merely sat down quite close to the subject and occasionally jiggled his keys. In the final, high-status invasion, the experimenter also sat down next to a subject but in this instance he was made to look like a staff member by actively making notes of the situation, looking pointedly at the subject on occasion, and jiggling his keys.

The data of interest in the study were simply the number of subjects that left their benches during the 20 minutes of the test. In the control group, no subjects left the spot on which they were sitting during the first minute of observation but, by the last minute, about 30 percent of them had moved off. The behavior of the experimental subjects was in sharp contrast. Fully 20 percent had fled as early as the first minute, and over 60 percent had moved by the end of the test period. Felipe and Sommer report at least a marginal effect ($p = .10$) for their status manipulation, with the high-status intruder having a somewhat more pronounced effect on the displacement of subjects.

Barash conducted a similar study, but used college students as subjects instead of institutionalized patients. Barash located individuals in a reference room of a library at a college with the requirements that the person be seated alone at a work table and be *actively* engaged in reading or writing. Subjects were then assigned to one of three experimental conditions that were defined in terms of the proximity and the status of the intruder (Barash). Proximity was varied by Barash's choice of seats at the table. In the close approach condition, he sat within 3 to 6 inches of the subject, while in the medium approach condition, he sat from 1 to 2 feet from the subject. Status was manipulated by dressing in faculty attire (jacket and tie = high status) or in student attire (jeans and casual shirt = low status). The three resulting experimental conditions were faculty-close approach, student-close approach, and faculty-medium approach. A fourth set of control subjects were not approached.

The findings of Barash are directly in line with those of Fellpe and Sommer. Over some 30 minutes of observation only about 30 percent of the control subjects abandoned their chairs. In the faculty-medium approach and the student-close approach conditions, the proportions of subjects leaving were about 52 and 72 percent, respectively. In the faculty-close approach condition, fully 84 percent of the subjects fled within 30 minutes of his arrival. These findings are all the more impressive, since the people who served as subjects for Barash doubt-less had a real reason for being in their seats (one does not go to a reference room for a lark), and the notion of *displacement* here has a good deal of face validity.

Barash provided some interesting ancillary measures of his subjects' behavior over and above the single response of leaving. Sometimes the subjects moved their chairs in what seemed to be an effort to turn away from the experimenter. This chair-moving tendency was a linear function of proximity and status. Also, the control subjects fidgeted on the average of once during the first 10 minutes of observation while those in the faculty-close approach group fidgeted over 7 times on the average. Another reaction of the subjects to the intrusion were pointed remarks to the experimenter. While there were rare, they were apparently related to experimental condition. Of interest are the student-close, and faculty-close approach conditions. In the former, 22 percent of the subjects protested, while in the latter only 10 percent vented their ire. Barash interprets the protests as aggressive responses and interprets the relatively low rate directed at the faculty member as evidence of inhibition by a dominant person. Several other studies have also shown that status differences produce greater distancing than status equivalencies (Duke, Johnson, & Nowicki, 1972; Hendrick, Giesen, & Coy, 1974; Lott & Sommer, 1967).

In the main, studies centering on status effects on actual displacement (departure) reactions in social distancing are consistent with other experimental procedures where people were either asked to report comfortable interpersonal distances by indicating where they or another approaching human should stop (Dabbs, Fuller, & Carr, 1973) or were asked for their reactions to an imaginary social situation (e.g., Lott & Sommer, 1967; Mehrabian, 1968). A general summing up over these studies (and others related to them) is that Hediger's hypothesis that there is such a thing as social distance has been convincingly confirmed.

Sex Differences in Spacing Behavior

On the other hand, a few apparent discrepancies were also discovered. Freedman, Levy, Buchanan, and Price (1972) investigated the relationship between crowding and human aggressiveness. Crowded or uncrowded situations were defined by having groups of people of constant size (4) and the same sex (male-male, female-female) discuss things in either a large room (625 square feet per person) or a small room (18 square feet per person). In order that the effect for crowding should be well established, subjects were kept in their respective situations for several hours. Then the data of interest were collected. Subjects were introduced to a "parlor game," in which each played against the other three members of his or her group. A detailed description of the game need not detain us (for a discussion of games see Jones & Gerard, 1967); it is sufficient to say that on any given trial a subject had to make either a cooperative or a competitive response. That is, he or she could try to share a modest outcome with the other (cooperate) or try to gain an advantage over the others at their expense (compete).

For the male subjects in the experiment, the results were clear and entirely consistent with other work that has demonstrated that intrusion of personal space, or crowding, is aversive. On the average, there were more competitive responses made in the small (crowded) room than in the large (uncrowded) room. To the contrary, the results for the females were the *reverse* of the pattern for males. Females gave more competitive responses in the large room than in the small room.

Freedman et al. were a bit puzzled by this interaction of sex with room size (see also Ross, Layton, Erickson, & Schopler, 1973), so they did another study to see if the sex difference was a reliable one. In the second experiment, the crowded-uncrowded conditions were retained, but the remaining procedure was modified. Here, subjects listened to taped transcripts of simulated jury trials, for which they were to act as anonymous jury members. It was the subjects' duty to assign prison sentences to individuals who were made to seem obviously guilty of certain violent crimes to persons such as purse snatching from an elderly woman, a hit-and-run death, a rape, and others. As a final experimental variation, half the subjects listened to tapes that were clearly audible and half listened to tapes that were marred by static. The static was intended as a supplementary source of irritation and was expected to enhance aggressive responses, that is, result in the assignment of larger prison sentences.

Again, for the males, the results of the second experiment were consistent with earlier research and the first experiment. There was a tendency toward longer sentences in the small room relative to the large room, and the longest average sentences were assigned by the men in the small room who had heard the static-marred tapes. And *again,* there were reversals in the data from the females. Women tended to give shorter sentences in the small room, and the shortest average sentences of all groups were assigned by the women in the small room who had heard the marred tape!

At this point, Freedman et al. (1972) were convinced of their findings, but no less puzzled. In a final attempt to understand the sex difference in crowding effects, they replicated the no-static condition of the second experiment with mixed-sex groups, males *and* females together in the large or small room. These latest data were exceptionally clear: there were *no* effects for either crowding conditions or sex. The only comparisons of interest were that females seemed to be as aggressive (assigned prison sentences about as large) in mixed groups as they were in same-sex groups of the second experiment, but that men were less aggressive in mixed company than in all male company.

Well, an understanding of the sex-crowding issue seemed to be more elusive than ever. Nevertheless, Freedman et al. offered several possible reasons for these differences. The reasons fall into two categories, those that are learned and those that are innate. First, it may be that:

1. We learn that there are different expectations about personal contact and that, among women, contact is more acceptable.

2. Crowding tends to intensify initial reactions to situations, and we have somehow come to expect that groups of men are more threatening than groups of women (see Freedman, 1975, for further discussion of the intensification hypothesis).

On the other hand, it may be that:

1. Since men are constitutionally larger (on the average) than women, they may require more room and feel more uncomfortable for the lack of it.

2. Men and women are innately different in many ways, one of which is their response to intrusions of personal space or crowding.

The reader is perhaps by now well aware of how difficult it would be to run critical tests on this facet or any other of the nature-nurture controversy. However, the evidence for sex differences in spatial dispersion or social distance is not limited to humans, and an examination of the behavior of some selected infrahumans may illuminate our own (human) condition.

The first set of species to be examined will be old world monkeys. Kummer (1974) studied the spatial arrangement of groups of captive patas monkeys and groups of captive gelada baboons. These animals inhabit open country in the wild and were therefore tested in a very spacious (100 by 400 feet) enclosure. Particular animals were observed in all combinations of male-male, female-female, and mixed pairs over several days.

The results from the observation of both species were clear. Within each species there was a greater mean distance between paired males than between paired females or mixed pairs. These differences (paired males versus either of the other combinations) were on the order of a factor of 5 for the patas and a factor of 8 for the geladas. In both cases the distances between paired females and mixed pairs was negligible. In some sense, these data are quite parallel with the findings of Freedman et al. (1972). Males showed most spatial intolerance to one another but were tolerant of females, as were females of females. Now this comparison *proves* nothing, but it suggests that for the baboons and monkeys at least, some of the factors governing interindividual distance may be innate. In the first place, since both types of animals occupy about the same sort of habitat, it would seem that the relatively wider dispersion of geladas males, compared to patas males, could represent traits inherent in those species. Second, the spacing of given members of a species were probably not learned reactions to particular individuals, because all but two of the subjects were unknown to one another (that is, they were strangers) prior to being placed in the test enclosure.

New world monkeys also space themselves and provide some interesting data on species and sex differences in spacing. Mason and Epple (1969) also used a 100-by-400-foot enclosure to observe interindividual distances between squirrel monkeys and between titi monkeys. One species at a time was introduced to the enclosure in combinations of male-male, female-female, and mixed pairs. The results for the squirrel monkeys were consistent with Kummer's observations of patas monkeys and gelada baboons. The greatest average distance was between male-male pairs, the least distance was between female-female pairs, and the mixed pairs were generally intermediate between the extreme same-sex pairs.

The data from the titi monkeys, however, were in stark contrast to *all* the sex differences reviewed so far. For the titis the mixed-sex pairs were also intermediate in social distance, but the female-female pairs showed the *greatest* social dispersion while the male-male pairs showed the *least* spacing (Mason & Epple, 1969). The pattern for sex differences in the titi might lead the reader to either of two wildly divergent conclusions. The more reasonable-appearing conclusion would be that spacing proclivities are not universally linked to sex differences in the monkey's world and, therefore, an argument for an innate basis for interindividual distance is discredited. A second conclusion is more interesting, albeit more looney. This conclusion would be that sex differences *do* determine spacing tendencies and that male titis are in some ways more feminine than females, thus the argument for an innate basis gains support.

It turns out that the second conclusion, despite its implausibility, is probably the more correct one. In some ways male titis *are* more feminine (or at least more maternal) than females, according to the observations of Mason (1974):

> Sex and parenthood also had their unusual aspects in [the titi monkey] . . . . After babies arrived there was an intriguing division of labour in which the male carried the infant most of the time. The mother took the baby to suckle it and clean it, and

when she had finished, the baby either returned to the male under its own power — aided and abetted by the mother who usually sat close to her mate — or the male simply lifted it off its mother's back (p. 157).

Obviously the act of carrying an infant presupposes an organism that is tolerant of social contact, at least of infants. It is my guess that this tolerance for infants is part of a generalized relative tolerance of conspecifics, and that is why the child carriers (if not the child bearers) in our universe get together in tighter groups. Actually, the titi is not the only new world primate in which the father literally carries the burden of his offspring. This behavior has also been reported by Pola and Snowdon (1975) and Jolly (1972) for pygmy marmosets. It would be interesting to determine whether these other species showed the sex-linked patterns of social distancing shown by the titis.

Before we return to the consideration of human social distancing, we can profit by a quick glance at some data on a small English songbird, the chaffinch. Marler (1956) was able to measure the spatial intolerance of this animal in a very simple and precise way. Birds were housed in groups of 8 in cages that had only 2 food hoppers. Each hopper could only accommodate one bird at a time. Marler varied the location of the two hoppers to estimate the distance required to provoke fighting between any two subjects. Apparently, the very proximity of another bird is enough to provide full-blown aggressive reactions in the chaffinch, even when both animals have free access to food.

Marler presented his results as a ratio of nonaggressions (N), that is, no fight during an encounter, to total encounters (T), for each of the several distances between hoppers. The closer the ratio N/T approaches 0.00 for a given distance, the more likely fighting occurred at that distance. A ratio approaching 1.00 indicates that fighting never occurred. For both male and female chaffinches, the maximum distance between the hoppers (125 inches) resulted in a ratio of over .95 which means that fighting rarely occurred, while for both sexes the shortest possible separation between hoppers (0 inches) produced a ratio of less than .05, which means that fighting almost always occurred there.

Intermediate distances did, however, provide evidence for sex differences. A ratio of .50 for a given distance means that there was a 50-50 chance for fighting to erupt at that separation. This so-called .50-distance for males was 56.25 inches, while for females it was 17.5 inches. These spatial differences may speak for differences in aggression between the males and females. Marler also caged birds in mixed-sex groups and observed male-male, female-female, and mixed-sex reactions at the hoppers. Under these circumstances the .50-distance was 48.75 inches for the male-male encounters, 27.5 inches for female-female encounters, and 25 inches for encounters between males and females. Apparently, if males are more aggressive they are so only toward other males.

As another variation, Marler colored the breast feathers of some female chaffinches so that they looked like males. The resulting .50-distance between normal males and the red-females went up to about 50 inches. In other words, the dyed females provoked reactions as if they *were* males. In fact, for red females tested with red females the .50-distance was 62.5 inches.

The effects for colored females plus some ancillary observations led Marler (1956) to state the following:

> This leads to a conclusion of the greatest interest, that using the distance at which others are attacked as a measure of aggressiveness, females are no less aggressive than males . . . The behavior of disguised (red) females is to be explained, not by a direct effect of colouring on their own aggressiveness, but by their responsiveness to the changed behaviour of others towards them. (p. 27)

What we can make of this statement for our present purpose is that, if there are sex differences in spacing behavior, these differences are not only mediated by one's own sex, but also by the sex of the others in interaction.

This idea brings us back to a human study conducted by Dabbs and Johns (under review). Pairs of college-student subjects were seated facing one another. The ostensible task was to discuss aspects of a lawsuit they had recently read about. These discussions took place with their chairs some 5 feet apart, or with their chairs moved together so that the subjects' knees almost touched. These two distances defined the "uncrowded" and "crowded" conditions, and each subject participated in each condition with crowding following the uncrowded situation. During discussions, the percent of time subjects maintained eye contact was recorded by covert observers, since eye contact reflects affiliation (see Rubin, 1970). After two minutes of discussion at the 5-foot distance, subjects were asked to rate several aspects of the situation, including the quality of the discussion and their own and their partner's feelings. They then moved to the crowded situation, and identical measures were taken during and after the appropriate time periods. The membership of the pairs was varied in the typical male-male, female-female, and mixed fashion.

When Dabbs and Johns analyzed their data in terms of the major conditions of sex (male-male, female-female, mixed), they found some parallels with the earlier Freedman et al. (1972) study. There was a trend for males to think somewhat less highly of their disucssion when crowded than when uncrowded, but the females thought even more of theirs, as did the mixed pairs. For the males, eye contact during discussions dropped over 8 percent of the total test time from the uncrowded to the crowded conditions, whereas for the female and mixed pairs, the average drop was less than 4 percent. But the data in this form do not add any understanding to the mediating factors in human sex differences in distancing.

However, when Dabbs and Johns evaluated their data from a different point of view, some rather interesting new information did emerge. In the new analysis the subjects' initial assignment to experimental condition was ignored, and a new breakdown was created by simply asking if a subject had been crowded with a man or a woman. The data of interest were change-scores on the various

TABLE 4.2

Subject's Response to Crowding as a Function of Sex of Partner
in the Dabbs-Johns Experiment

	Subjects with male partners	Subjects with female partners	p
Change after crowding in:			
Rating of discussion	.0	1.8	$p < .01$
Rating of own feelings	1.4	3.5	n. s.
Rating of partner's feelings	.8	2.7	$p < .05$
Percent eye contact	−8.5	−2.2	n. s.
Overall final liking	3.9	4.3	$p < .05$

Note: Higher scores indicate more positive ratings, eye contact, or liking.
(Reprinted with permission of the author.)

measures from the uncrowded to the crowded condition.[5] At least one of the mediating factors in spacing within sexes now became clearer. Table 4.2 shows that while subjects crowded with a man may or may not have evidenced a positive shift on a measure those crowded with a woman showed (on the average) relatively more positive shifting. As this effect was not dependent on the sex of the subject, but on the characteristics of the other, these findings are quite parallel to some of the data from chaffinches. Also, some of the earlier human findings are illuminated: women weren't less upset during crowding necessarily because they were women, but in part because they were crowded *with* women.

Now let me be the first to admit that none of the studies in this section begin to tap the nature-nurture origins of sex differences in social distance, much less any feature of interpersonal distancing in animals or man. Nonetheless, the finding of such consistent sex differences in so many species does leave one with a feeling that innate factors could be operating to produce this phenomenon. In any event, the continued study of sex effects with respect to proxemics in humans has revealed more such findings. In a recent study, under "crowded" conditions, both men and women had more positive feelings toward fellow members when in mixed-sex compared to same-sex groups (Marshall & Heslin, 1975), although in this instance males had more positive feelings toward males in same-sex collectives than did females toward females under the same condition. It must be pointed out, however, that subjects in this study were involved in a

[5]This procedure raises a problem because subjects run in pairs ought not be considered two independent observations. Dabbs and Johns get around this problem in their analysis of variance by reducing the degrees of freedom in the error term by half.

joint problem-solving activity, so that these results are not strictly comparable to findings produced by the procedure of Freedman et al. (1972). But it is worth mentioning that another study, using the Sommer-Barash "invasion" procedure found that men, for some reason, were more aversive to face-to-face intrusions while, in contrast, women reacted more negatively to intrustions from the side (Fisher & Byrne, 1975).

Closing Thoughts on Social Distance

"Nature" seems to have put a lot of emphasis on keeping proper distance between the ambulatory objects of her creation. This brings us back to Carpenter's (1958) point that optimal distancing provides benefits for the species. However, Christian (1970) goes considerably beyond this idea, by suggesting that the government of population density through the mechanisms of territorality, dominance hierarchies, and, at base, simple spatial intolerance may also provide a basis for the evolution of species (that is, mammalian evolution, at least). Christian's reasoning is simple and appealing. When an animal is forced from an ecologically preferred locale because of social pressure, it must, of course, go someplace else, even if the new locale is not ecologically preferred. Obviously, most of the social subordinates will not survive this displacement. But those that do might do so simply because they possessed a mutation that permitted them to survive in the somewhat alien conditions. As this mutation is passed on, a new species or subspecies will have developed apart from the original population. Ironically, in a sense, the new mutation would not necessarily prosper differentially in the original ecologically preferred locale, simply because it would not enjoy any special advantage for survival in that benign situation.

But the study of proxemics brings us to an apparent paradox: we feel — or we are told, at least — that the world is becoming too crowded for human habitation. Why aren't all these "innate" mechanisms of territoriality, dominance hierarchies, and proximal intolerance working? Where are they when we need them? The answer to these questions has three parts.

First, there is no evidence that spacing mechanisms are *not* working. We may not be aesthetically moved by all the garbage and clutter, but we are not yet standing on one another's toes. I don't want to preach social Darwinism, but those that can afford them buy or rent sets of rooms of fair proportion and the rule in America is still one man, one car.

Second, in a society like our own we survive through a technological system of food distribution, as do dogs in a kennel. Should that system (I rather like it myself) fail or be removed, I think we would see spacing mechanisms in abundance — and rather quickly.

Finally, distance between free-ranging animals is largely mediated by signals and rarely by physical aggression (see below). However, if one cannot see these signals, one cannot be influenced by them. As Kummer (1971) put it, "the wall is a substitute for distance" (p. 227). We can't begin to test this idea for man, since apparently he's always had access to walls, beginning with the cave. But monkeys don't normally use walls, and we can ask of them: is a wall really a substitute for distance?

The answer, in part, is yes. Certain of the rhesus monkeys that live here in Madison are housed in groups at the Wisconsin Regional Primate Research Center. Sometimes dominant animals threaten subordinates, presumably in an effort to displace them. However, since the subordinate animals cannot leave the cage, severe and damaging fighting can break out. One of the remedies to reduce the chronic state of stress and fighting in a group cage is to install several sheets of sturdy material. In a real sense, the subordinate animal will hide behind one of the panels, and the absence of visual access to the subordinate seems to calm the dominant or aggressive monkey, even though the subordinate is merely *behind* something and not enclosed safely in some container.

Still, much more evidence will be required before we can begin to decide if spacing mechanisms in humans are innate or learned. It is interesting to ask the question, though, whether there are walls because there is a human society, or whether there is a human society because there are walls?

SOCIAL COMMUNICATION

It is clear from the data presented by Kaufmann (1967) and others on the rhesus monkey that animal societies are by no means egalitarian. Competition and strife are commonplace, with winners and losers clearly identified to one another, and to us. Such aggressiveness is presumed to be of advantage to the species since it insures the robust and vigorous organism a degree of success at obtaining scarce resources and thus, in a real sense, the survival of the fittest. In fact, aggression in one form or another is one of the most widespread types of social behavior and should be of interest to the camparative social psychologist. To convey some idea of the extent of aggressiveness in the animal kingdom, Southwick (1970) has noted that:

> Aggressive behavior is virtually universal in some form or another in almost every animal which has the necessary motor apparatus to fight or inflict injury. It is absent or rare in only those invertebrates such as some worms and oysters which have no means of inflicting physical damage, whereas it is common in most arthropods and vertebrates which have appendages, claws, teeth, or other structures capable of damaging movements. Lobsters, crayfish, most insects, and most vertebrates are all capable of severe aggressive behavior, which can be seen in both natural and experimental conditions (p. 2).

If we can imagine, for the moment, an idealistic or utopian group of humans that aspired to a completely nonviolent life, it would seem that they would have few animals to choose from as emblems, mascots, or pets. Namely, worms and oysters. However, these gentle people might well be cautioned against *any* choice, since they may be disappointed in the end. For a long time it was assumed that certain toothless and clawless amphibia were not aggressive simply because they lacked the wherewithal. More recently, Test (1954) has questioned this assumption by reporting the discovery of a species of territorial frog. These animals defend their claims by leaping into the air and falling on their victim's back. Alas, it may be that the seemingly pacific worm and oyster are also aggressive, but have been able to conceal this darker side from the biologist or naturalist.

But if there is anything more remarkable than the fact that aggression is ubiquitous in the animal kingdom, it is the fact that animals are *rarely* injured or killed by one another in naturalistic settings (Eibl-Eibesfeldt, 1961; K. R. L. Hall, 1964; Lorenz, 1966; Matthews, 1964). The reason violent injury or death is rare in aggressive encounters is that apparently all species have evolved (possess) means of signalling their aggressive or other dispositions. The very signal of an aggressive intent often has the same result as an overt act of aggression, with the result that the overt act is obviated. These intention signals come under the heading of the social releasers introduced in an earlier section. As noted, some of the most striking examples of releasers are available in aggressive or sexual interactions between organisms. We will begin our discussion of social communication by considering releasers seen in aggressive contexts. Oftentimes this variety of releasers or social signals are called *agonistic displays.*

Agonistic Displays

Recall that subordinate animals are literally on the fringe of their society. The peripheral monkeys observed by Kaufmann (1967) were rarely seen in the privileged circle of the central group. But it probably would not be the case that an interloper would be physically mauled for his presumptuousness, or even dragged protesting by an ear or the tail from the area. Rather, it is more likely that such an intruder would be given a certain sort of *look,* as illustrated on the left in Figure 4.4. This facial configuration, sometimes called the scandalized expression, is one of a number of agonistic displays available to male and female rhesus. If this threat is effective in intimidating the threatened animal, a complementary facial configuration may ensue on the face of the intruder, called the fear grimmace or appeasement smile (right side of Figure 4.4). At this point the exchange would terminate, with the threat and submission signals serving in lieu of an actual physical contest between the two animals (see Wickler, 1969, for a photographic record of such an exchange).

However, a simple appeasement expression may not be satisfactory to a threatening animal, as might be the case when a dominant individual was intolerant of the nearness or position of a subordinate or an intruder. In this instance, a more intense agonistic display might be forthcoming, such as an abrupt forward lunge by the dominant. Other more intense threats in rhesus include slapping the

FIG. 4.4   Rhesus monkey threat (left) and appeasement (right) facial expressions employed in the Sackett (1966) research. (With permission of the author and the American Association for the Advancement of Science.)

ground with the forepaws or branch shaking, where the threatening individual holds on to a limb (or a chain, in captivity) and heaves itself up and down. These postural and gestural signals may also be accompanied by vocal signals of various intensities. Were all these signals to fail, the threatening individual might then resort to chasing and biting, but such chases are relatively infrequent and rarely result in anything but superficial wounds (cf. Hinde & Rowell, 1962; Rowell, 1972; Sade, 1967; van Hooff, 1969; Wickler, 1969). Of course, if the status of the individuals was close, or if the status of one was being challenged, more or less severe fighting could be expected.

Such agonistic exchanges are not limited to the rhesus monkey, although Wilson (1972) claims these macaques possess the widest repertoire of all infrahuman animals. Elaborate complementary signal patterns reflecting threat and appeasement in many species have been reviewed by Eibl-Eibesfeldt (1961), Johnson (1972), Tinbergen (1967), and Mayr (1974). Further, not all agonistic displays and gestures are for the purpose of displacing unwanted subordinates. Another common function of social releasers is that some are acts of greeting, which, in the final analysis, may also be acts of appeasement, but which have the result that the interacting organisms can remain in proximity.

The advantage of ritualized greetings is especially obvious in the case of the spotted hyena (Kruuk, 1972). This African plains animal obtains food in two distinct ways. First, the hyena is a famous scavenger and is known to be able to eat (and apparently relish) anything including skin, hair, bones, offal, and carrion. These scavenging trips are solitary junkets, with both males and females proceeding on their own. On the other hand, hyenas are also very adept at social hunting and literally cooperate in felling eland, wildebeest, and zebra, among other prey. Once an ungulate is downed, there is a good bit of socializing with hyenas eating while standing shoulder to shoulder, or actually laying on one another near (or in) the carcass.

The problem here is the stage of transition between the condition where hyenas have been solitary and the condition where they become social. When two formerly isolated hyenas meet, or when one joins an existing grouping, it is an occasion of considerable tension as these are quite high-strung animals, who are also cannibals, incidentally. This tension is reduced when the beasts in question have had an opportunity to examine (smell and lick) each other's genital area. Access to the genital area is facilitated by one or both animals raising a hind leg. Since the genital inspection reduces tension and allows social proximity, it is of interest here to learn the status of the animal that initiates the exchange by first lifting its leg. It should be recalled that in hyena society females are clearly dominant over males and that in general the larger animal in a same-sex pairing would be likely to be dominant. Obviously, adult hyenas are dominant over cubs.

Kruuk (1972) observed a number of meetings where he could clearly decide which of two hyenas initiated the greeting exchange by being the first to raise a leg, and *low* status was clearly implicated in such initiations. In male-female encounters, 80 percent of the initiations were undertaken by the males, as were 91 percent of the initiations undertaken by the cubs in cub-adult meetings. All of the smaller animals lifted their leg first in the same-sex meetings.

Leg-lifting is not the only greeting signal available to the hyena. According to Kruuk, as one approaches another, the stationary animal will often turn its head away, thus averting its stare. This turning away of the head has also been observed as a component of animal social greeting or acknowledgement in foxes and wolves (Fox, 1969), chickens (McBride, James & Schaffner, 1963), and gulls (Tinbergen, 1959). This brings us back to the role of physiognomy, and especially the stare, in agonistic exchanges and signalling.

Agonistic Facial Signals In Humans

Goffman (1963) set the ground rules for the assessment of the effects of gazing on human social interaction when he distinguished between focused and unfocused interaction between people. Focused interaction refers to a condition where there are assemblies of individuals who extend to one another the right to communicate or converse, or otherwise engage in some sort of mutual activity. Unfocused interaction, on the other hand, is a condition where persons are merely present in the same situation. In the case of focused interaction, glances and stares can take on many specific meanings. But in unfocused interaction, gazing is governed by the principle Goffman termed *civil inattention.* For example, when passersby meet on the street they grant each other civil inattention thusly: "What seems to be involved is that one gives another enough visual notice to demonstrate that one appreciates the other is present (and that one admits openly to having seen him), while at the next moment withdrawing one's attention from him so as to express that he does not constitute a target of special curiosity or design (Goffman, 1963, p. 84).

This means that we do not (*ought* not) stare at strangers in unfocused interactions. To stare would imply a wish to be hostile or to mark the person as one to be avoided. Goffman reminds us that for certain cultures at various times in our human history this business of not staring was taken pretty seriously, with a glance at an emperor or his agents being a punishable offense.

It is in the sense of the unfocused interaction that we will examine the role of the stare in human social communication. This does not mean that there have been no studies of gazing or eye contact in focused interactions. To the contrary, these are abundant (e.g., Argyle & Dean, 1965; Ellsworth & Carlsmith, 1968, 1973; Scherwitz & Helmreich, 1973; among others). But it seems truer to our ethological purpose to limit our attention to circumstances that somehow match what might befall our unfortunate friend in Figure 4.4, the subordinate monkey. That is, how do people react when they discover that they are the object (for no apparent reason) of a pointed stare? Does the presence of a staring individual have any systematic effect on the object of his attention?

The preferred locale to look for the answer to this question would be in a naturalistic or field setting, as espoused by the early ethologist, E. Geoffroy-Saint-Hillaire. However, we will defer to his adversary, Cuvier, for the moment, and review some findings from a laboratory study. There is the possibility of detecting minute variations in the movement of seated subjects with a radarlike ultrasonic motion detector. Dabbs and Clower (1973) used such a device to record subjects spontaneous movements during a 15-minute period of observation. It should be pointed out that the subjects were unaware that their spontaneous movements were being recorded; they thought they were in a time-estimation study.

In essence, there were three conditions in the Dabbs-Clower study: control, restriction and staring. During the first 5 minutes of observation, all conditions were equivalent, while during the second 5-minute interval, the control condition continued as usual, but the experimental conditions varied. In the restriction condition, the subjects were asked to sit as still as possible. Any movement they made was revealed to them by a light wired to the motion detecting device. For the staring condition, the experimenter merely turned in his chair and looked pointedly at the subject without explanation. During the last 5 minutes of testing, the conditions were again equivalent, with no special instructions or treatments for any of the groups.

The results of the Dabbs-Clower study were quite clear. For the control group, the average units of movement is fairly stable in the absence of interference. By contrast, the units of movement were 10, 3, and 18 for the restriction group and 8, 6, and 20 for the stare group. The patterns for both experimental groups indicate there was a regular decline during staring and voluntary restraint and that subjects seemed inclined to loosen up or shake off the restraint or the effect of staring when terminated. While a stare might have a different effect in some other situation, it seems that here the experimenter did gain a degree of control over the subjects with his stare and that this control was powerful enough to have measurable effects and aftereffects.

One characteristic of the Dabbs and Clower (1973) study is that it placed subjects in a "reactive" situation. That is, subjects knew they were under observation and may have felt they were expected to do *something* in reaction to the experimenter's stare (cf. Webb, Campbell, Schwartz, & Sechrest, 1966; Orne, 1962). It would seem that tests of ethological notions would be more reasonably carried out in nonreactive situations where subjects do not necessarily know they are under special observation, although this proposition raises ethical questions about the protection of subjects' rights (which will have to be solved elsewhere). Fortunately, there is a series of nonreactive, naturalistic studies on record, and it is to these we will now turn.

Ellsworth, Carlsmith, and Henson (1972) reviewed laboratory studies that showed that subjects tended to avoid eye contact with hostile interviewers. They rightly point out, however, that the avoidance of eye contact is not quite the same thing as an escape (flight) reaction, as in the case of a subordinate animal. Further, eye contact is not equivalent to a stare, where staring is defined as a look that continues regardless of the reactions of the object of the stare. In Goffman's sense, such concerted inspection would violate the norm of civil inattention.

Ellsworth et al. undertook a series of five field experiments to examine the effects of staring on flight reactions in humans. In the first study they chose a traffic intersection as the experimental setting and automobile drivers (in their cars) as subjects. The experimenters were able to arrange events so that one of their confederates (either a man or a woman on a motor scooter) stopped at the traffic light before the arrival of any other vehicle. When an unsuspecting motorist (male or female) did arrive, the confederate did one of two things, either glanced at the driver casually and looked away, or stared fixedly at the person for the duration of the red light. The data of interest in the study were the lengths of time it took the drivers to pass completely through the intersection when the light turned green. And, for the most part, the results clearly indicated that staring did have an influence on the flight reactions of the subjects. Those in the no-stare condition showed an average crossing time of 6.5 seconds while those in the stare condition took only 5.3 seconds, a highly significant ($p < .001$) effect.

Although the differences in the first Ellsworth et al. study were clear, interpretation of them was difficult. It could well be, they pointed out, that the drivers in the stare condition may have thought that they had been challenged to a drag race, even though the motor scooter involved was described as dilapidated. Hence, the relatively high rates of acceleration for the stare group may have merely reflected a desire on the part of the subjects to show off their prowess as drivers or the power of their cars. To rule out the possibility of challenges, the location of the second study was changed to a corner on a one-way street. In this case the confederate simply stood on the street corner and went through the stare or no-stare routines. And in this case the results matched those of the first experiment perfectly. Drivers in the no-stare condition spent 6.7 seconds crossing the intersection when the light changed whereas the drivers in the stare condition got through in 5.5 seconds, again a highly significant difference.

An interesting finding emerged from an internal analysis of the data from these first two of the Ellsworth et al. (1972) studies. It turned out that the actual duration of the stare, in the stare condition, was not the same for all subjects. This was so simply because the researchers had no way of completely controlling the arrival time of the subjects, nor the changing of the traffic light. Nevertheless, in both experiments the correlations between amount of staring time and crossing time were nearly zero ($r = .09$ in the first and .06 in the second). This can be interpreted to mean that it was sufficient for the drivers to realize that they were the object of a stare (where staring is defined as a look that is not influenced by the object's reactions) for the stare to have its impact.

In a sense, a stare may be an all-or-none signal.

For their third experiment, Ellsworth et al. (1972) introduced some procedural refinements in a replication of their second experiment. The point of interest here is that the findings from the third study exactly duplicated earlier observations, which represents a valuable confirmation. It was in their *fourth* study that the researchers introduced a major change by shifting their attention from drivers to pedestrians. The distinction between drivers and pedestrians is perhaps an important one: drivers may accelerate quickly to demonstrate prowess or bravado as mentioned earlier, but hurried walking is hardly a sign of assurance.

Pedestrians were located as subjects using the same procedure that selected motorists. A confederate stood on a street corner at a red light until someone walked up. Then the stare or no-stare routine took place. Again, the dependent measure was the amount of time subjects spent crossing the street when the light turned green. And again, the results were entirely consistent with the foregoing studies. The people who had been stared at walked across the intersection faster (11.1 seconds) than those who had not (12.1 seconds).

At this point Ellsworth et al. realized that while staring *appeared* to be a sufficient stimulus for avoidance or flight, an alternative explanation was still possible. It may have been, they cautioned, that a stare was also an incongruous event (cf. Goffman, 1963), and the mere incongruity of the situation may have caused people to withdraw. That is, people in the stare condition may not have been reacting to the stare per se, but to the total inappropriateness of the situation. To try to rule out the incongruity interpretation, the researchers first had to develop a situation that was incongruous, but that did not also have frightening, such a confederate cracking a whip, sexually distracting, such as a confederate in a state of undress, or other irrelevant implications. They finally chose to have a female confederate sit down at an intersection and hit the sidewalk with a hammer (?). When this condition was matched against stare and no-stare treatments in a fifth experiment with drivers as subjects, the incongruity and no-stare conditions proved to be equivalent (mean crossing times of 5.5 and 5.7 seconds, respectively) while the staring produced the usual accelerated departures (4.0 seconds). Thus the researchers were able to rule out incongruity as a main motivating factor in flight reactions.

There is additional support for the idea that the stare is a stimulus for flight in humans. Bakken and Bromley (1973) either stared or didn't stare at drivers in a replication of some of the Ellsworth et al. experiments. Further, they *smiled* at some of their motorist subjects. The average crossing times in the smile, no-stare, and stare conditions were, respectively, 6.07, 5.80, and 4.79 seconds. It is also interesting to note that the Bakken and Bromley design produced an interaction between sex of experimenter and sex of subject in their smile condition. When the male experimenter smiled, female subjects drove off more slowly (6.55 seconds) than did male subjects (5.60 seconds). Conversely, when the female experimenter smiled it was the male subjects who dallied (7.00 seconds), when compared to the female subjects (5.15 seconds). If we are inclined to accept the stare as an innate flight stimulus, we may also wish to consider the smile (from the appropriate sex) as an innate approach stimulus.

Human Prosocial Facial Signals

As indicated by the Bakken-Bromley data, not all faces are threatening all of the time. In fact, for human infants the adult face seems to hold special appeal when compared to other patterns of visual stimulation. In this section, we will consider the issue of form preferences in infancy. This concern is distinct from the earlier discussion of attachment, primarily because most tests for visual preferences were conducted prior to the time that specific attachments are known to form and the stimuli employed were typically schematized facts, or photographs of persons unknown to the children.

There have been a number of studies that examined the reactions of infants (from 1 to 13 months of age) to facial and other stimuli (Kagan & Lewis, 1965; Kagan, Henker, Hen-Tov, Levine, & Lewis, 1966; Lewis, 1969; McCall & Kagan, 1967; Thomas, 1965; among others). For parsimony's sake, only the Kagan & Lewis study will be considered in some detail, since the findings from all the works cited are generally consistent. The infants in the Kagan-Lewis research were exposed to a series of visual stimuli when they were 6 months of age. The series included a male face, a female face, a bulls-eye, a checkerboard, a nursing bottle, and the face of a panda bear. These were presented five times each (for 12 seconds) in different orders. During each projection, the amount of time the child fixated on the visual array was recorded. The results showed that the male and female face did not differ from one another, but that each elicited significantly more looking than any of the other projections. As for the nonsocial items, the panda bear (humanoid configuration) was looked at longer than the geometric figures, and the nursing bottle elicited significantly less looking time than *any* of the other configurations. So much for the drive-reduction view of early social interest, one might easily think, but Kagan and Lewis don't tell us if the babies were bottle or breast fed.

Still, one might question the motivation behind the child's glances. After all, these children were of relatively advanced age, and all came from normal families. It is doubtless correct that they had spent some time in interaction with both female and male adults, and such physiognomies may have taken on signal value during those interactions, as opposed to having some inherent signalling or attention-getting properties. For example, there is at least one report (Carpenter & Stechler, 1967) that infants can discriminate their mother's real face from other objects (a mannikin's head or a nonsense shape) as early as 14 *days* after birth. To test this distinction between learned and inherent signals, one would have to examine the reactions of much younger infants without extensive social experiences.

But the question then becomes: how much can the young child be expected to see? One of the most famous quotes in psychology is William James' assertion that the neonate enters a world alleged to be a "booming, buzzing confusion," at best. Well, it turns out that it's probably not all confusion for the infant after all. Fantz, Ordy, and Udelf (1962) discovered that infants less than a month old could apparently resolve 1/8-inch lines at a distance of 10 inches, and that they preferred patterns over solid surfaces. These findings prompted Fantz et al. to observe even younger children and to include some quasi-social stimuli in their selection of visual material.

Infants less than 48 *hours* of age were tested for duration of gaze at six different stimuli: a schematic face, a bulls-eye, a circular section of newsprint, and three unpatterned surfaces of white, yellow, or red color. The attention-getting value of each stimulus was expressed as the proportion (relative duration) of gazing devoted to it. For these neonates, the face was prepotent in eliciting fixation (29.5 percent), the bulls-eye was next in attractiveness (23.5 percent), with the newsprint a poor third (13.1 percent). The solid colors were least effective and received an average of less than 12 percent of all gazing. This pattern of visual preferences was also replicated exactly for children as old (or young) as 2 to 5 days (Fantz, 1961, 1963, 1965).

While these findings do not rule out a learning interpretation of the attractiveness of human faces for infants, they at least render such an interpretation questionable and seem to shift the burden of proof onto the learning theorist. Now, it should be pointed out that Fantz did not make any claims for a schematized face as a sign stimulus, nor am I. It is interesting, though, that such configurations do interest the child, and that human parents possess such configurations. This suggests that the infant's very interest in the parent may influence aspects of early social interactions. This possibility will be considered below.

Robson (1967) gave thought to what features of the adult face might be most engaging to the offspring, and settled on the eye. He reminds us that the eye is shiny and movable while also fixed in space (making it easy to localize), shows contrast in the pupil-iris-cornea configuration, and has its own internal motility in the dilation and contraction of the pupil. In fact, there is a certain amount of evidence that the pupillary activity itself is an indicator of social reactivity. Recall that Harlow could elicit gasps in female audiences by showing them a picture of a lovable monkey, but that this response was not on record for males. Other research has uncovered responses in the eye itself that parallel the gasp data.

Hess (1965) was able to measure the amount of pupil dilation adult subjects gave in reaction to certain pictures. His hypothesis was that attitude (or interest) and pupil size were related, and rather convincingly showed that this was so. In response to pictures of female "pinups," male subjects showed more pupil dilation than female subjects. In a complementary fashion, female subjects showed more dilation in response to male pinups that did male subjects. Most interesting for our current concern, however, was that when shown a picture of an infant, women showed a marked average dilation, while men showed none (see also Hindmarch, 1973). When the infant was shown in the company of its mother, the female subjects were all the more interested (showed even greater pupil dilation), while the males began to evince only the slightest interest, presumably in reaction to the mother. Clearly, the women in the study were more interested in the pictures of the baby than were the men.

More importantly, it may be the case that such dilation is detectable by the child, as suggested by Robson (1967), and that dilation would enhance the appeal of the adult. Grown men, at least, are attracted to women with dilated pupils (Hess, 1965, Hindmarch, 1973). Further, dilation in response to social stimuli is not restricted to adults, but is also in evidence as a response in infants. Fitzgerald (1968) measured the pupillary response in babies 1, 2, or 4 months of age. He exposed these children to photographs of their own mother, a stranger, checkerboards, and a triangle, and found consistent results in all age groups. One or the other face always produced the most dilation in each of the sub-samples.

This possibility of mutual signalling via pupillary responses raises the fascinating possibility that something like chaining (see above) could go on between adult and infant. That is, as the sight of the child provoked a dilation in the mother, this very dilation might provoke a dilation in the child, which in turn would provoke a reaction in the mother — and so on.

The results of one study, while not compelling in and of themselves, are at least in line with the hypothesized reciprocal stimulation of pupil dilation between adult and child. Ashear (1975) recorded the reactions of 2- to 4-month-old infants during two different 7-minute periods in which she interacted with individual babies by smiling, touching, and talking to them. For one of the test periods, Ashear had caused her own pupils to constrict to 2 to 3 mm by an application of pilocarpine hydrochloride; in the other test period, this researcher caused her own pupils to dilate to 7 to 8 mm by applying phenylephrine hydrochloride. The results of this rather heroic procedure were that under the dilated condition babies were more socially reactive and smiled more than under the constricted condition. Although these findings are interesting and in line with the reciprocated gaze hypothesis, it must be pointed out that the differences produced by these two conditions were not statistically significant. However, Ashear has suggested some refinements of her procedures that may result in reliable findings in the future.

There are, moreover, a fair number of anecdotal accounts on record that show that the recognition of gross mutual eye contact between a parent and a child is an extremely important milestone in the social integration of the child, of which one casual recounting from Robson (1967) will suffice:

> Most of [a sample of primaparous] women describe some initial feelings of "strangeness," "distance," and unfamilarity toward their offspring which persists for at least the first few weeks of life. When one inquires as to when the mother first felt love,

when she ceased feeling "strange" with her child and when he "became a person" to her, the answer to these questions frequently involves the baby's "looking," as if recognizing objects in the environment. A small number specifically articulate that eye-to-eye contact releases[6] strong positive feelings. These feelings have something to do with "being recognized" in a highly personal and intimate way (p. 16).

According to the above quote, a certain quality of the relationship between the mother and child is determined by the responsiveness of the child (see also Wolff, 1963). Obviously, though, the mother is more likely to set the tone of their relationship and, everything else equal, we would expect that her attitude toward childbearing or the birth of a particular child might figure largely in her actions.

In order to examine this proposition, Moss and Robson (1968) interviewed primaparous mothers during the final stages of their pregnancy to determine whether the forthcoming child was viewed positively (or not) and whether the mother looked forward to affectionate contact with it (or not). One month after the birth, Moss and Robson arranged a 6-hour visit in the family's home and made a record of the number of times the mother and infant simultaneously looked at one another's faces (termed vis-à-vis). They then compared the vis-à-vis scores with the mothers' attitudes during pregnancy, and found significantly positive correlations for both girl and boy babies. That is, the more the mothers thought of their infants before they were born, the more likely it was they would engage in face-to-face contact with them later. This result seems to tie in with the findings (see above) from Ainsworth et al. (1971) that insensitive mothers don't have children that are normally attached. Perhaps it is lack of eye contact, as opposed to the care of physical needs, that mediated the effect reported by Ainsworth and her colleagues.

Origin of Social Expressions in Men and Other Primates

The analysis of virtually every complex behavioral phenomenon has led to a nativist-empiricist debate at some time or other, and this is also true of the study of emotional expressions (compare Asch, 1952; Tomkins, 1962, with Bruner & Taguiri, 1954; Birdwhistell, 1963). The empiricists argue that we learn which facial configurations are appropriate to what internal emotive states, and base their arguments on the differences in emotive expressions across or even within cultures. The nativists, on the other hand, argue that cultural differences are apparent only in terms of learned affect evokers, or rules governing the control of emotional displays in social contexts. At base, in the nativist view, emotional expressions find their origin in the evolutionary history of our species. These days, as we shall see, the balance of evidence seems to be swinging to the side of the nativists. This evidence from man and other primates is of three main types: (a) pan-cultural recognition of emotive states; (b) fine-grained cinematic analysis of greetingss and other gestures, also pan-cultural in scope; and (c) ex-

[6]Robson does not mean "releases" in the ethological sense.

pression and recognition of emotive states within the framework of deprivation experimentation.

As noted, there is only one recognized species of living man: *Homo sapiens.* If emotional expressions are innate or culture-free at base, then individuals from different cultures, but from the same species, should be able to recognize each others' feelings. One method to test this notion involves photographs of posed or actual affective displays. Such pictures are obtained from members of one culture and then are shown to people of some other culture for identification. Using this technique, Ekman, Sorenson, and Friesen (1969) found that people in Brazil and Japan were quite adept at identifying pictures of (Caucasian) Americans who were happy, fearful, disgusted, angry, surprised, or sad. Correct identifications ranged from 63 to 97 percent across the various categories of emotion. But this hardly constitutes evidence for any innate ability at recognition since both Brazilians and Japanese doubtless have access to American books and films, as well as Americans in the flesh, and therefore had opportunities to learn about our emotional way of life.

To get around this problem, Ekman and Friesen (1971) took their emotion-pictures to a remote spot in New Guinea and tested people from the Fore linguistic-cultural group. Apparently, this society was an isolated, Neolithic, material culture until its discovery in the late 1950s. Ekman and Friesen were able to locate over 300 of these people (men, women, and children) that met some fairly stringent criteria. Selected individuals: (a) had never seen a movie; (b) neither spoke nor understood English or Pidgin; (c) had not lived in any Western settlement or government town; and (d) had never worked for a Caucasian.

At first, the actual test for the Fores' recognition of Western emotional expression proved difficult for linguistic reasons, so a story-telling method was finally used. While a subject viewed several of the pictures, he or she heard a story (in the Fore language) depicting some person in one or another emotional state. Since these "stories" are quite brief, several will be presented in their entirety:

> Happiness: "His friends have come, and he is happy."
> Sadness: "Her child has died, and she feels very sad."
> Disgust: "He is looking at something which smells bad."

The respondent's task was to then pick the photograph that matched the story.

In general, the Fore were *excellent* judges of Western emotional expressions, especially where happiness and anger were concerned, and the results from the children matched the results from adults. Moreover, when American college students saw videotapes of Fore emotional expressions, they also had no difficulty in correctly identifying them. In the view of Ekman and Friesen (1971), it is extremely implausible that the Fore had any preconceptions of what Westerners might have "learned" regarding appropriate affective displays and that their data support the notion of pan-cultural elements in such displays.

A second approach to the study of expressions also involves a cross-cultural perspective, but uses a considerably different methodology. Eibl-Eibesfeldt

(1970) has used a variety of motion-picture techniques to capture the behavior of his subjects. Where humans are involved he sometimes shoots frames at a slow rate, which allows him to see the processed sequence speeded up, or shoots at high speeds, which permits seeing the sequence in slow motion. Eibl-Eibesfeldt, along with his associate H. Hass, also uses a modified lens to make unobtrusive films of behavior. This lens contains a prism so that photos can be taken from a direction 90° from the apparent orientation of the camera. People realize that photographers are in the vicinity, but when they assume that the camera is not focused on them they relax and act more naturally than they would when "on camera." This is indisputably a useful technique in field studies where spontaneity is desired, as evidenced in some of the brilliant portraits accomplished by Paul Strand, the famous creative photographer. Strand used such a lens in 1931 (Tomkins, 1974), which somewhat discredits Eibl-Eibesfeldt's (1970) contention that Hass first developed the technique.

Nevertheless, such a technique contributed to the discovery of the "eyebrow-flash," which looks like it could well be an innate human social signal. Women who are engaged in harmless flirting or men who are in the act of greeting raise the two eyebrows simultaneously and maximally. This flash is completed within one second of time and is perfectly obvious from film taken at 48 frames per second. It appears that the eyebrow flash is another pan-cultural feature of emotive expression. Eibl-Eibesfeldt (1970, pp. 417-422) presents stills of eyebrow-flashes by a woman from Kenya, a French woman, a flirting girl from Samoa, a Balinese man, two men from different tribes in New Guinea, and a man from a primitive tribe on the Orinoco (in South America).

A final form of evidence that might allow a decision between the nativist and empiricist views of the origins of expressive behavior comes from what has been described earlier as deprivation experimentation. Experiments, or quasi-experiments, have controlled the experience of certain subjects in such a way that their reactions can be evaluated for their possible innate basis. These researchers have focused on two complementary features of communication: the organism as a *receiver* of social signals and the organism as a *transmitter* of social signals.

Sackett (1966) employed rhesus monkey infants in a study of the effects of social isolation on reactions to agonistic displays. The monkeys were separated from their mothers at birth and were placed singly in cages that contained a ground-glass screen onto which slides could be projected. Beginning at two weeks of age the infants were shown slides of different classes of stimuli. As a matter of fact, these slides included the very pictures shown in Figure 4.4, except that the slides were in full color. The slide from the picture on the left in Figure 4.4 was considered a threat stimulus, and reactions to it will be our major concern here. Other slides, including the one of the appeasement grin (Figure 4.4, right) and views of infants and landscapes, will be considered control stimuli.

The measure of primary interest was the incidence of "disturbance" behavior patterns during brief presentations of the slides. Disturbance included rocking, huddling, self-clasping, fear, and withdrawal. For the first few weeks of tests none of the slides, threat included, produced any disturbance. In fact, the control stimuli produced no disturbance during the whole of the seven months of tests. By the tenth week of testing, however, presentation of the threat slide had a marked effect of disturbing the infants, and such disturbances reached a peak when they were about three months of age. Thereafter, the impact of the threat slide diminished somewhat, but it still produced measurable disturbance until the experiment was over.

Sackett's (1966) conclusion was that the fear reactions of the monkeys were probably produced by the maturation of an innate releasing mechanism or an "innate recognition mechanism" that was influenced by the threat slide. Here, then, is evidence from a highly complicated primate species with an elaborate social structure that certain reactions to a species-wide social signal (releaser) are innate. This means that capacities of a receiver of visual signals are inherent in the organism. There is also evidence for innate recognition of auditory signals in this species. Young rhesus monkeys, hand-reared by humans in the absence of adult animals, showed marked behavioral reactions to tape recordings of the bark of an adult male. These included marked decreases in environmentally-oriented responses such as oral or manual contact with the test unit and increases in self-oriented responses such as clinging to self and huddling (Waldrop, 1975).

Evidence for an innate capacity as a transmitter of social signals comes from a study of humans with profound and permanent deprivation experiences. There was a group of deaf-blind residents observed by Eibl-Eibesfeldt (1973) at the *Landesblindenanstalt* in Hanover, Germany. For one reason or another (thalidomide contamination, meningitis, mother's german measles, or unknown physical deficiency), these children had been blind *and* deaf for all, or the greater part of, their lives. They were severely retarded in many ways and required a vast amount of attention and care. They were not comatose, however, and appeared to be in contact with many elements in their environment, especially people. Depending on their disabilities (some did not possess limbs), they were more or less active and more or less mobile and purposive. Eibl-Eibesfeldt lists many functional and nonfunctional motor patterns (eating, drinking, rocking, scratching, and others) that were observed as characteristic activities.

Most interesting to us were the expressive behavior patterns, which included smiling, laughing, crying in distress and anger, frowning, pouting, surprise reactions, headshaking as a gesture of refusal, clenching teeth and fists, stamping feet, biting of own hands and lips, strong exhalation, signalling by the hand with palm outward, and affectionate nibbling, among others! These expressive movements did not occur haphazardly, as reference to "laughing" will show. "Laughing occurs during rougher social play (wrestling) and when the deaf-blind children are tickled. In the latter case initial smiling often turns into laughing. Beatrice often laughed when she ate a chocolate. Harald laughs during tugging games, and in particular when he wins" (Eibl-Eibesfeldt, 1973, p. 177).

Eibl-Eibesfeldt argued that the study of the expressive behavior of blind and deaf people is of great theoretical importance, since these movements are possibly the best evidence to date that ethological principles and concepts apply directly to human behavior. That is, the meaningful expressive behavior of the deaf-blind constitutes a kind of proof that certain aspects of man's social behavior are innate. Of course, there is the criticism that some of the expressive behaviors noted could have been acquired by learning or associations, as the child may have reached out and touched the mother's face while the mother laughed, for example. Eibl-Eibesfeldt anticipated this criticism by pointing out that the thalidomide children in his sample all showed varied and adequate facial expressions, despite the fact that they had no arms to reach out with.

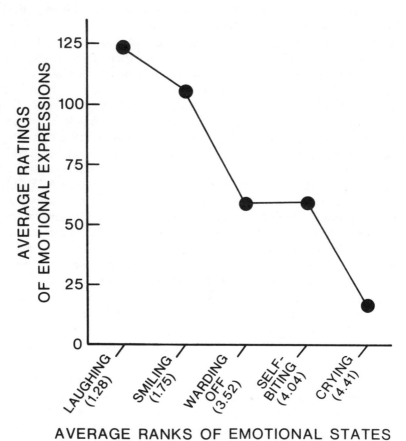

FIG. 4.5   Subjects' average ratings of slides of a deaf-blind person depicted as laughing, smiling, etc. The rank values are the same subjects' personal preferences for those states. (From Rajecki & Hayse, in preparation.)

Included in Eibl-Eibesfelt's report on the deaf-blind were a number of photographs of one of the children, a girl named Sabine. These photos show Sabine's face expressing a wide range of emotions, each contextually defined as in the examples of laughing by Beatrice and Harald (noted earlier). Although I myself was convinced of the ability of Sabine to display different emotions, I was curious whether other persons (who perhaps did not share my bias) could identify them, or even distinguish between them. Accordingly, permission was obtained to prepare slides from Eibl-Eibesfeldt's photographs.

In all, there were five categories, each based on a contextually defined emotional state as follows: (a) Sabine *laughing;* (b) *smiling* from pleasure; (c) *warding off* a repellent object (a tortoise, in this case) with arms extended and palms outward; (d) *biting her fingers* in frustration or anger; and (e) *crying* because of unhappiness. A large number of undergraduates at the University of Wisconsin were asked to give their impression of all categories of slides by rating them on 150-mm bipolar adjective scales. One end of each scale stated "negative emotion, extremely bad mood," while the other end stated the opposite. Additionally, the students rank-ordered the five expressions (laughing, smiling, warding off, biting oneself, and crying) in terms of how much the students themselves enjoyed those respective experiences. These rankings were obtained simply to arrive at a dimension against which to plot the students' ratings of Sabine's expressions.

The results of this simple test can be seen in Figure 4.5, where ratings are plotted against rankings. With the exception of a failure to distinguish between Sabine's enjoyment of warding off or biting herself, there were clear-cut distinctions made between the other emotional expressions presented. Moreover, there was a great deal of consistency across raters on most of the slides. In this connection it is perhaps worth noting that an analysis of the data points depicted in Figure 4.5 produced an F ratio in excess of 2000 (Rajecki & Hayse, in preparation).

Closing Thoughts on Social Communication

I should like to point out an additional finding from the Ellsworth et al. (1972) report. These authors apparently did not observe any motorist or pedestrian who "jumped" the light by crossing completely before it turned green.[7] This means that however much the subjects in the stare conditions were prompted to flight, this impulse may have been held in check by a learned inhibition. This suggests that social signals as discussed here would have the clearest influence in situations where cultural constraints or instigations were minimal or absent. We

[7]As a matter of fact, only some seven of the pedestrians under study so much as stepped off the curb and began to ease their way across the intersection during the red light. Interestingly, five of the seven were in the stare condition (Ellsworth, personal communication, 1975).

humans are, after all, civilized to a degree, and what civilization largely represents is a codification of powerful restraints on aggressive, sexual, and other emotional expressions. But I do not mean that the study of social signals is irrelevant to understanding contemporary social behavior. Adults in simple social situations (for example, Zajonc's 1965, mere-presence condition), and children in general, are probably quite susceptible to such influence.

As noted, certain social stimulus configurations seem especially important when seen through the eyes of an infant. Facial configurations are interesting to the newborn, and this interest stands in contradistinction to the secondary reinforcement interpretation (i.e., Dollard & Miller, 1950) of early social responsiveness in humans. What may be in order is a reevaluation of the important factors in the feeding situation for the process of socialization. In discussing the role of distance receptors in human attachment, Walters and Parke (1965) cite evidence (Haynes, White, & Held, 1965) that during the first weeks of life infants have a fixed point of clearest vision at eight or nine inches. Walters and Parke suggest that it may be more than a coincidence that, in caretaking situations, the mother's face is presented at an optimal distance for patterned vision. Hindmrach (1973) makes a related speculation that the changes in coloring of the areolae of lactating women may enhance the signal value of the nipples as "eye spots." What this analysis suggests is that feeding situations are certainly for feeding, but their main socializing impact may come from what the infant sees, not what he eats.

CONCLUSION

In the foregoing discussion, the concepts of ethology have been given fairly generous treatment. That is, while viewing them critically, I have tried to avoid skepticism. However, ethological theory (like any theory) has not gone unchallenged, and some of the most sacrosanct of its empirical findings have been contradicted. For example, we have seen in some detail that the process of imprinting is not solely determined by any exclusive sign stimulus. Further, the seemingly indisputable "fact" that the red of the sticklebacks belly is the sign stimulus for aggression has been revised. Muckenstrum (1969) found that red models were more likely to be attacked than grey ones, but that male stickleback fish even more avidly attack violet and yellow dummies. Do findings such as these mean, then, that the notions of sign stimulus and innate releasing mechanism are invalidated?

In an attempt to resolve such apparent discrepancies, Mayr (1974) has postulated two conceptually distinct forms of genetic programs for behavior. These are *closed* and *open* programs. In his scheme, a closed program is one that does not allow modifications during the translation of genotype to phenotype. For Mayr, closed means that experience cannot contribute to (or influence) the phenotypic expression of a genetically programmed response or reaction. In this sense, a closed program is conceptually similar to the sign stimulus, innate releasing mechanism, and fixed action pattern framework of ethology.

To the contrary, an open genetic program allows for additional input (information) during the lifespan of the organism. This additional information is acquired through experience and is integrated into the original genotype at the level of the nervous system, which itself is a phenotypic expression of that genotype. Obviously, open programs permit what is conventionally termed learning, although the advantage of retaining a distinction between learning and an open program is that the latter is not necessarily constrained by the principle of reinforcement.

The point is that both types of behavior program are innate, with the main question becoming: what conditions favor the evolution of one type of program over the other? Mayr (1974) argues that closed programs would evolve in the case of intraspecies communication since there would be a definite advantage if signals became unmistakable. For behaviors that exploit environmental resources, on the other hand, there would be an advantage if the program allowed some flexibility and an opportunity to adjust to changes or contingencies. Hence maintenance behaviors would evolve as open programs.

Mayr's (1974) scheme appears to be an advance over the much debated issue of whether any particular behavior is innate or learned, especially where the use of the word "learn" seems to divorce the behavior in question from its biological basis. In this view, *all* behavior is innate, or at least delimited by innate factors. Some of these factors are simply more plastic than others.

Ethological theory would benefit by the serious incorporation of the distinction proposed by Mayr. We might then see that some problematic findings are not so troublesome after all. For instance, if imprinting (attachment) as a distinct process was the product of an open behavior program, then this phenomenon could be viewed as no less innate in man than in the chick or duckling. We would simply recognize that there was an apparent advantage for the newborn to be initially unselective regarding loved ones, while at the same time having a disposition toward an attached state that was independent of reinforcement schedules.

Now it is not to be thought that a given species has either all open or all closed behavioral programs. In the case of the rhesus monkey, the social signalling system we have seen is probably a product of a closed system, but the matter of habitat selection most certainly is not. From a survey conducted in Northern India in 1959 and 1960, Southwick et al. (1965) reported on the various niches employed by the rhesus. Of the animals in that area, 76 percent lived in cities, town, or villages, while only 12 percent lived in forests. Canal banks and roadsides accommodated another 9 percent of the monkey population, with the remaining fraction living in temples and railroad stations. Therefore, habitat selection is probably governed by an open behavioral program for this animal.

In closing, if the points in this chapter have any merit, it would seem to follow that the continued study of phylogenetically adaptive (innate) social behavior patterns in man would certainly be a worthwhile endeavor. But an equally valuable recommendation (in my view) would be to encourage social psychologists to pursue the study of infrahuman social phenomena with increased vigor. With careful research and theorizing, the two bodies of knowledge — human and infrahuman — should come to complement and illuminate each other more and more.

However, I would not go so far as to suggest that the development of a comparative approach to an understanding of social psychology will be easy, or immediately fruitful. In the first place, the vast majority of social psychologists seem to have little interest in anything but people. An index of this indifference to other species is found in a simple count of the papers on animals in certain social-psychological journals. According to a series of bibliographies prepared by Clyde Hendrick and his associates, of the 1353 papers appearing in the *Journal of Personality and Social Psychology,* the *Journal of Experimental Social Psychology,* the *Journal of Applied Social Psychology, Representative Research in Social Psychology,* and the *Journal for the Theory of Social Behavior* between 1971 and 1975, a grand total of three reported on the behavior of infrahumans. This number represents an exceedingly small proportion of total articles, and one is left with the uneasy feeling that a behavioral subdiscipline that is interested in only a single species might very well be a lopsided discipline.

In the second place, even in our time, society in general may still not be receptive to the idea that man can further his understanding of himself through the study of other animals. The possibility of this negativism was recently brought forcefully to my attention in reading *The Chicken Book,* by Page Smith and Charles Daniel (1975), an historian and a biologist, respectively. According to these gentlemen:

> The point worth noting here is that, as with rats, the study of chickens under laboratory conditions by psychologists has been, for the most part, intended to reveal patterns of behavior relevant to the understanding of human reactions, individual and social. Wherever this presumption has existed it has resulted in research of little validity. Chickens are not people; therefore experiments — such as that on the pecking order — which suggest or intimate some connection are for the most part quite meaningless. . . .
>
> Indeed, looking back on the thousands of such experiments it is hard to escape the feeling that it represents one of the greatest wastelands of modern science or social science or pseudoscience. When the history of laboratory experiments on animal behavior is written, it will be a story of almost unparalleled stupidities and horrors which have, in toto, contributed little or nothing to man's knowledge of himself as an individual or as a social creature and very little to our knowledge of the animals that have been the objects of these experiments (p. 164).

Well, we can only hope that the Smith-Daniel appraisal is largely incorrect. But perhaps we can benefit from their point of view. After all, they are definitely correct on at least one point: *Chickens are not people.* And their insight can be extremely valuable since in places there has been a tendency to *over*generalize findings across species, especially where popularization is concerned. Therefore, let me end by proposing a slogan for the comparative ethologist or the comparative social psychologist of the future. Remember: *Whereas people are sometimes chicken, chickens are never people.*

REFERENCES

Ainsworth, M. D. S. Object relations, dependency, and attachment: A theoretical review of the infant-mother relationship. *Child Development,* 1969, *40,* 969-1025.

Ainsworth, M. D. S., Bell, S. M. V., & Stayton, D. J. Individual differences in strange-situation behaviour of one-year-olds. In H. R. Schaffer (Ed.), *The origins of human social relations.* New York: Academic Press, 1971.

Altman, I., & Lett, E. E. The ecology of interpersonal relationships: A classification system and conceptual model. In J. E. McGrath (Ed.), *Social and psychological factors in stress.* New York: Holt, Rinehart, & Winston, 1969.

Argyle, M., & Dean, J. Eye contact, distance and affiliation. *Sociometry,* 1965, *28,* 289-304.

Argyle, M., & Kendon, A. The experimental analysis of social performance. In L. Berkowitz (Ed.), *Advances in experimental social psychology* (Vol. 3). New York: Academic Press, 1967.

Asch, S. *Social psychology.* Englewood Cliffs: Prentice-Hall, 1952.

Ashear, J. B. Infants' reactions to dilated and constricted pupils of an adult stranger in a naturalistic setting: A preliminary investigation. Paper presented at the meetings of the Society for Research in Child Development, Denver, April, 1975.

Baer, D. M., & Gray, P. H. Imprinting to a different species without overt following. *Perceptual and Motor Skills,* 1960, *10,* 171-174.

Bakken, C. A., & Bromley, B. L. Effects of facial expression on eliciting an avoidance response among humans. Paper presented at the Meetings of the Midwestern Psychological Association, Chicago, 1973.

Barash, D. P. Personal space reiterated. *Environment and Behavior,* 1973, *5,* 67-72.

Barrett, J. E., Hoffman, H. S., Stratton, J. W., & Newby, V. Aversive control of following in imprinted ducklings. *Learning and Motivation,* 1971, *2,* 202-213.

Bateson, P. P. G. Relation between conspicuousness of stimuli and their effectiveness in the imprinting situation. *Journal of Comparative and Physiological Psychology,* 1964, *58,* 407-411.

Bell, S. M. V., & Ainsworth, M. D. S. Infant crying and maternal responsivess. *Child Development,* 1972, *43,* 1171-1190.

Bem, D. *Beliefs, attitudes, and human affairs.* Belmont: Brooks/Cole, 1970.

Bernstein, I. S. Role of the dominant male rhesus monkey in response to external challenges to the group. *Journal of Comparative and Physiological Psychology,* 1964, *57,* 404-406.

Birdwhistell, R. L. The kinesis level in the investigation of the emotions. In P. H. Knapp (Ed.), *Expressions of the emotions in man.* New York: International University Press, 1963.

Blair, W. F., Blair, A. P., Brodkorb, P., Cagle, F. R., & Moore, G. A. *Vertebrates of the United States.* New York: McGraw-Hill, 1968.

Blurton-Jones, N. (Ed.). *Ethological studies of child behaviour.* London: Cambridge University Press, 1972.

Bowlby, J. Grief and mourning in early infancy and early childhood. *Psychoanalytic Study of the Child*, 1960, *15*, 9-32.

Bowlby, J. *Attachment and loss* (Vol. 1). New York: Basic Books, 1969.

Brackbill, Y., Adams, G., Crowell, D. H., & Gray, M. L. Arousal level in neonates and pre-school children under continuous auditory stimulation. *Journal of Experimental Child Psychology*, 1966, *4*, 178-188.

Brodbeck, A. J. An exploratory study on the acquisition of dependency behavior in puppies. *Bulletin of the Ecological Society of America*, 1954, *35*, 73.

Bruner, J. S., & Taguiri, R. The perception of people. In G. Lindzey (Ed.), *Handbook of social psychology* (Vol. 2). Cambridge: Addison-Wesley, 1954.

Cairns, R. B. Development, maintenance, and extinction of social attachment behavior in sheep. *Journal of Comparative and Physiological Psychology*, 1966, *62*, 298-306.

Caldwell, B. M. The usefulness of the critical period hypothesis in the study of filiative behavior. *Merrill-Palmer Quarterly*, 1962, *8*, 229-242.

Carmichael, L. A further experimental study of the development of behavior. *Psychological Review*, 1928, *35*, 253-260.

Carpenter, C. R. Sexual behavior of free ranging rhesus monkeys. *Journal of Comparative Psychology*, 1942, *33*, 113-142.

Carpenter, C. R. Territoriality. In A. Roe & G. G. Simpson (Eds.), *Behavior and evolution*. New Haven: Yale University Press, 1958.

Carpenter, G. C., & Stechler, G. Selective attention to the mother's face from week one through week eight. *Proceedings of the 75th Annual Convention of the American Psychological Association*, 1967, *75*, 153-154.

Carr, A. *Handbook of turtles.* Ithaca: Cornell University Press, 1952.

Chivers, D. J. On the daily behaviour and spacing of howling monkey groups. *Folia Primatologica*, 1969, *10*, 48-102.

Christian, J. J. Social subordination, population density, and mammalian evolution. *Science*, 1970, *168*, 84-90.

Cofoid, D. A., & Honig, W. K. Stimulus generalization of imprinting. *Science*, 1961, *134*, 1692-1694.

Collias, N. E., & Collias, E. C. Some mechanisms of family integration in ducks. *Auk*, 1956, *73*, 378-400.

Collias, N. E., & Joos, M. The spectrographic analysis of sound signals of the domestic fowl. *Behaviour*, 1953, *5*, 175-187.

Craighead, J., & Craighead, F. Bright dyes reveal secrets of Canada geese. *National Geographic Magazine*, 1957, *113*, 817-832.

Crook, J. H. (Ed.). *Social behaviour in birds and mammals*. New York: Academic Press, 1970.

Dabbs, J. M. Jr., & Clower, B. J. An ultrasonic motion detector, with data on stare, restriction of movement, and startle. *Behavior Research Methods and Instrumentation*, 1973 *5*, 475-476.

Dabbs, J. M., Jr., Fuller, J. P. H., & Carr, T. S. Personal space when "cornered:" College students and prison inmates. *Proceedings of the 81st Annual Convention of the American Psychological Association*, 1973, *81*, 213-214.

Dabbs, J. M., Jr., & Johns, C. J. On being crowded with a man or a woman. (Under review.)

Dollard, J., & Miller, N. E. *Personality and psychotherapy*. New York: McGraw-Hill, 1950.

Drees, O. Untersuchungen uber die angeborenen verhaltensweisen bie springspinnen *(Salticidae). Zeitschrift fur Tierpsychologie*, 1952, *9*, 169-207.

Driver, P. M. Field studies on the behaviour of sea-ducklings. *Arctic*, 1960, *13*, 201-204.

Duke, M. P. Johnson, K., & Nowicki, S., Jr. Differential effects of authority role cues on interpersonal distancing as mediated by locus of control. Unpublished manuscript, Emory University, 1972.

Duke, M. P., & Nowicki, S., Jr. A new measure and social-learning model for interpersonal distance. *Journal of Experimental Research in Personality*, 1972, *6*, 119-132.

Edney, J. J. Human territoriality. *Psychological Bulletin*, 1974, *81*, 959-975.

Eibl-Eibesfeldt, I. The fighting behavior of animals. *Scientific American*, 1961, *205*, 112-222.

Eibl-Eibesfeldt, I. Concepts of ethology and their significance for the study of human behavior. In H. W. Stevenson, E. H. Hess, & H. L. Rheingold (Eds.), *Early behavior*. New York: Wiley, 1967.

Eibl-Eibesfeldt, I. *Ethology: The biology of behaviour*. New York: Holt, Rinehart, & Winston, 1970.

Eibl-Eibesfeldt, I. The expressive behaviour of the deaf- and blind-born. In M. von Cranach & I. Vine (Eds.), *Social communication and movement*. New York: Academic Press, 1973.

Einsiedel, A. A., Jr. The development and modification of object preferences in domestic white leghorn chicks. *Developmental Psychobiology*, 1975, *8*, 533-540.

Eiserer, L. A., & Hoffman, H. S. Imprinting of ducklings to second stimulus when a previously imprinted stimulus is occasionally presented. *Animal Learning Behavior*, 1974, *2*, 123-125.

Ekman, P. (Ed.) *Darwin and facial expression: A century of research in review*. New York: Academic Press, 1973.

Ekman, P., & Friesen, W. V. Constants across cultures in the face of emotion. *Journal of Personality and Social Psychology*, 1971, *17*, 124-129.

Ekman, P., & Sorenson, E. R., & Friesen, W. V. Pan-cultural elements in facial displays of emotion. *Science*, 1969, 86-88.

Elliot, O., & King, J. A. Effects of early food deprivation upon later consummatory behavior in puppies. *Psychological Reports*, 1960, *6*, 391-400.

Ellsworth, P. C., & Carlsmith, J. M. Effects of eye contact and verbal content on affective response to a dyadic interaction. *Journal of Personality and Social Psychology*, 1968, *10*, 15-20.

Ellsworth, P. C., & Carlsmith, J. M. Eye contact and gaze aversion in an aggressive encounter. *Journal of Personality and Social Psychology*, 1973, *28*, 280-292.

Ellsworth, P. C., & Carlsmith, J. M., & Henson, A. The stare as a stimulus to flight in human subjects: A series of field experiments. *Journal of Personality and Social Psychology*, 1972, *21*, 302-311.

Fabricius, E. Zur ethologie junger anatiden. *Acta Zoologica Fennica*, 1951, *68*, 1-178.

Fabricius, E. Experiments on the following response of mallard ducklings. *British Journal of Animal Behaviour*, 1955, *3*, 122.

Fabricius, E., & Boyd, H. Experiments on the following reactions of ducklings. *Wildfowl Trust Annual Report, 1952-53*, 1954, *6*, 84-89.

Fantz, R. L. Form preferences in newly hatched chicks. *Journal of Comparative and Physiological Psychology*, 1957, *50*, 422-430.

Fantz, R. L. The origin of form perception. *Scientific American*, 1961, *204*, 66-72.

Fantz, R. L. Pattern vision in newborn infants. *Science*, 1963, *140*, 296-297.

Fantz, R. L. Pattern discrimination and selective attention as determinants of perceptual development from birth. In A. J. Kidd & J. L. Rivoire (Eds.), *Perceptual development in children*. New York: International University Press, 1965.

Fantz, R. L., Ordy, J. M., & Udelf, M. S. Maturation of pattern vision in infants during the first six months. *Journal of Comparative and Physiological Psychology*, 1962, *55*, 907-917.

Felipe, N. J., & Sommer, R. Invasions of personal space. *Social Problems*, 1966, *14*, 206-214.

Finger, S. Child-holding patterns in Western art. *Child Development*, 1975, *46*, 267-271.

Fischer, G. J. Auditory stimuli in imprinting. *Journal of Comparative and Physiological Psychology*, 1966, *61*, 271-273.

Fischer, G. J. Chick *(Gallus domesticus)* approach preferences for natural and artificial sound stimuli. *Developmental Psychology*, 1976, *12*, 39-46.

Fisher, A. E. The effects of differential early treatment on the social and exploratory behavior of puppies. Doctoral dissertation, Pennsylvania State University, 1955.

Fisher, J. D., & Byrne, D. Too close for comfort: Sex differences in response to invasions of personal space. *Journal of Personality and Social Psychology*, 1975, *32*, 15-21.

Fitzgerald, H. E. Autonomic pupillary activity during early infancy and its relation to social and nonsocial visual stimuli. *Journal of Experimental Child Psychology*, 1968, *6*, 470-482.

Fox, M. W. The anatomy of aggression and its ritualization in Canidae: A developmental and comparative study. *Behaviour*, 1969, *35*, 242-258.

Freedman, D. G. Hereditary control of early social behavior. In B. M. Foss (Ed.), *Determinants of infant behaviour* (Vol. 3). New York: Wiley, 1966.

Freedman, J. L. *Crowding and behavior*. San Francisco: W. H. Freeman, 1975.

Freedman, J. L., Levy, A. S., Buchanan, R. W., & Price, J. Crowding and human aggressiveness. *Journal of Experimental Social Psychology*, 1972, *8*, 528-548.

Freud, A. The psychoanalytic study of infantile feeding disturbances. *Psychoanalytic Study of the Child*, 1946, *2*, 119-132.

Fullard, W., & Reiling, A. M. An investigation of Lorenz's "babyness." *Child Development*, 1976, *47*, 1191-1193.

Goffman, I. *Behavior in public places*. New York: Free Press, 1963.

Gottlieb, G. Following-response initiation in ducklings: Age and sensory stimulation. *Science*, 1963, *140*, 399-400.

Gottlieb, G. Prenatal behavior of birds. *Quarterly Review of Biology*, 1968, *43*, 148-174.

Gottlieb, G. *Development of species identification in birds*. Chicago: University of Chicago Press, 1971.

Gottlieb, G., & Simner, M. L. Auditory versus visual flicker in directing the approach response of domestic chicks. *Journal of Comparative and Physiological Psychology*, 1969, *67*, 58-63.

Gray, P. H. Theory and evidence of imprinting in human infants. *Journal of Psychology*, 1958, *46*, 155-166.

Gray, P. H. Evidence that retinal flicker is not a necessary condition of imprinting. *Science*, 1960, *132*, 1834-1835.

Gray, P. H. A checklist of papers since 1951 dealing with imprinting in birds. *Psychological Record*, 1963, *13*, 445-454.

Gray, P. H., & Howard, K. I. Specific recognition of humans in imprinted chicks. *Perceptual and Motor Skills*, 1957, *7*, 301-304.

Grier, J. B., Counter, S. A., & Shearer, W. M. Prenatal auditory imprinting in chickens. *Science*, 1967, *155*, 1692-1693.

Grohmann, J. Modifikation oder funktionsreifung? *Zeitschrift fur Tierpsychologie*, 1939, *2*, 132-144.

Guhl, A. M. The social behavior of the domestic fowl. *Technical Bulletin of the Kansas Agricultural Experimental Station*, 1953, *73*, 3-48.

Guhl, A. M. The development of social organization in the domestic chick. *Animal Behaviour*, 1958, *6*, 92-111.

Guyomarc'h, J-Ch. Contribution a l'etude du comportement vocal du poussin de *Gallus domesticus. Journal de Psychologie Normale et Pathologique,* 1962, *3,* 283-306.

Hailman, J. P. *The ontogeny of an instinct.* Leiden: Brill, 1967.

Hall, E. T. *The hidden dimension.* Garden City: Doubleday, 1966.

Hall, K. R. L. Aggression in monkey and ape societies. In J. D. Carthy & F. J. Ebling (Eds.), *The natural history of aggression.* New York: Academic Press, 1964.

Harlow, H. F. *Learning to love.* San Francisco: Albion, 1971.

Harlow, H. F. Induction and alleviation of depressive states in monkeys. In N. F. White (Ed.), *Ethology and psychiatry.* Toronto: University of Toronto Press, 1974.

Harlow, H. F., Gluck, J. P., & Suomi, S. Generalization of behavioral data between non-human and human animals. *American Psychologist,* 1972, *27,* 709-716.

Harlow, H. F., & Zimmerman, R. R. Affectional responses in the infant monkey. *Science,* 1959, *130,* 421-432.

Harper, I. V. Role of contact and sound in eliciting filial responses and development of social attachments in domestic guinea pigs. *Journal of Comparative and Physiological Psychology,* 1970, *73,* 427-435.

Haynes, H. M., White, B. L., Held, R. Visual accommodation in human infants. *Science,* 1965, *148,* 528-530.

Hebb, D. O. *The organization of behavior.* New York: Wiley, 1949.

Hediger, H. *Studies of the psychology and behavior of captive animals in zoos and circuses.* London: Butterworths, 1955.

Hendrick, C., Giesen, M., & Coy, S. The social ecology of free seating arrangements in a small group interaction context. *Sociometry,* 1974, *37,* 262-274.

Hess, E. H. Natural preferences of chicks and ducklings for objects of different colors. *Psychological Reports,* 1956, *2,* 477-483.

Hess, E. H. The relationship between imprinting and motivation. In M. R. Jones (Ed.), *Nebraska Symposium on Motivation.* Lincoln: University of Nebraska Press, 1959. (a)

Hess, E. H. Two conditions limiting the critical period for imprinting. *Journal of Comparative and Physiological Psychology,* 1959, *52,* 515-518. (b)

Hess, E. H. Attitude and pupil size. *Scientific American,* 1965, *212,* 46-54.

Hess, E. H. Ethology and developmental psychology. In P. H. Mussen (Ed.), *Carmichael's manual of child psychology.* New York: Wiley, 1970. (a)

Hess, E. H. The ethological approach to socialization. In R. A. Hoppe, G. A. Milton, & E. C. Simmel (Eds.), *Early experiences and the processes of socialization.* New York: Academic Press, 1970. (b)

Hess, E. H. *Imprinting.* New York: Van Nostrand, 1973.

Hess, E. H., & Schaefer, H. H. Innate behavior patterns as indicators of the "critical period." *Zeitschrift fur Tierpsychologie,* 1959, *16,* 155-160.

Hinde, R. A. The biological significance of the territories of birds. *Ibis,* 1956, *98,* 340-369.

Hinde, R. A. The nest-building behaviour of domesticated canaries. *Proceedings of the Zoological Society of London,* 1958, *131,* 1-48.

Hinde, R. A. Energy models of motivation. *Symposium of the Society for Experimental Biology,* 1960, *14,* 199-213.

Hinde, R. A. *Animal Behaviour.* New York: McGraw-Hill, 1970.

Hinde, R. A. *Biological bases of human social behaviour.* New York: McGraw-Hill, 1974.

Hinde, R. A., & Rowell, T. E. Communication by postures and facial expressions in the rhesus monkey *(Macaca mulatta). Proceedings of the Zoological Society of London,* 1962, *138,* 1-21.

Hinde, R. A., Thorpe, W. H., & Vince, M. A. The following response of young coots and moorhens. *Behaviour,* 1956, *11,* 214-242.

Hindmarch, I. Eyes, eye-spots and pupil dilation in nonverbal communication. In M. von Cranach & I. Vine (Eds.), *Social communication and movement.* New York: Academic Press, 1973.

Hoffman, H. S. The control of distress vocalizations by an imprinted stimulus. *Behaviour,* 1968, *30,* 175-191.

Hoffman, H. S., & Boskoff, K. J. Control of aggressive behavior by an imprinted stimulus. *Psychonomic Science,* 1972, *29,* 305-306.

Hoffman, H. S., & Ratner, A. M. A reinforcement model of imprinting: Implications for socialization in monkeys and men. *Psychological Review,* 1973, *80,* 527-544.

Hoffman, H. S., Ratner, A. M., & Eiserer, L. A. Role of visual imprinting in the emergence of specific filial attachments in ducklings. *Journal of Comparative and Physiological Psychology,* 1972, *81,* 399-409.

Impekoven, M. Response-contingent prenatal experience of maternal calls in the Peking duckling *(Anas platyrynchos). Animal Behaviour,* 1973, *21,* 164-168.

James, H. Flicker: An unconditioned stimulus for imprinting. *Canadian Journal of Psychology,* 1959, *13,* 59-67.

Jaynes, J. Imprinting: The interaction of learned and innate behavior. *Journal of Comparative and Physiological Psychology,* 1956, *49,* 201-206.

Jaynes, J. The historical origins of "ethology" and "comparative psychology." *Animal Behaviour,* 1969, *17,* 601-606.

Johnson, R. N. *Aggression in man and animal.* Philadelphia: Saunders, 1972.

Jolly, A. *The evolution of primate behavior.* New York: MacMillan, 1972.

Jones, E. E., & Gerard, H. B. *Foundations of social psychology.* New York: Wiley, 1967.

Kagan, J., Henker, B., Hen-Tov, A., Levine, J., & Lewis, M. Infants' differential reactions to familiar and distorted faces. *Child Development,* 1966, *37,* 519-532.

Kagan, J., & Lewis, M. Studies of attention in the human infant. *Merrill-Palmer Quarterly,* 1965, *11,* 95-127.

Kaufman, I. C., & Rosenblum, L. A. Depression in infant monkeys separated from their mothers. *Science,* 1967, *155,* 1030-1031.

Kaufmann, J. H. Social relations of adult males in a free-ranging band of rhesus monkeys. In S. A. Altmann (Ed.), *Social communication among primates.* Chicago: University of Chicago Press, 1967.

Klopfer, P. H. Parameters of imprinting. *American Naturalist,* 1964, *98,* 173-182.

Kovach, J. K., & Hess, E. H. Imprinting: Effects of painful stimulation on the following response. *Journal of Comparative and Physiological Psychology,* 1963, *56,* 461-464.

Kruuk, H. *The spotted hyena.* Chicago: University of Chicago Press, 1972.

Kummer, H. Spacing mechanisms in social behavior. In J. F. Eisenberg & W. S. Dillon (Eds.), *Man and beast: Comparative social behavior.* Washington: Smithsonian Institution Press, 1971.

Kummer, H. Distribution of interindividual distances in patas monkeys and gelada baboons. *Folia Primatologica,* 1974, *21,* 153-160.

Lack, D. *The life of the robin.* London: Cambridge University Press, 1943.

Lehrman, D. S. A critique of Konrad Lorenz's theory of instinctive behavior. *Quarterly Review of Biology,* 1953, *28,* 337-363.

Leibman, M. The effects of sex and race norms on personal space. *Environment and Behavior,* 1970, *2,* 208-246.

Leopold, F. A study of nesting wood ducks in Iowa. *Condor,* 1951, *53,* 209-220.

Lett, E. E., Clark, W., & Altman, I. A propositional inventory of research on interpersonal distance. Research Report No. 1. Naval Medical Research Institute, Bethesda, Maryland, 1969.

Lettvin, J. Y., Maturana, H. R., McCullock, W. S., & Pitts, W. H. What the frog's eye tells the frog's brain. *Proceedings of the IRE,* 1959, *47,* 1940-1951.

Lewis, M. Infants' responses to facial stimuli during the first year of life. *Developmental Psychology,* 1969, *1,* 75-86.

Lindsay, P. H., & Norman, D. A. *Human information processing.* New York: Academic Press, 1972.

Lorenz, K. Z. Der kumpan in der umwelt des vogels. *Journal fuer Ornithologie*, 1935, *83*, 137-413.

Lorenz, K. Z. The companion in the bird's world. *Auk*, 1937, *54*, 245-273.

Lorenz, K. Z. Die angeborenen formen moglicher erfahrung. *Zeitschrift fur Tierpsychologie*, 1943, *5*, 235-409.

Lorenz, K. Z. The comparative method in studying innate behavior patterns. *Symposia of the Society for Experimental Biology*, 1950, 14, 199-213

Lorenz, K. Z. The evolution of behavior. *Scientific American*, 1958, *199*, 67-78.

Lorenz, K. Z. *Evolution and modification of behavior.* Chicago: University of Chicago Press, 1965.

Lorenz, K. Z. *On aggression.* London: Methuen, 1966.

Lott, D. F., & Sommer, R. Seating arrangements and status. *Journal of Personality and Social Psychology*, 1967, *7*, 90-95.

Macdonald, G. E. Imprinting: Drug-produced isolation and the sensitive period. *Nature*, 1968, *317*, 1158-1159.

Marler, P. Studies of fighting in chaffinches (3): Proximity as a cause of aggression. *British Journal of Animal Behaviour*, 1956, *4*, 23-30.

Marshall, J. E., & Heslin, R. Boys and girls together: Sexual composition and the effect of density and group size on cohesiveness. *Journal of Personality and Social Psychology*, 1975, *31*, 952-961.

Mason, W. A. Differential grouping patterns in two species of South American monkey. In N. F. White (Ed.), *Ethology and psychiatry.* Toronto: University of Toronto Press, 1974.

Mason, W. A., & Epple, G. Social organization in experimental groups of *Samiri* and *Callicebus*. In C. R. Carpenter (Ed.), *Proceedings of the Second International Congress of Primatology* (Vol. 1). Basil: Krager, 1969.

Mason, W. A., & Kenney, M. D. Redirection of filial attachments in rhesus monkeys: Dogs as mother surrogates. *Science*, 1974, *183*, 1209-1211.

Matthews, I. H. Overt fighting in mammals. In J. D. Carthy & F. J. Ebling (Eds.), *The natural history of aggression.* New York: Academic Press, 1964.

Mayr, E. Behavior programs and evolutionary strategies. *Scientific American*, 1974, *62*, 650-659.

McBride, G., James, J. W., & Schaffner, R. N. Social forces determining spacing and head orientation in a flock of domestic hens. *Nature*, 1963, *197*, 1272-1273.

McCall, R. B., & Kagan, J. Attention in infants: Effects of complexity, contour, perimeter, and familiarity. *Child Development*, 1967, *38*, 939-952.

McGrew, W. C. *An ethological study of children's behavior.* New York: Academic Press, 1972.

Mehrabian, A. Relationship of attitude to seated posture, orientation, and distance. *Journal of Personality and Social Psychology*, 1968, *10*, 26-30.

Melvin, K. B., Cloar, F. T., & Massingill, L. S. Imprinting of bobwhite quail to a hawk. *Psychological Record*, 1967, *17*, 235-238.

Moltz, H. Imprinting: Empirical basis and theoretical significance. *Psychological Bulletin*, 1960, *57*, 291-314.

Moltz, H. Imprinting: An epigenetic approach. *Psychological Review*, 1963, 70, 123-128.

Moltz, H., & Stettner, L. J. The influence of patterned-light deprivation on the critical period for imprinting. *Journal of Comparative and Physiological Psychology*, 1961, *54*, 279-283.

Mortenson, F. J. *Animal behavior: Theory and research.* Monterey: Brooks/Cole, 1975.

Moss, H. A., & Robson, K. S. Maternal influences in early social visual behavior. *Child Development*, 1968, *39*, 401-408.

Muckenstrum, B. La signification de la livree nuptiale de l'epinoche. *Revue du Comportement Animal*, 1969, *3*, 39-64.

Nice, M. M. Development of behavior in precocial birds. *Transactions of the Linnaean Society*, 1962, *8*, 1-211.

Orne, M. T. On the social psychology of the psychological experiment: With particular reference to demand characteristics and their implications. *American Psychologist,* 1962, *17,* 776-783.

Parke, R. D. (Ed.). *Readings in social development.* New York: Holt, Rinehart, & Winston, 1969.

Patterson, M. Spatial factors in social interactions. *Human Relations,* 1968, *21,* 351-361.

Pitz, G. F., & Ross, R. B. Imprinting as a function of arousal. *Journal of Comparative and Physiological Psychology,* 1961, *54,* 602-604.

Pola, Y. V., & Snowdon, C. T. The vocalizations of pygmy marmosets *(Cebuella pygmaea).* *Animal Behaviour,* 1975, *23,* 826-842.

Rajecki, D. W. Imprinting in precocial birds: Interpretation, evidence, and evaluation. *Psychological Bulletin,* 1973, *79,* 48-58.

Rajecki, D. W. Effects of prenatal exposure to auditory or visual stimulation on postnatal distress vocalizations in chicks. *Behavioral Biology,* 1974, *11,* 525-536.

Rajecki, D. W., & Eichenbaum, H. Distress and contentment calls of the Peking duckling *(Anas platyrynchos):* Duration and intensity. *Perceptual and Motor Skills,* 1973, *37,* 547-551.

Rajecki, D. W., Eichenbaum, H., & Heilweil, M. Rates of distress vocalizations in naive domestic chicks as an index of approach tendency to an imprinting stimulus. *Behavioral Biology,* 1973, *9,* 595-603.

Rajecki, D. W., & Hayse, B. Recognition of the facial expressions of a deaf-blind child, in preparation.

Rajecki, D. W., Ivins, B., & Rein, B. Social discrimination and aggressive pecking in domestic chicks. *Journal of Comparative and Physiological Psychology,* 1976, *90,* 442-452.

Rajecki, D. W., & Saegert, S. Effects of methamphetamine hydrochloride on imprinting in white leghorn chicks. *Psychonomic Science,* 1971, *23,* 7-8.

Rajecki, D. W., Suomi, S. J., Scott, E. A., & Campbell, B. Effects of social isolation and social separation on domestic chicks. *Developmental Psychology,* 1977, *13,* 143-155.

Reese, E. P., Schotte, C. S., Bechtold, R. E., & Crowley, V. L. Initial preferences of chicks from five rearing conditions for a hen or a rotating light. *Journal of Comparative and Physiological Psychology,* 1972, *81,* 76-83.

Richards, J. L., & Finger, S. Mother-child holding patterns: A cross-cultural photographic survey. *Child Development,* 1975, *46,* 1001-1004.

Riesen, A. H. Sensory deprivation. In E. Stellar & J. M. Sprague (Eds.), *Progress in physiological psychology.* New York: Academic Press, 1966.

Robson, K. S. The role of eye-to-eye contact in maternal-infant attachment. *Journal of Child Psychology and Psychiatry,* 1967, *8,* 13-26.

Ross, M., Layton, B., Erickson, B., & Schopler, J. Affect, facial regard, and reactions to crowding. *Journal of Personality and Social Psychology,* 1973, *28,* 69-76.

Rowell, T. *Social behaviour of monkeys.* Baltimore: Penguin Books, 1972.

Rubin, Z. Measurement of romantic love. *Journal of Personality and Social Psychology,* 1970, *16,* 265-273.

Sackett, G. P. Monkeys reared in isolation with pictures as visual input: Evidence for an innate releasing mechanism. *Science,* 1966, *154,* 1468-1473.

Sade, D. S. Determinants of dominance in a group of free-ranging rhesus monkeys. In S. Altmann (Ed.), *Social communication among primates.* Chicago: University of Chicago Press, 1967.

Saegert, S., & Rajecki, D. W. Effects of prior exposure to animate objects on approach tendency in chicks. *Behavioral Biology,* 1973, *8,* 749-754.

Salk, L. The role of heartbeat in the relations between mother and infant. *Scientific American,* 1973, *228,* 401-408.

Salzen, E. A. Imprinting and environmental learning. In L. R. Aronson, E. Tobach, D. S. Lehrman, & J. S. Rosenblatt (Eds.), *Development and evolution of behavior.* San Francisco: Freeman, 1970.

Salzen, E. A., & Meyer, C. C. Imprinting: Reversal of a preference established during the critical period. *Nature,* 1967, *215,* 785-786.

Salzen, E. A., & Meyer, C. C. Reversibility of imprinting. *Journal of Comparative and Physiological Psychology,* 1968, *66,* 269-275.

Salzen, E. A., & Sluckin, W. The incidence of the following response and the duration of responsiveness in domestic fowl. *Animal Behaviour,* 1959, *7,* 172-179.

Schaffer, H. R., & Emerson, P. E. The development of social attachments in infancy. *Monographs of the Society for Research in Child Development,* 1964, *34,* Serial 94.

Schenkel, R. Zur deutung der phasianidenblaz. *Ornithologische Beobachter,* 1956, *53,* 182.

Schenkel, R. Zur deutung der blazleistungen einiger phasianiden und tetraoniden. *Ornithologische Beobachter,* 1958, *55,* 65-95.

Schenken, L. I. An application of ethology to aspects of human behaviour. *British Journal of Medical Psychology,* 1973, *46,* 123-134.

Scherwitz, L., & Helmreich, R. L. Interactive effects of eye contact and verbal content on interpersonal attraction in dyads. *Journal of Personality and Social Psychology,* 1973, *25,* 6-14.

Schjelderup-Ebbe, T. Social behavior of birds. In C. Murchison (Ed.), *A handbook of social psychology.* Worcester: Clark University Press, 1935.

Schnierla, T. C. Behavioral development and comparative psychology. *Quarterly Review of Biology,* 1966, *41,* 283-302.

Scott, J. P., & Fuller, J. L. *Dog behavior.* Chicago: University of Chicago Press, 1965.

Seay, B., Alexander, B. K., & Harlow, H. F. Maternal behavior of socially deprived rhesus monkeys. *Journal of Abnormal and Social Psychology,* 1964, *69,* 345-354.

Seay, B., Hansen, E. W. & Harlow, H. F. Mother-infant separation in monkeys. *Journal of Child Psychology and Psychiatry,* 1962, *3,* 123-132.

Simner, M. L. The cardiac self-stimulation hypothesis and nonnutritive sucking in human infants. *Developmental Psychology,* 1969, *1,* 569-575.

Sluckin, W. *Imprinting and early learning.* Chicago: Aldine, 1965.

Sluckin, W. Imprinting in guinea pigs. *Nature,* 1968, *220,* 1148.

Sluckin, W. *Early learning in man and animal.* Cambridge: Schenkman, 1972.

Sluckin, W., & Fullerton, C. Attachments of infant guinea pigs. *Psychonomic Science,* 1969, *17,* 179-180.

Smith, F. V. Towards definition of the stimulus situation for the approach response in the domestic chick. *Animal Behaviour,* 1960, *8,* 197-200.

Smith, F. V., & Hoyes, P. A. Properties of the visual stimuli for the approach response in the domestic chick. *Animal Behaviour,* 1961, *9,* 159-166.

Smith, P., & Daniel, C. *The chicken book.* Boston: Little, Brown, 1975.

Smith, S., & Hosking, E. *Birds fighting: Experimental studies of the aggressive displays of some birds.* London: Faber & Faber, 1955.

Snapp, B. D. Recognition of maternal calls by parentally naive *Gallus gallus* chicks. *Animal Behaviour,* 1969, *17,* 440-445.

Sokolov, E. M. Neuronal models and the orienting reflex. In A. B. Brazier (Ed.), *The central nervous system and behavior.* New York: Josiah Macy Foundation, 1960.

Sommer, R. Sociofugal space. *American Journal of Sociology,* 1967, *72,* 654-660.

Sommer, R. *Personal space: The behavioral basis of design.* Englewood Cliffs: Prentice-Hall, 1969.

Southwick, C. H. (Ed.). *Animal aggression: Selected readings.* New York: van Nostrand, 1970.

Southwick, C. H., Beg, M. A., & Siddiqi, M. R. Rhesus monkeys in North India. In I. De Vore (Ed.), *Primate behavior.* New York: Holt, Rinehart, & Winston, 1965.

Spalding, D. A. Instinct with original observation on young animals. *MacMillans Magazine,* 1873, *27,* 282-283.

Spelt, D. K. The conditioning of the human fetus *in utero. Journal of Experimental Psychology,* 1948, *38,* 338-346.

Test, F. H. Social aggressiveness in an amphibian. *Science,* 1954, *120,* 140-141.

Thomas, H. An experimental study of infant visual fixation responses. *Child Development,* 1965, *36,* 629-638.

Thorpe, W. H. *Learning and instinct in animals.* London: Methuen, 1956.

Thorpe, W. H. *Animal nature and human nature.* Garden City: Anchor Press, 1974.

Tinbergen, N. Social releasers and the experimental method required for their study. *Wilson Bulletin,* 1948, *60,* 6-51.

Tinbergen, N. *The study of instinct.* London: Oxford University Press, 1951.

Tinbergen, N. Comparative study of the behavior of gulls *(Laridae):* A progress report. *Behaviour,* 1959, *15,* 1-70.

Tinbergen, N. On the aims and methods of ethology. *Zeitschrift fur Tierpsychologie,* 1963, *20,* 410-433.

Tinbergen, N. *The herring gull's world.* New York: Doubleday, 1967.

Tomkins, C. Profiles (Paul Strand). *The New Yorker Magazine,* September 16, 1974, 44-94.

Tomkins, S. S. *Affect, imagery, consciousness* (2 vols.). New York: Springer, 1962.

Truslow, F. K. Businessman in the bush. *National Geographic Magazine,* 1970, *137,* 634-675.

van Hooff, J. A. R. A. M. The facial displays of the catarrhine monkeys and apes. In D. Morris (Ed.), *Primate ethology.* New York: Doubleday, 1969.

van Kreveld, D. A selective review of dominance-subordination relations in animals. *Genetic Psychology Monographs,* 1970, *81,* 143-173.

von Cranach, M., & Vine, I. (Eds.). *Social communication and movement.* New York: Academic Press, 1973.

von Frisch, K. *The dance language and orientation of bees.* Cambridge: Harvard University Press, 1967.

Waldrop, M. K. Responses of human-reared monkeys to strange simian calls. *Developmental Psychobiology,* 1975, *8,* 269-273.

Wallbank, T. W., & Taylor, A. M. *Civilization past and present.* Chicago: Scott, Foresman, 1960.

Walters, R. H., & Parke, R. D. The role of distance receptors in the development of social responsiveness. In L. P. Lipsitt & C. C. Spiker (Eds.), *Advances in child development and behavior* (Vol. 2). New York: Academic Press, 1965.

Webb, E. J., Campbell, D. T., Schwartz, R. D., & Sechrest, L. *Unobtrusive measures: Nonreactive research in the social sciences.* Chicago: Rand McNally, 1966.

Weiland, I. H. Heartbeat rhythm and maternal behavior. *Journal of the American Academy of Child Psychiatry,* 1964, *3,* 161-164.

White, N. F. (Ed.). *Ethology and psychiatry.* Toronto: University of Toronto Press, 1974.

Wickler, W. Sociosexual signals and their intraspecific imitation among primates. In D. Morris (Ed.), *Primate ethology.* New York: Doubleday, 1969.

Wilson, E. O. Animal communication. *Scientific American,* 1972, *227,* 53-60.

Wilson, E. O. *Sociobiology: The new synthesis.* Cambridge: Belknap Press, 1975.

Wilson, W. R., & Rajecki, D. W. Effects of the presence of familiar objects on the tendency of domestic chicks to peck in a novel situation. *Revue du Comportement Animal,* 1974, *8,* 95-102.

Wolff, P. H. Observations on the early development of smiling. In B. M. Foss (Ed.), *Determinants of infant behavior* (Vol. 2). New York: Wiley, 1963.

Wynne-Edwards, V. C. *Animal dispersion in relation to social behavior.* New York: Hafner, 1962.

Yarrow, L. J. Separation from parents during early childhood. In M. L. Hoffman & L. W. Hoffman (Eds.), *Review of child development research* (Vol. 1). New York: Russell Sage Foundation, 1964.

Zajonc, R. B. Social facilitation. *Science,* 1965, *149,* 269-274.

5

Mathematical Models in Social Psychology

S. S. Komorita

University of Illinois, Urbana-Champaign

INTRODUCTION

The purpose of this chapter, unlike earlier reviews of mathematical models in social psychology, is to present a brief perspective on mathematical applications. Hence, it is addressed primarily to students who have had little exposure to mathematical models. In accordance with this intent, the mathematical applications in this chapter have been selected so that they can be readily understood without any knowledge of mathematics beyond elementary algebra and probability theory.

During the past twenty years, theory and research in social psychology involving mathematical applications have increased by leaps and bounds. Hence, no attempt will be made in this chapter to survey and describe all of these diverse types of applications. This would be an impossible task. Since there are several earlier reviews of mathematical models in social psychology, only a representative sample of models will be presented, and particular emphasis will be placed on recent developments appearing in the literature since the latest review by Rosenberg (1968). For a more extensive survey of mathematical models of social behavior, the interested reader is referred to earlier reviews by Abelson (1967); Berger, Cohen, Snell, and Zelditch (1962); Rapoport (1963), as well as the review by Rosenberg. In addition to the above reviews, there is an important collection of papers involving mathematical methods in small groups edited by Criswell, Solomon, and Suppes (1962).[1]

The development of mathematical models in social psychology can be traced directly to similar developments in psychology, sociology, and economics. With

[1]The mathematically sophisticated reader is also referred to the three-volume *Handbook of Mathematical Psychology*, edited by Luce, Bush and Galanter (1963), and *Introduction to Mathematical Sociology* by Coleman (1964a).

the increasing use of mathematics in psychology and sociology, social psychologists were strongly influenced by developments in the two disciplines and soon became aware of the advantages of mathematics — not only as a vehicle for communicating complex ideas — but as a tool for organizing and integrating a large body of data. Correspondingly, all three of these disciplines were influenced by mathematical applications in economics. Of the social science disciplines, the use of mathematics is far more advanced in the field of economics and can be traced to the classic treatise on utility by Bernoulli which was written in 1738 and translated by L. Sommer in 1954. However, mathematical developments in economics did not have much of an impact on psychology and sociology until the publication of von Neumann and Morgenstern's "Theory of Games and Economic Behavior" (1947). This book had a tremendous impact, not only in economics and mathematics, but in all of the social sciences. As might be expected, these inter-disciplinary influences led to many cross-disciplinary collaborations, for example, Hays and Bush (1954); Cartwright and Harary (1956); Suppes and Atkinson (1960); Siegel and Fouraker (1960); and Simon and Newell (1964).

In organizing the various mathematical applications in social psychology, there are several possible organizational schemes which might be used. In reviewing the history of mathematical psychology, George Miller states that, "Mathematical psychology is more an attitude than a topic" (1964, p. 1). Based on Miller's idea and in contrast to previous reviews of mathematical models, which have been organized around substantive topics (for example, attitude change, impression formation, conformity, etc.), we will attempt to illustrate different types of mathematical applications as a function of the state of knowledge in the area.

It is not mere coincidence that in a given scientific discipline, as the state of knowledge increases, the use of mathematics to represent the phenomena in the discipline also increases. With an increasing body of knowledge, theory and principles in the discipline become increasingly complex. Hence, one of the main reasons for the correspondence between mathematical applications and progress in a science is that concepts, principles, and theoretical assumptions can be made more precise. More importantly, the use of mathematics enables unambiguous predictions derived from the assumptions of a given theory and facilitates comparative tests of two or more competing theories.

The Nature and Role of Mathematics and Mathematical Models

In the social sciences (and in other sciences), when mathematical notation is used to represent empirical phenomena, we speak of "formalizing" the phenomena in question. Formalization, in this context, refers to the process of translating a set of verbal statements into a formal (symbolic, mathematical) language. In the early stages of theoretical development, one of the main purposes of formalization is simply to define, clarify, or quantify the basic concepts and variables in the area. Hence, the verbal statements may contain few, if any, assumptions from which to derive predictions about the empirical phenomena. We will refer to such applications as quasi-theoretical models.

In contrast to quasi-theoretical models, in the later stages of theoretical development, the set of verbal statements will typically include a systematic set of assumptions from which another set of statements (theorems) can be logically deduced. In this case, we will refer to each of the three classes of statements — definitions, assumptions, and logical derivations — as a mathematical model of the phenomena. This is consistent with the definition proposed by Neimark and Estes (1967): "A mathematical model is a set of assumptions together with implications drawn from them by mathematical reasoning" (1967, p. v).

In many instances, the proposed distinction between mathematical models and quasi-theoretical models (of some empirical phenomena) becomes blurred. To provide a more precise basis for distinguishing between the two classes of models, we will borrow Miller's (1964) criteria for distinguishing between "discursive applications" and mathematical models. According to Miller, discursive applications of mathematics are deficient in two ways:

1. The functional form of the relationship between the response measure (dependent variable) and the antecedent (stimulus) conditions are not specified.
2. No methods or units are specified for measuring the relevant variables.

Discursive applications simply use mathematical notation as a convenient extension of natural language, and Miller cites Lewin's *Principles of Topological Psychology* (1936) as one example of a discursive application of mathematics. Such applications,

> ... though they hold no mathematical interest, they often contain hints and anticipations that later psychologists can pick up and develop rigorously. ... Lewin's work *suggested,* but did not create, a kind of structural mathematics that is currently developing in the study of social groups. Between the suggestion and the actual accomplishment, however, the gap is larger than many people have been willing to admit (p. 31).

This distinction between quasi-theoretical models and mathematical models is consistent with Rapoport's (1963) distinction between "descriptive" and "predictive" models. In describing Harary and Norman's (1953) graph theory as a mathematical model in social science, Rapoport states that their model is a descriptive model, in that behavioral predictions are not derived. To be classified as a predictive model, the model must include a set of assumptions — apart from the formal properties of linear graphs — from which experimental hypotheses may be derived, so that the model may be "empirically falsifiable."

The label quasi-theoretical model is used here to include Miller's description of discursive applications and Rapoport's distinction between descriptive and predictive models; it also includes attempts to derive quantitative indices, or a classification scheme, to organize a set of independent (or dependent) variables. In the latter case, no attempt is made to formalize the relations between antecedent conditions and their consequences, but to formalize the relations within each set of variables. Indices of sociometric choice (Festinger, 1949; Luce, 1950), of large social structures (Rapoport, 1963), or measures of balance and the degree of balance (Cartwright & Harary, 1956) would fall in this category. The distinction proposed here is comparable to "explication models" proposed by Berger et al. (1962), in which they cite Cartwright and Harary's formalization of Heider's theory as an example. According to Berger et al., the main purpose of an explication model is to explicate, or render a precise meaning to some of the basic concepts of a theory.

This is not to imply that quasi-theoretical models are less important than mathematical models of the empirical phenomena. Frequently, the development of a mathematical model depends on the prior development of a quasi-theoretical model. Advances in the development of models — and in the development of theories in general — progress through a series of stages, and frequently, a theoretical breakthrough is made possible by the formulation of a quasi-theoretical model. Coleman (1960), for example, argues that most research in the area of small group behavior is still in the "variable-searching" stage. By this he means that the aim of most studies is to search for variables related to a given dependent variable, and are thus directed toward demonstrating that a relationship exists. Such efforts, according to Coleman, may be characterized as a "premathematical stage" in research in which the theorist attempts to search and identify the best concepts to represent the phenomena.

The Process of Modeling

At this point, it is important to distinguish between a mathematical system (or theory) and a mathematical model of some aspect of the real world (empirical phenomena). A mathematical system is an abstract system with no reference to objects in the real world, and it consists of a set of statements (definitions and axioms) and the logically derived consequences of these statements (theorems). Obviously, there are many types of mathematical systems: algebraic, geometric, probabilistic, etc. A mathematical model (of some empirical phenomena), on the other hand, is the application of a mathematical system to represent some aspect of the real world. Hence, many types of mathematical systems might be used as a model to represent the same aspect of the real world. One example of this is Cartwright and Harary's application of graph theory (1956) as a model of Heider's balance theory (1946, 1958) and Abelson and Rosenberg's "symbolic psychologic" (1958) to represent the same conceptual processes.

To illustrate this process of modeling, consider Figure 5.1. According to Coombs, Dawes and Tversky, (1970), the process of selecting a mathematical

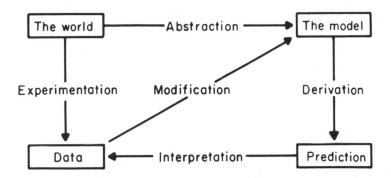

FIG. 5.1 Schematic illustration of a scientific investigation (from Coombs, Dawes, and Tversky, *Mathematical Psychology: An Elementary Introduction*, p. 3. ©1970. Reprinted by permission of Prentice-Hall, Inc., Englewood Cliffs, N.J.).

system to represent some aspect of the world is called abstraction. Abstraction is a critical phase of the entire process of modeling, and involves an assumption that a set of objects (and relations between the objects) in the world correspond to, or can be represented by, a set of objects and relations in the mathematical system. The process of abstraction is typically preceded by certain empirical relations between a set of independent and dependent variables, and the initial step in the process consists of formulating a set of assumptions from which the empirical findings can be derived (explained). This is, of course, an inductive process, and is identical to the process of theory construction. In the case of mathematical modeling, however, formal language is used to take advantage of the rules of deductive logic.

The exact specification of the correspondence between the objects and relations in the two systems, as the term implies, is sometimes called correspondence rules. The specification of correspondence rules in the process of abstraction (Fig. 5.1) can also be interpreted in terms of isomorphism between the objects in the world and objects in the mathematical system. According to Brodbeck (1959), *isomorphism* refers to the similarity between a thing and a model of it and requires a one-to-one correspondence between the elements of the model and the elements of the thing of which it is a model, and that certain relations between the elements are preserved.

Once the correspondence rules of the abstraction process are specified, all of the rules of logic in the mathematical system are also assumed to hold for the objects and relations in the real world. The consequences logically derived from these rules then constitute the predictions of the model. This is shown in Figure 5.1 as Derivation and Prediction. The predictions of the model are then compared with data collected through experimentation (Interpretation and Experimentation in Fig. 5.1). To the extent that the predictions correspond to the results of experimentation, the validity of the model is supported. If there are significant discrepancies between predictions and observed data, the model is typically modified by deleting or adding one or more assumptions, extending or limiting the boundary conditions (generality) of the model, or both. In some cases, of course, the discrepancies may be so serious that the model is abandoned altogether. Thus, the validity of a mathematical system is determined only on the basis of internal, logical criteria, while the validity of a mathematical model must meet external, empirical criteria as well (Coombs, Raiffa, and Thrall, 1954).

Figure 5.1 is obviously an oversimplification of the entire process of modeling and testing a model. Coombs, et al. (1970) state that the schematic illustration (Fig. 5.1) ". . . does not purport to describe the actual modeling process. Rather, it attempts to summarize, in schematic fashion, some of the relations among the various phases of this process. . . . The stages of research are typically interdependent and the directions of the arrows are often reversed" (p. 3). In addition, Coombs et al. also point out that, though a model can be rejected on the basis of data, the validity of a model cannot be proved: "If a model (M) implies certain characteristics (C) of the data, then the absence of these characteristics (not-C) is sufficient to reject the model, but the presence of these characteristics does give the model some inductive support" (p. 3). The main point here is that there may be other models, equally valid, which may predict the same results.

Functions of Formalization

The process of modeling depicted in Figure 5.1 illustrates one of the main advantages of formalizing a theory: it enables precise theoretical deductions from the assumptions of the theory and provides a more sensitive and unambiguous test of the theory. If something is wrong with one or more assumptions of the theory, we are more likely to detect it. Moreover, if there are serious discrepancies between predicted and observed results, it is much easier to identify the source of the problem and to revise the theory so as to correct the deficiency.

This advantage of formalization is based on the ability of formal language to translate complex verbal ideas into simple mathematical expressions (symbols). According to Miller (1964), "Ordinary language is frequently inefficient or even inadequate to express the full complexity of an author's ideas. In that situation a formal symbol can often summarize, if only metaphorically, what would take many long and tedious qualifying phrases" (p. 4). This function of formalization is analogous to the use of diagrams, figures, and tables, rather than words to communicate a complex set of ideas. And this is one of the main functions of quasi-theoretical models.

As an example illustrating this advantage of formalization, a verbal theory, upon closer examination, is sometimes found to make inconsistent predictions, or some purported derivations of the theory do not follow logically from the stated assumptions. A formal theory is more likely to reveal any internal contradictions of a theory — whether derivations from one subset of assumptions are inconsistent with the derivations from another subset of assumptions. As a case in point, Harris (1976b), in advocating greater use of formal (mathematical) approaches to theorizing in social psychology, cites an inconsistency in Festinger's original paper on social comparison processes (1950). However, Festinger may have been aware of the inconsistency because in his subsequent, expanded version of his theory (1954), the inconsistency seems to have been eliminated. This illustrates a point raised by Rosenberg (1968) that, "The deductions from a verbal theory are not necessarily less precise and rigorous than those from a mathematical model, although this is typically true in practice" (p. 184). Nonetheless, the important point is that when attempts are made to formalize a verbal theory, a theorist is forced to make explicit the assumptions underlying his theoretical ideas. A theorist may sometimes find that there are several hidden assumptions in his theory, which are necessary to derive certain predicted outcomes. Moreover, formalization of verbal theories will reduce the necessity of asking the author to determine whether a given hypothesis does or does not follow from his theory (Simon and Newell, 1964).

A final advantage of formalization is its heuristic value. Through the power of formal logic, it is possible to derive many non-obvious implications of a model, which may not have been possible, or immediately observed, from the verbal theory. One example of this advantage is Osgood and Tannenbaum's congruity model of attitude change (1955). In evaluating the congruity model, Roger Brown (1965) argues that many of the non-obvious derivations of the model are improbable and would be surprising if they were confirmed. Yet, Brown states that, "Each particular prediction that is improbable suggests some general addition to or correction of the model and these in turn suggest empirical tests. That is why a very explicit model can be useful even when it is inadequate" (p. 573).

Classification of Models

For expository purposes, there are two obvious ways to classify mathematical applications in social psychology: on the basis of mathematical systems, algebraic, probabilistic, graph theory, etc.; or on the basis of substantive topics, attitude change, impression formation, conformity, etc. Most earlier reviews of mathematical models in social psychology have used the latter scheme. Since the intent of this chapter is to present a brief perspective, in the following section, mathematical models will be organized around types of mathematical systems. This decision is based on acquainting the reader with a variety of mathematical systems which might be selected for application, rather than familiarizing the reader with the substantive topics.

Based on this decision, the following section will include an initial discussion of quasi-theoretic models and then a variety of mathematical systems that have been used as models of some substantive problems in social psychology will be presented. The various mathematical models will be classified in terms of algebraic, probabilistic, and stochastic models, and a brief section on computer models of social behavior will be discussed. This classification scheme is not mutually exclusive, and some readers may question the decision to organize this section in this way. However, given the intent of this chapter, this classification scheme was considered to be a reasonable compromise between a scheme based on substantive topics and one based on types of mathematical systems.

Finally, with regard to the selection of models to illustrate the various types of applications, several criteria were used: (a) simple models requiring a minimal level of mathematical sophistication; (b) emphasis on recent developments; and (c) the author's personal interests and biases. Therefore, the studies described in the following section are by no means the most important or the most elegant and rigorous contributions to the literature. Indeed, one of my colleagues facetiously remarked that a theorist should be flattered if his or her model were not included. As indicated earlier, for a more exhaustive (and perhaps unbiased) survey of mathematical applications in social psychology, the reader is referred to the excellent reviews by Rosenberg (1968) and Abelson (1967).

QUASI-THEORETICAL MODELS

The distinction between quasi-theoretical models and mathematical models (described earlier) is quite arbitrary and serves mainly to illustrate the progressive stages in the development of mathematical models and some of the problems encountered in the modeling process. In the early stages of theoretical development, a theorist may simply have a hunch about the relationship between one or more independent variables and one or more dependent variables. Though there may be considerable empirical support for his hunch, if the theorist does not specify the functional form of the relationship or does not specify how the variables are to be measured (or the class of measurement procedures for which the model applies), we will categorize the proposal as a quasi-theoretical model. Many models of this type have been proposed.

In addition to the above type of quasi-theoretical models, a second type of model, in which the main purpose is to derive indices of a concept (construct) or to classify a set of variables, will also be placed in this category. This type of model probably comes closest to what has been called "descriptive models" by Rapoport (1963) and "explication models" by Berger et al. (1962). Models of this type attempt to formalize a set of independent or dependent variables and make no attempt to specify the relation between the two sets. Hence, they might be more appropriately called measurement or classification models. In this context, it should be emphasized that quasi-theoretical refers to substantive theory and does not refer to theories of measurement. Though the problem of measurement and scaling is extremely important and closely related to progress in the development and tests of mathematical models (and of theories in general), a discussion of such theories is far beyond the scope of this chapter. For an elementary presentation of measurement theory, the reader is referred to

Coombs et al. (1970) or to the brief discussion and references cited in Abelson (1967).

Quasi-theoretical Models Lacking a Measurement Proposal

Despite the brief history of social psychology, probably hundreds of quasi-theoretical models have been proposed. Miller (1964), for example, cites a model proposed by William James (1890) in which he postulated that:

$$(1) \quad \text{Self-esteem} = \frac{\text{Success}}{\text{Pretensions}}$$

"Such a fraction," James remarked, "may be increased as well by diminishing the denominator as by increasing the numerator" (pp. 310-311). Since James did not suggest how the three variables should be measured, Miller (1964) classifies the proposal as a "discursive application."

Examples of quasi-theoretical models range in complexity from the simple model suggested by Heider (1958) that:

$$(2) \quad \text{Performance} = \text{Motivation} \times \text{Ability}$$

to the complex case of Lewin's topological (field) theory (1936; 1951). Both of these examples illustrate two important points: the heuristic value of quasi-theoretical models; and the fact that mathematical models of a social phenomenon are frequently anticipated by cruder, less formalized (quasi-theoretical) models. The impact of Lewin's model needs no discussion, and the impact of Heider's suggestion will be postponed to a subsequent section of this chapter.

The simple models proposed by William James and Heider suggest that it may be a simple matter (in some cases at least) to transform a quasi-theoretical model into an empirically testable mathematical model. Since the nature of the function is specified, all that is required is a proposal for measuring the basic variables of the model. In the case of simple models such as these, an investigator typically will simultaneously propose the nature of the function as well as the measurement method and proceed to test the model experimentally. In more complex situations where a large number of variables are involved (as well as complex relations between the variables), as an initial step, a theorist may attempt a formalization of a theory without specifying the measurement procedures. In this form, empirical tests of the model would not be possible and the intent of the theorist is to encourage others to test the model by formulating such measurement procedures. For example, Simon's (1952) formalization of Homans's (1950) theory of small groups would fall in this category.

In contrast, there are other situations in which the measurement procedures have been developed, but the nature of the functions relating the independent and dependent variables are in doubt. For example, in the early stages of research on impression formation (Asch, 1946; 1952) and implicit personality theories (Bruner and Tagiuri, 1954), measurement procedures had been developed, though they were somewhat crude, but the functional form of the relationship between the overall impression (response measure) and the individual stimulus traits were unspecified. Given this type of situation, if a theorist proposes a plausible functional relation between the impression and the list of stimulus traits, we would classify the proposal as a mathematical model of impression formation. Many models of impression formation have been proposed during the past ten years, but the exact nature of the function — averaging, summation, configural — is still uncertain. We will examine some of these models in detail in a subsequent section.

Models Used to Clarify Concepts and To Develop Indices

The previous examples of quasi-theoretical models were cases in which the functional form of the relationship between the independent and dependent variables was specified, but was lacking a specification of the measurement procedure. We now turn to the second type of model in which the response measure is clearly defined, and the main purpose of formalization is to clarify a concept, to develop indices, or to classify a complex set of independent variables.

Balance Theory

The first example of this type is Cartwright and Harary's (1956) formalization of Heider's balance theory (1946, 1958). Since their model has been reviewed in detail by many writers (Zajonc, 1968; Abelson, 1967; Rapoport, 1963; Berger et al. 1962), only a brief outline of their model will be presented. According to Cartwright and Harary (1956), the concept of balance has been defined to apply to a limited range of situations, and the concept contains several ambiguities. They list the following specific problems:

1. Should all relations be conceptualized as symmetric? If P likes O, O need not like P, and it should be possible for O to dislike P.

2. Theorizing about balanced states has been restricted to the triad (P, O, and X), and it would be desirable to define balance for larger units.

3. Is the negative relation the complement of the relation, or its opposite? The two types of relations are quite different, but discussions of balance do not distinguish between them. The complement of "liking," for example, is "not liking," but the opposite of "liking" is "disliking."

4. Though Heider makes a distinction between the two types of relations, liking and unit formation, a general formulation in which the two types of relations may be combined is lacking.

5. Though the balance concept has been used by Heider to refer to cognitive units of an individual, it would be desirable to extend the concept, " . . . to study the balance of sociometric structures, communication networks, patterns of power, and other aspects of social systems" (Cartwright and Harary, 1956, p. 281).

This list of problems indicates that there are indeed many ambiguities of the balance concept, and Cartwright and Harary attempt to define balance so as to overcome these limitations. Their formalization is based on a mathematical sys-tem called graph theory. A *graph* consists of a set of points $(A, B, C, \dots)$, to-gether with lines between all, some, or none of the pairs of points. In a *signed graph*, some of the lines are positive, while others are negative. In a *directed graph*, pairs of points are ordered, so that a line goes from one point to the other (for example, $\overrightarrow{AB}$ denotes A *to* B).

The correspondence rules to formalize Heider's theory involve the assumption that each point in a graph corresponds to an entity in Heider's theory (P, O, X), and that a line corresponds to a relation or bond between pairs of entities. A graph then represents, or is a model of, an individual's "cognitive structure."

To define balance and to provide indices of the degree of balance, Cartwright and Harary use the concepts of cycle and semi-cycle. A *cycle* is defined as a col-lection of lines of the form, AB, BC, CD, DA, where the points $A, B, C,$ and D are distinct. For a directed graph, a *semi-cycle* is defined as a collection of direct-ed lines obtained by taking exactly one from each pair of points $\overrightarrow{AB}$ or $\overrightarrow{BA}$, $\overrightarrow{BC}$ or $\overrightarrow{CB}$, $\overrightarrow{CD}$ or $\overrightarrow{DC}$, and $\overrightarrow{DA}$ or $\overrightarrow{AD}$.

To illustrate the concepts introduced thus far, consider Figures 5.2a and 5.2b, which illustrate two signed graphs with four elements. The solid lines denote positive bonds while the dotted lines denote negative bonds. In both of these cases there are seven cycles: one formed by the largest triangle (AB, BD, DA); three formed by the three smaller triangles (for example, AB, BC, CA); and three formed by combinations of pairs of triangles (for example, BC, CA, AD, BD). In such signed graphs, relations between pairs of points are assumed to be sym-metric, that is, if A likes B, B likes A. Figures 5.2c and 5.2d are examples of signed-directed graphs. In such graphs, symmetry is not assumed. In Figure 5.2c, for example, A likes B, but B dislikes A. In both of these cases, there are three semi-cycles: $(\overrightarrow{AB}, \overrightarrow{BA})$; $(\overrightarrow{AB}, \overrightarrow{BC}, \overleftarrow{CA})$; and $(\overrightarrow{AB}, \overrightarrow{BC}, \overleftarrow{CA})$.

Definition of Balance

Based on these concepts, balance is defined on the basis of the sign of its cycles or semi-cycles. The *sign of a cycle* (or semicycle) is the product of the signs of its lines. A signed graph, with any number of points, is balanced if all of its cycles are positive. In Figure 5.2a, for example, the signs of all cycles are pos-itive because all cycles have an even number of negative bonds of the form: $(+ + +)$; $(+ - -)$; or $(+ + - -)$. Hence, this is a balanced structure. In Figure 5.2b, on the other hand, the signs of the cycles formed by any three elements (ABC, ABD, ACD, BCD) are negative since they each contain one negative bond

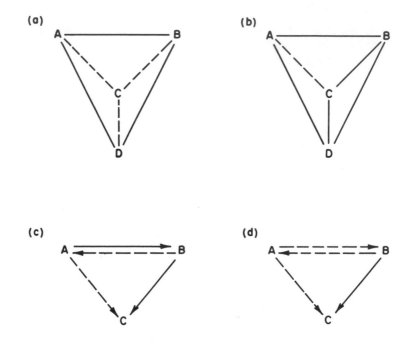

FIG. 5.2   Examples of signed graphs (a and b) and signed-directed graphs (c and d). Solid and dotted lines denote positive and negative bonds, respectively.

and two positive bonds. Hence, this is not a balanced structure. However, note that the signs of the remaining cycles are positive. For example, the cycle *AB, BC, CD, DA* are all positive in sign, so that the sign of the cycle is positive. Cartwright and Harary then propose an index (or scale) of the degree of balance based on the number of positive cycles (or semicycles) divided by the total number of cycles (or semicycles), that is, the proportion of positive cycles in the structure. For a completely balanced structure, as in Figure 5.2a, the index would be 1.0; for Figure 5.2b, since it contains three positive and four negative cycles, the index would be .43 (3/7).

Similarly, for the signed-directed graphs in Figures 5.2c and 5.2d, it is immediately obvious that the structure in Figure 5.2c is unbalanced because the sign of the *AB-BC* semicycle is negative. In the same way that we determined the index of balance for fhe signed graphs in Figures 5.2a and 5.2b, we can determine the index of balance for the structures in Figures 5.2c and 5.2d. Of the three semicycles in the structure in Figure 5.2c, one is positive and two are negative; hence, the index of balance is .33. For the structure in Figure 5.2d, the signs of all three semicycles are positive; hence, it is completely balanced with an index of 1.

In summary, it is clear that Cartwright and Harary's graph theoretical model has clarified many of the ambiguities of Heider's theory described earlier.

Despite this contribution of the model, it does not seem to have provided any additional insights into the processes underlying cognitive organization and change. This is why we have classified it as a quasi-theoretical model. However, we should mention that we have not included some of the theorems derived from the model, the extensions of the model by other investigators (e. g., Flament, 1963), nor the positive impact it has had as a model of social (group) structure.

Cartwright and Harary's model illustrates how a quasi-theoretical model is used to organize a set of independent variables and to clarify the nature of Heider's balance concept. Their model also illustrates another important function of such models, namely, the model may extend the generality of the underlying theory and may suggest additional hypotheses which might be tested. To examine and illustrate the nature of these functions, we will present two more examples in which models have been used for these purposes. In the typical situation, when models are used in this way, it is assumed that some of the independent variables are known to be relevant or have been shown to be related from previous research to one or more of the dependent variables. Thus, one of the purposes of the model is to organize a relatively large number of independent variables, and to reduce the number of variables which must be manipulated in subsequent research.

In the typical situation, the problem is to determine the functional interdependence among the set of independent variables and to derive a smaller set of variables as a function of the larger set of independent variables. The variables in the smaller set we label as intervening variables (constructs, indices). Assuming that the number of intervening variables is much smaller than the number of independent variables, in subsequent research, a much smaller number of variables would have to be varied and manipulated.

The Prisoner's Dilemma

To illustrate these ideas we have chosen a model derived from mathematical game theory called the Prisoner's Dilemma Game, hereafter denoted *PDG*.[2] As a result of the theories proposed by Thibaut and Kelley (1959) and by Homans (1961), who interpret social interaction in terms of the costs and rewards to the participants, many investigators have used two-person games as a research paradigm for the study of cooperation, competition, and interpersonal conflict. Though there are many types of games that might be used, the game that has been studied most extensively is the *PDG*. According to the notation scheme used by Rapoport and Chammah (1965), let *C* and *D* denote cooperative and competitive choices, respectively, and let *T, R, P,* and *S* denote the payoff values of the outcome matrix. Tables 5.1a and 5.1b show the nature of the game with

---

[2]For a detailed discussion of the PDG, and game theory in general, the reader is referred to Luce and Raiffa (1957); Rapoport (1965, 1966); and to Shubik (1964).

TABLE 5.1a

General Notation for Outcomes in PDG[a]

	C	D
C	R, R	S, T
D	T, S	P, P

[a]Left and right cell entries denote outcomes for row and column players, respectively. In the PDG, the following constraints must be satisfied: $T > R > P > S$; and $2R > (T + S)$.

TABLE 5.1b

PDG with $R = 3$; $S = 0$; $T = 5$; and $P = 1$

	C	D
C	3, 3	0, 5
D	5, 0	1, 1

the abstract notation scheme and an example with numerical values. Rapoport and Chammah systematically varied the values of $T, R, P,$ and S, and found that the proportion of cooperative choices over a long sequence of trials, hereafter denoted $P(C)$, varied directly with the magnitudes of R and S and inversely with the values of T and P. These results have been subsequently corroborated by other investigators (see Wrightsman, O'Connor, and Baker, 1972, for a review of such studies). At this point, these findings can be expressed in terms of four functions, one for each of the payoff values. The main point of this example is the problem of integrating these results by means of a model and, if possible, simplifying the four functions in terms of a single equation.

With suitable assumptions (which need not concern us here), Rapoport and Chammah show that $P(C)$ should not depend on the values of $T, R, P,$ and S individually, but on the ratio of their differences. With 4 values (or parameters), there are 30 possible ratios of differences; however, they also show that only 2 of them can be independent. They offer the following ratios as possible independent variables, and examine them in detail:

$$(3) \quad r_1 = \frac{R-P}{T-S} \text{ and } r_2 = \frac{R-S}{T-S}$$

Note that these ratios have the desirable property that: $0 < r_i < 1.0$, because the denominator consists of the difference between the largest and smallest values.

Also note that other ratios of differences can be expressed as functions of r_1 and r_2, for example, $(T-R)/(T-S) = 1-r_2$; or $(P-S)/(T-S) = r_2-r_1$.

In a subsequent paper, Rapoport (1967) proposes r_1 as an "index of cooperation," under the restrictions that: (a) $P(C) = 1$, if $T = R$ and $P = S$; (b) $P(C) = 0$, if $R = P$; and (c) the effects of $(T-R)$, the "temptation to defect," and the effects of $(P-S)$, "the fear of betrayal," are equal. In considering various possible indices, Rapoport (1967) states that "... one is forced for the time being to choose indices more or less arbitrarily and to justify them on 'untheoretical,' purely pragmatic grounds" (p. 103). However, on a social-psychological basis, it would be reasonable to postulate that $P(C)$ is a function of two motivational components: "greed" $(T-R)$; and "fear" $(P-S)$; and, based on these two components, the following index might be proposed:

$$(4) \quad K' = a\left|\frac{T-R}{T-S}\right| + b\left|\frac{P-S}{T-S}\right| + c$$

where a, b, and c denote parameters to be estimated.

The a and b parameters represent the weights (importance) of these components for an individual, and the desirable property of Equation 4 is that it directly incorporates greed and fear as motivational variables affecting cooperation. Equation 4, moreover, is consistent with Rapoport's index. If it is assumed that $a = b = -1$ (that the effects of greed and fear are equal, as did Rapoport in deriving his index), it can be shown that Equation 4 reduces to the following:

$$(5) \quad K' = \frac{R-P}{T-S} + k$$

where $k = c-1$. Hence, under the assumption that the two components are eqully weighted, the two indices differ by an additive constant (k).

Now, what has been accomplished by these theoretical formulations? First, we have reduced the number of independent variables from four (T, R, P, S) to two: $(T-R)/(T-S)$ and $(P-S)/(T-S)$. In the case of Rapoport's index, we have reduced it to one variable: $(R-P)/(T-S)$. Secondly, the model seems to provide a reasonably good fit in explaining previous empirical results (Rapoport & Chammah, 1965; Steele & Tedeschi, 1967). More importantly, we can ask to what extent the model can be generalized to other situations.

Extending the Generality of the Prisoner's Dilemma

To illustrate one possible extension of Equation 4 and to accommodate sequential processes, consider the following assumptions:

1. The reinforcing effect of the T-outcome (inhibiting the C-choice) is a function of $(T-R)$: the larger T, relative to R, the greater the reinforcing effect of T.

2. The punishing effect of the S-outcome (inhibiting the C-choice) is a function of $(P-S)$: the larger P, relative to S, the greater the inhibitory effect of S (on the C-choice).

Formally, these two assumptions can be expressed as follows:

(6) $\Delta P(C_i | T_{i-1}) = f_1(T-R)$

(7) $\Delta P(C_i | S_{i-1}) = f_2(P-S)$

where the ΔP's are conditional probabilities denoting the change in the probability of making a C-choice on trial i, given a T- or S-outcome on the previous trial; and f_1 and f_2 denote monotonically decreasing (inverse) functions.[3] Equations 6 and 7 imply that T- and S-outcomes extinguish (decrease the probability of) the C-choice, and these inhibitory effects are functions of the magnitudes of $(T-R)$ and $(P-S)$. Since the T-outcome is a consequence of making a D-choice, and the S-outcome is a consequence of making a C-choice, this means that the greater the value of T, relative to R, the greater the tendency to stay with the D-choice; and the greater the value of P, relative to S, the greater the tendency to switch to the D-choice.

This extension is consistent with the "win-stay, lose-change" hypothesis proposed by Kelley, Thibaut, Radloff, and Mundy (1962), for "minimal social situations." In a minimal social situation, neither subject is aware of the presence of the other nor that each person's outcome is completely determined by the response of the other. In this situation, two types of reinforcements were used: positive reward, consisting of points on a counter; and a negative reinforcement, consisting of shock to a finger. If the two subjects could coordinate their responses, it was possible for them to avoid the shock and mutually reward each other. In the experiments by Kelley et al., as a replication of the study by Sidowski, Wycoff, and Tabory (1956), when subjects made choices simultaneously, as in the PDG, they learned to reinforce each other, and were able to reach a mutually rewarding solution. Kelley et al. showed that the results of several variations of this situation could be explained by the hypothesis that subjects are likely to stay with the same response, if they are rewarded on the previous trial, and are likely to change their response, if they are punished on the previous trial. Hence, their hypothesis is frequently referred to as the "win-stay, lose-change," principle.

In the PDG, in contrast, the vast majority of subjects do not seem to learn and are generally unable to reach a cooperative solution. Now what accounts for this difference in results between the two situations? The most plausible explanation is that, in a minimal social situation, the magnitudes of positive and

---

[3]The model would not be complete, of course, without specifying the other functions: one each for the effects of R and P-outcomes. However, we shall not pursue this matter here.

negative reinforcements are not varied. In the *PDG*, there are four different out-comes, *T*, *R*, *P*, and *S*, while in the minimal social situation, there are only two, negative reinforcement (shock) and positive reinforcement (points on a counter). In effect, the minimal social situation corresponds to a game in which *T=R=* points on a counter, and *P=S=*shock. According to Equations 6 and 7, when *T=R* and *P=S*, the reinforcement value of the *T*-outcome should be negligible, and the punishment value of the *S*-outcome also should be negligible. Hence, a high level of cooperative choice would be predicted.

To illustrate the nature of this situation, Tables 5.2a and 5.2b show the re-ward structure of the minimal social situation and for a comparable two-person game with numerical values. It can be seen that a high level of cooperation would be predicted by the model based on Equation 4, because both the greed and fear components are nonexistent. The point of this digression was to show that the results of two different types of situations can be explained on the basis of a single model. Extending the generality of the model in this way may provide insights into the nature of processes that facilitate or inhibit the development of cooperative behavior.

The previous examples showed the value of a model in organizing the rela-tionship between a set of independent variables and its relationships with the de-pendent variable. Since the number of independent variables is typically reduced, the nature of the relationship(s) between the two variables is greatly simplified. We now turn to another type of model which bridges the gap between a quasi-theoretical and a mathematical model.

.TABLE 5.2a

Outcome Matrix for the Minimal Social Situation

	C	*D*
C	Points, points	Shock, points
D	Points, shock	Shock, shock

TABLE 5.2b

Outcome Matrix for Minimal Social Situation Assuming
Points and Shock Have Values of 1 and −5, Respectively

	C	*D*
C	1, 1	−5, 1
D	1, −5	−5, −5

Normative Theories: A Special Case of Quasi-theoretical Models

According to our classification scheme, a model is categorized as quasi-theoretical if it does not specify the nature of the relation between the independent and dependent variables. A special case of this classification scheme is a formal theory that attempts to specify the relationship between certain antecedent conditions and behaviors which achieve a certain goal. If the goal is to maximize reward, for example, such theories attempt to determine, on a logical basis, optimal behavior in such situations, and to prescribe what a person ought to do if he wants to maximize reward (or minimize loss). Such theories are called *normative models.* Note that the measurement procedures may be clearly defined for such situations, but since normative theories do not postulate what a person actually *will do* (only what a person ought to do), they represent models of "rational" man. In the next section we will examine some models that postulate how people will actually behave, rather than how they ought to behave. Such models are called *descriptive models* (theories).

Now what is the nature and role of such normative models? What useful functions do they serve? One of the main functions of such models is to provide a frame of reference or standard with which to compare behavior. In developing a descriptive model, a theorist may initially ask, "Do people behave rationally (as defined by the normative model)?" In many situations, it is not unreasonable to assume that people wish to maximize reward. If data are collected showing that the normative model yields inaccurate predictions, the interesting question is "why?" There are several possible explanations, and some of the obvious ones are: (a) the basic assumption that all people are motivated to maximize reward may be in error; (b) subjects may be motivated to maximize reward, but may be using poor strategies; (c) how the model defines reward may be different from how the subjects define (perceive) reward, hence, what is being maximized may not coincide. There may be other explanations, but the important point is that these alternative hypotheses are subject to empirical test, and normative models serve as a heuristic device to suggest new experiments. In the following section, we will present some examples of this use of normative models in the social sciences.

In an early stage of theoretical development — especially when little is known about the behavior in question — it would not be unreasonable to postulate that people are "rational," and to design experiments based on the predictions of a normative nodel. When such an assumption is made, according to our classification scheme, it would be classified as a mathematical model. Hence, there is a fine line between a quasi-theoretical and a mathematical model, and in this sense, a normative model can be considered to be a special case which bridges the gap between the two types of models.

As one example of a normative model, the two-person *PDG* (described earlier) was originally formulated as one class of games in the mathematical theory of games. One of the criteria of "rationality" proposed by game theorists is based on the idea of "dominating strategy." If one choice (act) yields outcomes that are greater than another, for all possible choices of the other person, then the first choice is said to *dominate* the second. In the *PDG* shown in Table 5.1b, it can be seen that the D-choice dominates the C-choice (for both players) because for each choice of the other person, the outcome for the D-choice is greater than for the C-choice *(T > R)* and *P > S)*. Hence, regardless of the choice of the other, it is better to choose D than C.

One of the prescriptive criteria (axioms of "rationality") is that choices that are dominated by another should be eliminated from consideration. Hence, if we accept this criterion, the model prescribes that both persons should make mutual D-choices. Moreover, in an iterated game, this outcome in the DD-cell, once it occurs, is called an *equilibrium outcome* — an outcome such that neither person is motivated to switch unilaterally, since the person who switches (to the C-choice) would receive a lower outcome than if he did not switch. The dilemma, of course, is based on the fact that this equilibrium outcome does not maximize mutual gain. Now if the goal of the players were to be changed so that they should maximize mutual reward, it would be possible to formulate a model that would prescribe that both persons should make C-choices in this situation. This variation would involve axioms of group rationality rather than individual rationality. However, such a model would still be a normative model and would not be descriptive of how people actually do behave.

The distinction between normative and descriptive models evolved from the economic literature and is usually associated with optimizing economic (monetary) reward. However, this distinction can easily be extended to bases other than economic ones. One example is the use of a formal, logical system as a model of attitude organization and change. Jones and Gerard (1967), for example, define an attitude in terms of a syllogism. A syllogism is a form of logical argument consisting of a major premise, minor premise, and a conclusion. Two examples cited by Jones and Gerard are as follows:

1. All Negroes are lazy.
   Lazy people are bad.
   Therefore, all Negroes are bad.

2. All nonwhites are lazy.
   Negroes are nonwhites.
   Therefore, Negroes are lazy.

With reference to the first syllogism, Jones and Gerard state, ". . . the attitude is the conclusion and the two premises generating it represent the structure of the attitude" (p. 159). They also state that many other forms of beliefs, values, and attitude statements fit the syllogistic paradigm and, in many communications, one or more of the premises may not be stated or stated without the conclusion being expressed. The second syllogism (above) illustrates the fact that, "A given belief may itself be the conclusion of a syllogism whose premises may be the conclusions of syllogisms, and so on (syllogisms can generate beliefs as well as attitudes)" (p. 160).

The main point of this example is that Jones and Gerard assume that an individual's attitude has a logical structure and use a formal system (syllogistic reasoning) as a model of cognitive organization. The formal system assumes that if one's goal is to make valid (rational) inferences from a set of premises, it prescribes the rules one ought to follow. In this sense, the syllogistic model is a normative model. But there is one important difference between their model and game theory as a normative model: Jones and Gerard postulate that the syllogistic model represents how people actually do behave (cognize, think, make inferences); therefore, it would not be classified as a quasi-theoretical model and would be classified as a formal model of cognitive organization. It is granted that an individual's conclusions (attitude) can be fallacious — but this is attributed to errors in one or more of the premises, and the underlying structure of the attitude is assumed to be logical and valid. In contrast, the symbolic-psychologic model of attitude organization proposed by Abelson and Rosenberg (1958) is assumed to be "psycho-logical" and not necessarily logical.

This interpretation of the syllogistic model as a normative model is consistent with the views of McGuire (1960), who first proposed and elaborated on such a model to represent cognitive and attitudinal relations. McGuire states,

> The "rational man" concept, long out of fashion in the behavioral sciences, is now undergoing a remarkable revival in the study of cognition. More and more, theory and research are being based on the postulate that a person's need to maintain harmony between his feelings, thoughts, and actions is a powerful determinant of his belief systems and of his gross behavior (p. 65).

McGuire then lists as ". . . modern versions of the 'rational man' concept" (p. 65) all of the theories based on the consistency principle: Heider's "balance" (1946, 1958); Newcomb's "strain toward symmetry" (1953); Osgood and Tannenbaum's "congruity principle" (1955); Festinger's "dissonance theory" (1957); and Abelson and Rosenberg's "Psycho-logic" (1958).

In McGuire's model, as in Jones and Gerard's formulation, a person's beliefs (expectations) are assumed to follow the rules of logic. The unique feature of his model is that a second principle of consistency, called "wishful thinking" is also assumed to be operating, that is, a person's beliefs on a given issue should be in accord with his desires on that issue. A second unique feature of his theory is the assumption that an individual's degree of belief in certain propositions, measured on a numerical rating scale, follow the axioms of probability theory. This is a very strong assumption and, in the next section, we will examine his "Socratic method of persuasion," and the theoretical extension of this approach by Wyer (1974).

Before concluding this section on normative models, one brief example will be presented to illustrate the application of a classic economic model: the normative model based on maximizing expected value. Given a risky situation, the expected value of an act (choice) is given by the expression,

(8)   Expected Value $(EV) = \Sigma p_i V_i$

where p_i and V_i denote the probability and value (consequence) of event i, and the summation is over all possible events. The normative model then prescribes that a rational economic man ought to behave so as to maximize expected value.

Mathematicians and economists soon discovered (over 200 years ago) that people do not always behave rationally, as prescribed by this model. Playing lotteries, gambling against the house (any gambling institution making a profit), and buying insurance are some of the many examples where people do not maximize expected value. Hence, it is a poor descriptive model of behavior. There have been several attempts to formulate descriptive models based on modifications of the EV-model, and a detailed discussion of such attempts are available in Edwards (1961); Becker and McClintock (1967); Lee (1971) and Rapoport and Wallsten (1972).

There are numerous examples where some variation of the EV-model has been used to formulate a descriptive model of social behavior, and we have selected Rosenberg's (1956, 1960) "affect-cognition" model to illustrate the generality of the model. Rosenberg's model conceptualizes an attitude as a function of: (a) the probability that the attitude object (issue, person) leads to good or bad consequences (called "perceived instrumentality"); and (b) the intensity of the affect associated with these consequences (called "value importance"). Numerical ratings of perceived instrumentality and value importance were obtained for each of 35 consequences or goals. For example, on the issue of whether members of the Communist party should be allowed to address the public, subjects were asked to rate the extent to which this policy would contribute to or inhibit the attainment of all human beings having equal rights, one of the 35 goals. Each of these goals was also rated for their value or importance. Based on these numerical values, Rosenberg proposed the following cognitive index of attitude structure:

(9)   Cognitive Index (attitude) $= \Sigma P'_i V'_i$

where P'_i and V'_i denote the perceived instrumentality and value importance, respectively, of the consequences or goals, and the summation is over the 35 goals. It can be seen that Rosenberg's model is a special case of the EV model, where no restriction is placed on the probability values, for example, the events need not be mutually exclusive nor exhaustive (the restriction that $\Sigma P_i = 1$). A similar model has been proposed by Fishbein (1963), where he defines an attitude as follows:

(10)   Attitude $= \Sigma B_i a_i$

where B_i denotes "the strength of belief i about the object" (the probability that the attitude object is related to object i); a_i denotes "the evaluative aspect of B_i" (the affect of "goodness-badness" of object i); and the summation is over the number of beliefs. Thus, Fishbein's model may also be interpreted as a special case of the EV model.

In summarizing this section on normative models, it should be noted that some writers do not distinguish between normative models and mathematical models. One of the reasons for this is that some theorists postulate that people are rational and are assumed to behave in accordance with the prescriptions of the normative model. In such instances, as we have seen, the normative model cannot be distinguished from a mathematical model. In the early stages of theoretical development, it is not unreasonable to ask whether people are rational, and after finding out that people are not rational, in many instances, a great deal of research was generated when attempts were made to determine why. Accordingly, normative models can be extremely useful even when they are not accurate representations of social behavior. Moreover, they provide a frame of reference with which to develop a more representative model, or to compare it with alternative models. We will examine such models in greater detail in the next section.

MATHEMATICAL MODELS OF SOCIAL BEHAVIOR

In the following section of this chapter, we will describe four types of formal mathematical systems that have been used as models of social behavior:

1. algebraic models based on simple arithmetic operations of addition, subtraction, multiplication, and division;
2. models based on probability theory;
3. stochastic models that make predictions about sequential processes;
4. computer simulation models in which a computer program is used to simulate a complex social process.

This list excludes some important formal systems such as graph theory as a model of social structure and models requiring differential equations and calculus. As indicated earlier, in the interest of keeping the mathematics as simple as possible and because of space limitations, such models have been omitted. The interested reader should consult Abelson (1967), Coleman (1964a), and Rapoport (1963) for detailed discussions of such models.

Algebraic Models

By far the largest number of mathematical models in social psychology are simple algebraic models. The main reason is probably because most research problems are in the early stages of theoretical development, and algebraic models are the simplest to formulate. For example, a frequently occurring situation is one in which a simple relationship is obtained between the dependent variable and one or more independent variables of the form: $y = f(X_1$ and $X_2)$. The natural question to ask is how the levels of X_1 and X_2 combine to yield levels of y. Is the combinatorial rule additive, multiplicative, or some other functional form? In some situations, a multiplicative, exponential function may seem to provide the best fit, and the nature of the relationship might be expressed as follows:

$$(11) \quad y = aX_1{}^b X_2{}^c$$

where a, b, and c denote parameters to be estimated.

It is not as easy to conceptualize such an expression as it would be if the relationship were additive. Moreover, for the purpose of analyses, it is more convenient to deal with additive functions. Hence, a common technique is to simplify such functions by taking the logarithms of both sides of Equation 11, to yield the following expression:

$$(12) \quad \log y = \log a + b \log X_1 + c \log X_2$$

With this transformation, it can be seen that $\log y$ is now a linear function of $\log X_1$ and $\log X_2$, with an additive constant $\log a$. This example not only illustrates the advantage of using mathematics as a language to communicate complex ideas, but its use in simplifying complex relations by means of logical transformation rules. The reader who is not convinced of this should try communicating the relation expressed in Equation 11 using ordinary language.

Turning to some examples of algebraic models, a controversial issue in the impression formation literature is how a set of stimulus traits presented to subjects is combined (integrated) to yield an overall impression. The problem of impression formation was first introduced by the classic study of Asch (1946), who found marked differences in impressions from the substitution of a single trait (warm-cold) in a longer list of traits. Using Gestalt principles of perceptual organization, Asch argued that the meaning or interpretation of the other traits in the list were transformed by the "central" traits of warm and cold. However, subsequent studies have shown that more simple combination rules (models) could explain his findings.

In contrast with Asch's original experiment, more recent studies assess the desirability (evaluation) of each trait in isolation and then use the same measuring instrument to assess the evaluation of the stimulus traits when presented together. For such purposes, Anderson (1968) has published "likeableness" ratings of over 500 trait adjectives. Such ratings of the individual traits can then be used to determine how the overall evaluation can be predicted as a function of the evaluation of each trait in the set.

Additive Models

A simple combination rule for impression formation is that the individual adjective traits combine additively. Such a simple, additive model can be expressed in the form:

(13) $E = \Sigma s_i$

where E denotes the overall (integrated) evaluation of the stimuli (traits), and s_i denotes the evaluation of the individual stimuli. Anderson (1962) and Levy and Richter (1963) showed that the simple additive model provided a reasonably good fit for the overall evaluation.

A more general case of the additive model is a weighted summation model, hereafter called the summation model, postulated by Triandis and Fishbein (1963), Fishbein and Hunter (1964), and Anderson and Fishbein (1965), expressed as follows:

(14) $E = \Sigma w_i s_i$

where w_i denotes the weights (importance, salience) of the stimuli. If $w_i = 1$, we have the simple additive model of Equation 13.

Another case of an additive model is Anderson's weighted averaging model (1965), hereafter called the averaging model, expressed as follows:

$$(15)\quad E = \Sigma \left| \frac{w_i}{\Sigma w_i} \right| s_i$$

the basic difference between Anderson's averaging model and Fishbein's summation model is that the averaging model requires that the weights sum to 1 ($\Sigma w_i = 1$), while the summation model places no restrictions on the weights.

The implication of this difference is illustrated by an example in which an individual is presented two positive traits, one very positive and the other only mildly positive. The summation model predicts that the two traits in combination should evoke an overall evaluation that is more extreme (more positive) than the very positive trait, while the averaging model predicts that the overall evaluation should be less extreme than very positive, between mildly and very positive.

Based on this paradigm, Anderson (1965) presented sets of two or four adjectives, varying in social desirability (likeableness ratings), and his results were clearly inconsistent with the summation model and supported the averaging hypotheses. However, he also found that the mean evaluation of four equally positive traits was more positive than the mean rating of two equally positive traits, and the mean evaluation of four equally negative traits was more negative then the mean rating of two equally negative traits. These results are inconsistent with the averaging hypothesis. In order to explain this discrepancy, Anderson extended the model to incorporate the individual's initial impression.

In subsequent work on the averaging model, Anderson has proposed a general information integration model (1974a), based on "functional measurement" (1970), and he reviews the applications of his general model in a variety of social situations (Anderson, 1974b).

Multiplicative Models

As the term implies, in a multiplicative model, the component variables are assumed to be multiplicative rather than additive. The simplest example of this is the effect of adverbs on adjectives. When intensifying adverbs, such as "extremely," "fairly," "slightly," are combined with adjectives ("kind," "cruel," etc.), the overall impression, unlike the combination of adjectives alone, seems to follow a multiplicative function (Cliff, 1959; Howe, 1962; Stilson & Maroney, 1966), of the form:

(16) $E = a_i s_i$

where a_i denotes the intensifying value of the adverb; and s_i denotes the adjective value. However, a recent study by McClelland (1974) suggests that both the additive and the multiplicative models are deficient, and a "single-peaked" model was proposed for adverb-adjective combinations.

The second example of a multiplicative model is Heider's suggestion (described earlier) that performance is a multiplicative function of motivation and ability (Equation 2). Based on functional measurement methodology, Anderson and Butzin (1974) showed that judgments of performance as a function of motivation and ability were indeed multiplicative. Paradoxically, however, judgments of motivation as a function of performance and ability, and judgments of ability as a function of motivation and performance, seemed to follow an additive process. In order to explain these results, Anderson and Butzin hypothesized that judgments of performance, in contrast with judgments of motivation and ability, may conform to a conjunctive-averaging model. In a conjunctive model (Coombs, 1964), some minimal level of each component is required, and an excess in one component cannot compensate for deficiencies in another. Another possibility is that judgments of performance are based on multiplying motivation and ability, whereas judgments of motivation and ability are based on division (performance/ability and performance/motivation, respectively). Hence, though the quantitative processes of multiplication and division are simply inverse operations, the psychological processes of attributions based on multiplication and division may be qualitatively different.

There are numerous other examples of multiplicative models in the psychological literature: Hull's habit strength = drive x habit, (1943); Rotter's social learning model (1954); behavior = expectancy x reinforcement value; and Atkinson's need-achievement model (1964); motivation $= P_s(1-P_s)(M_s-M_f)$, where P_s denotes probability of success, and M_s and M_f denote motive for success and failure, respectively. In addition, before turning to other types of models, we might mention the equity model formulated by Adams (1965).

According to Adams, equity is perceived by Person P, with respect to Person O, when:

$$(17) \quad O_p/I_p = O_a/I_a, \quad I_p \cdot I_a > O$$

where O_p and O_a denote the outcomes of P and O, respectively, and I_p and I_a denote the inputs of P and O, respectively.[4] The outcomes (O) and the inputs (I) both consist of the sum of outcomes and inputs perceived to be relevant to a particular exchange, and it is also assumed that these sum of outcomes and inputs are not necessarily weighted equally. Hence, Adams' model is a compound algebraic model involving both addition and division. Moreover, in the reward-allocation paradigm, a commonly used procedure to test the equity model (cf., Pritchard, 1969), an individual is led to believe that his inputs are greater (or less) than his partner's. He is then asked to divide a fixed amount of money between himself and his partner, and the model, as applied to the reward-allocation paradigm, may be expressed as follows:

$$(18) \quad O_p = (I_p/I_a)O_a$$

where $O_p + O_a$ = some constant. Expressed in this form, it can be seen that equity is achieved if an individual's outcome is directly proportional to his inputs. This variation of the equity formulation is identical to the "parity norm" postulated by Gamson (1961), as a basis for reward division in his minimum resource theory of coalition formation. Since Gamson attributes the parity norm to Homan's idea of "distributive justive" (1961), the equity model and the idea of distributive justice, mathematically at least, are virtually identical.

Probability Models

In a strict mathematical sense, models based on probability theory are also algebraic models; however, they will be treated as a different class of models because they make use of an elaborate and powerful mathematical structure. The advantage as well as the limitations of such models will be illustrated with the logical inference model proposed by McGuire (1960; 1968), and the extension of this model by Wyer (1974).

---

[4]In Adams's formulation, no restrictions were placed on the sign of I_p and I_a. However, Walster, Berscheid, and Walster (1973) showed that intuitively unreasonable predictions can result if one or both inputs are negative in value. They suggested an alternative formulation of equity to incorporate negative inputs, but Harris (1976a) showed that the formula proposed by Walster· et al. also leads to unreasonable derivations and proposed still another formulation. We will not pursue these alternative formulations here and will simply assume that I_p and I_a are nonnegative, as indicated in Equation 17.

Some Elementary Theorems

If two events, A and B, are mutually exclusive (cannot occur together), the probability that one or the other (A or B) will occur is given by the sum of the probability of each event:

(19) $P(A$ or $B) = P(A) + P(B)$

If the two events are not mutually exclusive,

(20) $P(A$ or $B) = P(A) + P(B) - P(AB)$

where $P(AB)$ denotes the probability of A and B, the joint occurrence of the two events.

If the two events are independent, the joint occurrence of the two events is given by the product of the probabilities of the events:

(21) $P(AB) = P(A)P(B)$

The conditional probability of event A, given that event B has occurred, denoted $P(A|B)$, is as follows:

(22) $P(A|B) = \dfrac{P(AB)}{P(B)}$

If events A and B are independent, substituting Equation 21 in 22, $P(A|B) = P(A)$. If the events are not independent, Equation 22 shows that $P(AB)$, the joint occurrence of A and B, equals $P(A|B)P(B)$.

If A is a given hypothesis and D is an observation (an item of information), then:

(23) $P(A|D) = \dfrac{P(D|A)P(A)}{P(D)}$

Equation 23 is called Bayes' Theorem (in its simplest form) and is the basis for a revolutionary movement in statistical decision making called the Bayesian approach. The term on the left, $P(A|D)$, is called the *posterior probability* of the hypothesis A, after observing D, while $P(A)$ is called the *prior probability* of A.

For the case of choosing between two hypotheses, A and B, Bayes' Theorem is expressed as the ratio of Equation 23, as follows:

(24) $\dfrac{P(A|D)}{P(B|D)} = \dfrac{P(D|A)P(A)}{P(D|B)P(B)}$

In the above ratio form, Bayes' Theorem is typically expressed as follows (Morgan, 1968; Slovic & Lichenstein, 1973):

(25) $\Omega_1 = LR(D)\Omega_0$

where $\Omega_0 = P(A)/P(B)$, and is called the *prior odds* — the odds of event A over B, prior to observation D; $LR(D) = P(D|A)/P(D|B)$, and is called the *likelihood ratio* of the observation D; and $\Omega_1 = P(A|D)/P(B|D)$, and is called the *posterior odds* — the odds of event A over B after observing D.

McGuire's Syllogistic Model

As indicated earlier, McGuire has proposed a model of logical consistency in which an individual's beliefs are assumed to conform to the laws of probability theory (McGuire, 1960, 1968). His syllogistic model is based on a paradigm in which two premises, A and B, logically imply a conclusion C. In addition, if there is another premise k, which also implies C but is independent of premises A and B, then the following equation is assumed to hold for an individual's belief system:

$$(26) \quad P(C) = P(AB) + P(k) \left[1 - P(AB)\right]$$

An example of such a syllogism would be:

Premise A: A major nuclear war would result in violent death to at least half the earth's population.

Premise B: A major nuclear war will occur within the next ten years.

Factor k: Factors other than nuclear war are going to result in violent death to at least half the earth's population within the next ten years.

Conclusion C: At least half the earth's population will meet violent death within the next ten years.

If it is assumed that premises A and B are independent, Equation 26 can be reduced to the following form:

$$(27) \quad P(C) = P(A) P(B) + P(k) \left[1 - P(A)P(B)\right],$$

and estimates of the likelihood of A, B, and C, and k can be obtained to test the model. As a model of attitude change, the basic hypothesis is that if a persuasive argument is made so as to change one or more of the premises, in accordance with Equation 26, an individual's belief in the conclusion should also change. Tests of his model indicated that though the predicted change was in the right direction, the magnitude of the change was not as great as predicted. McGuire also found that when subjects were administered the belief questionnaires one week apart, their responses were more logically consistent in the second session than in the first, and he called this increase in logical consistency the "Socratic effect." Though there is some support for his model, there are problems with the k-factor with regards to its relationship with the premises and the estimation of $P(k)$.

Wyer's Subjective Probability Model

Wyer (1974) has modified and extended McGuire's syllogistic model, so as to avoid the problems involving the k factor. The basic equation for the syllogistic model is given by:

$$(28) \quad P(B) = P(A)\,P(B|A) + P(\overline{A})\,P(B|\overline{A})$$

where $P(A)$ and $P(B)$ are the likelihood that beliefs A and B are true, respectively; $(\overline{A})$ is the likelihood that belief A is *not* true, i.e., $P(\overline{A}) = 1 - P(A)$; and $P(B|A)$ is the belief that B is true if A is true; and $P(B|\overline{A})$ is the belief that B is true if A is *not* true. In Equation 28, belief B is treated as the conclusion, with two logically related premises: one set consisting of, "A; if A, then B," and the other set consisting of "not-A; if not-A, then B."

The following is an example of his syllogistic paradigm (Rosen & Wyer, 1972):

A	Marijuana will be legalized within the next 10 years;
$B|A$	If marijuana is legalized, it will become as common as alcoholic drinks within the next 10 years;
$B|\overline{A}$	Even if marijuana is not legalized, it will become as common as alcoholic drinks within the next 10 years;
B	Marijuana will become as common as alcoholic drinks within the next 10 years.

Using a number of issues, judgments of the likelihood of each of these beliefs were obtained in a questionnaire administered one week apart. Though a Socratic effect was obtained, a relatively poor quantitative fit was obtained between predicted and observed values of $P(B)$. Wyer (1975) hypothesized that an individual's previously formed beliefs tend to be inconsistent, but when made salient by responding to a questionnaire, these beliefs change in the direction of consistency (the Socratic effect). Newly formed beliefs, in contrast, should be less inconsistent, and his model should be more accurate for such beliefs.

To test this hypothesis, abstract stimulus materials (for example, the likelihood that a person with a hypothetical gene would or would not have attribute X) were used, and levels of $P(A)$, $P(B|A)$, and $P(B|\overline{A})$ were manipulated (subjective probability of not-A was assumed to be the complement of A). Subjects were also asked to judge the likelihood of B, which were compared with the predicted values of $P(B)$, derived from the right hand side of Equation 27. A good linear fit was obtained between predicted and observed values, thus supporting the hypothesis.

Bayesian Models of the Attribution Process

Though there are numerous studies showing that normative decision models, such as the Bayesian model, are typically poor descriptive models of behavior

(Peterson & Beach, 1967; Becker & McClintock, 1967; Edwards, 1968), as indicated earlier, they are extremely useful heuristic devices to generate and guide empirical research. In this context, Messick (1971) and Ajzen (1971) have proposed Bayesian models of the trait inference process.

For the case of a single trait and a single behavior, Bayes' theorem (see Equation 23) can be expressed as follows:

$$(29) \quad P(T|B) = \frac{P(B|T)\,P(T)}{P(B)}$$

where T and B denote trait and behavior, respectively, $P(T|B)$ is the posterior trait probability, and $P(T)$ is the prior trait probability.

It can be seen that the posterior trait probability is an inverse function of $P(B)$, the probability of the behavior, and is a positive function of the prior trait probability, $P(T)$. This is consistent with the predictions of attribution theory (Heider, 1958; Kelley, 1967), and Ajzen (1971) found empirical support for both of these relations: trait inference (strength of attribution) was negatively correlated with behavior probability, and positively correlated with trait probability prior to observing behavior B.

Trope (1974) has extended Ajzen's Bayesian approach to trait inference and has proposed a model that accommodates any number of traits and behaviors. Let $T_1, T_2, \ldots T_n$ denote a mutually exclusive and exhaustive set of traits, and let $B_1, B_2, \ldots B_n$ denote a mutually exclusive and exhaustive set of behaviors. For the case of two traits, T_1 and T_2, Bayes' theorem (see Equations 24 and 25) states that:

$$(30) \quad \frac{P(T_1|B_j)}{P(T_2|B_j)} = \frac{P(B_j|T_1)\,P(T_1)}{P(B_j|T_2)\,P(T_2)}$$

where B_j is a particular act of the individual (an item of information).

Based on the work of Messick (1971) and Ajzen (1971), Trope used the Bayesian model to predict observer's inferences about an actor's traits in a forced compliance situation. Subjects, as observers, were presented both written and video taped descriptions of an experiment similar to the one reported by Helmreich & Collins (1968), and were asked to make subjective probability estimates of the terms in Equation 30. Though the model received only partial support, the model suggests several important variables, which can be used to conceptualize the attribution process.

The Lorge-Solomon Model

Our final example of a model based on probability theory is the Lorge-Solomon (1955) group problem-solving model. In reanalyzing Shaw's classic study comparing individuals and groups in problem solving (1932), Lorge and Solomon found that a simple model (Model A) could account for the data on two of the three problems used by Shaw. Though Lorge and Solomon also proposed a sequential stage model (Model B) to account for the third problem used by Shaw, we will only present the simple model (Model A), given as follows:

$$(31) \quad P_G = 1 - (1 - P_i)^n$$

where P_G denotes the probability that a group of size n will be able to solve the problem, and P_i denotes the probability that a given individual in isolation can solve the problem.

Based on probability theory, the term $(1 - P_i)$ is the complement of P_i, and denotes the probability that an individual cannot solve the problem, and $(1 - P_i)^n$ denotes the probability that no one in a group of size n can solve the problem, assuming subjects behave independently of one another. Hence, P_G simply specifies the probability that at least one person in a group of size n can solve the problem, and the model implicitly assumes that if one person in the group can solve the problem, the solution will be communicated to the remaining members of the group. The important point is that the model provides a simple explanation of Shaw's findings that the group is superior to the individual, and it also suggests that group discussion may be less important than previously believed, at least for some types of problems.

Stochastic Models

All of the previous examples of models are static models, in the sense that they make predictions about the outcomes (or probabilities of outcomes) of social situations and do not make assumptions about the sequential stages in which these outcomes are reached. In most social situations, however, social interaction is a sequential process in which the responses of one individual serve as stimuli for other persons, and their reactions in turn serve as stimuli for the first individual, etc. Though social-psychological theories must ultimately deal with such sequential dependencies, both the conceptualization and methods of analyzing such dependencies are extremely complex and intractable. Hence, most of the attempts to study such processes have been restricted to simple, idealized social situations. As in previous sections, in order to keep the mathematics as simple as possible, one simple example will be presented.

Some Definitions

A sequence of experiments in which the outcome of each experiment is based on some random (chance) element is a *stochastic process*. For example, tossing a coin 100 times (where each toss is an experiment) is a stochastic process in which the outcome of each experiment is independent of the outcomes on previous experiments. Since most social interaction involves sequential dependencies, we will restrict ourselves to Markov models, which assume such dependencies.

A *Markov chain* is a special class of stochastic processes in which the outcome on any given experiment (trial) depends only on the outcome of the previous experiment (trial). Let $a_1, a_2, \ldots a_r$ denote a finite number of possible outcomes, and let p_{ij} denote the probability of outcome a_j on a given trial — given that outcome a_i occurred on the previous trial. Hence, p_{ij} is a conditional probability of the form, $p(a_j|a_i)$. The outcomes $a_1, a_2, \ldots a_r$ are called *states*, and the p_{ij}'s are called *transition probabilities*.

In a Markov chain, it is assumed that the process moves (changes) over a sequence of steps, such that if the process is in State a_i, it will move to State a_j, with probability p_{ij}. To illustrate this idea, consider the *transition diagram* shown in Figure 5.3. Figure 5.3 illustrates a two-state Markov chain (a_1 and a_2) with transition probabilities $p_{12} = \frac{1}{2}$ and $p_{21} = \frac{1}{4}$. It can also be seen that p_{11}, the probability of remaining in State a_1 (not changing) is $\frac{1}{2}$, and the probability of remaining in State $a_2 (p_{22})$ is $\frac{3}{4}$.

A more common way of expressing the transition probabilities is through a *transition matrix*, as shown in Figure 5.4. In a transition matrix, the rows represent the preceding state (a_i), while the columns represent the succeeding state (a_j). Hence, the sum of each row of a transition matrix must equal 1. Also, if one of the diagonal entries is equal to 1 $(p_{ii} = 1)$, since it would be impossible to leave that state, the State a_i is called an *absorbing state*. A Markov chain is called absorbing if it has at least one absorbing state, and if it is possible to move to an absorbing state (not necessarily in one step) from any other state. And finally, it can be shown that in an absorbing Markov chain, it is certain that the process will end up in one of the absorbing states (Kemeny, Snell, & Thompson, 1957).

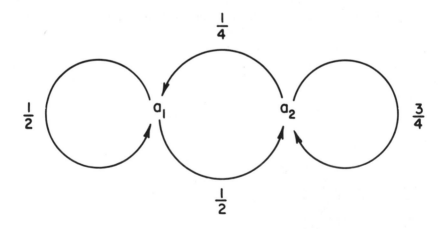

FIG. 5.3   Transition diagram for a two-state Markov chain.

$$P = \begin{array}{cc} & \begin{array}{cc} a_1 & a_2 \end{array} \\ \begin{array}{c} a_1 \\ \\ a_2 \end{array} & \left[\begin{array}{cc} \dfrac{1}{2} & \dfrac{1}{2} \\ \\ \dfrac{1}{4} & \dfrac{3}{4} \end{array} \right] \end{array}$$

FIG. 5.4   Transition matrix for two-state Markov chain in Figure 5.4.

In a Markov chain, once the initial state and the transition probabilities are specified, the process is completely determined. For example, for the transition probabilities in Figure 5.4, if the starting state is a_1, we can determine the probability that it will be in State a_2, after any number of steps, n. This probability is denoted $p_{ij}^{(n)}$, where the subscripts represent the starting State i, and the terminal State j, after n steps. The tree diagram in Figure 5.5 illustrates the process of determining these probabilities after two steps ($n = 2$), with starting state a_1. It can be seen that after one step, the probability of being in State a_2 is $\frac{1}{2}$. After two steps, $p_{12}^{(2)} = (\frac{1}{2})(\frac{1}{2}) + (\frac{1}{2})(\frac{3}{4}) = 5/8$. In general, $p_{ij}^{(n)}$ is equal to the sum of the probabilities of all branches of the tree diagram that end in State j, where the probability of each branch is the product of the transition probabilities through the branch.

Conformity as a Markov Process

Cohen (1958, 1963) developed a Markov model for predicting responses in the Asch conformity paradigm (1951, 1956). Based on a variation of Asch's paradigm, except for the first two trials, the confederates responded "erroneously" on all trials, and the naive subject responded last. Assuming that subjects in this situation are placed in a conflict between yielding to social pressure and maintaining "personal integrity," Cohen wished to describe the process of resolving this conflict as a Markov chain.

For this purpose, Cohen postulated the following four-state Markov chain:

State 1. *Absorbed Nonconformity:* The subject does not conform if in this state, is not in conflict, and will not conform on all subsequent trials.

State 2. *Temporary Nonconformity:* The subject does not conform when in this state, but is in conflict and may or may not conform on subsequent trials.

State 3. *Temporary Conformity:* The subject conforms when in this state, but is in conflict and may or may not conform on subsequent trials.

State 4. *Absorbed Conformity:* The subject conforms when in this state, is not in conflict, and will conform on all subsequent trials.

States 1 and 4 are absorbing states, and once a subject enters one of these states, it is assumed that he never leaves this state. States 2 and 3 are temporary states through which the subject eventually enters one of the absorbing states (resolves the conflict). Hence, the model predicts that all subjects should eventually become consistent conformers or nonconformers.

As the starting state, Cohen assumed that all subjects would be in State 2, Temporary Nonconformity. This is not an unreasonable assumption since subjects have not been exposed to social pressures before Trial 1. Assuming that the transition probabilities are the same for all subjects, the transition matrix and diagram for this situation are shown in Figure 5.6. Note that $p_{24} = 0$. This means that a person cannot move from State 2 (temporary nonconformity) to State 4 (absorbing conformity) and must first move to State 3 (temporary conformity) before moving to State 4. This is also implied in the transition diagram, showing that there is no arrow from State 2 to State 4. Similarly, note that a person cannot move from State 3 to State 1 ($p_{31} = 0$) and must first move to State 2 before moving to State 1.

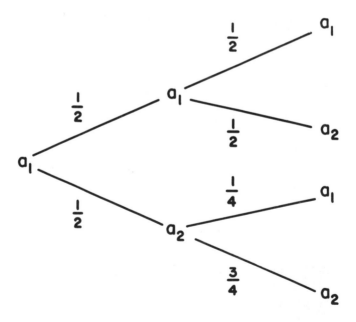

FIG. 5.5   Tree diagram for two-state Markov chain in Figure 5.4, with starting state a_1.

(a)

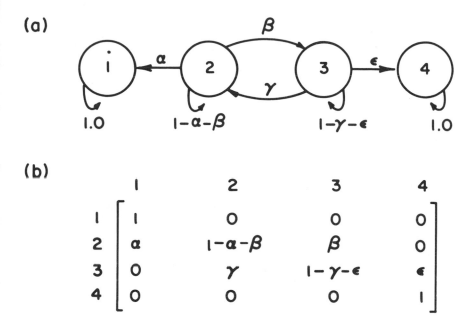

(b)

FIG. 5.6   Transition diagram (a) and transition matrix (b) in Cohen's model of conformity (from Berger, Cohen, Snell, and Zelditch, *Types of Formalization in Small Group Research*, 1962, p. 49. Reprinted by permission of authors and Houghton Mifflin Company, Boston, Mass.).

Cohen then estimated the transition probabilities such that the estimates would yield a theoretical response curve that would be as close as possible to the mean response curve. Using these estimated transition probabilities, predictions were made about the sequential properties of the data, for example, the average number of switches (changes) from one response to the other, and the distribution of error scores. Though the model provided a reasonably good fit, there were several discrepancies between the predicted and observed data. One notable discrepancy was the fact that not all subjects became consistently conforming or nonconforming, as predicted by an absorbing Markov chain. One possible reason for this discrepancy is that Cohen used only 36 trials, and perhaps not enough trials were administered so that all subjects would reach one of the absorbing states.

These and other discrepancies led Kemeny and Snell (1962) to reanalyze Cohen's data using other sets of assumptions. For example, one attempt to improve the fit was to change the assumption of the starting state. Instead of assuming that all subjects start as temporary nonconformists (State 2), they examined what would happen if it is assumed that 80% of them started in State 2, while 20% of them started in State 1 (absorbing nonconformity). This change in the probability distribution of the initial state significantly reduced the discrepancies between predicted and observed results.

It is reasonable to ask what has been accomplished by Cohen's Markov model. Probably the main contribution of the model is that with a small number of parameters (four), the model reduces the number of variables for a complex situation and describes the sequential processes in the Asch conformity situation. The main limitation of this application is that the model does not incorporate any social-psychological assumptions regarding the internal processes of conflict resolution. Hence, as in Cartwright and Harary's graph theory model of balance, strictly speaking, Cohen's model should be classified as a quasi-theoretical model. To be treated as a mathematical model, assumptions must be made regarding how the transition probabilities vary as a function of certain experimental manipulations. This is consistent with the fact that Berger et al. (1962) classify Cohen's model as a representational model (descriptive) rather than a theoretical construct model (explanatory).

There are, of course, many types of stochastic models, and there are numerous applications of Markov models in the social psychological literature. There are also more elegant and probably more fruitful and promising applications of Markov models than the model we have presented here. However, such models are much more complicated, and, in the interest of brevity and simplicity, they will not be discussed here. The interested reader is referred to the reviews by Rosenberg (1968); Abelson (1967); Rapoport (1963); and the selections in Coleman (1964a), and in Criswell, Solomon, and Suppes (1962).

Computer Simulation of Social Processes

One of the criticisms of mathematical models is that most models deal with simple, highly idealized situations and do not simulate (represent, mirror) complex, real-life social processes. When attempts are made to extend the generality of simple mathematical models, in many cases, rigorous analytic solutions are not possible. But one of the main purposes of a mathematical model is to enable precise, logical predictions from a set of assumptions. Hence, in such cases, a number of investigators have employed computers to simulate such complex social processes. Another criticism of mathematical models is that they deal mainly with the outcomes and ignore the processes of social interaction, and another advantage of computer simulation is that it is amenable to the analysis of such processes. Both of these criticisms of mathematical models will be discussed in the concluding section of this chapter.

Abelson (1968), in reviewing the literature on computer simulation, defines *simulation* as, ". . . the exercise of a flexible imitation of processes and outcomes for the purpose of clarifying or explaining the underlying mechanisms involved" (p. 275). The process of imitation itself is not the goal of computer simulation; the intent is that successful imitation may reveal insights into the nature of the object or process being simulated. Although there are different types of simulations (for example, man-machine, internation, gaming, artificial intelligence), as the term implies, in computer simulation, a computer is used to represent (imitate) some aspect of an individual or group process. For example, Newell, Shaw, and Simon (1959) have developed a computer program called the "General Problem Solver" to represent the cognitive activity of an individual attempting to solve problems.

As an extension of this idea of simulating human problem-solving, Abelson and Carroll (1965) have developed an "Ideology Machine," which simulates how an individual's belief system accepts or resists attitude change. The computer is programmed with a belief system stored in memory, and, when it is fed an "input assertion" (a simple sentence), the computer searches its memory to accept or reject (agree or disagree) with the input assertion. Moreover, it gives its reason for its action. One mechanism simulated by the Ideology Machine is that of "denial." As a process of resisting attitude change, denial consists of a search in memory for evidence supporting the negation of the input assertion. However, according to Abelson (1968), ". . . the Ideology Machine stands in need of considerable further improvement before it is fully satisfactory as a simulation. Nevertheless, a start has been made in an interesting direction" (p. 312).

Though most computer simulation studies have been directed at simulating complex human thought processes, in recent years, there have been several attempts to simulate social interactional processes (cf. review by Abelson, 1968). Gullahorn and Gullahorn (1963, 1964), for example, attempted to apply reinforcement principles in social situations, based on Homans's theory of social exchange (1961). However, such attempts at simulating social interaction have encountered serious difficulties, and it is too early to determine the future prospects of this approach. Judging from developments in simulating human cognitive processes, such attempts may prove to be invaluable in suggesting hypotheses for experiments. As one example to support this conjecture, Gullahorn and Gullahorn found that simulated social triads tended to develop into a friendly pair and an isolate. This outcome could be traced to a process in which the pair of individuals mutually reinforced each other early in the interaction sequence and gradually led to the exclusion of the third person. Kirk and Coleman found the same tendency in an independent simulation, and Coleman (1964b, 1965) argues that coalition formation in the triad can be explained on the basis of early mutual reinforcement, and one need not invoke more complicated assumptions to explain such outcomes. The point of this example is, of course, that Coleman's hypothesis is subject to empirical test using traditional experimental procedures.

SOME CONCLUDING REMARKS

In this chapter we have repeatedly stressed the advantages and values of mathematical models in social psychology. It is appropriate now to warn the reader of some of the dangers of this approach. A frequent criticism of mathematical models in social psychology — and of laboratory experiments in general — is that models are typically restricted to very simple experimental situations and are typically quite removed and abstracted from the real-life situation we want to understand. As a case in point, some critics have argued that the Prisoner's Dilemma Game (*PDG*) as an experimental paradigm will not tell us anything about cooperative behavior in real-life situations. But such a criticism is analogous to criticizing a geneticist that experiments with fruitflies have little relevance for genetic principles of humans. We have argued elsewhere (Davis, Laughlin, and Komorita, 1976) that such critics fail to realize that

> ... the *PDG* paradigm represents an intermediate stage between a "minimal social situation" (Kelley, Thibaut, Radloff, and Mundy, 1962) and more real-life situations. This research strategy is based on the assumption that insights into the nature of behavior in complex social situations depend, partly at least, on the discovery of principles underlying behavior in simple (artificial, idealized) social situations. This approach is consistent with the arguments made by Guyer and Rapoport (1972) when they state that, "... the fundamental laws of physics were developed in terms of the behavior of ideal objects moving through frictionless space" (p. 410), (p. 517).

There are, of course, other limitations of mathematical models in social psychology. Rosenberg (1968) cites three main disadvantages in the use of mathematical models:

1. The formalization of a substantive area is premature in that not enough data are available to formulate a reasonable and precise model.
2. A related disadvantage is the substitution of an elegant mathematical theory for a vigorous program of empirical research.
3. The initial formalization of a substantive problem often results in a highly simplified and idealized model, and there is the danger that a theorist may fixate upon an oversimplified theory.

It can be seen that the main disadvantage in the formulation of models depends to a large extent on timing. An investigator may adopt an elegant mathematical model because the model happens to be readily available. However, there may be an insufficient data base to determine its adequacy, and it may be more fruitful to develop a quasi-theoretical model. The danger here is that, if the initial tests of the model demonstrate its inadequacies because of the elegance of the model, an investigator may be reluctant to abandon it. Thus, Kaplan (1964), in describing the dangers of models, cites the danger of overemphasis on form. The theorist may become committed to and preoccupied with his model so that empirical evidence inconsistent with the model may be distorted or overlooked. Coleman (1960) also states that, "There is a certain fascination in postulating a mathematical model and deducing consequences from it, a fascination akin to the delight one feels in constructing a mechanical toy with moving parts. Model builders often seem captivated by that fascination, forgetting that their major problem is explaining why people or aggregates of people behave as they do" (p. 112).

A problem related to the danger of fixating on a given model is that, in the process of testing the model, it serves as a guide to suggest new experiments. However, the derivations of the model may not lead to the most fruitful research questions, and the most important and informative experiments may not be conducted. These observations suggest that preoccupation with a model may divert our attention from investigations of the processes underlying social behavior. For example, Miller (1964), in evaluating stochastic models of learning, asks, "But is a model of learning data necessarily the same thing as a model of the learning process?" (p. 220). Similarly, Wyer (1975) admits that, "We have tended to focus on the mathematical properties of the formulations we have proposed, while ignoring the implications of these models for what subjects are actually doing" (p. 2).

Despite these dangers, as we emphasized earlier in the chapter, the advantages of formalization far outweigh the disadvantages. This is especially true when there is a large data base on which to build a model. Just as premature formalization may be a disadvantage, there is the opposite danger that formalization is not attempted soon enough. Once a large body of data has been accumulated – and especially if a verbal theory of the phenomena becomes increasingly complex – there are disadvantages in *not* making attempts to formalize the verbal theory. As we emphasized earlier, mathematics offers a precise language with which to express the assumptions of a theory, and, not uncommonly, verbally stated theories are so ambiguous that the research hypotheses (presumably derived from the theory) do not necessarily follow from the assumptions of the theory (cf. Harris, 1976b).

If this chapter has motivated the reader to increase his or her knowledge of mathematical applications in social psychology – or to attempt a formalization of some theoretical ideas – the reader is strongly urged to consult some of the reviews of mathematical models in social psychology cited earlier in this chapter.

ACKNOWLEDGMENTS

The preparation of this chapter was partially supported by Grant SOC74-13399 from the National Science Foundation. The author expresses his appreciation to Jim Davis, Bob Wyer, and Pat Laughlin for many helpful suggestions on earlier drafts of the manuscript. They are not responsible of course for any errors or deficiencies in the final version.

REFERENCES

Abelson, R. P. Mathematical models in social psychology. In L. Berkowitz (Ed.), *Advances in experimental social psychology* (Vol. 3). New York: Academic Press, 1967.

Abelson, R. P. Simulation of social behavior. In G. Lindzey & E. Aronson, (Eds.), *Handbook of social psychology* (Vol. 2). Reading, Mass.: Addison-Wesley, 1968.

Abelson, R. P., & Carroll, J. D. Computer simulation of individual belief systems. *American Behavioral Scientist*, 1965, *8*, 24-30.

Abelson, R. P., & Rosenberg, M. J. Symbolic psycho-logic: A model of attitudinal cognition. *Behavioral Science*, 1958, *3*, 1-13.

Adams, J. S. Inequity in social exchange. In L. Berkowitz (Ed.), *Advances in experimental social psychology* (Vol. 2). New York: Academic Press, 1965.

Ajzen, I. Attribution of dispositions to an actor: Effects of perceived freedom and behavioral utilities. *Journal of Personality & Social Psychology*, 1971, *18*, 144-156.

Anderson, N. H. Applications of an additive model to impression formation. *Science*, 1962, *138*, 817-818.

Anderson, N. H. Averaging versus adding as a stimulus-combination rule in impression formation. *Journal of Experimental Psychology*, 1965, *70*, 394-400.

Anderson, N. H. Averaging model analysis of set size effect in impression formation. *Journal of Experimental Psychology*, 1967, *75*, 158-165.

Anderson, N. H. Likeableness ratings of 555 personality-trait words. *Journal of Personality & Social Psychology*, 1968, *9*, 272-279.

Anderson, N. H. Functional measurement and psychophysical judgment. *Psychological Review*, 1970, *77*, 153-170.

Anderson, N. H. Integration theory and attitude change. *Psychological Review*, 1971, *78*, 171-206.

Anderson, N. H. Information integration theory: A brief survey. In D. H. Krantz, R. C. Atkinson, R. D. Luce, & P. Suppes (Eds.), *Contemporary developments in mathematical psychology*. San Francisco: Freeman, 1974. (a)

Anderson, N. H. Integration theory applied to social attribution. In L. Berkowitz (Ed.), *Advances in experimental social psychology* (Vol. 7). New York: Academic Press, 1974. (b)

Anderson, N. H., & Butzin, C. A. Performance = motivation x ability: An integration-theoretical analysis. *Journal of Personality & Social Psychology*, 1974, *30*, 598-604.

Anderson, R., & Fishbein, M. Prediction of attitude from the number, strength, and evaluative aspect of beliefs about the attitude object: A comparison of summation and congruity theories. *Journal of Personality and Social Psychology*, 1965, *2*, 437-443.

Asch, S. E. Forming impressions of personality. *Journal of Abnormal and Social Psychology*, 1946, *41*, 258-290.

Asch, S. E. Effects of group pressure upon the modification and distortion of judgment. In H. Guetzkow (Ed.), *Groups, leadership, and men*. Pittsburgh: Carnegie Press, 1951.

Asch, S. E. *Social psychology*. New York: Prentice-Hall, 1952.

Asch, S. E. Studies of independence and conformity: I. A minority of one against a unanimous majority. *Psychological Monographs*, 1956, *70*, No. 9 (416).

Atkinson, S. *An introduction to motivation*. Princeton: Van Nostrand, 1964.

Bartos, O. J. *Simple models of group behavior*. New York: Columbia University Press, 1967.

Becker, G. M., & McClintock, C. G. Value: Behavioral decision theory. In P. R. Farnsworth (Ed.), *Annual Review of Psychology* (Vol. 18). Palo Alto: Annual Reviews, 1967.

Berger, J., Cohen, B. P., Snell, L., & Zelditch, M. *Types of formalization in small group research*. Boston: Houghton-Mifflin, 1962.

Bernoulli, D. [Exposition of a new theory on the measurement of risk.] L. Sommer (Trans.). *Econometrica*, 1954, *22*, 23-36.

Brodbeck, M. Models, meaning, and theories. In L. Gross (Ed.), *Symposium on sociological theory*. Evanston, Ill.: Row, Peterson, 1959.

Brown, R. *Social psychology*. New York: Free Press, 1965.

Bruner, J. S., & Tagiuri, R. The perception of people. In G. Lindzey (Ed.), *Handbook of social psychology* (Vol. 2). Cambridge: Addison-Wesley, 1954.

Cartwright, D., & Harary, F. Structural balance: A generalization of Heider's theory. *Psychological Review*, 1956, *63*, 277-293.

Cliff, N. Adverbs as multipliers. *Psychological Review*, 1959, *66*, 27-44.

Cohen, B. P. A probability model for conformity. *Sociometry*, 1958, *21*, 69-81.

Cohen, B. P. *Conflict and conformity*. Cambridge: M.I.T. Press, 1963.

Coleman, J. S. The mathematical study of small groups. In H. Solomon (Ed.), *Mathematical thinking in the measurement of behavior*. New York: Free Press, 1960.

Coleman, J. S. *Introduction to mathematical sociology*. New York: Free Press, 1964. (a)

Coleman, J. S. Mathematical models and computer simulation. In R. E. L. Faris (Ed.), *Handbook of modern sociology*. Chicago: Rand McNally, 1964. (b)

Coleman, J. S. The use of electronic computers in the study of social organizations. *European Journal of Sociology*, 1965, *6*, 89-107.

Coombs, C. H., Raiffa, H., & Thrall, R. M. Some views on mathematical models and measurement theory. *Psychological Review*, 1954, *61*, 132-144.

Coombs, C. H., Dawes, R. M., & Tversky, A. *Mathematical psychology: An elementary introduction*. Englewood-Cliffs: Prentice-Hall, 1970.

Coombs, C. H. *A theory of data*. New York: Wiley, 1964.

Criswell, J., Solomon, H., & Suppes, P. (Eds.). *Mathematical methods in small group processes*. Stanford University Press, 1962.

Davis, J. H., Laughlin, P. R., & Komorita, S. S. The social psychology of small groups: Cooperative and mixed-motive interaction. *Annual Review of Psychology*, 1976, *27*, 501-541.

Edwards, W. Behavioral decision theory. In P. R. Farnsworth (Ed.), *Annual Review of Psychology* (Vol. 12). Palo Alto: Annual Reviews, 1961.

Edwards, W. Conservatism in human information processing. In B. Kleinmuntz (Ed.), *Formal Representation of Human Judgment*. New York: Wiley, 1968.

Festinger, L. The analysis of sociograms using matrix algebra. *Human Relations*, 1949, *2*, 153-158.

Festinger, L. Informal social communication. *Psychological Review*, 1950, *57*, 271-292.

Festinger, L. A theory of social comparison processes. *Human Relations*, 1954, *7*, 117-140.

Festinger, L. *A theory of cognitive dissonance*. Stanford: Stanford University Press, 1957.

Fishbein, M. An investigation of the relationships between beliefs about an object and the attitude toward that object. *Human Relations*, 1963, *16*, 233-239.

Fishbein, M., & Hunter, R. Summation versus balance in attitude organization and change. *Journal of Abnormal and Social Psychology*, 1964, *69*, 505-510.

Flament, C. *Applications of graph theory to group structure*. Englewood Cliffs: Prentice-Hall, 1963.

Gamson, W. A. A theory of coalition formation. *American Sociological Review*, 1961, *26*, 373-382.

Gullahorn, J., & Gullahorn, J. E. A computer model of elementary social behavior. *Behavioral Science*, 1963, *8*, 354-362.

Gullahorn, J., & Gullahorn, J. E. Computer simulation of human interaction in small groups. *American Federation of Information Processing Societies Conference Proceedings*, 1964, *25*, 103-113.

Guyer, M. J., & Rapoport, Anatol. 2 x 2 games played once. *Journal of Conflict Resolution*, 1972, *16*, 409-432.

Harary, F., & Norman, R. *Graph theory as a mathematical model in social science*. Ann Arbor: University of Michigan Press, 1953.

Harris, R. J. Handling negative inputs: On the plausible equity formulae. *Journal of Experimental Social Psychology*, 1976, *12*, 194-209. (a)

Harris, R. J. The uncertain connection between verbal theories and research hypotheses in social psychology. *Journal of Experimental Social Psychology*, 1976, *12*, 210-219. (b)

Hays, D. G., & Bush, R. R. A study of group action. *American Sociological Review*, 1954, *19*, 693-701.

Heider, F. Attitudes and cognitive organization. *Journal of Psychology*, 1946, *21*, 107-112.

Heider, F. *The psychology of interpersonal relations.* New York: Wiley, 1958.

Helmreich, R., & Collins, B. E. Studies in forced compliance: Commitment and magnitude of inducement to comply as determinants of opinion change. *Journal of Personality and Social Psychology*, 1968, *10*, 75-81.

Homans, G. C. *The human group.* New York: Harcourt Brace, 1950.

Homans, G. C. *Social behavior: Its elementary forms.* New York: Harcourt Brace, 1961.

Howe, E. S. Probabilistic adverbial qualifications of adjectives. *Journal of Verbal Learning and Verbal Behavior*, 1962, *1*, 225-242.

Hull, C. L. *Principles of behavior.* New York: Appleton-Century-Crofts, 1943.

James, W. *The principles of psychology* (Vol. 10). New York: Holt, 1890.

Jones, E. E., & Gerard, H. B. *Foundations of social psychology.* New York: Wiley, 1967.

Kaplan, A. *The conduct of inquiry.* San Francisco: Chandler, 1964.

Kelley, H. H. Attribution theory in social psychology. In D. Levine (Ed.), *Nebraska Symposium on Motivation.* Lincoln: University of Nebraska Press, 1967.

Kelley, H. H., Thibaut, J. W., Radloff, R., & Mundy, D. The development of cooperation in the "minimal social situation." *Psychological Monographs*, 1962, *76* (19, Whole No. 538).

Kemeny, J. G., Snell, L., & Thompson, G. L. *Introduction to finite mathematics.* Englewood Cliffs: Prentice-Hall, 1957.

Kemeny, J. G., & Snell, L. *Mathematical models in the social sciences.* Boston: Ginn, 1962.

Lee, W. *Decision theory and human behavior.* New York: Wiley, 1971.

Levy, L. H., & Richter, M. L. Impressions of groups as a function of the stimulus values of their individual members. *Journal of Abnormal and Social Psychology*, 1963, *67*, 349-354.

Lewin, K. *Principles of topological psychology.* New York: McGraw-Hill, 1936.

Lewin, K. *Field theory in social science.* New York: Harper, 1951.

Lorge, I., & Solomon, H. Two models of group behavior in the solution of Eureka-type problems. *Psychometrika*, 1955, *20*, 139-148.

Luce, R. D. Connectivity and generalized cliques in sociometric group structure. *Psychometrika*, 1950, *15*, 169-190.

Luce, R. D., & Raiffa, H. *Games and decisions.* New York: Wiley, 1957.

Luce, R. D., Bush, R. R., & Galanter, E. (Eds.). *Handbook of mathematical psychology* (3 vol.). New York: Wiley, 1963.

McClelland, G. H. Non-metric tests of composition rules in impression formation. *Michigan Mathematical Psychology Program*, Report No. 72-7, 1974.

McGuire, W. J. A syllogistic analysis of cognitive relationships. In C. I. Hovland & M. J. Rosenberg (Eds.), *Attitude organization and change.* New Haven: Yale University Press, 1960.

McGuire, W. J. Theory of the structure of human thought. In R. P. Abelson, et al., *Theories of cognitive consistency: A sourcebook.* Chicago: Rand-McNally, 1968.

Messick, D. M. Logical aspects of social inference. Paper presented at Third Research Conference on Subjective Probability, Utility, and Decision Making. Brunel University, Uxbridge, England, 1971.

Miller, G. A. *Mathematics and psychology.* New York: Wiley, 1964.

Morgan, B. W. *An introduction to Bayesian statistical decision processes.* Englewood Cliffs: Prentice-Hall, 1968.

Neimark, E. D., & Estes, W. K. *Stimulus sampling theory.* San Francisco: Holden-Day, 1967.

Newcomb, T. M. An approach to the study of communicative acts. *Psychological Review*, 1953, *60*, 393-404.

Newell, A., Shaw, J. C., & Simon, H. A. Report on a general problem-solving program. *Proceedings of International Conference on Information Processing.* Paris: UNESCO, 1959.

Osgood, E. E., & Tannenbaum, P. H. The principle of congruity in the prediction of attitude change. *Psychological Review,* 1955, *62,* 42-55.

Peterson, C. R., & Beach, L. R. Man as an intuitive statistician. *Psychological Bulletin,* 1967, *68,* 29-46.

Pritchard, R. D. Equity theory: A review and critique. *Organizational Behavior and Human Performance,* 1969, *4,* 176-211.

Rapoport, Amnon, & Wallsten, T. S. Individual decision behavior. In P. Mussen & M. R. Rosenzweig (Eds.), *Annual Review of Psychology* (Vol. 23). Palo Alto: Annual Reviews, 1972.

Rapoport, Anatol. Mathematical models of social behavior. In R. D. Luce, R. R. Bush, & E. Galanter (Eds.), *Handbook of mathematical psychology* (Vol. 2). New York: Wiley, 1963

Rapoport, Anatol, & Chammah, A. *Prisoner's dilemma.* Ann Arbor: University of Michigan Press, 1965.

Rapoport, Anatol. *Two-person game theory: The essential ideas.* Ann Arbor: University of Michigan Press, 1966.

Rapoport, Anatol. A note on the index of cooperation for Prisoner's Dilemma. *Journal of Conflict Resolution,* 1967, *11,* 101-103.

Rosen, N. A., & Wyer, R. S. Some further evidence for the "Socratic effect," using a subjective probability model of cognitive organization. *Journal of Personality and Social Psychology,* 1972, *24,* 420-424.

Rosenberg, S. Mathematical models of social behavior. In G. Lindzey & E. Aronson (Eds.), *Handbook of social psychology* (Vol. 1). Reading, Mass.: Addison-Wesley, 1968.

Rosenberg, M. J. Cognitive structure and attitudinal affect. *Journal of Abnormal and Social Psychology,* 1956, *53,* 367-372.

Rosenberg, M. J. An analysis of affective-cognitive consistency. In C. I. Hovland & M. J. Rosenberg (Eds.), *Attitude organization and change.* New Haven: Yale University Press, 1960.

Rotter, J. B. *Social learning and clinical psychology.* New York: Prentice-Hall, 1954.

Shaw, M. E. A comparison of individuals and small groups in rational solution of complex problems. *American Journal of Psychology,* 1932, *54,* 491-504.

Shubik, M. *Game theory and related approaches to social behavior.* New York: Wiley, 1964.

Sidowski, J. B., Wyckoff, L. B., & Tabory, L. The influence of reinforcement and punishment in a minimal social situation. *Journal of Abnormal and Social Psychology,* 1956, *52,* 115-119.

Siegel, S., & Fouraker, L. E. *Bargaining and group decision making.* New York: McGraw-Hill, 1960.

Simon, H. A. A formal theory of interaction of social groups. *American Sociological Review,* 1952, *17,* 202-211.

Simon, H. A., & Newell, A. The uses and limitations of models. In M. II. Marx (Ed.), *Theories in contemporary psychology.* New York: Macmillan, 1964.

Slovic, P., & Lichenstein, S. Comparison of Bayesian and regression approaches to the study of information processing judgment. In L. Rapoport & D. A. Summers, *Human judgment and social interaction.* New York: Holt, 1973.

Steele, M. W., & Tedeschi, J. Matrix indices and strategy choices in mixed-motive games. *Journal of Conflict Resolution,* 1967, *11,* 198-205.

Stilson, D. W., & Maroney, R. J. Adverbs as multipliers: Simplification and extension. *American Journal of Psychology,* 1966, *79,* 82-88.

Suppes, P., & Atkinson, R. C. *Markov learning models for multiperson interactions.* Stanford: Stanford University Press, 1960.

Thibaut, J. W., & Kelley, H. H. *The social psychology of groups.* New York: Wiley, 1959.

Triandis, H. C., & Fishbein, M. Cognitive interaction in person perception. *Journal of Abnormal and Social Psychology,* 1963, *67,* 446-453.

Trope, Y. Inferential processes in the forced compliance situation: A Bayesian analysis. *Journal of Experimental Social Psychology,* 1974, *10,* 1-16.

von Neumann, J., & Morgenstern, O. *Theory of games and economic behavior* (2nd ed.). Princeton: Princeton University Press, 1947.

Walster, E., Berscheid, E., & Walster, G. W. New directions in equity research. *Journal of Personality & Social Psychology,* 1973, *25,* 151-176.

Wrightsman, L. S., O'Connor, J., & Baker, N. J. *Cooperation and competition: Readings on mixed-motive games.* Belmont, Calif.: Brooks-Cole, 1972.

Wyer, R. S. *Cognitive organization and change: An information processing approach.* Potomac, Md.: Erlbaum, 1974.

Wyer, R. S. The role of probabilistic and syllogistic reasoning in cognitive organization and social inference. In M. Kaplan & S. Schwartz (Eds.), *Human judgment and decision processes.* New York: Academic Press, 1975.

Zajonc, R. B. Cognitive theories in social psychology. In G. Lindzey & E. Aronson (Eds.), *Handbook of social psychology* (Vol. 1). Reading, Mass.: Addison-Wesley, 1968.

Author Index

•

The numbers in *italics* refer to the page on which the complete reference is cited.

Subject Index